God
Laughed

God Laughed

Sources of Jewish Humor

Hershey H. Friedman
Linda Weiser Friedman

Transaction Publishers
New Brunswick (U.S.A.) and London (U.K.)

Library of Congress Catalog Number: 2013036452
ISBN: 978-1-4128-5376-7
Printed in the United States of America

Library of Congress Cataloging-in-Publication Data

Friedman, Hershey H.
  God laughed : sources of Jewish humor / Hershey H. Friedman and Linda Weiser Friedman.
      pages cm
  Includes bibliographical references and index.
  ISBN 978-1-4128-5376-7
  1. Jewish wit and humor—History and criticism. 2. Wit and humor in the Bible. 3. Wit and humor in rabbinical literature. I. Friedman, Linda Weiser. II. Title.
  PN6231.J5F77 2014
  809.7'935203924—dc23
                                        2013036452

This book is dedicated to my late father and teacher, Avraham Shlomo b. Yitzchak Asher Friedman Z"L, who instilled in me a great love of the sages in the Talmud. I will always remember his wonderful stories of the Talmudic sages, and I am certain that he is now enjoying their company in the "world of truth."
—Hershey H. Friedman

Also dedicated to our children and grandchildren, who somehow manage to always keep us laughing.
—Linda and Hershey H. Friedman

Contents

Preface

Among the major works that have influenced the Jewish people are the Hebrew Bible (i.e., *Tanach*), the Talmud, and the Midrash, all of which are replete with humor and wit. (Really!) This humor has had a profound effect on the way the Jewish people see the world and has sustained them through millennia of hardships and suffering. Inevitably, it has influenced a tremendous body of humor that is uniquely Jewish. Jewish humor has, itself, influenced several generations of comics, as well as many genres of humor.

This book is a work of love for us and has been a joy to create. In it, we first examine the Hebrew Bible. True, there are no jokes in the Bible but there is an abundance of wit and humor. Some of the types of humor found in the Hebrew Bible include sarcasm, irony, wordplays, humorous imagery, and humorous stories and situations. Much of this humor can only be appreciated if read in the original Hebrew and is lost in a translation. Since, to the believer, the Bible is a moral document, not merely an entertaining "storybook," one might be moved to consider the purpose of using humorous devices in the Holy Scriptures. An examination of the collection in this book brings at least one important purpose to mind: Humor narrows the distance between teller and listener, and thus brings God closer to humankind. In addition, laughter is frequently employed as an effective way of indicating the folly of idolatry and other sins.

The Talmud and Midrash are also replete with humor. This is not surprising given that the Talmud and Midrash are oral traditions based on the Torah, the written law. Spalding[1] notes that both the Talmud and the Bible have a fair share of wit and humor. Some of the humor of the Talmud may be found in popular books such as William Novak and Moshe Waldoks's *Big Book of Jewish Humor* and Hyam Maccoby's *The Day God Laughed.*

A note about the translations in this book is in order. Yevgeny Yevtushenko once famously said, "Translations are like women. When they are faithful they are not beautiful, and when they are beautiful they are not faithful." We decided to go for translations that are closely faithful to the texts from which they are taken. This results in passages that may seem a bit stilted to our ears.

Most of the jokes in this book are old—uhmm, classics. Where we used a reference for the particular rendering of the joke cited, the reference is named as source. For the most part, there is no definitive source for any of these jokes.

We hope you have as much fun reading this book as we did writing it!

Hersh and Linda Friedman
New York City

Acknowledgements

This book is a long time in the making. Much of the research has been conducted over the past twenty years and some of the writing goes back almost that far. Some of the material has had earlier incarnations in print. For example, Friedman (2000), Friedman (1998), and Friedman and Lipman (1999). Many thanks to the journal *Humor: International Journal of Humor Research* for permission to reuse much of the material included in Chapter 4.

A project such as this one cannot be completed without the assistance of a great many individuals: editors, reviewers, encouragers, readers—you know who you are. In particular, the authors wish to thank Rachel F. Adler, William D. Adler, Deborah Friedman, Esther Friedman, Jeffrey Helmreich, William Helmreich, Daniel Hoffman, Sarah F. Hoffman, Steve Lipman, Ryan Shapin, Avi Weisel, Pearl Weisel, and Norman Weiser. And a very sincere thank you to the helpful and professional team of editors at Transaction Publishers.

Part I
Introduction

1

Studying Jewish Humor

Engaging in scholarly discourse on humor is probably the surest way to put one's audience to sleep and—uhm—to actually *not* be funny. Still, we try in this volume to walk the admittedly very fine line between scholarship and entertainment.

What is humor? The bottom line is that humor has the ability to make people laugh, smile, or chuckle, at least inwardly. There are, of course, many different types of humor, including puns, wordplay, riddles, jokes, satire, lampoon, sarcasm, irony, wit, black humor, slapstick, farce, burlesque, caricature, and parody. The differences among these are not always great. In particular, burlesque, caricature, and parody are very much alike and refer to literary or dramatic works that mimic serious works in order to achieve a humorous or satiric effect. Likewise, the difference between satire and lampoon is not great.

Human beings seem to naturally gravitate toward all forms of humor. Indeed, humor has been shown to be useful and effective in many different areas of human endeavor, including medicine, counseling, education, advertising and, of course, communication.[1] Humor has many functions, both positive and negative. Humor has been found to be an important de-stressing device.[2] One important function of humor, according to Meritt Conrad Hyers, is to minimize the distance between the sacred and the profane.[3]

Scholars and other mavens return repeatedly to consider whether there is such a thing as Jewish humor. While opinions vary, we prefer to believe that Jewish humor exists, and that it has its own peculiar characteristics and unique elements. Conversely, if the Jews in a joke can easily be replaced by individuals of some other ethnicity, that should not really be considered Jewish humor. Examples that fail this test can be found among many supposedly Jewish jokes about sex and marriage.

Wikipedia, the online encyclopedia, notes that Jewish humor is rooted in several traditions.

3

Jewish humour is the long tradition of humour in Judaism dating back to the Torah and the Midrash from the ancient mid-east, but generally refers to the more recent stream of verbal, self-deprecating, crude, and often anecdotal humor originating in Eastern Europe and which took root in the United States over the last hundred years.[4]

One thing is certain, a very high percentage of major American comics are Jewish. A traditional number mentioned is 80 percent.[5] And here is what some well-known Jewish humorists have to say about Jewish humor:[6]

David Steinberg: Ethnic groups are attracted to comedy. When the Jews were in the ghetto, they became the comedians because they were the outsiders.

Roseanne Barr: If you make fun of your own in front of the dominant culture here, you can live next door to them.

Mel Brooks: My comedy comes from the feeling that as a Jew, even though you're better and smarter, you'll never belong.

Mel Brooks: One of my lifelong jobs has been to make the world laugh at Adolf Hitler, because how do you get even? There's only one way to get even, you have to bring him down with ridicule.

In fact, according to Mel Gordon, the humor industry in pre-Nazi Berlin was almost entirely Jewish. The Nazi propaganda machinery considered self-deprecating Jewish humor a way to fool the public with regard to the Jewish proclivity toward criminality and was "yet another tool in the Jews unending quest for world domination."[7]

Robin Williams tells the story of the time he was interviewed in Germany:

I was once on a German talk show, and this woman said to me, "Mr. Williams, why do you think there is not so much comedy in Germany?" And I said, "Did you ever think you killed all the funny people?"

Philologos, a columnist for *The Forward*, expounds on the derivation of the Yiddish expression "Man plans and God laughs." According to his timeline, this modern proverb, originally based on a passage from Proverbs 16:9, first appeared in Latin rhyme as "Man proposes, God disposes," then emerged in German as "Man thinks, God directs," rhyming *denkt* (thinks) with *lenkt* (directs). Interestingly, there was no easy way to translate this rather serious proverb into Yiddish, as Yiddish did not have the word *denkt*, but rather, *trakht* (thinks). So, what to rhyme with trakht? Of course, *lakht* (laughs).[8]

William Novak and Moshe Waldoks provide an extensive discussion on Jewish humor.[9] They conclude that "Jewish humor is too rich and too diverse to be adequately described by a single generalization." They argue quite convincingly that the belief that traditional Jewish humor is "laughter through tears" is incorrect. Many Jews, especially those from Eastern Europe, had to deal with "persecution, poverty, and uprootedness" and it found its way into the humor. However, Jewish humor is much richer than that and deals with so much more including *schlemiels*, God, matchmaking, marriage, family, *schnorrers*, Talmudic reasoning, rabbis, business, etc. They try to define Jewish humor but admit that this may be an exercise in futility. In a similar vein, Stephen Whitfield observes that Jewish humor is like pornography, in the sense that: "I know it when I see it."[10]

Jewish humor covers such a broad spectrum it may be futile to try to create a unified framework for classifying humor as "Jewish." We feel strongly that any attempt to define Jewish humor will fail. Jewish humor is broad, invoking specific experiences and universal values, often at the same time. Sometimes Jewish humor may appear to be self-deprecating, but then it can appear to be poking fun at the non-Jew, for example, in the *goyishe kopf* brand of Jewish joke. Whitfield[11] correctly observes that some note its aggressiveness and some talk of its kindness. As we shall see, the Yiddish curse is actually both aggressive and sweet at the same time.

The range of prototypes in Jewish humor includes the schlemiel, the wise men of Chelm, the snide waiter, the arrogant beggar, the matchmaker, the anti-Semite, the shrew, the pompous fool, and many more. There are Chassidic stories and strange Yiddish curses. There is gallows humor, referencing centuries of oppression, the Holocaust, and assimilation. Many examples are sprinkled throughout this volume.[12] To include a joke from every conceivable category of Jewish humor would make this book much too long and, regardless, there are a number of excellent compilations[13] as Jewish humor has been the subject of many treatises, for both scholarly and entertainment purposes.

Do you have to be Jewish to appreciate Jewish humor? Well, sometimes it helps:

In a small village in the Ukraine, a terrifying rumor was spreading: A Christian girl had been found murdered. Realizing the dire consequences of such an event, and fearing a pogrom, the Jewish community instinctively gathered in the synagogue to plan whatever defensive actions were possible under these circumstances. Just as the emergency meeting was being called to order, in ran the president of the synagogue, out of breath and all excited. "Brothers," he cried out, "I have wonderful news! The murdered girl is Jewish!" [14]

Not everyone will find this bit of tragic humor funny. Focusing a joke on the tragedy of the notorious blood libel—that Jews killed Christian children and used their blood in the *matzot* eaten on Passover—which led to numerous pogroms in Jewish history, might be considered by some to be in poor taste. In fact, this is the problem Steve Lipman had when writing his fascinating work on the use of anti-Nazi humor during the Holocaust, [15] and he has the same problem today with a book he is working on dealing with humor used by those afflicted with chronic or life-threatening illnesses. [16] Those that do not suffer from these kinds of ailments find it hard to believe that, for example, cancer patients can make jokes about chemotherapy; in fact, a simple search of the Internet brings up many such jokes.

Much Jewish humor is self-deprecating. On the other hand, the joke may be about outwitting an oppressor or, even, outwitting each other. In many jokes, the Jew, using his "superior" intelligence, outwits the oppressor *du jour*. For example,

During the Second World War, a southern matron calls up the local army base.

"We would be honored," she tells the sergeant who takes her call, "to accommodate five soldiers at our Thanksgiving dinner."

"That's very gracious of you, ma'am," the sergeant answers.

"Just please make sure they're not Jews."

"I understand ma'am."

Thanksgiving afternoon, the woman answers the front doorbell and is horrified to find five black soldiers standing in the doorway.

"We're here for the Thanksgiving dinner, ma'am," one of the soldiers says.

"Bu . . . bu . . . but your sergeant has made a terrible mistake, " the woman says.

"Oh no, ma'am," the soldier answers. "Sergeant Greenberg never makes mistakes." [17]

and

Two Arab men board a short commuter flight to New York, one at the window, one in the middle of a three-seat row. At the last moment, a little Jewish man arrives, and takes the aisle seat. He kicks off his shoes, stretches his feet out and gets comfortable. At this point, the Arab sitting in the window seat says, "I think I'll go to the galley and get a Coke."

The Jew stands up and says "No problem. I'll get it for you." While he is gone, the Arab picks up the Jew's shoe and spits in it.

As soon as the Jew returns with the Coke, the other Arab says, "Would you mind? I think I'll have one too."

"No problem," the Jew says, and he goes to get another Coke. The Arab in the middle seat quickly picks up the Jew's other shoe and spits in it. The Jew returns with the Coke, and they all sit back and enjoy the flight.

A short while later, the plane prepares to land, and the Jew slips his feet into his shoes. Immediately, he realizes what his seatmates had done. "How long must this go on?" he exclaims. "This enmity between our peoples . . . this hatred . . . this spitting in shoes and peeing in Cokes?"[18]

As we will see, humorous anecdotes of this sort can even be found in the ancient Jewish sources. Well, maybe not references to peeing in Coke, but certainly to outwitting the enemies of the Jewish people. In the Talmud and Midrash, some humor shows that wicked people are outsmarted by the good people. In fact, the entire Book of Esther can be seen in that light.

Joseph Telushkin makes a powerful point about Jewish humor when he says that Jewish humor must express a Jewish sensibility.[19] It must deal with a subject that is of great concern to the Jewish people. As such, many Jewish jokes address such sensitive issues as intermarriage, anti-Semitism, and assimilation, and many incorporate logic and argumentation. Novak and Waldoks also believe that Jewish humor is often substantive, that is, it is about *something* and is especially fond of topics such as food, anti-Semitism, family, wealth, health, and survival.[20]

An old Jew on his death bed insists that he wishes to convert immediately to Catholicism. His friends and family argue the matter with him to no avail. Finally, they call in his Rabbi, who leans close to the dying man and asks him why he wants to convert—why now?

The old Jew whispers feebly, "If someone has to die, let it be one of those bastards."

Sometimes the style, more so than the subject, is what makes a joke "Jewish." The television show "Seinfeld," arguably the best television comedy of all time,[21] made use of many elements of strikingly Jewish humor. For example, the "soup Nazi" episode, has its antecedents not in the gallows humor of the Holocaust era but in jokes featuring the sarcastic Jewish waiter who believes that he is better than the customers he serves. The family of George Costanza (a character not so loosely based on co-creator Larry David, a Jew) is so Jewish in its mannerisms, attitudes, relationships and—yes—humor, that the actor Jerry Stiller, who played Frank Costanza, George's father, once described his character's family as a Jewish family in the Witness Protection Program, that is, they are only pretending to be Gentiles.

Jokes involving extreme examples of Talmudic-type logic are, naturally enough, uniquely Jewish. For example, the famous rabbi who explained the *halachic* basis for his reluctance to give speeches in synagogues around the country by saying, "It might lead to men and women sleeping together." Certain other styles, for example, satire, sarcasm, and exaggeration, may be used by other groups, but not to the same degree. It is interesting to observe (as we do later in this book) that many of the styles "typical" to modern Jewish humor were used hundreds of years ago in Talmudic discourses.

One night, a Jew gets so drunk that he wanders out of the town and goes up to the cemetery, where he falls unconscious into a freshly dug grave. The morning sun awakens him. He looks around, mystified as to his whereabouts and, finally, he decides to think it through Talmudically.

"If I see the sky above me, then I must be lying down. If I'm lying down and see earth on all four sides around me, then I must be in a grave. If I'm in a grave, then I must be dead. But, if I'm dead, why do I have to pee so bad?"[22]

Even Yiddish curses are humorous and, indeed, they are vaguely reminiscent of some of the sarcastic remarks found in the Talmud. Yosef Guri, chronicler of Yiddish blessings and curses[23] has said that "Wit is the essence of the Yiddish curse"[24] and

> "Eastern European Jews would walk a mile for a good job. For a witticism they'd give away their mother and father."[25]

In reviewing Guri's book, the *Jewish Week* noted that since Jews were steeped in the Bible and the Talmud, as well as other Jewish lore, these became ready sources for curses.[26] Guri's collection includes, "May your bones be broken as often as the Ten Commandments and may you have Pharaoh's curses decorated with Job's boils." It is interesting to note that the Torah prohibits curses, even cursing a deaf person who, presumably, would not even know about the curse and could not be hurt by it. This may be why Yiddish curses are so witty, and more colorful than merely nasty.

May you back into a pitchfork and grab a hot stove for support.[27]

They are a way of blowing off steam, or a way of getting even with someone who has slighted you, as did the television repairman in an episode of *All in the Family*:

It is Friday near sundown, and Archie Bunker has been trying to convince a television repairman, who is an Orthodox Jew, to fix his television right away instead of waiting for Monday.

Repairman: I just can't go against my religion.

Archie Bunker: Hey, turning down business. THAT'S against your religion.

Repairman: Mr. Bunker, I can only answer that insult with an old Jewish expression: Tzun a leben in a hoyz mit a toyznt tsimers aye zolt hobn a boykhveytik un yeder tsimer.

Archie Bunker: What the hell does that mean?

Repairman: You'll never know, but believe me, I got even.[28]

Also,

May your enemies get cramps in their legs when they dance on your grave.[29]

May you get passage out of the old village safely, and when you settle, may you fall into the outhouse just as a regiment of Ukrainians is finishing a prune stew and twelve barrels of beer.

May your two sons grow up happy and strong. And may they become a doctor and a lawyer. And may each marry a wonderful woman and have wealth. And may they each have many children and may they all name someone after you already![30]

Are these traditional Yiddish curses aggressive, sweet, or just plain clever? Marnie Winston-Macauley recognizes the poetry and uniqueness of the Yiddish curse as "a juicy, literate malediction that no mere obscene word could possibly convey."[31] The most clever ones—like those cited here—start out sounding like a blessing, lulling the listener into complacency until the turnaround occurs at the very end. Similarly, a sarcastic remark attributed to Groucho Marx builds on the structure of the Yiddish curse:

I've had a perfectly delightful evening. Unfortunately, this wasn't it.

Others forms of Jewish humor, while perhaps not totally unique, have a distinctly Jewish character, for example, Chassidic tales.

The famous Preacher of Dubno was once journeying from one town to another delivering his learned sermons. Wherever he went he was received with enthusiasm and accorded the greatest honors. His driver, who accompanied him on this tour, was very much impressed by all this welcome.

One day, as they were on the road, the driver said, "Rabbi, I have a great favor to ask of you. Wherever we go people heap honors on you. Although I'm only an ignorant driver I'd like to know how it feels to receive so much attention. Would you mind if we were to exchange clothes for one day? Then they'll think I am the great preacher and you the driver, so they'll honor me instead!"

Now the Preacher of Dubno was a man of the people and a merry soul, but he saw the pitfalls awaiting his driver in such an arrangement.

"Suppose I agreed—what then? You know the rabbi's clothes don't make a rabbi! What would you do for learning? If they were to ask you to explain some difficult passage in the Law you'd only make a fool of yourself, wouldn't you?"

"Don't you worry, Rabbi—I am willing to take that chance."

"In that case," said the preacher, "here are my clothes." And the two men undressed and exchanged clothes as well as their callings.

As they entered the town all the Jewish inhabitants turned out to greet the great preacher. They conducted him into the synagogue while the assumed driver followed discreetly at a distance.

Each man came up to the "rabbi" to shake hands and to say the customary: "Shalom Aleichem, learned Rabbi!"

The "rabbi" was thrilled with his reception. He sat down in the seat of honor surrounded by all the scholars and dignitaries of the town. In the meantime the preacher from his corner kept his merry eyes on the driver to see what would happen.

"Learned Rabbi," suddenly asked a local scholar, "would you be good enough to explain to us this passage in the Law we don't understand?"

The preacher in his corner chuckled, for the passage was indeed a difficult one.

"Now he's sunk!" he said to himself.

With knitted brows the "rabbi" peered into the sacred book placed before him, although he could not understand one word. Then, impatiently pushing it away from him, he addressed himself sarcastically to the learned men of the town, "A fine lot of scholars you are! Is this the most difficult question you could ask me? Why, this passage is so simple even my driver could explain it to you!"

Then he called to the Preacher of Dubno: "Driver, come here for a moment and explain the Law to these 'scholars!'"[32]

Jews tend to see the world through the prism of Jewishness. Hey, don't knock it, we've survived fairly well over several, often difficult, millennia.

The class had been asked to write an essay on the elephant, and the teacher was happy to note that every student's submission was different from the others.

The Englishman's was titled, "The Elephant and the British Empire."

The Frenchman wrote about "The Love Life of the Elephant."

The German student wrote a large treatise called "A Brief Introduction to Elephants." It was subtitled "Volumes I–III."

The Jewish student's essay was titled, "The Elephant and the Jewish Problem."

Many feel that Jewish humor is a "weapon for survival" that has enabled Jews to overcome numerous oppressors.[33] The idea that Jewish humor is a weapon of the oppressed has been noted by scholars.[34] Stanley Schachter, taking a psychoanalytic approach to Jewish humor, believes that it is an "escape hatch" for the evil inclination (*yetzer hara*). According to Jewish tradition, every person has a *yetzer hara* and a *yetzer tov* (good inclination); the two are constantly fighting each other. The *yetzer hara* is the trickster who does everything in his power to convince us to sin. He asserts that the struggle between the two powerful forces is an important part of Jewish humor. Schachter avers that Jews generally do not use violence as a way of dealing with anger and frustration. Instead, these repressed urges emerge through sarcasm and insulting humor.[35] For example, according to Robert Rothstein, a common Yiddish insult was to call someone a fifty-second-er (*Er iz a tsvey-un-fuftsiker*), that is, a dog, in *gematria* code, the sum of the numerical values of the letters in Hebrew word for dog, *kelev*.[36] This is a very witty, sarcastic insult requiring specialized knowledge. The wit, the sarcasm, the use of Hebrew—all these things make it Jewish.

Novak and Waldoks state that Jewish humor tends to be anti-authoritarian and "ridicules grandiosity and self-indulgence, exposes hypocrisy, and kicks pomposity in the pants. It is strongly democratic, stressing the dignity and worth of common folk." They also make the point that it mocks everyone including God. It affirms rituals and traditions but frequently satirizes and mocks rituals, religious personalities, and institutions.[37] As we shall see, arguing with God goes all the way back to the Torah. The Talmud and Midrash also have no problem finding fault with how God runs the world. Ruth Wisse said the following about Jewish humor:

> Reversal, displacement, and turning the tables are the wellsprings of a tradition that mocks the contradictions of Jewish experience—the gap between accommodation to foreign powers and promise of divine election. Although many religions acknowledge a tension between the tenets and confutations of their faith, few have had to balance such high national hopes against such a poor political record. Jewish humor at its best interprets the incongruities of the Jewish condition.[38]

Sigmund Freud posited that there was something unique about Jewish humor. He observed: "I do not know whether there are many other instances of a people making fun to such a degree of its own character."[39] Self-disparaging humor is indeed something Jews excel at. Larry David, the driving force behind *Seinfeld* and *Curb Your Enthusiasm* repeatedly engages in humor of this sort. The shows have featured a blabbermouth rabbi, an incompetent *mohel*, Jews who renounce their religion for a *shiksa*, a dentist who converts to Judaism for the jokes, an observant Jewish woman who covers her hair but has no problem smoking on the Sabbath or committing adultery, a newly observant Jew who will not play golf on the Sabbath but insists on wearing a yarmulke when eating in a non-kosher restaurant owned by Palestinians, and more.

Not everyone is a fan of self-directed Jewish humor. Abraham Foxman of the Anti-Defamation League (ADL) has, over the last several years, repeatedly taken Jewish comedians—for example, Sacha Baron Cohen—to task for making fun of their own group. He feels that it encourages anti-Semitism.

Still, of all the characteristics of Jewish humor, perhaps the one that is most definitive is the ability of Jews to laugh at themselves—and, of course, at each other. Most ethnicities and nationalities have a group they poke fun at. In America, there are those odious Polish jokes; the North has Southern jokes, and everyone loves those redneck jokes. The humor of just about every country has a group that it makes fun of and to which it feels superior. In Jewish humor, the thing is, Jews make fun of themselves. Even in the jokes about the "wise" men of Chelm, which sound very much like, say, Polish jokes, the Chelmites are themselves Jews. So who do Jews get to feel superior to? To the not-so-wise men of Chelm, for one. And, of course, to each other. With so many Jewish sub-cultures, it's easy to find someone to make fun of.

What happened when the Jews received the Torah at Mount Sinai?

The Yekkes (German Jews) came early, and therefore they got the man-ners. After all, we know that derech eretz kodma leTorah[40] *(literally, manners preceded the Torah).*

The Litvaks came exactly on time and got Torah.

The Chassidim were so awed with this great spiritual gift the Lord was giving them, that they spent a long time preparing themselves for this awesome event and thus, arrived late (as Chassidim are wont to do) missing the entire thing. And, so, the Chassidim got the Kiddush!

Yekkes, the German Jews, are known to be very proper. *Litvaks*, Jews from Lithuania, are considered to be Torah intellectuals, over-ly consumed with the letter of the law. Chassidism is a movement that arose in opposition to the cold, intellectual approach of the *Litvaks*, and its members traditionally are more interested in the spiritual and the metaphysical. They are also known to enjoy a good *kiddush* or two.

Joseph Telushkin devotes a section of his book, *Jewish Humor: What the Best Jewish Jokes Say About the Jews*, to "Jewish Civil Wars," about the very serious battles among different Jewish denominations, eth-nicities, and nationalities that nonetheless provide fertile inspiration for much of Jewish humor. For example:

A new rabbi comes to a well-established congregation.

Every week on the Sabbath, a fight erupts during the service. When it comes time to recite the Sh'ma Yisra'el, "Hear, O Israel, the Lord Is Our God, the Lord Is One," half of the congregation stands and the other half sits. The half who stand say, "Of course we stand for the Sh'ma Yisrae'el: It's the credo of Judaism. Throughout history, thousands of

Jews have died with the words of the Sh'ma on their lips." The half who remain seated say, "No. According to the Shulkhan Arukh (the Code of Jewish Law), if you are seated when you come to the Sh'ma you remain seated." The people who are standing, yell at the people who are sitting, "Stand up!" while the people who are sitting yell at the people who are standing, "Sit down!" It's destroying the whole decorum of the service, and driving the rabbi crazy.

Finally, it's brought to the rabbi's attention that at a nearby home for the aged is a ninety-eight-year-old man who was a founding member of the congregation. So, in accordance with talmudic tradition, the rabbi appoints a delegation of three, one who stands for the Sh'ma, one who sits, and the rabbi himself, to go interview the man. They enter his room, and the man who stands for the Sh'ma rushes over to the old man and says: "Wasn't it the tradition in our congregation to stand for the Sh'ma?"

"No," the old man answers in a weak voice. "That wasn't the tradition."

The other man jumps in excitedly. "Wasn't it the tradition in our congregation to sit for the Sh'ma?"

"No," the old man says. "That wasn't the tradition."

At this point, the rabbi cannot control himself. He cuts in angrily. "I don't care what the tradition was! Just tell them one or the other: Do you know what goes on in services every week—the people who are standing yell at the people who are sitting, the people who are sitting yell at the people who are standing—"

"That was the tradition," the old man says.[41]

Why We Laugh

While many hypotheses as to why people laugh have been postulated, humor studies scholars posit three major schools of thought. *Incongruity theory* posits that humor results from a contrast between what is logically expected and what actually takes place or what is said.[42] Although Alexander Gerard[43] and James Beattie[44] first proposed this theory (some claim that it was actually proposed even earlier, by Blaise Pascal in the seventeenth century), it is usually associated with Immanuel Kant[45] and Arthur Schopenhauer.[46]

A rabbi and a minister were sitting together on a plane.

The stewardess came up to them and asked, "Would you care for a cocktail?"

"Sure," said the rabbi. "Please bring me a Manhattan."

"Fine, sir," said the stewardess. "And you, Reverend?"

"Young lady," he said, "before I touch strong drink, I'd just as soon commit adultery."

"Oh, miss," said the rabbi. "As long as there's a choice, I'll have what he's having."[47]

The *Relief/Release theory* of humor focuses on the fact that laughter is a socially acceptable way to release pent-up tension and nervous energy, and to relieve stress. This theory was first developed by Herbert Spencer[48] but was made famous by Freud.[49] Many people may be afraid or find it difficult or uncomfortable to talk about certain subjects, for example, such topics as impotence, homosexuality, violence, racism, rape, or incest. Humor is a socially acceptable way of relieving one's tension about sensitive issues.

Much gallows humor, or dark humor, falls into this category. For example,

Hitler, not being a religious man, was inclined to consult his astrologers about the future. As the tide of war worsened, he asked, "Am I going to lose the war?"

Answered affirmatively, he then asked, "Well, am I going to die?" Consulting their charts, the astrologers again said, yes.

"When am I going to die?" was Hitler's next question. This time the answer was, "You're going to die on a Jewish holiday."

"But when . . . on what holiday?" he asked in agitation.

The reply: "Any day you die will be a Jewish holiday."[50]

Superiority theory suggests that the purpose of humor is to demonstrate one's superiority, dominance, or power over others. Mocking humor that belittles the stupidity, infirmities, or weaknesses of other groups would certainly be a way of demonstrating the "superiority" of one's own reference group and thus boosting one's ego. Superiority theory is associated with Thomas Hobbes[51] but was also discussed by many others including Aristotle, Plato, and Cicero. A variation of superiority theory is posited by Charles Gruner[52] who believes that humor should be seen as a type of game in which there is a winner and a loser. The winners are the parties doing the laughing and the losers are the ones being laughed about or at. Not all proponents of the superiority theory of humor see it as belittling and denigrating others. Some assert that this type of humor may also be sympathetic, empathetic, and congenial.[53]

Two wise men of Chelm were deep in conversation, discussing the intricacies of modern travel.

"Let me understand you correctly," said the first man. "it takes a horse and carriage only four hours to go from here to Pinsk, is that right?"

"Exactly," said his friend. "But if you had a carriage with two *horses, then it would take you only two hours."*

"I see," replied the first. "And I suppose, then, that if you had a carriage with four horses, you'd get there in no time at all. Is that right?"

"Precisely," answered his friend. "But in that case, why bother to go to Pinsk in the first place? Better to just harness up your four horses and stay right here!" [54]

Jokes about the "wise" men of Chelm are sometimes compared to the odious "Polish" type of joke, in which members of some particular nationality or ethnicity are mercilessly ridiculed as being extremely stupid. However, this analogy is mistaken. True, we laugh at (rather than with) the less-than-wise foibles of the folks of Chelm who think they are, indeed, quite wise. But we appreciate these jokes with a warmth reserved for the less talented members of our own family. In their foibles, we recognize extreme versions of our own faulty reasoning. Polish jokes, racist jokes, blonde jokes and their ilk denigrate the "other" toward the simple goal of making oneself feel superior; they have no redeeming value.

Humor is Culture Specific

As culture moderates all human endeavors, it should come as no surprise that these general abstract theories of humor are moderated by cultural factors. One of the underpinnings of humor and humor research is that all humor will not necessarily be funny to all people. In other words, there is really no such thing as pure humor.[55] All humor is to some extent cultural and, perhaps to that same extent, humor serves to define, explain, and enhance our understanding of a particular culture. Thomas Veatch[56] posits that the way in which people from diverse cultures are offended, amused, or even unaffected by different sets of events reflects different subjective moral systems. Hugh LaFollette and Niall Shanks[57] also note that all humor is context-dependent, some depending on the listeners' beliefs. Even in antiquity it was believed that it is possible to learn a great deal about a person by what he finds funny.[58] Much like the Indian parable of the blind men and the elephant,[59] in which several blind men approach the elephant and each "sees" it in a totally different way (a snake, a wall, a rope, etc.), humor is one of the ways with which we can grasp a level of understanding of a highly complex cultural environment.

Humor can be used to deride other groups (e.g., racist jokes, lawyer jokes) but it can also be used to enhance the image of a group. Of course, one joke can sometimes do both: mock one group while at the same time making another group appear smarter than everyone else. According to Martineau's model of in-group humor, when humor lauds the in-group, it functions to strengthen the group. When the humor belittles the in-group, it has one of four purposes: to control the behavior of the in-group; to strengthen the in-group, that is, using self-disparaging humor to laughingly talk of one's own group's weaknesses but in a congenial way that strengthens the rapport of the group; to introduce or encourage conflict that is already present; and to encourage the break-up of the group. When humor lauds an out-group, it functions to strengthen the group. The out-group may be seen as a reference group and the humor demonstrates that the two groups have much in common. When humor belittles an out-group, it enhances the morale of the in-group and introduces or encourages a negative attitude toward the out-group.[60]

With ethnic humor, it becomes crucial to know who is telling the joke and who is listening to it. Some jokes are very funny when told by a member of the group to a listener who is also of the group, about some real or perceived shortcoming of their shared ethnicity. This is a true bonding experience. The same joke, however, told by one outsider to another outsider is highly likely to be derogatory (deprecating, rather than self-deprecating). Racist humor often falls into this sinkhole. For example, the following:

Two Jews are about to face a Russian firing squad. The two condemned men are offered blindfolds. One of them accepts it, but the other does not, defiantly saying: "I don't want your blindfold." His friend urges: "Shh . . . don't make trouble."

When told by one Jew to another, this joke is a gentle acknowledgement of the tendency of Jews in the Diaspora to keep quiet at all cost, rather than attract unwelcome attention. On the other hand, when this joke is told by one non-Jew to another, especially with humorous Jewish-sounding names and dialect as in Gruner's book,[61] it definitely comes across as disparaging to Jews.

Certain behaviors that would be considered bigoted coming from a non-Jew are just fine—and even give us a warm, fuzzy, friendly feeling—when engaged in by a Jew. For example, Jews love to devise lists of well-known or important individuals—such as celebrities, scientists, athletes, etc.—who are Jewish; take Adam Sandler's "The Chanukah Song," for example. Many jokes about Jews are funny when told to one Jew by another Jew, but bigoted when told by one anti-Semite—er, non-Jew—to another. For example, many of the gags in Sacha Baron Cohen's movie, *Borat*, fall into this category.

Also:

Two Jews pass a Catholic church with a big sign outside that reads:
CONVERT TO CATHOLICISM—GET $100

Abe looks up and down the street, then turns to Izzy and says, "Let's do it—no one will know and we'll each make a hundred bucks."

"Okay," says Izzy, "but you go first."

Abe strides purposefully into the church and comes back out twenty minutes later.

"So," asks Izzy eagerly, "did you get the $100?"

Abe rolls his eyes and says, "Is that all you people think about?"

and

The El Al plane landed at Ben Gurion airport, and the Captain made the usual announcement: "We have landed successfully. Please remain seated with your seat belts fastened until the plane comes to a complete stop, and the seat belt sign has been turned off. Also, until that time, the use of cell phones on board this aircraft is strictly prohibited.

"To those of you who are still seated, we wish you a Happy Easter, and hope that you enjoy your stay in the Holy Land. And to those of you standing in the aisles and talking on your cell phones, we wish you a Happy Passover. And welcome back home."

Sometimes humor of this type seems to operate under the theory of superiority, as when another (outsider) group is the object of the joke. At other times, there is no superiority; the humor may be of the self-deprecating type. Sometimes it is hard to tell the difference. One popular category of Jewish humor involves the anti-Semite. This appears to be an example of self-deprecating humor. In fact, many believe that the Jewish penchant for self-deprecating humor arose from centuries of abuse and disparagement at the hands of anti-Semites. However, much like Cyrano's soliloquy about his nose, Jewish anti-Semite jokes are often taken to be examples of superiority-oriented humor. The victim shows up the oppressor by doing it himself—and doing it better. As Martin Grotjahn put it:

> One can almost see how a witty Jewish man carefully and cautiously takes a sharp dagger out of his enemy's hands, sharpens it so that it can split a hair in midair, polishes it until it shines brightly, stabs himself with it, then returns it gallantly to the anti-Semite with a silent reproach: now see whether you can do it half as well.[62]

Christie Davies[63] appreciates Grotjahn's imagery but considers it misleading. According to Davies, "the point of getting hold of the dagger is not only to demonstrate superior dexterity but to switch daggers so that an innocuous rather than a potentially envenomed weapon is used."

Hermetic Humor of the In-Group: Special Knowledge Required

Freudenheim was walking down the street in Nazi Germany in 1934, when suddenly a large black limousine pulled up beside him. Freudenheim looked up in astonishment and terror as Hitler himself climbed out of the car.

Holding a gun to Freudenheim, Hitler ordered him to get down on his hands and knees. And pointing to a pile of excrement on the curb, Hitler ordered the Jew to eat it.

Freudenheim, putting discretion before valor, complied. Hitler began laughing so hard that he dropped the gun. Freudenheim picked it up, and ordered Hitler to undergo the same humiliation. As Hitler got down on the sidewalk, Freudenheim ran from the scene as fast as he could.

Later that day, when Freudenhim returned home, his wife asked him "How was your day?"

"Oh, fine, dear," he answered. "By the way, you'll never guess who I had lunch with today!"[64]

Sure this joke is about oppression and anti-Semitism, but it also is appreciated on another, somewhat hermetic, level. To do this one must have some familiarity with the German Jew archetype who always tries to hobnob with the elite and demonstrate by any means possible what a high-class guy he is, in fact, much like the tragic namedropper in the above joke. In that sense, this may be considered an *in joke*.

Much humor has a social purpose. It serves as a bonding device. Indeed, there are several kinds of humor whose primary function appears to be the creation of a sense of belongingness and togetherness. Some of this humor is almost generic, in that the same joke works well for one subgroup and then can be reworked and recycled to be just as funny to another group of people; but much of it—the really good stuff—is not. This type of humor covers a wide variety of comic endeavors, including the humor of various ethnic groups, racial groups, religions, professions, scientific disciplines, indeed, any group of individuals who share a body of knowledge, rituals, experience, lore, and, of course, a sense of humor.[65] Ted Cohen[66] uses the term *conditional* for jokes that will work only with certain audiences—like the "Don't make trouble" joke, above—and *hermetic* for those jokes that presume particular knowledge or belief. Some of the most strongly conditional, hermetic jokes are those that make references to the jargon or knowledge of a particular profession, ethnic group, or religion. In-group humor, a kind of culture-specific humor, can be used, for example, to help new recruits or trainees develop a feeling of belonging. In general, this type of humor tends to bond together members of the profession. This type of bonding humor helps people find common ground.[67] Marvin Koller notes, "to share a laugh together is a major social bond,"[68] that is, humor builds rapport. In-group humor may be just as conditional as culture-specific bonding humor. It may also be hermetic, meant only for true insiders and, for the most part, might not even sound funny unless one has the necessary knowledge or experience to understand it. This type of humor cannot be recycled for use by other groups, as it depends on shared knowledge between the joke teller and the audience.

When bonding humor is hermetic, the listener must bring some kind of specialized knowledge to the joke-telling enterprise or the joke is meaningless, or, at least, not funny. This phenomenon can occur in tightly knit groups or groups that share similar experience or knowledge, for example, musicians, mathematicians, computer scientists or, even, families. Avner Ziv and Orit Gadish found that private jokes, phrases, sayings, and expressions constitute a kind of "secret language" for couples and serve to strengthen "feelings of belongingness and intracouple cohesiveness."[69]

How do we explain this type of humor? Although, at first glance, there seems to be a slight fit or overlap with the type of humor based on superiority theory, it is really quite different. With humor that is hermetic but derives its satisfaction from superiority, the payoff comes when the listener is baffled—an explanation is clearly *required*, whether or not it is offered. There is definitely a winner and a loser here, a sort of *gotcha*. Some humor of this type is so hermetic, that even the teller does not understand it but only pretends to, for example, the "elephant jokes."[70] This sort of joke requires a three-handed experience: the joke teller, an accomplice who laughs at the joke, and the baffled listener.

Conversely, the payoff for in-group humor, in fact, is in *not* needing to explain the joke. Both parties share the joke; they are both winners. Those who would not understand the joke—the presumed outsiders—are not relevant to this transaction;they are not even there. Superiority is not at play. It is this unstated bond, this implied wink, this *secret handshake* that informs the transaction: both parties are members of the "club."

Question: Why does Orthodox Judaism forbid premarital sex?
Answer: Because it might lead to mixed dancing.

To the world at large, this joke might require some explanation. It pokes fun at an ultra-Orthodox fastidious level of observance, namely, to stay away from any possible temptation, to place a "fence" around something that one must not do by adding even more "don'ts" into the mix than are already there. In the following, in which a Reform rabbi offers his congregant a solution very appropriate to the problem, references the practice among Orthodox Jews of checking the parchment of the *mezuzah* when tragedy strikes the family and has definite elements of incongruity.

A Reform Jew goes to his rabbi, very depressed.

"My son," he says, "has become very Orthodox. He goes full time to a yeshiva, and claims that everything in our house is unkosher, so he can never eat with us. And worst of all, he's influenced our daughter. She's left the house and gone to study at some super Orthodox seminary for women."

"And what about your younger son?" the rabbi asks. "The one who was at Stanford?"

"That's the worst case of all," the man answers. "He got hooked up with some Hasidim, and now lives at a yeshiva in Israel."

"Have you thought of checking your mezuzot?" the rabbi asks.[71]

Here, the Reform rabbi suggests to his congregant that he might wish to check his *mezuzah*, and this is an example of hermetic, incongruity-based, culture-specific humor. To appreciate the joke, one must know about the phenomenon of returnees (i.e., the *baal teshuva* movement) being more observant than their parents, as well as the practice among Orthodox Jews of checking (for possible errors) the parchment contained in the *mezuzah* case in times of crisis.

Another example of a Jewish joke that is conditional and hermetic is the following. This is an example of a joke that requires knowledge of Orthodox Jewish "types." In particular, one must know about the type of "Litvak" (a Jew with origins in Lithuania) who is very extreme in his observance of ritualistic details, to the point where the fellow in this joke somewhat misses the big picture.

A very devout Litvak is praying at the Kotel *(Western Wall) when, suddenly, an Islamic extremist grabs him from behind and puts a large knife to his throat. The Jew quickly recites the blessing for someone who is about to die for his religion:* "Baruch ata . . . al kiddush Hashem!"

The terrorist, impressed with his victim's piety, stops what he is doing and turns to leave.

The Litvak, pointing to his throat, calls out impatiently to the terrorist: "Nu! Nu!"

In order to understand this joke, one must know about the concept of a blessing made in vain, and how this "sin" might be very upsetting to someone who compulsively follows the letter of the law.

We have tried to demonstrate by our examples that we can find in the oeuvre of Jewish humor all these fundamental theories of why we laugh—whether it is the incongruity of the haughty beggar, the superiority (on the part of both the joke teller and the audience) in the stories of the wise men of Chelm, the relief/release in telling jokes about the Holocaust, the culture-specific Yiddish curses, or the hermetic jokes involving Talmudic logic.

Origins of Jewish Humor

Scholars, naturally, disagree on the origins of Jewish humor. How far back does Jewish humor go? A few hundred years? To Talmudic times? To the Bible? There are those who insist that Jewish humor is a modern manifestation not in evidence before nineteenth-century Europe.[72] Many individuals believe that the Bible, in particular the Hebrew Bible, is without any humor at all. For example, Alfred North

Whitehead was of the opinion that there is no humor in the Old Testament. He claimed that "the total absence of humor from the Bible is one of the most singular things in all of literature."[73] Whitehead attributed the humorlessness of the Bible to the fact that the ancient Jews were a "depressed people" because of their situation, that is, continually attacked and overrun by foreign powers.

Needless to say, many scholars disagree with Whitehead. In fact, tragedy and humor can and do exist side by side. Indeed, in Part II of this book, we demonstrate that the Hebrew Bible does include humor—and lots of it. However, to truly appreciate this humor one must be well versed in the Hebrew language. Language-based humor, like puns, alliteration, and wordplay, does not translate well.

Ziv discusses the question as to whether there is such a thing as Jewish humor.[74] He cites sources such as Ben-Amos[75] who feels that there really is no such thing as distinctly Jewish humor. Ziv notes, however, that there are those who disagree and assert that there is such a thing as Jewish humor. Wisse cites sources such as Elliott Oring[76] and others who believe that Jewish humor is a "late invention."[77] Some scholars believe that it has its roots in the *badchen* (wedding jester) that was prevalent in Eastern Europe for hundreds of years. Mel Gordon, a Professor of Theater, is one of the proponents of the view that Jewish humor started in 1661 when the Council of Four Lands (*Va'ad Arba' Aratzot*), the central governing institution that administered Jewish affairs in Poland, met to see why God punished the Jewish people with the horrific pogroms by Chmielnicki from 1648–1651 in which 100,000 Jews were butchered. The Council attributed this to a divine punishment and ruled that levity and luxury would be prohibited. The Council, however, exempted the *badchen* since he was more abusive than funny. The *badchen* was extremely sarcastic and would make fun of the bride, groom, and guests. For instance, he would tell the bride she was ugly and make fun of the gifts brought by guests. The *badchen* would use humor as a "leveling device" to put some of the affluent townspeople in their place; the powerful were subtly knocked by the less powerful (but witty) members of society. According to Gordon, this type of mocking humor that we refer to as Jewish humor is an offshoot of *badchan* humor, the only humor that remained after the Council forbade levity. Even Jewish waiter jokes, in which the waiter insults the customer, is essentially a kind of *badchan* humor.[78] The institution of *badchen* has not disappeared completely; many Chassidic weddings today feature a *badchen*.

What may have enriched Jewish humor for the last two thousand years is the persecution that has caused the Jewish people to move from country to country seeking a haven. A Jew going to a synagogue will find Jews with all kinds of backgrounds—Hungary, Poland, Romania, Lithuania, Russia, Germany, France, Syria, Morocco, Iran, Yemen, Argentina, Mexico, Columbia, and many other countries. This results in humor where one group makes fun of the peculiarities of another group—for example, Hungarian Jews making fun of the *Yekkes* (German Jews). After the Second World War, Hungarian Jews did not get along with the Polish Jews. There was friction between the *greener* (newly arrived Jew to America, a greenhorn) and the American Jews. This hostility often emerged in humor.

Wherever Jews have settled, they have taken on the trappings of the predominant culture. How, then, are we to talk about a Jewish sense of humor, or a Jewish sense of anything? How to come up with a framework for Jewish humor when Jews are Ashkenazi, Sepharadi, Bukharian, Iranian, Argentinian, Mexican, etc.? How can these diverse cultural groups have anything in common, let alone a common comic sensibility?

What does it mean to be Jewish? At the conclusion of this book we examine different paradigms of Jewishness—for example, race, religion, culture—all of which fall short. So, perhaps Jews are not quite a defined race, not quite a cohesive religion, not quite a distinct culture, not quite a nationality. There is no single common history, food, culture, dress, or daily language. We are, however, an identifiable people (*am*)—certainly, to the anti-Semite. What Jews everywhere and across the centuries have in common are the scriptures and the ancient writings containing their varied interpretations.

Wisse feels that the "seeds of Jewish skepticism" and "cognitive independence" are found in the verse in Genesis (18:12) when Sarah laughs and says: "After I have grown old shall I have pleasure, my Lord being old also?" Sarah appears to believe more in "biological probability" than "divine prophecy."[79] Sarah does give birth to a son and is told to name him Yitzchak. The commentaries make the distinction between the bitter, skeptical laughter of Sarah and the jubilant, joyous laughter of Abraham who never doubts that Sarah will give him a son. In any event, God tells Abraham what his son will be named, Yitzchak, meaning "he will laugh."[80] God gets the last laugh!

According to Jonathan Sacks, Chief Rabbi of Great Britain and a noted scholar, "Too little attention has been paid to the use of humor in the Torah. Its most important form is the use of satire to mock the pretensions of human beings who think they can emulate G-d."[81] Samson Raphael Hirsch, the great German commentator on the Torah, says that the reason the Torah mentions what the Jews said when they beheld the powerful Egyptian army advancing upon them when they were at the Sea of Reeds (or Red Sea) was to show us how witty the Israelites were even in times of great distress. The snide, but clever, remark made by them was: "Were there no graves in Egypt that you took us to die in the wilderness?"[82]

The Talmud and Midrash also have a great deal to teach us about how humor can be used. The type of logic used is very useful in humor. Even the strange stories and cases find themselves in Jewish humor. Those who want to have a deeper understanding of Jewish humor must first delve into the Torah and Rabbinic writings to understand what has shaped the Jewish persona. The Talmud itself notes that a person is known by his humor. The "People of the Book" have no choice but to be influenced by it.

Many scholars note that Jewish humor goes back to the Torah and/ or Talmud.[83] This makes a great deal of sense since the Torah and the Talmud are essentially what Jews from so many disparate parts of the world have in common. A Sephardic Jew from Iran does not have a common history, language, or culture with a Jew from Poland. What these Jews do have in common is the Torah and the Talmud. This is why it is important to examine the Torah, Talmud, and Midrash to have a better understanding of Jewish humor. Even the way we study the Torah and Talmud gives Jews from all parts of the world an appreciation of the written word. Commentaries on the Torah force us to examine each word and argue about its meaning.

God is supposed to be omnipotent and omniscient, yet there are numerous examples in the Hebrew Bible where mortals argue or disagree with Him. All in all, God does not do very well in these disputes. This, in itself, could be considered humorous. How does one even begin to have the temerity to disagree with an omniscient God? God knows exactly what you are going to say—why would He be swayed by your argument?

David Frank believes:

> The Jewish tradition offers much to the broader study of argumentation. Indeed, the process of argumentation is often more important than Truth. Ultimately, the Jewish tradition of argument teaches the

global community of the benefits of reasoned discourse and pluralism. We now know that ethical behavior is much more likely when argumentation and persuasion are taught as means of dealing with difference and disagreement.

Frank makes the point that "by arguing, rather than simply exercising raw power, God relinquishes control over and vests freedom to humans."[84] Frequently, the mortal wins, yet—how can a mortal even hope to win an argument with the omniscient One? It is this unspoken tension that makes these stories interesting—and, often, funny.[85]

Since the major purpose of the Talmud was to elaborate on the written laws of the Bible, there are a great number of legal disputes recorded in the Talmud; often one sage is pitted against another in attempting to demonstrate that the law agrees with his view. The sages of the Talmud, smart and sharp and educated, frequently employed various forms of humor in expressing themselves. These legal disputes often run across many pages in the Talmud and it takes many years to master Talmudic logic. Not surprisingly, perhaps, there is quite a bit of humor that involves Talmudic logic itself,[86] as well as at least one claim that yeshiva (Jewish school) study which emphasizes Talmud dialectics has produced "not only rabbis and religious scholars but also comedy writers and comedians."[87] Joseph Telushkin believes that parodies of Talmudic reasoning are the basis of numerous Jewish jokes.[88] And, Henry Spalding, in his work on Jewish humor, devotes an entire section to "Logic and Deduction."[89] Novak and Waldoks also dedicate a portion of their classic—and wonderful—work on Jewish humor to Talmudic logic. They note:

> If classic Jewish jokes share anything with the Talmud, it is in their process rather than their content. Improbable logic, slightly convoluted arguments, skepticism, and a remarkable desire to equate intelligence with common sense—these are some of the characteristics of the rabbinic mind, as well as of Jewish humor.[90]

When it comes to the practical application of Talmudic logic and argument, nothing compares to the vast oeuvre of material about the impudent Jewish *shnorrer* (beggar):

Beggar: "One kopek? Last week you gave me two kopeks."
Lazar: "I had a bad week."
Beggar: "So, if you had a bad week, why should I suffer?"[91]

A schnorrer *knocks at the door of a well-to-do household and is invited to share dinner with the host and hostess. A spread of many delicious foods is offered as well as both coarse black bread and fine white bread. The beggar quickly devours the white bread and asks for more.*

"You know," says the host carefully, not wanting to hurt the poor fellow's feelings, "white bread is quite expensive."

"Yes, I know" responds the schnorrer, *"but it's well worth it!"*

And this one referenced by Freud:

A shnorrer *is having heart problems and goes to a very expensive specialist. When the time comes to pay, the shnorrer says he has no money at all.*

"So why did you come to me?" the doctor asks angrily. "You know I am the most expensive doctor in Vienna."

"Because when it comes to my health, I want only the best." [92]

In fact, the similarity of these "modern classics" to the following Talmudic anecdote is extremely hard to ignore. This Talmudic passage illustrates that poor people are to be provided with a level of support that will maintain them in the style to which they had become accustomed before becoming impoverished.

> *A man came before Rava applying for assistance. Rava asked him: "What do you usually eat?" The man said: "Stuffed hen and old wine." Rava asked: "Are you not concerned that your extravagant taste will be a burden on the community?" He said: "Am I eating of theirs? I am eating of the Merciful One's bounty, for we learned,*[93] *'The eyes of all look hopefully to You, and You give them their food in his season.' The verse does not say 'in their season' but 'in his season,' teaching us that the Holy One provides for every individual in accordance with that to which one is accustomed." While they were talking, Rava's sister, whom he had not seen for thirteen years, arrived, bringing him stuffed hen and old wine. Rava said: "How remarkable! I apologize to you; please go and eat."*[94]

In this story, while the beggar uses Biblical sources to prove his argument, his attitude of entitlement makes him a direct genetic ancestor of the arrogant *schnorrers* of modern Jewish humor. And, in the passage above, his sense of entitlement to community support in the style to which he feels he deserves is upheld by God Himself, in the form of the "remarkable" occurrence.

Jews appreciate humor. At the risk of egregious generalization, the people of the book may truly be the people of the *joke* as well. Some believe that all you have to do to get a room full of Jews laughing is to shout out punch lines of old (er, classic) Jewish jokes. Not the entire joke, just the punch line.[95] Try it—our guess is that you'll get "hecklers" calling out punch lines of their own. There's even a series of jokes about *that*. For example:

Manny flies down to Miami Beach to visit his friend Abie.

His first day there, he finds Abie sitting with a group of his friends around the pool. As Manny watches in confusion, someone calls out a number, say, "42!" and everyone laughs hysterically. Then another one: "65!" More raucous laughter. He quietly asks Abie, "what are you guys doing?"

Abie replies, "Well, we sit out here every day, telling old jokes. A while back we realized that we are telling the same jokes over and over again. So, in the interest of efficiency and to save time, we cataloged them and now we just have to say a number instead of telling the whole joke." And with that, Abie calls out, "57!" which promptly results in a round of guffaws.

Manny likes the idea and, after watching a while, decides to give it a try. He thinks a moment and calls out, "38!"

Silence. Nothing.

Abie pats his friend on the back and whispers, "Don't worry about it, Manny. It's just that we heard that one already."

2

A Word on the Sources: Biblical, Talmudic, and Midrashic Literature

Jewish tradition[1] organizes the Hebrew Bible or *Tanach*—an acronym of *Torah, Neveim*, and *Ketubim*—into three categories of the canon. The *Five Books of Moses*, also called the Pentateuch or the *Torah*, are Genesis, Exodus, Leviticus, Numbers, and Deuteronomy. The *Prophets* (*Neveim*) consists of eight books, including Joshua, Judges, Samuel, Kings, Jeremiah, Ezekiel, Isaiah, and the Twelve Minor Prophets (e.g., Haggai, Zechariah, and Malachi). The *Writings* (*Ketubim*) is composed of eleven books, namely, Ruth, Psalms, Job, Proverbs, Ecclesiastes, Song of Songs, Lamentations, Daniel, Esther, Ezra (and Nehemiah), and Chronicles. The traditional Jewish view is that the Torah (and all the commandments) were divinely revealed to Moses at Mount Sinai.

The Jewish oral law elaborates on the written law contained in the Torah. The Talmud is the compilation of Jewish oral law, consisting of the *Mishna*, compiled and redacted by Rabbi Yehuda Hanasi, known as Rebbi, about the year 189 C.E. in Israel; and the *Gemara*, commentaries and discussions on the *Mishna*. The Mishna consists of six orders (*sedarim*). The names of these orders are: *zera'im*—seeds—dealing with agricultural laws; *mo'ed*—season—dealing with festivals; *nashim*—women—dealing with marriage and divorce; *nezikin*—damages—dealing with civil and criminal law; *kodashim*—sanctities—dealing with sacrifices and Temple offerings; *teharot*—purities—dealing with ritual purity and impurity. Each order is composed of tractates (*massektot*) and there are a total of sixty-three tractates.

The pre-Tannaitic period known as *zugot*—literally, pairs, the most famous pair being Hillel and Shammai—started about 200 B.C.E.

The Tannaitic period started with Rabbi Yochanan b. Zakkai[2] and his colleagues, and lasted from about the year 40 to 200 C.E., five generations of *Tannaim*. This was followed by a transition period from 200 to 220 C.E., and then the Amoraic period from 220 to 500 C.E., eight generations of *Amoraim* (*see* Appendix B). Many statements of the *Tannaim* which are not part of the *Mishna* are found in *Baraitot* (literally meaning outside, i.e., external and not part of the *Mishna*) which were edited and redacted by Rabbi Chiya and Rabbi Oshiyah. Even though the *Baraitot* are not part of the *Mishna*, they are still quite authoritative and are frequently discussed in the *Gemara*.

There were academies in Israel and Babylon independently studying and researching the *Mishna*. Thus, there are two versions of the Talmud: the Jerusalem Talmud (*Talmud Yerushalmi*), a product of the academies in Israel, and the Babylonian Talmud (*Talmud Bavli*), a product of the academies in Babylon. The *Gemara* of the Babylonian Talmud is considerably larger than that of the Jerusalem Talmud, and it is more authoritative. References to the Talmud without qualification are usually to the Babylonian Talmud. The Babylonian Talmud, compiled by Ravina and Rabbi Ashi, was completed around the year 500 C.E., and the Jerusalem Talmud was completed circa 400 C.E.

The Talmud is mainly concerned with *halacha* (Jewish law) but also provides a detailed record of the beliefs of the Jewish people, their philosophy, traditions, culture, and folklore, that is, the *aggada*(homiletics). The *aggada* is basically moralistic and in it we find attempts to explain such concepts as the afterlife, God, Satan, the Messiah, why good people suffer, penitence, and how to lead the ideal life. The Midrash, a separate scripture, recorded the views of the Talmudic sages and is mainly devoted to the exposition of Biblical verses. There are two types of Midrash: Halachic Midrash which is mainly concerned with Jewish law and Aggadic Midrash which is homiletic and is mainly concerned with morality. The sages quoted and discussed in the Midrash are generally the same sages as in the Talmud.

Zevi Hirsch Chajes[3] states that the aim of the homiletic portion of the Talmud was to inspire people to serve the Lord. In addition, if a lecturer noticed that the audience was not paying attention or was dozing off, he might tell stories which "sounded strange or terrifying or which went beyond the limits of the natural and so won the attention of his audience for his message."

The stories told in the Talmud and Midrash, many of which are referenced in this book, were not necessarily meant to be taken literally.

Maimonides[4] describes individuals who take the homiletics of the Talmud literally as simple-minded fools, since there are hidden inner meanings in the stories, riddles, and parables used in *aggada*. Literal or not, the stories have had a profound effect on the Jewish people. The *aggadic* material in the Talmud sheds light on how Judaism views such diverse issues as God, Satan, the afterlife, marriage, good and evil, death, and, even, laughter. As one might expect, most of the humor of the Talmud and Midrash is found in the *aggadic* portions.

Part II
Heavenly Humor

3

Does God Have a Sense of Humor?

A Reform rabbi was so compulsive a golfer that once, on Yom Kippur, he left the house early and went out for a quick nine holes by himself. An angel who happened to be looking on immediately notified his superiors that a grievous sin was being committed on earth.

On the sixth hole, God caused a mighty wind to take the ball directly from the tee to the cup for a miraculous and dramatic hole in one. The angel was horrified. "Lord," he said, "you call this a punishment?"

"Sure," answered God with a smile. "Who can he tell?"[1]

Somewhere in the wide range of characters that appear in Jewish humor—the schlemiel, the Wise Men of Chelm, the snide waiter, the sarcastic beggar, the matchmaker, the anti-Semite, the pompous fool, and many more—is, believe it or not, the Creator Himself. In fact, Jewish humor is rather unique in the way God is portrayed: God is often blamed, criticized, haggled with, and sometimes seems almost like a Lower East Side haberdasher.

Does God have a sense of humor? With all the humor *about* God, in both modern and ancient times, He'd better be able to take a joke— for our sake, of course! In fact, the Psalmist states: "He who sits in Heaven shall laugh."[2] Since we are supposed to emulate God in all his attributes—this is the principle of *imitatio Dei*—why not laugh along with Him?

William Novak and Moshe Waldoks assert that "Jewish humor mocks everyone—including God."[3] *Mock* may be too strong a word. Jewish humor involving God often tries to make a point, such as the unfairness of life or the unjustness of the Diaspora. Since God is the One to blame for the plight of His people, He is fair game for this sort of humor. This humor is generally not meant to show disrespect or defiance toward God. On the contrary, it demonstrates a great love for God, even though God is blamed for the unhappy plight of His people. The affection of God for His people and that of the Jewish people for God are manifested in this type of humor. One important function of humor according to Conrad Hyers is to minimize the distance between the sacred and the profane.[4] Jewish humor involving God may serve the function of making the Almighty seem closer to mankind.

A close Jewish friend of the authors who has had many problems often states his intention to run against God in a future election. He declares that he can easily beat God. When asked to state his platform, this friend responds: "Platform? Who needs a platform? I'll run on His record!" In other words, wars, AIDS, the Holocaust, famine, cancer, Alzheimer's disease, etc. In this friend's words: "God hasn't got a chance." This is typical Jewish humor and, believe it or not, is not perceived as blasphemous. It is a very Jewish way of saying: When will God end mankind's troubles and keep the promises made via numerous prophets regarding world peace and happiness?

The Talmud and Midrash, which have had a strong influence on the Jewish people, are filled with different types of humor, including humor involving God. Treating God in such an informal and familiar manner is also common in Chassidic tales, which were certainly influenced by the Talmudic stories. In Chassidic stories, God is often chided, albeit in a warm manner, for the harshness of the Diaspora and for not helping His people. For example, in one classic story, three Chassidic rabbis—Rabbi Elimelech of Lizhensk, Rabbi Israel of Koznitz, and the seer of Lublin—act as the Jewish court (a *beit din*) in a suit brought by an individual against God. Their verdict—that the plaintiff was right and God was wrong for allowing the emperor to issue an edict against the Jews. In this story, God, of course, had no choice but to obey the final verdict of the court: The decree was annulled.[5]

In another story, the famous Rabbi Levi Yitzchak of Berditchev once declared to God that if He did not forgive the Jewish people their sins, then he would tell the whole world that God's *tefillin* (phylacteries) were invalid. How could that be? Well, according to the Talmud,[6] God's *tefillin* contain the verse: "And who is like Your people Israel, a unique nation on earth."[7] Rabbi Levi explained that if God did not forgive the people of Israel their sins, then they were not a "unique nation on earth," thus making His *tefillin* invalid! On another occasion he scolded God and said: "The Jewish people are your *tefillin*. When one of the *tefillin* of a simple Jew falls on the ground he picks it up carefully and kisses it. Dear Lord!" Rabbi Levi cried, "Your *tefillin* have fallen to the ground."[8]

In Jewish literature too, God is quite frequently portrayed in a warm, amicable and, indeed, almost disrespectful, manner. For example, Sholom Aleichem's unforgettable character, Tevye the dairyman, had Job-like conversations with God: "O God, All-powerful and All-Merciful, great and good, kind and just, how does it happen that to some people you give everything and to others nothing?"[9] Even in the middle of his prayer, Tevye would interject his own personal comments: "*Thou sustainest the living with loving kindness*— and, sometimes, with a little food."[10] Yes, Tevye could be somewhat sarcastic at times: "With God's help, I starved to death . . . three times a day, not counting supper."[11]

It would be difficult to imagine members of another religion being able to joke about God to the degree that Jews can. At least as far back as Talmudic times, Jews saw God in a very different way than did other peoples. God could be treated like a member of the family—criticized, argued with, negotiated with—and He would not mind. Sometimes, He argued back. Sometimes, He even won.

A matron once asked one of the Talmudic sages what God has been doing since He created this world. The response was that God matches up people, that is, God is a matchmaker.[12] Apparently, matchmaking is so difficult that only God Himself can do it properly. Of course, if God is a matchmaker, we know that he sometimes has to tell white lies. On at least one occasion, God diplomatically manages to avoid friction between husband and wife.

> *The School of Rabbi Yishmael taught: Great is peace, for even the Holy One altered what was said for peace. It is written: "Sarah laughed to herself saying . . . My husband is old."*[13] *God, however, said to Abraham:*[14] *"Why did Sarah laugh and say . . . I am too old."*[15]

Even the great matriarch Sarah could be vain and act like other women. Sarah, who was eighty-nine years old when she heard that she would have her first child, laughed because she felt *Abraham* was too old. He was ninety-nine. Apparently, even at her advanced age she was reluctant to admit to herself that she was old too. What is more, God lied to Abraham, so as not to cause friction between husband and wife. The Talmud derives from this the principle that it is permitted to tell a white lie in order to preserve peace.[16] This story demonstrates that truth is not always the best route in human relationships. If God can tell a white lie, sometimes we should too.

In the Bible, we see that even though God is perfect, He seems to accept and even welcome criticism. Thus, Abraham had the temerity to say to God: "Shall the Judge of the whole world not act justly?"[17] Perhaps this is where Tevye learned to criticize God.

On the other hand, when Job demanded to confront God and know the reason for all his suffering, his wish was granted and God answered him with magnificent sarcasm: "Where were you when I laid the foundations of the earth?. . . Have you ever in your life commanded the morning, or told the dawn its place?"[18] God's sarcastic response to Job was basically a version of "Could you do my job?"

Shlomo was walking through a forest, observing nature, pondering life, and feeling very close to God. Shlomo said aloud, "God, are you listening?" And, amazingly, God replied, "Yes!"

Shlomo looked towards the heavens and said, "God, what is a million years to you?" God replied, "Shlomo, a million years to you is like a second to me."

Shlomo considered this for a while and then asked, "God, what is a million dollars to you?" And God replied, "Shlomo, a penny to me is like a million dollars to you."

"In that case," Shlomo said, "can I have a penny?" "Sure," God replied. "Just a second."

God appears to enjoy negotiating with mortals. The most famous example is that of Abraham "haggling" with God to save Sodom and Gomorrah from destruction:

> Abraham: "What if there are 50 innocent people in the city? Will you still destroy it?"
>
> God: "If I find 50 innocent people in Sodom, I will spare the entire area."
>
> Abraham: "Suppose there are 45. . . .?"
>
> God: "I will not destroy it if I find 45. . . ."
>
> Abraham: "What if there are 40?"
>
> God: "I will not act if there are forty. . . ."[19]

As this conversation continues, Abraham proposes and God agrees to allow for thirty, twenty, ten in succession, until Abraham finally gives up, presumably because ten innocents could not be found in those evil towns.

How different is that exchange from the following, more—uh—modern anecdote?

"Good morning. I came to this store because I don't like to bargain."

"Well, you've come to the right place. We're strictly a one-price outfit."

"Excellent. I like that blue suit over there. What will it cost?"

"Like I said, I don't fool around with bargaining. So I'm not going to ask two-fifty for this suit, or even two thirty-five. I'm going to give you my best price: two hundred and twenty dollars."

"Well, you're my kind of businessman, and that's why I'm here. I won't fool around and offer you one-sixty for that suit, or even one seventy-five. I'll give you two hundred dollars for that suit."

"You can have it for two hundred and ten."

"I'll take it."[20]

In a somewhat similar vein, the following Midrash portrays God trying to sell his "wares" to the nations of the world. This Midrash depicts God as a door-to-door salesman trying to peddle His Torah to each of the nations successively. In the end, God only finds one customer for His Torah.

When God revealed Himself to give the Torah to Israel, He did not only reveal Himself to Israel but also to all the nations.

First, He went to the descendants of Esau and asked them: Do you wish to receive the Torah?

They said to Him: What is written in it?

He said to them: Thou shalt not murder.

They said to Him: Creator of the Universe, The very essence of our forefathers was murder, as it says: "The hands are the hands of Esau."[21] And regarding this, his father Isaac assured him: "And by the sword shalt thou live."[22]

God then went to the children of Ammon and Moab, and said to them: Do you wish to receive the Torah?

They said to Him: What is written in it?

He said to them: Thou shalt not commit adultery.

They said to Him: Creator of the Universe, The very essence of our forefathers was incest, as it says: "And both daughters of Lot were made pregnant by their father."[23]

God went and found the children of Ishmael, and said to them: Do you wish to receive the Torah?

They said to Him: What is written in it?

He said to them: Thou shalt not steal.

They said to Him: Creator of the Universe, The very essence of our forefathers is robbery, as it says: "And he shall be a wild ass of a man."[24]

There was no nation among the nations that God did not go to, speak to, and knock at their door.[25]

The above Midrash is cited in numerous places and demonstrates that God had no success with any nation other than Israel in getting them to accept the Torah. A version of the Midrash appears to have morphed into a joke that ends with the Jews asking God "How much does it cost?" God says, "It's free." "Okay," the Jews respond. "We'll take two." Meaning, the two tablets that Moses carried down from Mount Sinai.

The next Midrash shows how the Jewish people later used this in an argument to justify their "impudence" in praying to God after the Temple was destroyed and the people were driven out of Israel.

The Holy One said to Israel: You are acting impudently.

They replied: Creator of the Universe, it is appropriate and proper that we do so, for no other nation accepted your Torah except for us.

God replied: I was the One who disqualified all the nations for your sake.

The Jewish people said to God: If so, why did you take your Torah around to every nation and they did not accept it?[26]

This sounds almost like an old married couple having an argument as to who had been pursuing whom during their courtship. Indeed, the Midrash uses the parable of a king who ousts his queen and, then, seeing her later clinging to the pillar of the palace, says to her: You are acting impudently. She tells the king: I am acting appropriately since no other woman would accept you except for me. The king says to her: I was the one who disqualified all women for you. She replies to the king: If so, why did you enter that street, that yard, and that place? Were you not rejected by all the women there?[27]

God appeared to Moses at the burning bush and told him to return to Egypt and free his people. Moses refused his mission five times using five different arguments.[28] Moses's fifth objection, "Oh Lord, send, I pray Thee, by the hand of whom Thou will send," made it clear that

Moses was not interested in going—this was possibly because of his great humility—and it was only then that God got angry at him.[29] Jonah was another reluctant prophet who had to be coerced into prophesying to the people of Nineveh.

After Moses finds out that he will not be the one to lead the Israelites into the Promised Land, he asks God to appoint a successor. In explaining the verse,[30] the Midrash presents the following parable:

> *A king saw a woman who was an orphan, and wanted to take her for a wife. He sent messengers to ask for her hand. She responded that she was not worthy of being married to a king. He asked for her hand seven times, and still she refused him. Eventually, she married him. Subsequently, the king got angry at her and wanted to divorce her. She said, I did not seek to marry you; you sought to marry me. Since you have decided to divorce me and take someone else, don't do to her what you did to me.[31]*

The Midrash goes on to say that this is what Moses told God: "Seven days you tried to convince me to lead the Israelites out of Egypt and I kept refusing you. Now you decide that I will not be the one who brings them into the Promised Land. Please don't treat my successor the way you treated me."

The Talmud[32] describes a situation in which God admitted that He made a "mistake." The Talmud explains the meaning of God's reply (as to His name) to Moses in Exodus, "I Will Be What I Will Be."[33] God instructed Moses to tell the Israelites that, "I shall be with them in this servitude just as I will be with them in other servitudes." Moses told God: They have enough troubles now; You do not have to tell them about future troubles. God agreed with Moses and instructed Moses to tell the Israelites: "I Will Be has sent me."[34]

As this next passage from the Talmud demonstrates, God can be sarcastic and expects to be greeted just as any mortal would. God was said to be insulted when Moses, who went up to heaven for forty days, ignored Him and did not wish Him well on His handiwork.

> *Rabbi Yehoshua b. Levi said: At the time that Moses ascended to Heaven, he found the Holy One tying crowns on the letters of the Torah.*
>
> *God said to him: "Moses, in your town people do not give greetings?"*
>
> *Moses replied: "Is it then proper for a servant to extend greetings to his master?"*
>
> *God said to him: "You should have wished me success."*

Moses then said to Him:[35] *"And now let the power of the Lord be great,' as You once declared."*[36]

Moses's response was close to the traditional Jewish way of congratulating someone on a job well done by blessing him with strength to continue (*yishar cochacha*). Moses's dilemma of what to wish God is reminiscent of the joke: What do you say when God sneezes? (You bless You?)

When the Israelites made the golden calf, only a short time after hearing the Ten Commandments, it looked very bleak for the Israelites. The Bible states that God said to Moses: "Now therefore let Me alone (*hanicha li*), that My wrath will flare up against them and that I may consume them."[37] According to the Talmud, it is as though Moses took hold of God —impossible, since God is incorporeal— and said that he would not let go until God forgave the Jewish people. This is derived from the expression "*hanicha li*" which can also be stretched to mean let go of me or release me, although it is more accurate to say that it means "let Me alone."[38]

The Talmud offers a wonderful explanation of why God told Moses to leave Him alone even though Moses had not yet started to pray on behalf of the Jews. Indeed, Moses had just been told that the Israelites had sinned by making the golden calf. The Talmud states that this is similar to a situation in which a king was beating the prince in front of a friend. The friend was afraid to say or do anything until the king said: "Were it not for this friend of mine who is before us, I would kill you." So too, Moses was afraid to do anything until God said to him: "let Me alone." Moses had not yet spoken up on behalf of his people and God was telling him to leave Him alone. Moses then understood that God really wanted Moses to defend the Israelites.[39]

Moses used every possible argument to convince God to forgive the Israelites. In the next selections we see Moses using some outlandish arguments with God to get Him to change His mind about destroying the Israelites after they made the golden calf in the wilderness. Moses even played "gotcha" with God in one of the selections.

When the Israelites made the golden calf, Moses tried to convince God to forgive them.

God said: "Moses, I have already sworn that, 'he that sacrifices unto the deities other than God alone shall be utterly destroyed,'[40] *and I cannot take back an oath which emanates from My mouth."*

> *Moses replied: "Creator of the Universe, did you not grant me the power of annulling oaths . . .?"*
>
> *. . .*

A scholar may absolve one's oath under certain situations. And now Moses, referring to God, is in effect telling God to practice what He preaches.

> *. . . Any elder that passes judgment, who desires that his pronouncement should be accepted, should be the first to accept the pronouncement. You, who commanded me regarding annulling oaths, it is only right that I should be able to annul your oath the way you commanded me to annul the oaths of others."*
>
> *Immediately, Moses wrapped himself in his prayer shawl and sat as an elder of the court, and God stood as one asking about his oath. . . .*[41]

The way an oath is usually annulled by a court is by ascertaining that the individual making the oath did not have perfect knowledge and made the oath without considering every ramification. How do you annul the oath of God, who is omniscient? For that matter, how do you tell God—in effect—to practice what He preaches? We are reminded here of the Chassidic tale referred to in Chapter 1 in which God is actually summoned to appear before a *beit din*—and loses.

According to the Midrash, Moses tried several good arguments on God to convince Him not to punish the Jewish people for the sin of the golden calf. For example,

> *Moses said to God: Why are you angry with the Israelites? Is it not because they made an idol? You never told them not to do this.*
>
> *God replied to Moses: Did I not say in the second commandment, "Thou shalt have no other gods before me?"*[42]
>
> *Moses replied: You did not command them, you commanded me, since You did not say, "You (plural) shalt not have. . . ." It was thus only me that You commanded. Hence, if I have made an idol, "Blot me, please, out of Your book"*[43,44]

The second commandment states: *Lo yihyeh lecha* not *Lo yihyeh lachem. Lachem* (to you) is plural and *lecha* (to you) is singular. Moses's argument was the kind that a clever lawyer might use when looking for a loophole in a legal document.

Moses said to God: This (golden) calf that the Israelites made can now be of assistance to You. It will send down the rain and You will produce the dew.

The Holy One said to him: Is there any substance to it?

Moses then retorted: If there is no substance to it, then why are you angry with the Israelites?[45]

Moses to God: Gotcha.

In the following Talmudic passage, Moses not only tries to exculpate the Israelites for the sin of the golden calf that they made, he also blames God Himself for it. Apparently, God even gets blamed for the sins of mortals. The Talmud compares God to a father who sets his son up in business in a perfume store on a street frequented by prostitutes. Knowing that prostitutes are likely customers for perfume, can he really blame his son for falling into bad ways?

The verse states: "Moses began to plead before God his Lord, and said, Lord, why unleash your wrath against Your people, that You brought out of Egypt . . ."[46] *Why did Moses decide to mention here the exodus from Egypt?*

Moses said: Creator of the Universe, from where did You bring them out? From Egypt, where everyone worships lambs.

Rabbi Huna said in the name of Rabbi Yochanan: This can be compared to a wise person who opened a perfume store for his son in a street of prostitutes. The street did its part, the business did its part, and the young man did his part and fell into bad ways. His father came and caught him with prostitutes. He started yelling, saying: I will kill you! A friend was there who said to the father: You caused the boy's ruination, yet you are screaming at him. You ignored all other occupations and taught him perfumery, you ignored all other streets and could only open the store in the street of prostitutes.

So too did Moses say: Creator of the Universe, You forsook the whole world and caused your children to be enslaved only in Egypt, where lambs are worshipped. That is from whom your children learned and made the golden calf.

This is the reason Moses said: ". . . that you brought out of Egypt."[47]

This is a clever way of blaming God for the sin of the golden calf. The implication is that the idol worship was all God's fault since it was He who made sure the Israelites would live in Egypt, where they learned to worship idols.

God sometimes blames too; but, according to the Midrash, Moses does not let Him get away with it, as the following shows.

> At first, the Holy One said to Moses: "Now go, and I will send you to Pharaoh, and take my people, the children of Israel, out of Egypt."[48]
>
> After they made the golden calf, what does it say there? "Go down, because your people whom you have brought out of Egypt have become corrupt."[49]
>
> Moses exclaimed before the Holy One: Creator of the Universe, when they are sinners, they are mine, and when they are righteous, they are Yours? Whether they are sinners or righteous they are Yours, since it is written:[50] "They are Your people and Your heritage."[51]

In this Midrash, God seems like a parent, who, when disappointed in the actions of a child, tells his or her spouse, "Look what your child has done."

Morris is having problems with his son and goes to his rabbi for advice. "I sent him to Hebrew School and gave him a very expensive Bar Mitzvah. Now he tells me he's decided to become a Christian! Rabbi, what should I do?"

"Funny you should come to me," said the Rabbi. "I also gave my son the very best Jewish education. Then one day he, too, told me he decided to become a Christian."

"So what did you do?" asked Morris.

"I turned to God for the answer," replied the Rabbi.

"What did He say?"

The Rabbi sighed, "God said, 'Funny you should come to me. . . .'"

> The verse states: "Because the Lord was not able (yecholet) to bring his people into the land which He swore to them."[52] It should state yachol.
>
> Rabbi Elazar said: Moses said to God, Master of the Universe, now the nations of the world will say, He has grown weak as a woman and cannot save His people.[53]

The word *yecholet* is feminine. Moses defended the Israelites after the incident with the spies[54] using this unusual argument.

It was in the late 1970s and President Jimmy Carter, Egyptian President Anwar Sadat and Israeli Prime Minister Menachem Begin were meeting at Camp David. Suddenly, a Heavenly voice called out, " In reward for your efforts toward peace, you may each ask me any one question and I will answer it."

President Carter went first. "Dear God," he asked, "when will we have a nuclear-free world?"

"In the year 2048," God replied. And President Carter began to cry. "Why do you cry?" asked God. "Not in my administration," sobbed President Carter.

Egyptian President Sadat asked his question. "Dear God," he asked, "when will my Arab brothers finally be united?"

"In the year 4004," God replied. And then Sadat began to cry. "Why do you cry?" asked God. "Not in my administration," wailed Sadat.

Then it was Prime Minister Begin's turn. "Dear God," he asked. "When will Israel finally begin to get fair treatment in the world media?"

And then God began to cry. "Dear God, why do You cry?" Begin asked.

And the Lord replied, "Not in my administration."

According to the Talmud, King David made a bet with God that he could withstand any spiritual test. He lost the bet. David, however, was a bit of a sore loser:

> *Rabbi Yehuda said in the name of Rav: A person should never bring himself to be tested because David, King of Israel, asked to be tested and failed.*
>
> *David asked God: Creator of the Universe, why do we say in the (amidah) prayer, "The God of Abraham, the God of Isaac, and the God of Jacob" and do not say the God of David?*
>
> *God replied: They were tested and you were not.*
>
> *David said: Examine and test me, as it is written, "Examine me, God, and test me."* [55]
>
> *He answered: I will test you and do something special for you. For they were not informed beforehand as to the nature of the test, but I will tell you beforehand that the test will involve sexual immorality. . . .* [56]

Apparently, David thought he would free himself from sexual desire by having intercourse with his wives during the daytime, but as the Talmud points out, controlling one's sexual urges doesn't really work that way:

> *There is a small organ in a person. When it is hungry, it is satisfied; when it is satisfied, it is hungry.* [57]

David failed the test and ended up cohabiting with Bathsheba, a married woman. With that, he lost his wager with God, but not gracefully:

> *David said to God: "You know very well that had I wished to overcome my desire I could have done so, but I did not want people to say the slave defeated his Master."*[58]

David knew that if he had not sinned with Bathsheba then he would have been right in his assertion that he deserved to be included in the aforementioned prayer. And that is why he so magnanimously "let" God win the bet.

In Talmudic stories, God is very close to mankind and even laughs when they "best" Him. He has a great deal of warmth for His creations and sometimes seeks mortal blessing. In one case, God asked for a blessing of Rabbi Yishmael b. Elisha, a High Priest, who came up with an appropriate response:

> *Rabbi Yishmael b. Elisha said: I once entered the innermost part of the Temple to offer incense and I saw that God, the Lord of Hosts, was seated on a high and lofty throne.*
>
> *He said to me: Yishmael, My son, bless me.*
>
> *I said to Him: May it be Your will that Your compassion should suppress Your anger and that Your compassion prevail over all Your other attributes so that You should treat Your children with the attribute of mercy and You should stop short of the strict letter of the law for them.*
>
> *And God nodded to me with His head.*[59]

This poignant story not only depicts God as asking a mere mortal for a blessing, but this mortal then turns the tables on God because the blessing he gives is one that will benefit the Jewish people, and God is happy with this.

In the following story we see God admitting that the world is sometimes unjust and that he would have to remake it to change the sad plight of some unfortunates. He tells Rabbi Elazar b. Pedat that He will make it up to him in the next world and describes the reward, but Rabbi Elazar is not that thrilled with his future reward.

> *Rabbi Elazar b. Pedath was in dire poverty. Once, after bloodletting, he had nothing to eat so he took some garlic peel and placed into his mouth. He grew faint and fell asleep.*

The rabbis came to ask him something and noticed that he was crying and laughing and that a spark of fire came out of his forehead. When he awoke, they asked him: Why did you cry and laugh?

He said to them: Because I saw that God was sitting with me and I asked Him, How long will I continue to suffer in this world?

He said to me: Elazar, my son, would it please you if I turned the world back to its very beginnings? Perhaps then you might be born at a more auspicious time for achieving sustenance.

I said: All this and only "perhaps"? I then asked: Which is longer, the time I have already lived, or the time I am still to live?

God said: The time you have already lived is longer.

That was why he cried.

I then said to God: If so, then I do not require that you remake the world.

God then said to me: As a reward for saying that you do not require it, I will provide for you in the next world thirteen rivers of pure balsam oil, which you will be able to enjoy.

So that was why he laughed.

I said to Him: Only that and nothing more?

He said to me: Then what will be left for Me to give to your colleagues?

I said to God: Am I asking from someone who has nothing?

He then flicked me on my forehead with his finger and said: Elazar, My son, I shot My arrow at you.[60]

Thus, the sparks. Rashi, the major commentator on the Bible and Talmud, explained this last statement as an expression of love. God was telling Elazar that He loved him. Apparently, God enjoyed Rabbi Elazar's retort that He could "afford" to give him a better reward.

It was a hot day at Jones Beach. Bessie Cohen was there with her three-year-old grandson; she had bought him a cute little sailor suit with a hat, and she watched with delight as he played with his toys at the edge of the water.

Suddenly a giant wave swept onto the shore and before Bessie could even move, the boy was swept out into the cold Atlantic.

Bessie was frantic. "I know I've never been religious," she screamed to the heavens. "But I implore You to save the boy! I'll never ask anything of You again!"

The boy disappeared from view, and Bessie was beside herself. He went under a second time, and Bessie began to wail. As he went under for the third time, she screamed mightily, appealing to God to save the boy's life.

Her final supplication was answered, as the sea suddenly threw the child on to the shore. He was badly shaken but clearly alive. Bessie picked him up and put him down gently on a blanket, far from the water. After looking him over, she turned her face toward the heavens, and complained loudly, "He had a hat!"[61]

In this well-known joke, making one small change—replacing God with, say, a lifeguard—transforms the humor from a warm, Jewish joke into a nugget of anti-Semitism. With a mortal, being a complainer and a cheapskate is not attractive. Put God in the joke, though, and we're all family. We understand each other. And similarly,

Every week, Moishe would pray to win the lottery. "Please God," he would say, "let me win the lottery. I need to win the lottery." After several years of this, God finally replied and His booming voice rattled Moishe more than a little bit. "Moishe," God said, "meet me half way. Buy a ticket."

God is open to suggestions from mortals and is even willing to change His mind when proven "wrong," a state that ought to be impossible for God, who is perfect:

> *Rabbah b. Shila once encountered Elijah the Prophet. He asked him: What is the Holy One doing?*
>
> *Elijah answered: He is quoting legal decisions in the names of all the Rabbis, but not in the name of Rabbi Meir.*
>
> *Rabbah asked: Why?*
>
> *Elijah answered: Because Rabbi Meir studied laws from the mouth of Acher.*
>
> *Rabbah explained: Rabbi Meir found a pomegranate, he ate the fruit on the inside and discarded the peel.*
>
> *Elijah answered: Now God is saying, Meir, my son, says . . .*[62]

This story portrays a God who studies the law and quotes mortals. This, despite the fact that God Himself gave the law to the Israelites. Who ought to know better what the law entails, the giver or the receiver? Who ought to know best what is in the heart of man, God or Rabbah? Yet, when Rabbah explains that Rabbi Meir only culled the good in learning from *Acher*—literally, the other, a name given to Rabbi Elisha b. Avuyah who became a heretic—and discarded the bad, God accepts this and starts quoting Rabbi Meir along with everyone else.

Rabbi Eliezer b. Hyrkanos, who was of the Shammai school, refused to go along with the majority in a famous dispute regarding an oven of Aknai, and whether it could become ritually unclean. To prove his point, Rabbi Eliezer performed various miracles which were all ignored. Finally:

> *Rabbi Eliezer said: If the law is as I say, let it be proven from Heaven.*
>
> *A Heavenly voice then rang out and exclaimed: What do you want with Rabbi Eliezer, since the law is in agreement with him in all areas.*
>
> *Rabbi Yehoshua then got up on his feet and declared: "The Torah is not in Heaven."* [63]
>
> *What does "not in Heaven" mean? Rabbi Yirmiyah has said: Since the Torah was already given at Sinai, we therefore pay no attention to Heavenly voices. After all, it is written in the Torah itself:* [64] *"After the majority one must follow."* [65]

This passage in question refers to the Torah and its commandments. This story portrays God as being interested in law and even—ineffectively—trying to influence the outcome of a legal debate. The Talmud adds this coda to the "not in Heaven" story to explain how God handled it when His Heavenly voice was disregarded:

> *Rabbi Nathan met Elijah the Prophet and asked him: What was God doing at that time?*
>
> *Elijah answered: He laughed and said, My children have triumphed over me. My children have triumphed over me.* [66]

God laughs when He realizes that mortals refuse to accept Him as the final authority on religious matters since once given to mankind the Torah is no longer "in heaven" but, rather, on earth.

Four rabbis argued passionately about a particular aspect of Jewish law. Three were on one side of the issue, the fourth was adamantly on the other. Sure of his opinion, he decided to appeal to a higher authority.

"Oh, God!" he cried. "Please give me a sign to prove that I am right and they are wrong!"

It was a beautiful, sunny day. As soon as the rabbi finished his prayer, a storm cloud moved across the sky until it stopped directly over them.

It rumbled once and dissolved. "A sign from God! See, I'm right, I knew it!" But the other three disagreed, and insisted that he follow the majority, as the law directed.

So the rabbi prayed again: "God, I need a bigger sign to show that I am right and they are wrong!"

This time four storm clouds appeared, rushed toward each other to form one big cloud, and a bolt of lightning slammed into a tree on a nearby hill. "I told you I was right!" cried the rabbi, but his friends insisted that nothing had happened that could not be explained by natural causes. Whereupon, the sky turned pitch black, the earth shook, and a Heavenly voice boomed, "He's right!"

The rabbi put his hands on his hips, turned to the other three, and said, "Well?"

"So," shrugged one of the other rabbis, "now it's 3 to 2."

The Talmud describes how Rabbah b. Nachmeni died. The government did not like the fact that Rabbah's lectures resulted in thousands of Jewish people not being in their homes during the two months preceding the holidays of Rosh Hashanah and Passover, and thereby making it difficult for the tax collectors to collect the monthly tax. The government sent agents to capture him. He managed to escape and was hiding in a swamp, totally exhausted and sitting on the stump of a tree and studying Torah. Meanwhile, a dispute arose in Heaven regarding the accurate diagnosis of leprosy. This is important because an individual who has leprosy is deemed to be "impure":

> *There was a dispute in Heaven regarding laws of leprosy:*
>
> *If the bright spot on the skin precedes the white hair, the person is impure; if the white hair precedes the bright spot, the person is ritually pure. What if there is a doubt as to which one came first? God said "pure" and the entire Heavenly Academy said "impure."*
>
> *They decided to ask Rabbah b. Nachmeni to resolve this dispute, since he once said, I am unique in my knowledge of leprosy and tents.[67] They sent a messenger to get him, but the Angel of Death could not approach him, since Rabbah did not cease his Torah studies.[68] Meanwhile, a wind began to blow which made the reeds rustle. Rabbah thought it was a company of soldiers that were coming to get him. He said: It is better that I die than be delivered into the hands of the government. While he was dying he exclaimed: It is pure! It is pure![69]*
>
> *A Heavenly voice declared: Happy are you Rabbah b. Nachmeni, your body is pure and your soul departed in purity.[70]*

. . . Sometimes God wins the argument. How did God win this argument? He needed the help of a mortal who was "unique in his knowledge of the laws of leprosy . . ." Did Rabbah know more than God? Apparently, this story illustrates that when it comes to a legal dispute, even one between God and the angels in Heaven, a well-trained expert must be brought in to resolve the dispute.

Interestingly, Maimonides, who wrote the encyclopedic compilation of Talmudic law, concluded that when there is uncertainty as to which came first, the white hair or the bright spot, the law is that the person is impure.[71] Thus, Maimonides disagreed with God.

A very pious rabbi dies at a ripe old age and goes straight to Heaven. There, he finds a large table, surrounded by several learned men, all studying the Talmud. Many are his former teachers and students. The table is laden with all kinds of wonderful food— kishke, kugel, knaidlach and much more. The men noshed as they studied.

One of his former students exclaims, "Rebbe, we're so happy you've finally joined us! Come, have something to eat!"

The Rabbi surveys the scene, looks over the food and asks, "Who's the mashgiach *here?"*

The man looks at the rabbi incredulously and replies, chuckling, "This is Heaven! God is the mashgiach!"

The old man ponders this for a long, long time, stroking his beard, eyes closed, deep in thought. The others regard him with great anticipation, awaiting his learned words. At last, the rabbi speaks. "OK," he finally says, "I'll have some fruit. On a paper plate."

In the next selection from the Talmud, God is seen as arguing with the sages as to whether Solomon deserved to be listed as a king without a share in the World to Come, meaning Paradise. God wins the argument, but barely. Of course, God has an advantage: He controls both Paradise and Hell and thus decides who will be allowed to enter each place.

> *Rabbi Yehuda stated in the name of Rav that they wished to add one more king—Solomon—to the list of kings that have no share in the World to Come. A vision resembling Solomon's father, King David, appeared before the sages and prostrated itself in supplication, but they ignored it.*
>
> *A fire from Heaven came and singed their benches, but they ignored it.*

A Heavenly voice proclaimed to them: "Do you see a man diligent in His work? He will stand before kings, but he shall not stand before the lowly."[72] King Solomon built My home[73] before his own, and furthermore, he built My home in seven years and his own palace in three years. He should stand before kings, and should not stand before the lowly.

They ignored this Heavenly voice.

The Heavenly voice then proclaimed: "Shall his compensation be as you wish it? . . . Should you choose and not I?"[74,75]

Looks like God won this one; Solomon was not added to the list. God, it seems, sometimes has to tell the sages on earth to mind their own business. He alone decides who will go to Paradise and who to Hell. The story is even more humorous when one considers that the Heavenly voice quoted Proverbs which was, after all, written by King Solomon.

Rabbi Haim of Romshishok was a preacher who traveled from town to town delivering religious sermons that stressed the importance of respect for one's fellow man. He often began his talks with the following story:

"I once ascended to the firmaments. I first went to see Hell and the sight was horrifying. Row after row of tables was laden with platters of sumptuous food, yet the people seated around the tables were pale and emaciated, moaning in hunger. As I came closer, I understood their predicament. Every person held a full spoon, but both arms were splinted with wooden slats so he could not bend either elbow to bring the food to his mouth. It broke my heart to hear the tortured groans of these poor people as they held their food so near but could not consume it.

Next I went to visit Heaven. I was surprised to see the same setting I had witnessed in Hell—row after row of long tables laden with food. But in contrast to Hell, the people here in Heaven were sitting contentedly talking with each other, obviously sated from their sumptuous meal. As I came closer, I was amazed to discover that here, too, each person had his arms splinted on wooden slats that prevented him from bending his elbows. How, then, did they manage to eat?

As I watched, a man picked up his spoon and dug it into the dish before him. Then he stretched across the table and fed the person across from him! The recipient of this kindness thanked him and returned the favor by leaning across the table to feed his benefactor.

I suddenly understood. Heaven and Hell offer the same circumstances and conditions. The critical difference is in the way the people treat each other.

*I ran back to Hell to share this solution with the poor souls trapped
there. I whispered in the ear of one starving man, "You do not have
to go hungry. Use your spoon to feed your neighbor, and he will surely
return the favor and feed you." "You expect me to feed the detestable
man sitting across the table?" said the man angrily. "I would rather
starve than give him the pleasure of eating!"*

*I then understood God's wisdom in choosing who is worthy to go to
Heaven and who deserves to go to Hell."*[76]

In many of the Talmudic tales, we have seen human beings argue,
negotiate, even best God. Here is one in which God finally pokes fun
at mankind.

*In the future, the Holy One will take a Torah onto his lap and say:
Anyone who has occupied himself with it should come and take his
reward.*

*Immediately, all the nations will gather together and arrive in disorder,
as it says: "All the nations will gather together."*[77]

*The Holy One will say to them: Do not enter in disorder, but allow
each nation with its sages to enter separately. . . .*

*Immediately, Rome will enter first. The Holy One will say: With what
have you occupied yourself? They will say: Creator of the Universe,
many marketplaces have we established, many bathhouses have we
constructed, and much silver and gold have we accumulated. All this
we have done only for Israel in order that they should be able to occupy
themselves with the study of Torah. The Holy One will say: Fools of the
World, everything that you have done, you have done for yourselves.
You established marketplaces in order to place prostitutes there. You
constructed bathhouses for your own enjoyment, and the silver and
gold is mine. . . .*

*The Romans will depart with a disheartened spirit and the Persians
will enter. The Holy One will say: With what have you occupied
yourself? They will say: Creator of the Universe, many bridges have
we erected, many cities have we conquered, and many wars have we
waged. The Holy One will say: Everything that you have done, you
have done for yourselves. You erected bridges in order to collect tolls.
You conquered cities in order to use them for forced labor; as for wars,
I wage them, as it is written: "The Lord is a Master of war."*[78] *. . . They
too will depart with a disheartened spirit. . . . The same will happen
with every nation.*

*The nations will then say: Creator of the Universe, give the Torah to
us now and we will observe it.*

*The Holy One will say to them: Fools of the World, one who works
hard on the eve of the Sabbath will have something to eat on Sabbath,*

but one who has not worked hard on the eve of Sabbath, from where will he eat on Sabbath? However, I have one easy commandment by the name of sukkah,[79] *go and perform this precept. . . . Immediately, each one will go and make himself a small* sukkah *on his roof. The Holy One will make the sun blaze and penetrate as it does during the summer solstice. Each one of them will kick contemptuously at his* sukkah *and go away. . . .*

The Holy One will sit and laugh at them, as it is written:[80] *"He who sits in Heaven shall laugh."*[81]

In this story, God has the last laugh on all the nations by proving that He made the right choice in giving His Torah to the Jewish people because they are the only ones who follow the commandments regardless of their personal comfort.

We see that God is portrayed in Rabbinic literature in a very respectful yet unique manner, with warmth, wit, and affection. He is an omnipotent God but still wants to be blessed; He is an omniscient God but laughs when bested by His children. Even the Almighty, Omnipotent and Omniscient One needs to be noticed. One can easily see why Tevye feels entitled to talk constantly to Him. This warm attitude vis-à-vis God has had a profound effect on Jewish humor and Jewish literature, even to this day.

Does God have a sense of humor? Perhaps the best way to address that question is to examine the works that He has authored. And so, to the next chapter.

4

Biblical Humor: From Irony, Sarcasm, Wordplay to Humorous Imagery

Moses asks God to explain the kosher laws.

"THOU SHALT NOT SEETHE A KID IN ITS MOTHER'S MILK."

"Does that mean that we should wait six hours between eating meat and drinking milk?"

"THOU SHALT NOT SEETHE A KID IN ITS MOTHER'S MILK."

"Does that mean we should have two sets of dishes?"

"THOU SHALT NOT SEETHE A KID IN ITS MOTHER'S MILK."

"Does that mean we should check the label of everything we buy and use only those items made with pure vegetable shortening?"

"THOU SHALT NOT SEETHE A KID IN ITS MOTHER'S MILK."

"Does that mean—"

"OKAY, HAVE IT YOUR WAY!"[1]

Many individuals—and this includes many scholars—believe that the Bible, in particular the Hebrew Bible, is without any humor. As noted previously, the philosopher Alfred North Whitehead was of the opinion that there is no humor in the Old Testament. Other scholars disagree. Israel Knox, for one, believes that there is much humor in the Hebrew Bible, and that it consists mainly of irony.[2] Knox points out that the prophets, in particular, used irony to warn the Jews against the "allurements of pagan civilization." Thomas Jemielty[3] demonstrates that Hebrew prophecy makes use of satire. A major purpose of the satire and sarcasm in the Hebrew Bible was to ridicule the evildoer and idolater. Jakob Jonsson rejects the opinion that there is no humor in the Hebrew Bible and discusses several examples of Biblical humor, for example, the story of Jacob and Laban.[4] William Whedbee also demonstrates that there is much humor in the Hebrew Scriptures,[5] as does Tal Bonham, who argues that examining the Bible proves that "God has a sense of humor."[6]

While it is true that the Hebrew Bible employs many sorts of humor, its primary purpose is not to entertain. The major goal of the Hebrew Bible is to teach humanity how to live the ideal life. Much of the humor found in the Hebrew Bible has a single purpose: To demonstrate that evil is wrong and even, at times, ludicrous. The punishments meted out to wrongdoers are often designed to mock them and to hoist them by their own petards.

This chapter will demonstrate that the Hebrew Bible contains a lot of humor, although much of it is quite subtle and requires a knowledge of the original language of the Bible, Hebrew. The goal here is not to exhaustively enumerate all instances of humor in the Bible but, rather, to demonstrate that humor permeates the Holy Scriptures. The humorous verses and situations collected here may be characterized as belonging to one of several broad categories of humor: irony, sarcasm, wordplay, exaggerated imagery, and humorous situations.

Irony

In many cases, the irony of the Hebrew Bible demonstrates that individuals should be careful regarding what they say or do. Their deeds or words can come back and haunt them years later. Using this device, the Bible hints at a divine plan, one in which bad deeds do not go unpunished. Punishment in the Hebrew Bible often fits the crime measure for measure, and we are repeatedly shown that, in a sense, what goes around comes around.

In a classic work, Edwin Good shows how the Bible uses different types of irony. In particular, Good focuses on six instances in which irony is employed: the Book of Jonah, the story of Saul (in Samuel), the Book of Genesis, Isaiah, Ecclesiastes, and Job.[7] Israel Knox also finds a great deal of irony in the Hebrew Bible. For instance, he notes that there is irony in the story of Jacob and Laban and how they try to outwit each other. He also discusses how prophets such as Elijah and Isaiah used irony to mock idolatry.[8] Lillian Klein cites numerous examples of irony from the Book of Judges.[9]

The classic example of irony in the Hebrew Bible is in the story of Joseph, the dreamer, who was sold as a slave by his brothers and eventually turned out to be his brothers' salvation during a time of famine. Joseph dreamed that his family bowed to him as their leader and, with eerie similarity, the Hasid in the following Jewish joke evokes Joseph's dream and possibly how his brothers should have responded, rather than selling him into slavery to get rid of him.

A Hasid comes to see his Rabbi: "Rabbi, I have had a dream in which I am the leader of three hundred Hasidim."

The Rabbi replies: "Come back when three hundred Hasidim have a dream that you are their leader."[10]

According to the tale told in Genesis, Judah and his brothers had perpetuated one of the most horrible crimes one can imagine: They sold their own seventeen-year-old half-brother into slavery. Twenty-two years later the brothers had all but forgotten the evil they had done but, of course, God did not forget. There was a famine in the land of Canaan and the brothers were forced to go to Egypt to purchase food. Joseph, unbeknownst to his brothers, was by then the Grand Vizier of Egypt. Joseph's silver chalice was found among Benjamin's possessions and Joseph declared that Benjamin would have to remain in Egypt as his slave. Judah, in an attempt to gain sympathy, told the Grand Vizier (in actuality, Joseph) that they had an elderly father, and that Benjamin, the youngest child, was the only one of his mother's children who was alive, since he had had a brother who *died*. It is quite comical and ironic since the reader knows what Judah does not—that Judah was actually talking to this brother (Joseph), who was far from dead. There is even more irony in the words of Judah whose plea before the Grand Vizier was: "For how can I go up to my father if the lad (Benjamin) is not with me? I cannot bear to look upon the evil misery that shall come on my father."[11] Twenty-two years earlier, Judah had had no problem looking upon his father's suffering when he conspired with his brothers to sell their seventeen-year-old brother. Indeed, Judah was the one who had said: "What profit will there be if we kill our brother . . ."[12] It is also quite ironic—and fitting, in a measure-for-measure sense—that whereas at first Judah was the one who advised that one brother (Joseph) be sold into slavery, twenty-two years later, Judah offered himself as a slave in lieu of another brother (Benjamin). Judah redeemed himself by this noble act and thus we learn two important lessons: First, bad deeds can boomerang and cause one much harm in the future and, second, one can repent and be forgiven for even the worst of crimes.

This is one of the grand themes of Genesis: The one who deceives is ultimately, in turn, deceived. Jacob deceived his nearly blind father

Isaac by pretending to be his older brother Esau. Several years later, Laban fooled Jacob and substituted Leah, his elder daughter, for Rachel, his younger daughter whom Jacob wished to wed. Further, Jacob was deceived by his children into believing that his favorite son, Joseph, was devoured by a wild animal. Years later, Joseph, as Grand Vizier of Egypt, deceived his brothers who did not recognize him. Joseph's coat of many colors was dipped in goat's blood in order to deceive Jacob and make him think Joseph was devoured by a wild animal.[13] Judah, in turn, was deceived by Tamar, his daughter-in-law, by means of a kid (a young goat). The Bible states that: "Judah sent the young kid" to the prostitute; actually, Tamar disguised as a prostitute.[14] The Midrash notes that the same wording is used in both stories: *haker nah* (do you recognize). Jacob was asked by the brothers whether he recognized the bloody coat of many colors and Judah was asked by Tamar whether he recognized the seal, wrap, and staff.[15]

After noticing that his father-in-law Laban was not treating him as in the past, Jacob decided to flee with his family. Rachel, by now one of Jacob's wives, stole her father Laban's *teraphim*—small statues used for idolatry and/or divination. Laban pursued and intercepted them in the Gilead mountains. "Why have you stolen my gods?" Laban said to Jacob.[16] The Midrash comments that it cannot be much of a God if it can be stolen.[17] Jonsson suggests that there is humor (albeit "rough" humor) in the fact that, not only was Laban deceived, but his idols were actually underneath his daughter Rachel's posterior while she claimed that the "manner of women" was upon her.[18] Those idols did not get much respect.

It is ironic that when the brothers sold Joseph, he was taken by a caravan of Ishmaelites carrying "spices, balsam, and ladanum"[19] and, then, twenty-two years later, Jacob sent a gift to the Grand Vizier (who was actually Joseph) which included balsam, spices, and ladanum.[20] It is also somewhat strange that Jacob's gift to Egypt consisted of food (honey, pistachio nuts, and almonds) when there was a great famine in Jacob's country, the land of Canaan.

In an exquisitely tragic example of irony in the Hebrew Bible, Rachel, still childless, "envied her sister and said to Jacob, 'give me children or else I die.'"[21] The irony is that Rachel subsequently died in childbirth while giving birth to Benjamin.

Pharaoh's words to Joseph regarding his family are filled with irony. Pharaoh said: ". . . take your father and your households and come to me; and I will give you the best of the land of Egypt."[22] Rashi, a leading

Jewish commentator on the Hebrew Bible and Talmud, notes that Pharaoh unknowingly alluded to what was going to happen centuries later when the Israelites left Egypt and emptied it out after the final plague. At that time, the Egyptians gave the Israelites vessels of silver and gold and clothing and the Israelites "despoiled the Egyptians."[23]

There is irony in the Song at the Red Sea, sung by Moses and the Israelites, which described the miracles wrought by God on behalf of the Israelites. One verse in the song declares: "You shall bring them in and plant them on the mountain of Your inheritance."[24] The Midrash points out that Moses and the Israelites inadvertently prophesied in saying "them" rather than "us."[25] As we know, this generation, including Moses, did not make it to the Promised Land.

There is irony in the words of Moses when he tells the Israelites regarding the commandments: "It is not in the heaven, so that you should say, 'Who shall go up for us to the heaven and bring it to us so that we can hear it and perform it.'"[26] Indeed, the Torah *was* in heaven and had to be brought down to the Israelites.

And when Moses summoned Dathan and Aviram in the hope of preempting a serious rebellion started by Korach, Dathan and Aviram said: "We will not go *up*."[27] They were right. A few verses later, the text states that they died by being swallowed up by the earth; they went straight *down*.[28]

Clearly, there is irony in the fact that many of the punishments meted out by God in the Hebrew Scriptures are measure for measure. The reader immediately notes that divine punishment fits the crime. For instance, the Egyptians drowned children in the river, so God drowned them in the sea. Miriam, Moses's sister, disparaged Moses "because of the Cushite woman he had married."[29] The Cushites (Ethiopians) were very dark-skinned, and Miriam's punishment was that she became leprous or "white as snow." Here, Miriam became deathly white for making critical remarks of a dark-skinned person. The Israelites whined that the manna was not sufficient and demanded meat in a most despicable way. They went on to say that they remembered (evidently, fondly) the free fish they were accustomed to eat in Egypt. God's punishment was to give them meat until "it is coming out of your nose and makes you nauseous." The ingrates died "while the meat was still between their teeth."[30]

In the Book of Judges, Deborah's song depicts Sisera's mother looking out the window to see why her son's chariot was late. The wisest of her princesses eased her mind: "Are they not finding and dividing the spoils; a woman, two women for every man."[31] The irony is that while the mother of Sisera was told that her son was being delayed because he was ravishing the women of Israel, a young woman, Jael, killed him in his bed by hammering the tent pin through his temple while he was sleeping.

When King David slept with Bathsheba and made her pregnant, she was still married to Uriah. In what is probably his least noble moment, King David sent a letter to his general, Joab, telling him to place Uriah at the front where the battle was the most fierce, so that he would be killed. The irony is that David sent this letter via the hand of Uriah, who unwittingly carried his own death warrant to Joab.[32] The tables were later turned on David when the prophet, Nathan, told David a parable, making it seem as if the event it described had actually occurred. Nathan's parable involved a poor man who owned nothing but a lamb that he loved dearly. A rich man took the lamb and slaughtered it to make a meal for a guest. David, who took the story literally, swore that the person who did this was deserving of death.[33] Since the parable referred to David himself, who had taken away Uriah's wife, David had also in effect signed his own death warrant.

Amnon became sick because of his infatuation with Tamar, his half sister. The verse states: "And Amnon suffered to the point of becoming ill on account of (his lust for) Tamar, his sister."[34] It is ironic that Jonadab advised Amnon to: "Lie on your bed and feign sickness, and when your father comes to visit you, say to him: 'Please let my sister Tamar come and serve me some bread.'"[35] Amnon was already almost sick from lust and did not have to pretend too hard at being ill. In fact, there is a lot of irony in the entire story.

Good claims that the word *hevel*, used many times in Ecclesiastes (the word is used five times in the second verse alone), means something very close to irony.[36] Of course, the traditional translation of *hevel* is vapor, steam, or hot air—and, therefore, the word is often translated as vanity or futility. Kohelet, the author of Ecclesiastes, points out the various ironies of life: the fact that the same fate awaits the wise man and the fool, the beast and the human; the fact that man's arduously acquired wealth often goes to fools who squander it; that the lover of money is not satisfied with money; etc.

The foundation and structure of the entire Book of Esther is steeped in irony. Those individuals who are on top when the Book opens are at their lowest point when the Book closes, and *vice versa*. For example, by the end of the story, Haman and his sons were hanged on the very gallows which Haman had prepared earlier for Mordechai. King Ahasuerus deposed a queen for disobedience and ended up with a queen who violated the king's rules herself, entering the inner court without being summoned. Esther continued to assert herself and by the end of the story asked the king to grant additional time for the Jews to kill their enemies. At the turning point of the story, the king asked Haman "What should be done to the man the king especially wants to honor?" Haman thought the king must surely mean him and described the way he most wanted to be honored: wearing the royal robe, riding the royal horse, etc. Haman was then instructed to do all these things for Mordechai. Picture Haman parading his archenemy Mordechai through the city square crying, "This is what is done for the man whom the King especially wants to honor."[37] Finally, Mordechai may have been instrumental in saving the Jews but he was also the cause of the problem. His refusal to bow to Haman caused Haman's anger. It is explicitly stated: "And when Haman saw that Mordechai bowed not down nor prostrated himself before him, then Haman was filled with wrath."[38] This may explain why the story ends with a very strange statement, namely, that Mordechai was "accepted by most of his brethren."[39] Why *most*? Perhaps, some Jews felt that the problems would not have occurred if Mordechai would have simply bowed to Haman—or at least stayed out of his way.

Sarcasm

Philosopher Sidney Morgenbesser was known for his sharp, witty, verbal ripostes. Possibly the most famous of these occurred during a talk by Oxford philosopher J. L. Austin, who noted that it was peculiar that although there are many languages in which a double negative makes a positive, no example existed where two positives expressed a negative.

Morgenbesser, in a dismissive voice, replied from the audience, "Yeah, yeah..."

In keeping with their characters, the evil people of the Bible are often very sarcastic. Even so, Biblical sarcasm is not limited to evildoers; ordinary people, leaders, and even God may occasionally indulge.

Rhetorical questions are essentially sarcastic, and lend themselves very easily to humor. The Midrash, noting that there are four rhetorical questions in the Torah itself that should have been responded to more appropriately, says, "God banged on their barrels and found them to be full of urine,"[40] that is, rather than wine. This is an idiomatic way of saying that God tested these four individuals and found them wanting, as they did not know how to respond to God. These are: Adam, Cain, Balaam, and Hezekiah (who responded inappropriately to a prophet of God).

When God asks a question it is a pretty good bet that he probably already knows the answer. God, upset that Adam and Eve have eaten from the fruit of the Tree of Knowledge, asked Adam about it.

> *God to Adam: Did you eat the fruit of the tree that I commanded you not to eat?*
> *Adam to God: The woman whom you gave to me . . .*[41]

Similarly, God actually does know that Cain has just murdered his brother Abel when he asks him about it.

> *God to Cain: Where is Abel, your brother?*
> *Cain: I do not know. Am I my brother's keeper?*[42]

In the following, God knows that Balak intends to hire Balaam to curse the Israelites. So, this wasn't a social visit.

> *God to Balaam: Who are these people with you?*
> *Balaam: Balak, son of Zippor, king of Moab."*[43]

Finally, Hezekiah has been flaunting his wealth to his Babylonian guests. They came to hear about God, who had miraculously cured Hezekiah of a dire illness, and instead he showed off his wealth.

> *Isaiah, God's prophet, said to Hezekiah: What did those people say? And from where did they come?*
> *Hezekiah: From a distant land they came to me, from Babylon.*
> *Isaiah responded: "The day will come when everything in your palace will be carried off to Babylon . . ."*[44]

All four did not understand that the questions were rhetorical or, if they did, they answered disingenuously. All should have known that God, who is omniscient, already knew the answer. The answers they gave were not what God wanted to hear. In fact, each individual would have done better had he simply answered, "Well, you are God. Don't you know?" Okay, maybe a better answer would have been "I sinned and I am sorry."

The Bible tells us very little about Dathan and Aviram. They were just two Israelites of the many who complained during the forty-year sojourn in the wilderness. It is the way they complained, however, that made them stand out, even amongst a group of perpetual complainers. When Korach's rebellion against Moses started, Moses in an attempt to make peace, summoned Dathan and Aviram, Korach's co-conspirators. Their complaint to Moses dripped with so much sarcasm that it caused Moses to immediately protest to God about them. They told Moses:

> *"Is it but a small thing that you have brought us up out of a land flowing with milk and honey to kill us in the wilderness, but you also have to lord over us?"*[45]

The evocative term "land of milk and honey," used repeatedly to describe the Promised Land of Israel, here refers unbelievably to the land of Egypt. We learn a good deal about the personalities of Dathan and Aviram from their nasty remark to Moses.

We also learn much about the character of the newly freed Israelites from their way of asking Moses for help seven days after their triumphant exodus from Egypt. They saw Pharaoh's army approaching behind them, and all that loomed ahead was the sea. The nascent Jewish nation asked Moses:

> *"Was there a lack of graves in Egypt, that you took us away to die in the wilderness?"*[46]

This impudent remark made when all seemed hopeless for the Israelites sheds much light on their character. It would seem that humility and prayer might have been a more appropriate response in a time of great danger than sarcasm. One is not surprised to learn that eventually these complainers went too far with their sarcastic and loathsome remarks and came to an ignominious end. The Israelites, totally demoralized by the report of the spies sent to reconnoiter their future homeland, complained to Moses that the inhabitants of Canaan were clearly much too strong to defeat, and said: "We wish we had died in the land of Egypt, or in this desert would we had died."[47] God's response to Moses and Aaron was to tell the Israelites that: "Surely as you have spoken in My ears, so I will do to you. In this desert your carcasses shall fall."[48] The text indicates that the Israelite adults did indeed die in the desert over the next thirty-nine years; their children made it to the Promised Land.

In Samuel I, when David found out that King Saul wished to kill him, he fled from Israel and went to Gath. Fearful that Achish, King of Gath, would have him killed, David pretended to be insane. David scribbled on the doors of the gates and allowed saliva to dribble down into his beard. When his servants brought David to him, Achish said:

> *"Why did you bring him to me? Do I lack lunatics that you have brought this one to carry on insanely in my presence?"*[49]

Rabshakeh joined the Assyrian King Sennacherib in his military action against the Israelite King Hezekiah. Rabshakeh impudently offered King Hezekiah's officers two thousand horses "if you can put riders on them."[50] When King Hezekiah's officers asked Rabshakeh not to speak the Judean language (Hebrew) but Aramaic, a language the soldiers on the wall did not understand, not only did Rabshakah not comply with this request, but his reply—in Hebrew—was: "Is it to your master and to you that my master has sent me to speak these words? Is it not to the people sitting on the wall, who will eat their dung and drink their urine with you?"[51] that is, in the famine that would result from a siege.

God is sometimes sarcastic, especially when upset or exasperated with the Jewish people, who manage to continually test Him. When the Jewish people, who were engaging in idol worship, cried to God about the neighboring people (such as the Philistines) oppressing them, God told them:

> *"Go and cry to the gods which you have chosen; let them rescue you in the time of your torment."*[52]

This sounds very mortal-like, much like the woman saying to her husband who has strayed and then wants to return: *"Now* you come to me. Why don't you go back to what's-her-name?" Also, parents have said similar words to children who return when they need help and realize that their so-called friends are not there for them in times of trouble. By using sarcasm in this way, the text makes God seem more understandable and less aloof. Apparently, even omniscience and omnipotence do not prevent one from being hurt by straying children.

Throughout the Hebrew Bible, idolatry is often targeted with sarcasm. Elijah's remarks to the prophets of Baal are steeped in sarcasm. Referring to their false deity, Elijah told them:

Call with a loud voice, for he is a god. Perhaps he is talking, or he is pursuing enemies, or he is relieving himself, or perhaps he is sleeping and will awaken.[53]

Knox cites this as well, but considers this an example of irony.[54]

When King Ahaziah became ill, he sent for messengers and said to them: "Go inquire of Baal-zebub, the god of Ekron, whether I will recover from this illness." An angel of God told Elijah to go to these messengers and tell them: "Is it because there is no God in Israel that you go to inquire of Baal-zebub the god of Ekron?"[55] Again we note the sarcasm in this rhetorical question.

Jeremiah was also quite sarcastic when referring to the idolatrous ways of the Israelites. He said to them:

"They say to the wood 'You are my father' and to the stone 'You gave birth to us'... Now where are the gods that you made for yourself? Let them get up if they can save you at the time of your misfortune; for as the number of your cities were your gods, O Judah."[56]

Sarcasm is used in Psalms to ridicule idolaters. The Psalmist says:

"Their idols are silver and gold, the handiwork of man. They have a mouth, but they cannot speak; they have eyes, but they cannot see. They have ears, but they cannot hear; they have a nose, but they cannot smell. Their hands cannot feel; their feet cannot walk; they cannot speak with their throat. Those who make them should become like them, all who put their trust in them."[57]

Job became quite sarcastic after his life became miserable and the Book of Job is replete with sarcastic remarks. Job's explanation regarding the righteous person who suffers was: "The completely righteous man is a laughingstock."[58] And, as we saw in the previous chapter, God could be sarcastic in return as when He said to Job: "Where were you when I laid the foundations of the earth?"[59] Or, in other words, when you create your own world, then you can tell me how to run mine.

Wordplays, Double Entendres, and Puns

One winter, Yankel's wife gave birth to a beautiful baby boy. The only problem was they lived out in the country, far from the nearest shtetl. And, wouldn't you know it, eight days later they were completely snowed in, and the mohel *couldn't get to them to perform the circumcision.*

67

The local galach *(Yiddish for priest) was a friendly sort and stopped by to wish the happy couple well. When Yankel explained the problem, the priest said he would be happy to help out with the baby's circumcision.*

God was with them and all went well. The boy flourished. Several years later, the priest bumped into Yankel on the road and stopped to ask after his son's welfare.

"Oh, he's fine." Yankel said. "There's only one small problem. At night when he says his bedtime prayers he gets mixed up and, instead of saying "hamalach hagoel," he says "hagalach hamoel."

Much of the humor in the Hebrew Bible is in the form of wordplay which, as it is language dependent, can only be appreciated in the original Hebrew. These wordplays will not be evident in translations. Many of the wordplays in the Bible are possible because the written Hebrew of the Bible contains neither vowels nor punctuation. In Hebrew, the vowels are marks that appear beneath the letters. Vowels were developed much later in history, probably even after the Talmud was completed. A word written without vowels can often be read in a variety of ways. To this very day, Torah scrolls are written without vowels or punctuation.

Wordplays are an interesting type of humor. The reader feels that the author is being mischievous and purposely using a word in a clever or cute manner. For the believer, the wordplays in the Bible make God seem closer to mankind. A stern, patrician (hence, humorless) authority figure is not likely to use wordplays in His writings. When the Bible says, "The dove could not find a resting-place."[60] The Hebrew word for resting-place, *manoach*, is a play on Noah's name—*Noach*, in Hebrew. One might say, the dove could not find a *manoach*, so it had to return to *Noach*.

Like everything else in the Hebrew Bible, wordplays are there not merely to entertain, but to teach as well. Sometimes, wordplays serve to connect seemingly different situations or actions. For example, the word *arumim* is used in Genesis[61] to mean naked when Adam and Eve are described as naked in the Garden of Eden. The next verse[62] uses the word *arum* to mean cunning, that is, the serpent was cunning. There may very well be a connection between these two verses and the reader is challenged to find it. If the serpent is a metaphor for temptation, then the purpose of this wordplay might be to show that nakedness causes temptation which may ultimately result in expulsion from paradise. Another connection by wordplay uses the Hebrew root word *shachat*, which means ruin and destruction but can also connote corruption and decadence. The Bible first uses this word to describe the utter decadence of mankind just prior to the Great Flood in Noah's time.[63] Later this word is used to describe what the flood will wreak.[64] Thus, during the telling of an engrossing morality tale, the Bible uses wordplay to further emphasize the connection between decadence and destruction.

Wordplay is sometimes the subtle means by which the text shows its displeasure with someone's deeds. Later in Genesis, "Noah began to be a man of the soil,"[65] the word for began is *vayachel*. This word, however, can also mean to debase oneself or to act profanely. Using wordplay, the Bible shows its displeasure with Noah for first planting a grapevine (and getting intoxicated) after the flood rather than planting something else.[66] Calling Noah "a man of the soil" may also be a subtle affront in itself. Moses was called "a man of God" because of his concern with spiritual matters and Noah, the person whose priority was to plant a grapevine, was "a man of the soil."

Another example cited in the Midrash,[67] refers to the statement that Isaac loved Esau because he was: "*tzayid bapiv*."[68] This means that Esau the hunter provided his father with game for his mouth. The word *tzayid* can mean game (*ba* means "in" and *piv* means "his mouth"), but it can also mean to hunt or trap. The Midrash and many commentators on the Bible believe that there is a double entendre here. The verse may be suggesting that Esau used his own mouth to trap (that is, deceive) his father. Esau was deceptive and made his father believe that he was a fine individual, and his father loved him more than Jacob.

It is written: "Do not turn to the idols (*elilim*)."[69] The word for deities is usually *elohim*. The word *elilim* is connected with the Hebrew word *al* which means not or naught.[70] A similar word is used in Job to mean worthless, in the phrase *rofeh elil*[71] ("a worthless doctor," a quack).

The Hebrew Bible often uses words with other meanings to describe idols. For instance, the root word *etzeb* is used to mean idol in numerous places in the Prophets and Writings; it is used several times in Psalms.[72] The word *etzeb* in Hebrew means sorrow, pain, and distress.[73] People who worship idols are in distress because their idols never listen to them. *Gilulim* is also used to mean idols in many places in the Bible.[74] It is derived from the Hebrew word *galal* which means dung and excrement. The word *toevah*, used numerous times in the text to refer to an abomination, something disgusting and loathsome, for example, incestuous relationships[75] and false weights and measures,[76] is also used to refer to idols in many places.[77]

The Hebrew Bible uses wordplay so extensively that this device could warrant a treatise of its own. What follows here is just a selection of the use of this device.

Lot's plea to the Sodomites after they found out that he had some guests was: "Do not do anything to these men (*ha-anashim ha-el*)."[78] The words "*ha-anashim ha-el*" mean "these men" but also can mean the "men of God." Indeed, the two "men" Lot was pleading for at that time were actually angels sent by God.

After the binding of Isaac, an angel called to Abraham and told him not to sacrifice his son. Abraham named the place "God Will See" (*yireh*).[79] However, the word *yirah*, spelled the same as *yireh* in Hebrew, has another meaning: it means fear and terror. This may be a play on words. Abraham may have been alluding to his new relationship with God, one now also based on the fear of God.

Rebeccah became pregnant with twins and she experienced great pain as the twins struggled within her. She inquired of the Lord and was told: "Two nations are in your womb . . . and the elder (*rav*) will serve (*yaavod*) the younger."[80] The word *rav* is in this case translated as elder, however, the word *rav* usually means much or many; the word for elder is usually *bechor*. One possible translation (that of Tosafot) is that the younger will work much (i.e., many years); indeed, Jacob worked hard for twenty years in the house of Laban. The Midrashic interpretation is as follows: If Jacob (the younger) is deserving, then Esau (the elder) will serve him; if not, then Esau will enslave him.[81] This play on words is possible because, without vowels, the word *yaavod* can be pronounced as *yaaved* (shall enslave) or *yaavod* (shall serve).

Esau was famished and showed his lack of manners by saying to Jacob: "Stuff into me *(haleateini)* some of that red, red stuff for I am exhausted."[82] The red, red stuff was a dish of lentils that Jacob had prepared. This is the only time in all of the Scripture that the word *haleateini* is used. The word is used to show how crass Esau was. According to commentators, he asked Jacob to pour the food down his throat the way an animal might be fed (*see* Rashi). Normally, one who is hungry would say "*hachil na li*" which means "please give me to eat."

Laban said to Jacob: "Designate (*nakvah*) to me your wages and I will give it."[83] The word "nakvah" means designate or specify and has exactly the same spelling as *nekevah* which means female. This is a clever pun and refers to the fact that previously Jacob's "wage" was a female, that is, he worked a total of fourteen years for the hand of Rachel.

Jacob had stolen his father's blessing (*bracha*) from Esau. Later, Esau, with four hundred men, came to meet Jacob upon his return from living with Laban. Jacob sent a present (*mincha*) to Esau to mollify him. The word *mincha* is used several times to describe this gift. However, when Jacob said to Esau: "Please take my gift,"[84] the word Jacob used for gift was *birchati* which can mean gift, but literally means "my blessing." Was this a Freudian slip? Was Jacob nervous about the blessing he "stole" twenty years ago and inadvertently used the wrong word? The more appropriate word would have been *minchati* (my gift).

The expression "will lift up your head" (*yisa et roshecha*) is used several times in describing Joseph's interpretation of the dreams of the butler and the baker.[85] The lifting of the head when referring to the Pharaoh's butler means to count, that is, that he will be restored again to his original position and will be counted again among Pharaoh's servants. However, the "lifting up your head" expression when referring to the baker is used to mean that the baker will be hanged. This is a clever play on the idiom "will lift up your head."

Joseph called his first-born Manasseh: "because God has made me forget (*nasheh*) all my troubles and all my father's house."[86] Joseph did indeed forget all of his father's house, since he did not communicate with his father or his full brother Benjamin. As a ruler of Egypt he must have had ample opportunity to send a messenger to his father and brother informing them that he was alive. In fact, they did not find out that Joseph was alive for nine more years.

Jacob's bequest to Joseph while in Egypt was: "I have given you one *shechem* above your brothers."[87] The word *shechem* means portion but also is the name of the actual place in Israel where Joseph was ultimately buried.

Jacob's deathbed blessing to his son Judah contains an interesting wordplay: "A young lion is Judah; from prey, my son, you ascended . . ."[88] The overt meaning is that Judah is like a lion cub: he takes his prey with none daring to challenge him. The phrase "my son" was a term of address aimed at Judah. However, if the word *teref* (prey) and *beni* (my son) are said together without any punctuation between them, then the meaning of the verse becomes that Judah ascended from the prey of Jacob's son (Joseph). It was, in fact, Judah who said "what profit will there be if we kill our brother . . ." Years earlier, when Jacob was shown Joseph's coat covered with blood, he said: "an evil beast has devoured (*tarof toraf*) Joseph."[89] The word used there (*tarof*) is from the same root as *teref*. Indeed, the major commentaries on the Bible argue as to whether the "my son" referred to in Jacob's blessing is Judah or Joseph (*see* Rashi and Rashbam).

Pharaoh asked the midwives, Shifra and Puah, to surreptitiously kill the newborn boys in order to keep the population of the Israelites down. The midwives feared God and did not comply with Pharaoh's request. When Pharaoh summoned them and asked them why they did not kill the newborns, their response was: "The Hebrew women are not like the Egyptian women, for they are vigorous (*chayot*); before a midwife comes to them, they give birth."[90] The Hebrew word *chayot* which is generally translated as lively or vigorous (and therefore giving birth easily and quickly) is spelled the same as the Hebrew word for animals. Perhaps, the midwives were calling the Hebrew women animals, that is, they are like animals and have no need for assistance in childbirth. Indeed, there is a debate in the Talmud as to whether the word *chayot* is related to the Hebrew word for midwife or animal.[91] By calling the Hebrew women "animals" they also most likely convinced Pharaoh that they hated the Israelites and were not really trying to help them.

"Moses looked all around, and when he saw that there was no man, he killed the Egyptian"[92] who had beaten the Hebrew. The Midrash notes that there was no one man enough to protect the Hebrew from the Egyptian tormentor.[93]

The verse states "See that evil (*raah*) is before your face."[94] One explanation of this difficult verse is that Pharaoh told Moses and Aaron that it is clear that your true intentions are evil, that is, that you wish to leave Egypt permanently. The Hebrew word *ra* or *raah* means evil. However, one Midrash explains this verse differently. Pharaoh warned Moses that the star known as Ra (probably the sun god, Ra) was going to cause the death of the Israelites in the wilderness.[95] After the Israelites made the golden calf, Moses pleaded on their behalf to God: "Why should the Egyptians speak, saying: 'With evil intent (*b'raah*) did He take them out to slay them in the mountains and to annihilate them from the face of the earth.'"[96] There may be a wordplay here. Moses may have been hinting to God: Why should the Egyptians say that their god Ra was responsible for killing the Israelites in the mountains?[97]

While the Israelites were preparing to leave Egypt, they were told to request gifts from the Egyptians. They were given gifts to encourage them to leave quickly, and the verse states: "They despoiled (*vayinatzlu*) the Egyptians."[98] The word for despoiled (*vayinatzlu*) is the same as the Hebrew word for rescued. The root *nitzail* can mean either rescue or despoil. This may suggest that the Egyptians saved themselves by providing the Israelites with gifts, for had they not given these gifts to their departing former slaves then more of them might have died in the tenth plague.

The Hebrew Bible warns the Israelites not to make themselves disgusting by eating repulsive creatures. The verse continues: "Because I am God that brought you up (*hamaaleh*) out of Egypt . . ."[99] The Talmud notes that the word that is normally used to describe the Israelites being taken out of Egypt (*hamotzie*) means "who brought you out" not "brought you up." The word *hamaaleh* (meaning brought up) that is used in this verse has a double meaning. Besides meaning that God took the Israelites out of Egypt, it also indicates that the purpose of these dietary laws was to elevate the Israelites in a spiritual sense.[100]

When Korach and his followers rebelled against Moses in the wilderness,[101] they said to Moses and Aaron: "It is too much (*rav*) for you." The Hebrew word "rav" means much or many and its antonym, *me'at*, means a little or a few. Their complaint was that Moses and Aaron had taken too much power for themselves. Moses's response was "You take too much (*rav*) upon you, you sons of Levi," that is, that they have gone too far. Moses then told them: "Is it but a small thing (*hame'at*) that the God of Israel has separated you . . ." Dathan and Aviram, Korach's associates in the rebellion, sarcastically used Moses's own phrase of "*hame'at*" to ridicule Moses. They told Moses: "Is it but a small thing (*hame'at*) that you have brought us up out of a land flowing with milk and honey to kill us in the wilderness . . ." Nechama Leibowitz points out that Dathan and Aviram mocked Moses not only by using his own words but also by using a sentence with a similar structure. Moses asked a rhetorical question: "Is it but a small thing that the God of Israel has separated . . . and will you seek the priesthood also?" Dathan and Aviram responded rhetorically: "Is it but a small thing that you have brought us up . . . that you must make yourself also a prince over us?" According to Leibowitz, what they actually meant was: "You concluded with a rhetorical question upbraiding us for our ambition. We too conclude with a rhetorical question which denounces your uppityness."[102]

Another use of similar words is seen in the following: Korach and his followers' complaint was: "Why do you lift yourselves (*tisnasu*) over the congregation of God?"[103] Moses told God: "I have not taken (*lo nasati*) one donkey from them."[104] The word that is normally used to mean "take" is *lakoch*. The word *nasah* means to lift or to carrry. In the first verse it means to exalt oneself and in the second verse it indicates to carry away or to take.

An interesting word is used in the verse, "Harass the Midianites and strike them."[105] Here the word *tzaror*, meaning harass, is used. Actually the Israelites were being commanded to go to war and eradicate the Midianite people for their part in having their women seduce the Israelites and get them to worship the idol Baal-Peor. One of the important royal families of the Midianites was the Tzur family. Cozbi, daughter of Tzur, successfully seduced Zimri, one of the leaders of the tribe of Shimon.[106] By the way, the name Cozbi is related to the Hebrew word for deception. Here the word *tzaror* is a wordplay to remind the reader of the evil that the Tzur family had wrought.

The well-known verse in Deuteronomy, ". . . in order to make you know that man does not live by bread alone, but by everything that emanates out of the mouth of the Lord does man live,"[107] contains an interesting wordplay. Food normally goes into a mouth. The verse speaks of things that come "out of the mouth." The verse could just as easily have said that man lives by things that come from the hand of the Lord rather than "mouth of the Lord."

God asked Moses to choose whatever promised land he wished. After weighing several factors, Moses settled on California. But Moses, according to legend, had a speech impediment, and he began to answer, "Ca- Ca-" whereupon God said, "Canaan, that wasteland? Well, okay, Mo. If you want it, you got it!"[108]

Samson used the Hebrew word *chamor* repetitively in two different ways in his declaration after killing a thousand Philistines with the jawbone of a donkey: *Bilchi hachamor chamor chamoratayim*— with the jawbone of a donkey I piled many piles. The Hebrew word *chamor* means both donkey and heaps.[109]

When the prophet Samuel asked King Saul why he spared the sheep of the Amalekites after being told by the Lord to eradicate everything, "Samuel said: 'What then (*meh*) is this bleating of sheep in my ears?'"[110] The word used for "what then" is *meh* which sounds uncannily like the bleating of sheep.

Achsah, wife of Otniel son of Kenaz, asked her father for a gift of springs of water since the land she and her husband were given was arid. Achsah said to her father: "Give me a gift (*bracha*) since you have given me an arid land: give me springs of water."[111] There may be a wordplay here since *braicha*, spelled the same as *bracha*, means a pond or pool. The prophet Hosea compared God to a lion and a leopard waiting to destroy the Jewish people for having forsaken Him: ". . . as a leopard by the way I will watch (stealthily)."[112] The word used to mean "watch stealthily" or "lie in wait" is *ashur*. This word is spelled exactly the same as the word *Ashur* which means Assyria except that it is missing a *dagesh*, a dot added to a consonant to indicate a difference in pronunciation. Interestingly, the prophet Hosea warned the Kingdom of Israel about *Ashur* (Assyria). He referred to the treaty made with Assyria[113] and told the Israelites that: "Assyria (*Ashur*) will not save us."[114] As a matter of fact, it was the Assyrians who drove the ten tribes out of Israel. Using the word *ashur* to describe the lurking leopard watching stealthily is a clever wordplay: God's tool for punishing the Israelites for idolatry and immorality was indeed Assyria.

Upon returning from Moab, where she lost her husband, two sons, and all her wealth, Naomi, whose name means the pleasant one, said to the residents of Bethlehem: "Do not call me Naomi; call me *marah*,"[115] that is, the bitter one. Boaz told Ruth: "May the Lord reward your actions and may your payment be full."[116] The word for full, *shlemah*, is spelled the same as *Shlomo* (Solomon) in Hebrew. And Ruth's most famous descendant was King Solomon.[117]

Plays on People's Names

Little Alice, the youngest of 5 girls, wanted to know how her parents came up with her name.

"Well," her mother replied. "It was the strangest thing. When you were born, your father just took one look at you and said: 'Dos is alles.'"

Names are very important in the Hebrew Scriptures. God told Abraham to name his soon-to-be-born son, *Yitzchak*,[118] because Abraham and Sarah laughed upon hearing that she would give birth to a son. The Hebrew word *tzachak* means laughed. An angel told Hagar to name her son Ishmael (God will hear), since God heard her prayer.[119] When Jacob's name was changed to Israel, a name which means to prevail over the divine, it referred to the angel with whom Jacob wrestled.[120] The Bible states the reason for each of Jacob's children's names. Given the important place of names in the Hebrew Bible, it is not surprising that there are numerous wordplays related to names. Just as wordplay is a large part of Biblical humor, plays on names are a large part of wordplay.

Noah's blessing to his son Japhet, "*Yaft Elohim La Yefet*"[121] meaning "May God enlarge Japheth" was a play on Japheth's name; the word *yaft* was used only because it is similar to *Yefet* (Japheth).

With regard to Jacob's birth, we see that: "And after that came forth his brother, and his hand was grasping Esau's heel; and his name was called Jacob,"[122] *Yaakov*, in Hebrew, means one that takes by the heel; the Hebrew word for heel is *ekev*. Later on, when Jacob took the blessing that was originally intended for his twin brother Esau by pretending to be him, Esau said: "Is he not rightly named Jacob (*Yaakov*), for he has deceived me (*vayaakveini*) these two times."[123] The word *akav* means deceived, and Esau was making a clever wordplay on Jacob's name.

Rachel's name for her first son has an interesting wordplay. The Bible states: "She conceived and bore a son and said, 'God has taken away (*asaph*) my reproach.' And she called him Joseph, saying, 'May the Lord add (*yoseph*) another son to me.'"[124] The word *asaph* means taken away, but with the addition of one letter it means to add. Even more interesting, this name hints at Joseph's future. He indeed was taken away from his family but later on (in Egypt) was added back to his family.

Jacob's blessing of Judah begins: "Yehuda, *atta yoducha . . .*"[125] *Yoducha* means to praise you. The Hebrew word *yodu* (to praise) is very similar to Yehuda's (Judah) own name. Jacob's blessing of Dan begins: "Dan *yadin amo . . .*"[126] *Yadin* means to judge and is similar to Dan's name. Also, Jacob's blessing to his son Gad contained a wordplay on his son's name: "Gad *gedud yagudenu.*"[127] ("Gad, a troop shall troop upon him.") The name Gad is similar to the Hebrew word *gedud* which means a troop or band.

When Abigail pleaded with King David to spare her husband's life, she said to David: "Let not my lord take to heart this scoundrel, Nabal; for like his name so is he. His name is Nabal, and disgracefulness is with him."[128] The Hebrew word *nabal* means vile, mean, scoundrel, disgrace, wickedness, degradation, and foolishness. Abigail was telling David that her husband's name suited him perfectly. It is interesting to note that David's eulogy over the general Abner was: "Should Abner die like a scoundrel (*nabal*)?"[129] Was it a coincidence that David used the word *nabal* to describe the way the vile individuals die (i.e., by the sword and without honor)?

Doeg the Edomite told King Saul that the priests living in Nob gave David food and a sword, when David was on the run from Saul who wanted David dead. Saul ordered Doeg to kill the priests of Nob. Doeg's name in Samuel I[130] is spelled differently than it is elsewhere. The letter *aleph* in Doeg's name was replaced with a *vav* and *yod*. The name Doeg spelled with an *aleph* means concerned, anxious, and worried. Doeg did not show any concern for the people of Nob and even slaughtered the women, infants, and cattle (Saul's order was to slay the priests). The letters *vav* and *yod* spell the Hebrew word meaning woe. Doeg went from being a man who showed concern to a man who caused woe. The Talmud[131] explains the change in Doeg's name somewhat differently. At first, God is concerned that a person will go astray (*doeg* means to be concerned). After a person has become evil, God exclaims, "Woe, that this person has set out an evil path."

In the days of Ahaz, the King of Judah, Aram and Ephraim made an alliance and were planning to attack Judah. They planned to install a new king to replace Ahaz. The verse in Isaiah describes what they planned to do after conquering Jerusalem: "and let us crown a king in its midst, Ben Taval."[132] The commentaries argue as to the meaning of "Ben Taval." Some claim that it is not a name but is a combination of two Hebrew words: *tov* (good) and *el* (unto), that is, good for us (the word *ben* means son or member of), and thus the meaning of the verse is that they wanted to crown a puppet king who would be good for them. On the other hand, many commentaries believe that Ben Taval is the actual name of a person from Ephraim or Aram. If so, the meaning of this name is *tov* (good) *al* (not), that is, good for nothing (see commentary of Ibn Ezra) or not good in the eyes of the Lord (see commentary of Rashi). The suggestion by Good that this is a wordplay and that the noble's real name was a contraction of *tov* (good) and *el* (God) but the vowelling was changed by the Masoretes to make fun of this individual[133] is quite plausible. The spelling is the same whether the name is read as Toval or Tovel; the only difference is in the vowels which tell us how to pronounce the word.

Pashchur the false priest struck Jeremiah and had him thrown into prison. The name Pashchur means spread (*pash*) with nobility (*chor*). When Jeremiah was released from the prison he declared: "Not Pashchur did the Lord call your name but Magor Misaviv."[134] Magor Misaviv means surrounded (*saviv*) with terror (*magor*).

In Genesis, Jacob refers to the "God of Abraham and the Dread (*Pachad*) of Isaac."[135] Later on, Jacob swears by the "Dread of his father Isaac."[136] Referring to God as a "Dread" is quite unusual. It is not inconceivable that Isaac after being bound and almost sacrificed, had a tremendous fear of God and therefore referred to Him as his Dread.

Shechem, the son of Chamor, raped Dinah, the daughter of Jacob.[137] *Chamor* means donkey in Hebrew. Was Shechem's father's real name Chamor or is the Bible purposely corrupting the name in order to make fun of Shechem? It is not inconceivable that the Bible is telling us that Shechem was a son-of-a-jackass.

King Josiah sent an entourage to a prophetess to inquire of the Lord regarding a scroll which had been found. The verse states: "Hilkiah the priest and Ahikam and Achbor and Shaphan and Asaiah went to Huldah the prophetess."[138] In Hebrew, the name Achbor is virtually the same as *achbar* meaning mouse, *shaphan* means a rock-badger or coney, and *huldah* means weasel (or mole). It is quite strange that half the people at the meeting had rodent names. This is probably not a coincidence since Achbor seemed to have a second name,[139] Avdon.[140] The author purposely used the rodent-like name, Achbor, rather than the other name, Avdon.

Humorous Imagery and Exaggeration

One friend told another, "Yesterday I went to the museum. They had an exhibit of the hammer that Cain used to slay his brother." Not to be outdone, his friend responded, "That's nothing. Last week the museum exhibited the ladder Jacob saw in his dream."[141]

According to Tal Bonham, many of the descriptions in the Book of Proverbs and the Song of Solomon are quite comical. In particular, he feels that the descriptions of the nagging woman and the lazy man in Proverbs are intentionally humorous.[142] Sometimes, underlying the humorous exaggerations is the principle that wicked people and whiners have a tendency to exaggerate their travails and to focus on the good times of the past while magnifying the horrors of the present.

The plague of frogs is certainly quite humorous. The image of a country overrun with frogs, including frogs in the palace, in the bedrooms of Egypt, in the ovens, and kneading bowels is quite funny. There is humor in the fact that the Egyptian magicians, in trying to downplay what Moses had done, "brought up frogs on the land of Egypt"[143] to show that they could do the same thing. So instead of eliminating the plague they just made it worse. There is even humor in the word used to describe Moses's prayer to God asking for the frogs to go away. Moses cried (*vayitzack*) to God. Moses had to cry because the noise made by all those frogs required that Moses scream to be heard.[144] This is another example of a clever play on words.

John Currid is of the opinion that the ten plagues mocked the deities of Egypt.[145] The plague of frogs might very well have mocked Hekhet, the Egyptian goddess of fertility, who was the protector of women in childbirth. She was depicted as either a frog-headed woman or a frog. The Egyptians were mocked when the frogs became superfertile instead of the people.

The Israelites' complaint to Moses in the desert was a ludicrous exaggeration: "If we had only died by the hand of the Lord in the land of Egypt, when we sat by the pots of meat."[146] This was obviously an absurd overstatement; it is highly unlikely that the Egyptians served their slaves pots of meat. Indeed, it is highly unlikely that they were served meat at all. This kind of exaggeration was used several times in the wilderness. Later on, the complaint shifted from pots of meat to free fish: "We remember the fish we used to eat in Egypt for free; the cucumbers, the melons, the leeks, the onions, and the garlic."[147] This complaint was also ludicrous. True, the slaves were probably given food for "free," but they had to perform backbreaking work and their children were murdered. Apparently, the text is trying to show us how this complaining mode of thought feeds on itself and results in worse and worse behaviors. Ultimately, this generation of Israelites wandered in the desert and died out; the next generation entered the Promised Land.

Ehud came to Eglon, King of Moab, while he was sitting alone and said: "I have a word (*dvar*) from God to you."[148] Ehud's message was a sword, which he stuck into Eglon's huge belly. Eglon was so obese that his fat completely covered the sword. Furthermore, there is a pun in Ehud's message to Eglon. He told him that he had a *dvar*. The Hebrew word *dvar* (or *davar*) means both thing and word or message. Ehud pretended to have a word but actually delivered a thing, that is, a sword.

The verse in Hosea, "To them say: 'They that sacrifice men kiss the calves'"[149] was a proverb used in ancient times to mock the idolaters. Normally, individuals kiss other people and slaughter calves for sustenance. Idolaters do the opposite and slaughter their fellow men and kiss the calves.[150]

Solomon's Song of Songs is a beautiful, romantic love poem, but it has some of the most unusual imagery in all of the Scriptures. Comparing a loved one to a horse may not have been strange in ancient times, but one has good reason to be skeptical. "I have compared you, my love, to a mare in Pharaoh's chariots."[151] Horses may indeed be beautiful but this is still an unusual way to describe one's love. "Your hair is as a flock of goats trailing down from Mount Gilead. Your teeth are like a flock of ewes all shaped alike, which have come up from the washing; all of them (*shekullam*) are paired, and none of them is missing (*shakullah*)."[152]

There is also a nice alliteration here. That word *shekullam* (meaning all of them) sounds similar to the word *shakullah* (meaning missing). "Your nose (*appech*) is like the tower of Lebanon, which overlooks Damascus."[153] The commentaries have problems with the translation of *appech* as nose since even in ancient times a prominent nose was not a sign of beauty. Therefore, some translate *appech* as face. Hmmm. A face like the tower of Lebanon. Much better.

The Book of Proverbs lampoons fools, lazy people, and quarrelsome women by using comical caricatures. These images describe the contentious woman and the woman who lacks discretion in a witty and clever manner.

> "As a gold ring in a swine's snout, so is a beautiful woman from whom sense has departed."[154]

> "It is better to live in a desert than with a contentious and angry woman."[155]

> "It is better to live on a corner of a roof, than in a house of companionship with a quarrelsome wife."[156]

> "A constant dripping on a rainstormy day and a quarrelsome woman are alike."[157]

The fool is also described in comical, ludicrous, and often graphical ways in Proverbs:

> "Like snow in the summer and like rain at harvest, so is honor unbefitting for a fool."[158]

Snow is a disaster in the summer when the crops need warmth and rain is a calamity during the harvest season. Giving a fool honor is also a catastrophe since it makes people think that there is value in folly.

> "A whip for the horse, a bridle for the donkey, and a rod for the body of fools."[159]

> "Like a thorn that goes into the hand of the drunkard, so is a parable in the mouth of fools."[160]

A thorn in the hands of a fool will hurt others, so too does the parable of the fool annoy others because it is nonsensical.

> "Like a dog that returns to his vomit, so does a fool repeat his folly."[161]

The fool shamelessly repeats his inanity just as the dog eats his own vomit Finally, regarding the indolent individual:

> "The lazy man says, 'there is a lion on the road, a lion is between the streets.'"[162]

He exaggerates in order to justify doing nothing.

> "The door turns on its hinges, and the lazy man on his bed."[163]

The door turns on its hinges but goes nowhere, so too the lazy man turns on his bed from side to side but does not get up.

> "The lazy man buries his hand in the dish; it wearies him to return it to his mouth."[164]

He is too lazy even to bring the food to his mouth.

> "A lazy man is wiser in his own eyes than seven men who give advice."[165]

The king had seven advisors in ancient times.

Toward the end of the Book of Esther, Haman, prostrating himself before Esther to beg for his life, fell on her bed. The king misinterpreted what happened and said: "Will he even force the queen while I am in the house?"[166] Haman, second to the king, to whom all bowed, the architect of the plot to viciously exterminate the Jews, suddenly became a klutz. The Jews were saved.

Humorous Stories and Situations

Morris Rabinowitz in the 1930s finally decided to flee the onslaught of the Nazis into his little piece of Eastern Europe. Rather than leave his holdings behind, he sold all his assets and converted it to gold and then had 5 sets of solid gold false teeth made.

When he arrived in New York the customs official was perplexed as to why anybody would have 5 sets of gold teeth.

Morris explained: "We Orthodox Jews have two separate sets of dishes for meat products and dairy products but I am so kosher and religious I also have separate sets of teeth."

The customs official shook his head and said, "Well that accounts for two sets of teeth. What about the other three?"

Morris then said "Vell us very religious Orthodox Jews use separate dishes for Passover, but I am so religious I have separate teeth, one for meat and one for dairy food."

The customs official slapped his head and then said, "You must be a very religious man with separate teeth for food and dairy products and likewise for Passover. That accounts for four sets of teeth. What about the fifth set?"

"Vell to tell you the truth, once in a while I like a ham sandwich."

While the primary purpose of the Hebrew Bible is to teach people how to live a spiritual life and serve God, many of the stories contained in the text are quite humorous. As we have seen, much of the humor of the Bible may be categorized as either sarcasm, irony, wordplay, or humorous images; however, some situations simply cannot be classified. They're just funny—situationally. Some of these situations result from a funny predicament and may include humorous imagery as well.

Abraham's wife Sarah died and Abraham needed a place to bury her. The negotiations between Abraham and Ephron over the Cave of Machpelah is a good example of humor used to show the difference between a truly good person and someone—er—somewhat less so. These negotiations are humorous and illustrate the concept that ignoble men promise much and deliver little. Ephron, posturing before his countrymen, said to Abraham:

> *No, my lord, listen to me! I have already given the field to you, and as for the cave that is in it, I have given it to you; in the view of my countrymen, I have given it to you. Bury your dead . . .*

However, Abraham refused to accept the land for free, probably suspecting that Ephron was only offering the land because his countrymen were watching. Abraham replied:

> *If only you would listen to me. I am giving you the money for the field . . .*

Ephron said:

> *My lord, hear me! Land worth four hundred silver shekels, between me and you what is it? Bury your dead.* [167]

Ephron, still pretending that he wanted to give away the land for nothing, cleverly mentioned its presumed value. Of course, Abraham understood what Ephron really wanted and ended up paying him the grossly outrageous sum of four hundred silver shekels. By way of comparison, Jeremiah paid seven shekels and ten silver pieces[168] for property that was better, and probably larger, than the Cave of Machpelah.

In a small shtetl, two Jews in shul on Shabbos during prayers.

"I saw your new calf; very nice animal. Nisht auf Shabbos geredt—if it weren't Shabbos—I would offer you a nice price for that calf."

"Nisht auf Shabbos geredt, I wouldn't sell it for a penny less than $1000."

"Nisht auf Shabbos geredt, I could probably go as high as $600."

"Nisht auf Shabbos geredt, I might be able to let her go for $850."

"Nisht auf Shabbos geredt, I wouldn't offer more than $750."

"Nisht auf Shabbos geredt, I would make a deal at $800."

"Nisht auf Shabbos geredt, I would agree to that."

"Nisht auf Shabbos geredt, you got it!"

The next humorous situation illustrates that an individual with a guilty conscience is always afraid regardless of numerous assurances of safety, even if the assurances come from angels and even from God. Jacob was afraid of his brother Esau because he "stole" the blessings intended for Esau. God saved him from Laban and on his way home, Jacob encountered angels of God.[169] God may have sent these angels to reassure Jacob and show that He was watching. Jacob heard that Esau, along with four hundred of his people, was coming to meet him and was terrified. Jacob prayed to God: "Rescue me, I pray Thee, from the hand of my brother, from the hand of Esau."[170] Jacob planned on running away and got his family across the Jabbok crossing. An angel sent by God wrestled with him, apparently to prevent him from fleeing so that Jacob could see that God would not allow Jacob to be hurt. They wrestled all night and Jacob was made lame by the angel. It appears that the purpose of the lameness was to demonstrate to Jacob that he should not run away. The angel even changed Jacob's name to Israel because "You have struggled with a divine being and man and you have prevailed."[171] When Esau saw Jacob, he embraced and kissed him, and they wept. Esau offered to accompany Jacob. Jacob replied that the children were weak and the flocks and herds could not be driven hard. Jacob then said: "Let my lord, please go ahead of me. I will journey on gently . . . I will eventually come to my lord in Seir."[172] Of course, Jacob never went to Seir. The Bible shows us that Jacob's fear overwhelmed him again and he was looking for an excuse to get rid of Esau. This is not so different from the person who tells the bully who challenges him to a fight, "why don't you step out," and then does not follow after the bully steps out.

Even God can become exasperated with His people. At first, the Holy One said to Moses: "Now go, and I will send you to Pharaoh, and take *my* people, the children of Israel, out of Egypt"[173] (emphasis added). After they made the golden calf, God said to Moses: "Go down, because *your* people whom *you* have brought out of Egypt have become corrupt."[174] This is much like parents who may say to each other when a child misbehaves: "Go speak to *your* son."

God says to Moses, after the golden calf was made, "Now therefore let Me alone, that My anger may flare up against them and I shall annihilate them."[175] What makes this surprising is that God had just informed Moses that the Jewish people had made a golden calf and Moses did not have a chance to speak up on their behalf. Parents often say to each other—for effect—after a child has been bad: "Hold me back before I . . ." The Midrash actually uses the metaphor of the angry parent to explain why God told Moses to leave him alone before Moses said anything in defense of the Jewish people.[176]

The expression "as God lives" is used numerous times throughout the Scriptures as an oath.[177] One may ask, what expression does God use when He vows? After the spies returned and convinced the people that they would not be able to conquer the Promised Land,[178] God vowed to destroy every Israelite over the age of twenty. The expression used by God was "as I live" (*chai ani*). Apparently, God swears by His own existence. This expression is also used in various places in the Prophets.[179]

Balak, the Moabite king, was afraid of the Israelites and sent messengers to Balaam whom he wished to hire to curse the Israelites. Balaam was an arrogant seer who wanted to profit from his powers, and he knew full well that God did not want him to go curse the Israelites. While the arrogant Balaam called himself: "one who hears the sayings of God and knows the knowledge of the Most High,"[180] God showed Balaam that his own donkey saw things that Balaam did not. The ass saw an angel standing in the way with his sword drawn, but Balaam saw nothing. You might say that God made an ass out of Balaam. Also humorous is the fact that Balaam said to his donkey: "Because you have mocked me; if only there were a sword in my hand, I would now have slain you."[181] Balaam was ready to eradicate an entire nation with his ability to curse but he suddenly needed a sword to kill his own helpless donkey.[182]

Balaam's donkey, suddenly endowed with the power of speech, did not talk like a lowly donkey and simply tell his master to stop beating him. Instead, God made the donkey speak like an intelligent and eloquent individual. His first comment to Balaam was a rhetorical question: "What have I done to you that you have beaten me these three times?"[183] Balaam said, "Because you have mocked me; if only there were a sword in my hand, I would now have slain you." The ass replied, "Am I not your donkey upon which you have ridden all your life until this day? Have I ever been wont to do such a thing to you?" Balaam's response reveals him as irrational and hot-tempered. The donkey's words, on the other hand, indicate a superior and rational intellect. Balaam's father's name was Be'or. *Be'or* is very similar to the Hebrew word *be'ir* meaning cattle or beasts. When Balaam referred to himself as the son of Be'or[184] he was confirming that he was little more than an animal. Moreover, referring to himself as "the man with the open eye" was ludicrous given that he could not see what his donkey saw.

Saul, the future king of Israel, was looking for the prophet Samuel. The young, handsome man encountered some young ladies and, using as few words as possible, asked them: "Is the seer here?"[185] To which the young ladies replied thus:

> *He is. Behold, he is before you. Hasten now, for on this day he has come to the city since the people will have today's sacrifice in the high place. When you come to the city, you will immediately find him, before he ascends to the high place to eat; for the people will not eat until he comes, since he blesses the sacrifice, and afterwards those that are invited shall eat.*[186]

The Talmud wonders about this strange and very lengthy response and concludes that the young maidens prolonged the conversation because Saul was a very good looking (albeit reticent) young man.[187]

After Abigail convinced King David not to kill her husband Nabal, she said: "And when the Lord will do good to my master (David), you should remember your maidservant."[188] The Talmud[189] feels that Abigail told David to remember her in marriage, knowing that God would eventually punish her husband Nabal for his misdeeds. This is indeed what happened. Once David heard that Nabal died, he sent messengers to Abigail asking her hand in marriage. Abigail's response was essentially positive, although she declared herself unworthy of being a wife but only worthy of washing "the feet of my master's servants." This was a very eloquent and humble response. However, in the next verse: "She hurried, mounted, and rode the donkey and her five maidens went with her."[190] Apparently, she was going to have help washing feet.

Many view the entire book of Jonah as a parody.[191] Jonah was sent by God to announce to the residents of Nineveh (capital of Assyria) its imminent destruction by the Lord. Jonah, unlike other prophets, refused to go and even tried to flee from God by taking a ship from Jaffa to Tarshish. Why was Jonah reluctant to prophesy to the Ninevites? Many commentators suggest that Jonah knew that in the future the Assyrians would attack Israel, as indeed they did, driving the ten tribes out of the country. Jonah was the reluctant prophet, unlike other prophets such as Jeremiah and Isaiah. His entire reluctant prophecy consisted of but five Hebrew words: "In another forty days Nineveh shall be overturned."[192] This prophecy had its desired effect and the people of Nineveh proclaimed a fast, and even the cattle and sheep were made to fast. The reluctant Jonah accomplished in five words what numerous eloquent prophets could not accomplish in thousands of words, and all this without even trying.

Boaz told Ruth: "Do not go and glean in another field. . . but stay close to my maidens." Boaz told Ruth to stay on the part of the field where the young women were working so that she would not be molested by any of the male harvesters. Ruth repeated Boaz's words to her mother-in-law Naomi but made a slight modification: "Yea, he even told me, 'stay close to my young men until they have ended all my harvest.'" In misquoting Boaz, Ruth replaced "maidens" with "young men" (the words are very similar in Hebrew: n'arim = young men and naaroth = young maidens). Naomi must have realized this because she said to Ruth: "It is good, my daughter, that you go out with his maidens."[193] Ruth's Freudian slip might have made Naomi realize that Ruth needed a husband and therefore immediately advised Ruth how to get married.

Among the most humorous and literary of the Holy Writings, the Book of Esther contains a great deal of irony and many humorous situations. The story begins with King Ahasuerus making a huge feast for the people of Shushan, the capitol of his realm. He ordered that Queen Vashti be brought to his party wearing the royal crown (some say only the royal crown) to "show off to the people and the officials her beauty." She refused, feeling that such a display was beneath her dignity, and the King had her deposed (and presumably killed). The king issued a decree to the effect that henceforth: "every man should rule in his own home and speak according to the language of his people."[194] This superfluous decree is clearly comical and the Midrash discusses whether this decree made Ahasuerus a laughingstock all over the world.[195]

Does God Have a Sense of Humor?

Looking at the abundance of humor in the Hebrew Scriptures, from irony to humorous images to wordplay and more, one is tempted to say that the author of these works has a terrific sense of humor. Is that statement blasphemous? We can be pretty sure it is not, since no less a source than Psalms declares, "He who sits in Heaven shall laugh."[196] Indeed, humor is frequently divine.

5

No Match for God: Satan as Trickster

David Ben-Gurion dies, and he is granted the unprecedented privilege of choosing where to spend eternity. Ben-Gurion thinks for a moment and then asks, "Can I have a tour first?"

The angels first show him around Heaven, which is very nice, but just a bit boring, not much going on. Hell, on the other hand, is a real blast—the food, the booze, the music, the weather—it's just fantastic. Finally, the moment comes when he has to make his choice. Ben-Gurion says, "I've definitely got to choose Hell." So be it, chant the angels.

Immediately, the floor drops out beneath him and Ben-Gurion tumbles into a dark, hot, fiery Hell with all kinds of otherworldly tortures visited upon the flesh of the eternally damned. "Wait a minute! Hey!" he calls out.

Satan appears and says in a booming voice, "What do you wish to ask?" Ben-Gurion is terrified but he counters, "When I was given the tour, Hell was such a nice place. What happened?"

Satan threw back his head and roared. "Before you were just a tourist! Now you're an oleh chadash *(new immigrant)!"*

Satan, condemned in Christianity as a fallen angel, as evil incarnate, is a more complex figure in Judaism, where he originated.[1] In the perspective of Judaism, Satan is just another angel, one who is constantly carping and who causes people to transgress the will of God. He is the angel who accused Joshua, the High Priest, of misdeeds before God[2] and who instigated David to sin in taking a census of Israel.[3] In *Job*, Satan diligently albeit unsuccessfully tried to get Job to blaspheme the Lord.[4]

In the Jewish tradition, Satan is not a fallen angel. He is not an evil force equal and opposite to God; in fact, he is merely another angel, obedient and subservient to God. The literal meaning of the Hebrew word *satan* is "accuser" or "adversary," a word that connotes the angel's task as prosecutor in the Heavenly court. It is interesting to note that the word Devil, a synonym for Satan, is derived from a corruption of the Greek word *diabolos*, meaning "slanderer" which may have been derived from the Hebrew.

Satan is a sort of archetype, often depicted in a somewhat humorous manner, not unlike the fox fables and trickster tales. In fact, of all the trickster figures in the folktales of various diverse cultures[5]—for example, the Native American Coyote, the African Trickster Rabbit, the Greek god Hermes, the Norse god Loki—Satan is probably the oldest.

Satan is often identified as a person's evil inclination in Jewish thought, an internal counterbalance to one's good inclination, both of which are under a person's control. Satan is also the Angel of Death,[6] an angel whose duty is to take the souls of mortals when their time has come. Finally, Satan is the angel who tests individuals, tempts them into sin, and then testifies against them in the Heavenly tribunal, hence the name "Accuser." The Accuser is the prosecutor who testifies against the recently departed in a Heavenly court regarding the individual's sins. Not only does this trickster get us to sin in the first place, he then stands up to accuse us, and to argue that our souls be sent to Hell because of these sins that he impelled us to do. It is the ultimate trick on mankind.

Evil inclination, angel of death, accuser, trickster: Are these distinct entities or merely facets of the same complex creation? Here is how the Talmud describes what this angel looks like:

> *It is said regarding the Angel of Death that he is full of eyes. When a sick person is about to die, he stands above his head with his sword drawn and a drop of poison hanging from the tip. When the sick person sees him, he trembles and opens his mouth (in terror). He then drops the poison into his (victim's) mouth.*[7]

The description of the Angel of Death as being full of eyes probably symbolizes mankind's insatiable greed, but it is also a striking metaphor for the complexity of Satan's persona and the multiplicity of modalities with which he goes about his business.

Some individuals sin easily, others Satan tests or tricks into sin, always working of course within the individual's own personal manifestation of the evil inclination.

The Evil Inclination

The Evil Inclination plays a major role in much of Jewish thought and modern Jewish literature, especially, for example, many of the works of Isaac Bashevis Singer.

Luckily, Satan in his guise as the evil inclination is not always successful in getting people to sin. In fact, the Talmud believes that overcoming the temptations of the evil inclination may be viewed as either incredibly difficult or incredibly easy, depending on one's point of view:

> *In the future, God will bring the Evil Inclination and slaughter him in the presence of the righteous and the wicked. To the righteous, he will appear as a tall mountain and to the wicked he will appear as a strand of hair. Both the righteous and the wicked will weep. The righteous will cry, saying: How were we able to overcome a mountain as high as this? The wicked will cry, saying: How were we not able to overcome this strand of hair?*[8]

Our outlook on the magnitude of the evil inclination depends on whether we have overcome it or not, whether we are looking forward or looking back.

According to Rabbi Assi:

> *The Evil Inclination at first is like the strand of a spider web and ultimately becomes like the rope of a wagon.*[9]

Rabbi Shimon Ben Lakish stated:

> *A person's Evil Inclination gathers strength against him every day and seeks to kill him.*[10]

And here is what Rava had to say:

> *First, the Evil Inclination is called a passerby, then he is called a guest, and ultimately he is called Master.*[11]

Satan, in the persona of the Evil Inclination, starts small, promoting the commission of small sins, then gathers strength until finally the individual is completely overwhelmed.

The Talmud believes that studying Torah enables one to overcome the evil inclination:

> *"The School of Rabbi Yishmael taught: My son, if that Degenerate One approaches you, drag him to the House of Learning. If he is like stone, he will dissolve and if he is like iron, he will melt."*[12]

The term Degenerate One—sometimes translated as Ugly One—was well known as a reference to Evil Inclination.

The Accuser

When the guise of the Evil Inclination is not sufficient to induce humankind to sin, Satan appears to his appointed prey as a trickster, a tester, a tempter. He seems to revel in the task of proving that good people aren't really that good.

In the *Book of Job*, Satan is permitted by God to test Job's faith by besetting him with a stream of afflictions of increasing intensity. By the time Satan is finished, Job, who started out as a righteous man living the idealized "good life" (good family, friends, prosperity, etc.) has experienced the worst string of bad luck ever conceived. Satan's argument to God was that it had been too easy for Job to be righteous because his life was charmed and easy. Satan never achieved his goal; poor Job remained a righteous man.

Some commentators[13] claim that the snake who tricked Adam and Eve to commit mankind's first sin was actually Satan in disguise. Others believe that the angel Samael, frequently identified as Satan, persuaded the snake to do the evil deed.[14]

The Talmud feels that David would not have sinned with Bathsheba were it not for the meddling of Satan. The Talmud describes what happened in this way: Bathsheba was washing her hair behind a screen that concealed her from public view. Satan appeared in the form of a bird. David shot an arrow at the bird as it flew passed the screen. The arrow missed the bird and broke the screen apart. Bathsheba stood revealed, and David saw her.[15] This is the Talmudic explanation of the verse: "And he (King David) walked upon the roof of the King's palace and from the roof he saw a woman bathing; the woman was very beautiful . . ."[16] Satan took the form of a bird in order to cause David to sin with Bathsheba. The assumption is that Bathsheba would not have bathed on an open rooftop visible to all.

Since even great people can be tempted by Satan, they should therefore be more understanding of sinners.

> *Rabbi Meir used to scoff at sinners for giving in to their desires. One day, Satan appeared to him in the guise of a beautiful woman on the other side of the river. There was no ferry, so Rabbi Meir grasped the rope-bridge and proceeded across. When he reached halfway, Satan left him saying: Had they not declared in Heaven, "Beware of Rabbi Meir and his Torah" your life would not have been worth two* maahs.[17]

A *maah* is a small coin. Thus, did Satan the trickster tempt and teach a great teacher of Israel an important lesson about hubris.

A similar incident is recounted involving another great sage, Rabbi Akiva:

> *Rabbi Akiva used to scoff at sinners for giving in to their desires. One day, Satan appeared to him in the guise of a beautiful woman on a tree. Rabbi Akiva grabbed the tree and began climbing it, but when he reached halfway, Satan left him saying: Had they not declared in Heaven, "Beware of Rabbi Akiva and his Torah" your life would not have been worth two* maahs.[18]

Would we ever think that Satan could teach us something about prayer? The next incident has Satan once again in disguise in order to teach a mortal an important lesson.

> *Plimo used to say every day, "an arrow in Satan's eyes" . . .*

Plimo was a Talmudic sage. The expression "an arrow in the eye of Satan" is referred to elsewhere in the Talmud as well and was probably an idiomatic curse of that time period. The story continues:

> *. . . One afternoon, before the Day of Atonement, Satan appeared to Plimo disguised as a poor man. He came to beg at Plimo's door and was brought some bread. He said: On a day like today when everyone is inside, should I be outside? He was brought into the house and given some bread. He said: On a day like today when everyone is eating at a table, should I be eating alone? They brought him in and sat him at the table. As he sat, he caused his body to be covered with boils and ulcers, and proceeded to behave in a most disgusting manner. Plimo told him to sit properly. He then asked for a cup of wine. When it was given to him, he coughed and spat his phlegm into the cup. They scolded him, so he pretended to die. Satan then caused Plimo to hear voices outside saying: Plimo killed someone. Plimo ran away and hid in an outhouse. Satan followed him there and Plimo (not realizing who it was) fell down before him. When Satan saw how much Plimo was suffering, he revealed his identity. Satan then said to Plimo: Why do you say this prayer (i.e., an arrow in Satan's eyes)? What should I say, asked Plimo? Say: May the Merciful Lord rebuke Satan.[19]*

This story illustrates somewhat humorously that one should be careful not to hurt anyone's feelings, even Satan's. And, if even the Angel of Death has feelings, all the more so do mortals. The Talmud emphasizes the principle elsewhere that praying for an enemy's repentance is always preferable to praying for his downfall, but never with a more untraditional teacher.

In the next story, Satan is compared to Peninah who, along with Hannah, was a wife of Elkanah. According to the Talmud, Peninah goaded the barren Hannah into praying for a child. Hannah eventually gave birth to the prophet Samuel.[20]

> *Rabbi Levi stated: Satan and Peninah both had intentions to please Heaven. When Satan saw that God was showing favor towards Job, he said: Heaven forbid! Shall Abraham's love of God be forgotten? . . . Rabbi Acha b. Yaakov lectured thus in Papunia. Satan came to him and kissed his feet.*[21]

Satan was happy that someone recognized his good intentions—that he denounced Job before God, in order to defend the patriarch Abraham. This story also demonstrates the importance of gratitude. Even Satan appreciated human recognition and was properly grateful for it.

The Midrash tells the tale of Satan's unsuccessful attempts to mislead, misguide, and misdirect Abraham while he was en route to carry out God's order to sacrifice his son Isaac on Mount Moriah. In this Midrash, Satan tries to trick Abraham and confuse him as to the source of the sacrificial commandment. Satan is brilliant in carrying out his task and this temptation, while unsuccessful, is viewed as an important test, an integral part of Abraham's trial.

> *On the way to Isaac's sacrifice, Satan ran ahead of Abraham and appeared before him disguised as an old man. Satan asked Abraham where he was going. Abraham replied: To pray. Satan asked Abraham: And does one who goes to pray have fire and a knife in his hand and wood on his shoulder? Abraham replied: We may tarry there a day or two, and we will have to slaughter (an animal for meat), bake bread, and eat. Satan said: Old man, was I not there when God told you to take your son? And an old man like you is going to go and destroy a son that was given to him at the age of one hundred? Did you not hear the proverb: "That which he had in his hand he destroyed and (now) seeks from others." . . .*

Seeing his arguments were not working, Satan, in the guise of the old man, tried another tactic, attempting to convince Abraham that the commandment actually came to him not from God, but from Satan, the Accuser. One thing that makes this pretty funny is that it actually comes from Satan himself, in disguise as an old man.

> *. . . You listen to the Accuser (i.e., not God) and destroy a soul for which you will be judged guilty in court. Abraham said: I did not*

hear it from the Accuser but from the blessed Lord; I will not listen to you . . .

Satan does not give up that easily. He left Abraham and went to work on Abraham's son, Isaac.

> *. . . Satan then appeared as a young man and stood on the right side of Isaac. He asked Isaac where he and his father were going. Isaac replied: To study Torah. Satan asked: While you are alive or dead? Isaac said: Is there then a person who can learn after death? Satan said: Humiliated one, son of a humiliated one, how many fasts did your mother fast until you were born? And that old man went crazy and he is going to slaughter you. Isaac replied: Despite this, I will not violate the will of my creator or the command of my father.[22]*

A similar story is told in the Midrash Rabbah. There Satan told Abraham: "Old man, have you lost your heart? A son that was given to you at the age of one hundred, you are going to slaughter?" When that did not work, he tried another approach and told Abraham: "Tomorrow God will say you are a murderer and are guilty for shedding the blood of your son."[23] In both stories Satan is unsuccessful in deterring the patriarchs from their Heavenly task.

Satan was a bit more successful with Noah. According to the Midrash, Satan was a partner of Noah in the planting of the first post-Flood vineyard. Satan's contribution was the addition of the blood of a sheep, a lion, a pig, and a monkey.[24] This is the Talmudic way of explaining the effect alcohol has on people. The drinker, initially as innocent as a sheep, after a few drinks becomes as bold as a lion. Eventually, as the drinks flow, the person becomes as filthy as a pig and acts like a monkey. Indeed, the Bible relates how Noah debased himself when he became intoxicated.[25]

The Angel of Death

As we can see, in the Talmud, the Angel of Death is not always seen as a frightening figure. In one story, when commanded by God to bring back the soul of Moses, Satan is yelled at and chased away by Moses. Eventually, the Almighty Himself has to take the soul of Moses.[26]

In the next selection, the Talmud demonstrates that good people do not have to fear Satan. It also shows how easy it is to fool Satan. Here Satan appears as the Angel of Death, with instructions to first carry out the will of his intended victim before taking his soul.

When Rabbi Yehoshua ben Levi was about to die, the Angel of Death was instructed to carry out his will. He appeared before Rabbi Yehoshua and revealed himself. Rabbi Yehoshua said to him: Show me my place in the world to come. He replied: All right. Rabbi Yehoshua said: Give me your slaughtering knife since you might frighten me with it on the way. He gave him his knife. Upon arriving in Paradise, the Angel of Death lifted up Rabbi Yehoshua and showed him his place. Rabbi Yehoshua jumped over to the other side but the Angel of Death grabbed him by the hem of his garment and was about to pull him back. Rabbi Yehoshua swore that he was not going to return. Thereupon, the Holy One said: If he has ever had an oath annulled (while on earth) then he must go back; if not, he can remain here . . .

Since Rabbi Yehoshua never had a vow annulled he was allowed to stay.

. . . The Angel of Death then said: Give my knife back to me. Rabbi Yehoshua refused to return it. A Heavenly voice declared: Return it to him for it is needed for mortals.[27]

A lesson to be learned from the story is that death is necessary for mortals. Only in a world where everyone is good and no one lies can there be immortality. Henry Wadsworth Longfellow used the story of Rabbi Yehoshua ben Levi as the basis of the poem "The Spanish Jew's Tale: The Legend of Rabbi Ben Levi" in *Tales of a Wayside Inn*.

So, the trickster was tricked. But, apparently, judging from the following story, it only works once.

Rabbi Chaninah ben Papa was a friend of the Angel of Death and when he was about to die the Angel of Death was instructed to carry out his will before taking his soul. He went to Rabbi Chaninah and revealed himself. Rabbi Chaninah said: Give me thirty days so that I can review my studies since it says, "Happy is he who comes here (the next world) with his learning in hand." He left him and returned in thirty days. Rabbi Chaninah said to him: Show me my place in the world to come. He replied: All right. Rabbi Chaninah said: Give me your knife since you might frighten me on the way. The Angel of Death said: Do you wish to do to me as your friend did?[28]

The Angel of Death is even quoted in the Talmud. For instance, Rabbi Yehoshua b. Levi states three things he was taught by the Angel of Death;[29] Abba, the father of Shmuel, a well known Talmudic sage, quotes him too.[30] Quoting the Angel of Death is a sure way of getting people to listen to your ideas.

The Talmud and Midrash record the Angel of Death conducting conversations with many sages, even befriending several. For instance, in one story, Satan became very disconcerted over the response of a group of rabbis, headed by Rabbi Shimon ben Chalafta, who were invited to a circumcision. The father of the baby said to the rabbis: "Drink of this old wine because I am confident in the Lord in Heaven that I will give you to drink of this same wine at my son's wedding." The rabbis' response to the father was: "As you brought him into the covenant (of Abraham, i.e., circumcision), so too may you bring him to Torah and the marriage canopy." The Angel of Death subsequently met Rabbi Shimon, who left late in the evening towards home. The Angel of Death was critical of Rabbi Shimon for traveling at such a late hour. He said: "Because you rely on your good deeds, you venture out at a time which is not a time to travel." Rabbi Shimon asked the Angel of Death why he looked so upset and found out that he had been going to kill the child who had just been circumcised, and was concerned that the rabbis' prayer would annul the decree against the child. Rabbi Shimon asked him how much longer he himself would live. The Angel of Death replied that he did not know because he had no jurisdiction over the life spans of Rabbi Shimon and the other sages. Rabbi Shimon asked him the reason for this. The Angel informed him that God adds years to the lives of those engaged in Torah study and acts of righteousness. Rabbi Shimon then prayed for the child, who survived.[31] In this story, the Angel of Death is seen as a less than frightening figure who has little power over a pious sage.

The following story which, as we will see, we may decide to call "Appointment in Luz," demonstrates that an individual cannot escape his or her destiny and must inevitably die. The Angel of Death is depicted as simply performing a necessary task, and doing it any way he can.

> *There were two Cushites that attended on King Solomon, Elichoreph and Achiyah, sons of Shisha, who were scribes of Solomon. One day, Solomon noticed that the Angel of Death looked sad. Solomon asked him: Why are you sad? He replied: Because they have demanded from me the two Cushites that dwell here. Solomon had demons take them to the city of Luz (a legendary city where no one dies). However, as soon as they reached the gates of Luz, they died. The next day, Solomon noticed that the Angel of Death was happy. He asked him: Why are you so happy? He replied: Because you sent them to the very place where they were supposed to die.[32]*

Solomon, the wisest man who ever lived,[33] discovered himself outsmarted by Satan. There are obvious similarities here to the well known "Appointment in Samarra" story, a retelling of which was made famous by William Somerset Maugham in his play *Sheppey*. Some scholars believe that the origin of the Maugham tale is "When Death Came to Baghdad," a ninth-century Arabian Sufi story in Fudail ibn Ayad's *Hikayat-I-Naqshia*. This similar story in the Talmud is several hundred years older.

The next selection was probably used to explain why good people often die young.

> *Rabbi Yosef wept when he came to the verse:*[34] *"But there is one that is swept away without justice." He exclaimed: Is there anyone who passes away before his time? Yes! As in the story told by Bibi ben Abaye, who was often visited by the Angel of Death. The Angel of Death told his agent to bring him the soul of Miriam the hairdresser and was brought the soul of Miriam, the children's nurse. The Angel of Death told his messenger: I told you to bring me Miriam the hairdresser. The messenger replied: If so, I will return her. The Angel of Death said: Since you already brought her, then let her be included in the quota.*[35]

That is, the quota of people scheduled to die that day. Apparently, even Satan has trouble finding good help. The story concludes with Bibi asking The Angel of Death what he did with the extra years that Miriam the hairdresser should have lived. He was told that it was given to scholars who overlook being slighted. And the Angel of Death cooks the books.

In the Talmud, Shmuel's father quotes the Angel of Death as saying: "If I did not care for the dignity of human beings, I would cut open the throat of man as (wide and gaping as) that of a slaughtered animal."[36] In other words, Satan prefers using the poison on the tip of his sword rather than the sword itself to kill mortals because he does not feel that people should be mutilated by death.

The following selection demonstrates the importance of dying with dignity. More importantly, it shows that good people have nothing to fear of death.

> *The Angel of Death appeared to Rabbi Sheshet in the marketplace. Rabbi Sheshet said to him: Will you kill me in the marketplace as though I were an animal? Come to my house.*[37]

The Angel of Death apparently complied with Rabbi Sheshet's request. As noted above, Satan respects people's feelings for a dignified demise. In the next selection we note that the Angel of Death understood that Rabbi Ashi needed some time to complete his studies. No one likes to leave an unfinished masterpiece behind after death.

> *The Angel of Death appeared to Rabbi Ashi in the marketplace. Rabbi Ashi said to him: Grant me thirty days respite in order that I may go over my studies, since it says, "Happy is he who comes here (the next world) with his learning in hand." On the thirtieth day, the Angel of Death returned. Rabbi Ashi asked him: What is the urgency? The Angel of Death replied: Rabbi (Huna) bar Nason is close on your heels (to succeed you as the President of the Sanhedrin) and no sovereignty encroaches upon another even by as little as a hair's breadth.*[38]

John Milton, in *Paradise Lost*, has Satan saying: "Better to reign in hell than serve in heaven." From what we see of the Satan described in the Talmud and Midrash, he is not all that interested in being one of the ruling elite. He revels in his work as a tempter of mankind, a tester of the righteous. He glories in his persona as the Evil Inclination, performs brilliantly as Angel of Death, and awaits every opportunity to function as the Accuser in the Heavenly tribunal. He is a trickster *par excellence*.

Because the Talmudic Satan is not overly intimidating, he figures in many Jewish jokes and sayings. For instance,

The great Rabbi Nachman of Breslau is supposed to have said: "It was difficult for Satan alone to mislead the entire world, so he appointed rabbis in various communities."

The Trickster of the Talmud and Midrash strikes again.

Part III
Humor in the Talmud and Midrash

6

Humor in the Talmud and Midrash: An Overview

After months of negotiation, a Jewish scholar from Odessa was granted permission to visit Moscow. He boarded the train and found an empty seat. At the next stop a young man got on and sat next to him. The scholar looked at the young man and thought:

This fellow doesn't look like a peasant, and if he isn't a peasant, he probably comes from this district. If he comes from this district, he must be Jewish because this is, after all, a Jewish district. On the other hand, if he is a Jew, where could he be going? I'm the only one in our district who has permission to travel to Moscow.

Wait—just outside Moscow there is a little village called Samvet, and you don't need special permission to go there. But why would he be going to Samvet? He's probably going to visit somebody there, but how many Jewish families are there in Samvet? Only two—the Bernsteins and the Steinbergs. The Bernsteins are a terrible family, so he must be visiting the Steinbergs. But why is he going?

The Steinbergs have only girls, so maybe he's their son-in-law. But if he is, then which daughter did he marry? Sarah married that nice lawyer from Budapest and Esther married a businessman from Zhadomir, so he must be Sarah's husband. Which means that his name is Alexander Cohen, if I'm not mistaken. But if he comes from Budapest, with all the anti-Semitism they have there, he must have changed his name. What's the Hungarian equivalent of Cohen? Kovacs. But if he changed his name, he must have some special status. What could it be? A doctorate from the university.

At this point the scholar turned to the young man and said, "How do you do, Dr. Kovacs?"

"Very well, thank you, sir," answered the startled passenger. "But how is it that you know my name?"

"Oh," replied the scholar, "it was obvious."[1]

The Talmud not only records the legal opinions of hundreds of individuals but also relates stories about many of them. These sages had much in common: love of God, of the Torah, the Jewish people, the land of Israel, and of knowledge. They believed that humanity, and the Jewish people in particular, has a purpose in the world—to make the world a better place by spreading Torah values. These include such important values as kindness, justice, and a strong family.

The Talmud contains many types of humor, not surprising given that the opinions and stories of many individuals living over a period of hundreds of years are recorded. Some of the major types of humor found in the Talmud include:

Satire: The Talmudists used satire to poke fun at heretics and non-believers and so demonstrate that the Torah way of life was ideal. The hilarious story of Abraham's servant, Eliezer, in Sodom, demonstrates what happens to a xenophobic society that repudiates the Torah values of justice and charity.[2]

Irony: The Talmud contains many examples of irony. The Talmud notes that God punishes measure for measure. Ironic punishments are a clever way of teaching the public the importance of living a Torah way of life. Mistreat the stranger in your land and you will become a stranger. Do not take care of the widow and orphans, and your wife will become a widow and your own children orphans. The classic story of Joseph-who-honors-the-Sabbath (*Yosef-Makir-Shabbat*) is an inspiring and memorable parable demonstrating the reward for honoring the Sabbath.[3]

Sarcasm: Sarcasm, too, is used in the Talmud as a way of deriding heretics and nonbelievers. Many of the ancient prophets used sarcasm to ridicule idolaters and false prophets. The Talmudists often had to deal with heretics who tried to prove their superiority by asking difficult questions, and Rabbis Gamliel, Yehoshua b. Chananiah, Akiva, and Abuhu were especially skilful at being able to answer nonbelievers. There seems to have been a healthy competition between sages living in Israel and those living in Babylon. Some of the sages living in Israel would often make fun of the opinions of the Babylonian scholars. The Israeli scholars even kidded their counterparts in Babylon about their strange diet. The Israeli sages were the superior scholars. They attributed this to the fact that "the climate of Israel makes one wise."[4] Ulla was an Israeli scholar who traveled frequently between the two countries. As we will see later, he often made sarcastic remarks regarding Babylon and the Babylonian way of doing things.

Exaggeration: The Talmud takes note of where the Hebrew Bible uses hyperbole. Clearly, hyperbole and exaggeration were tools used to emphasize points or to get the attention of an audience. For instance, one Talmudic sage tried to demonstrate how horrible was the Temple's destruction. He claimed that 600,000 cities consisting of 600,000 individuals each were killed (except for three cities which each had 1.2 million inhabitants). Ulla, a sage known to be sarcastic on occasion, ridiculed this and said that there was not even enough room for that many reeds in the places described, let alone people.[5]

In another story Og, a giant killed by Moses, is described as being as tall as a huge mountain. He was so tall that he was able to lift a mountain the size of the entire Israelite camp and attempt to crush them underneath.[6] Moreover, Rabbah Bar Bar Chanah describes some incredible sights that he saw on his travels. His stories are obvious exaggerations, for example, a dead fish cast out of the sea which destroyed sixty towns. Many scholars believe that his stories are parables, and virtually no one takes them literally.[7]

Wordplay: Both the Hebrew Bible and the Talmud are written in languages (Hebrew and Aramaic, respectively) that do not use vowels;vowels may optionally be added as diacritical marks near a letter. This makes it easy for words to be read in different ways. The Talmudists used this as a device to teach the public important lessons. For instance, the Hebrew word for tithing (*asser*) is similar to the word for rich (*asher*). The lesson the Talmud learns from this is "Give tithes in order to become wealthy."[8] Similarly, wordplays on names are used to indicate an individual's true character. For example, the Talmud notes that Korach, who started a rebellion against Moses and Aaron, deserved his name. His name is similar to the Hebrew word meaning baldness (*kerach*) and he created "defoliation in Israel."[9]

Humorous Sayings: The Talmud respected the popular sayings of the people and even demonstrated that many aphorisms can be derived from the Bible. The Talmud itself is a rich source of wonderful sayings about all types of people and situations. For instance, the Talmud describes four kinds of people the mind cannot tolerate: arrogant paupers, crooked rich people, lecherous old men, and leaders who enjoy being bosses but do not help their followers in time of difficulty.[10] Sayings of this type are teaching devices that describe how good people should behave. Many of the Talmudic aphorisms contain important advice on how to live a good and happy life.

Allegories, Parables, and Fables: Several of the Talmudic sages were expert at fox fables. One third of Rabbi Meir's lectures consisted of parables and fables. The Talmud relates that, "Rabbi Meir had three hundred parables of foxes, and we have only three left."[11] These parables and fables were used to teach important lessons and also to make lectures interesting. The sages used allegories, parables, and fables to explain or elaborate on various ideas. For example, to explain the idea that all Jews suffer when one Jew sins, a sage used the parable of the individual who bored a hole in his part of the boat. Everyone in the boat started to yell at him. This individual told everyone in the boat to mind their own business, since he was only drilling in his section of the boat.[12]

Humorous Anecdotes: The Talmud is replete with stories. Many are true stories and describe an incident that actually happened. Some are probably describing dreams or are in parable form. Regardless, many of the stories were meant to teach the public important lessons. Some of the stories illustrate that even great sages can have weak moments. The Talmud tells stories of sages who came very close to committing sexual transgressions but just managed to control themselves before sinning. One scholar was saved from sinning with a prostitute by his *tzizit* (fringes worn on the corners of a four-cornered garment), which *tzizit* got caught on the steps leading to her bed.[13]

One of the classic stories of the Talmud describes a bet an individual made with a friend to make Hillel lose his temper. The individual keeps returning all throughout Friday afternoon, asking foolish questions, while Hillel was busy preparing for the Sabbath. Still, Hillel did not lose his temper.[14]

Humorous Cases, Absurd Questions, and Strange Proofs: Rabbi Yirmiyah was known as a sage who asked his teacher humorous questions in order to make him laugh.[15] Many absurd questions and cases are humorous but were discussed in order to derive important legal principles. The fact that the case is impossible is not relevant since the principle is what counts. For instance, "towers flying in the air" may not have existed in Talmudic times but Talmudic sages could still imagine hundreds of legal questions were they to exist.[16] Plimo's question regarding a two-headed man and on which head should his *tefillin* be worn is actually quite interesting.[17] It is surprising that Rebbi was not pleased with the question. Perhaps Rebbi, known as an individual who did not want to laugh, thought Plimo was trying to be funny.

The Talmudic sages were educators. They taught their students and the public Torah. Like most good educators they used various approaches, some involving humor and wit, to make their points. This may partially explain why more than 1,500 years after the "closing" of the Babylonian Talmud, the Talmud is still a fascinating and interesting work.

Question: It is said that an established custom is stronger than the law. What is the proof for this principle?

Answer: The proof is simple. The law is that if one borrows money from another, he must repay the loan. However, the custom is—he doesn't!

Is Humor Even Permissible?

A Talmudic dictum states that a person's true character may be determined from his "wine-cup, his purse, his anger."[18] In the original, this dictum is humorous due to the alliteration of the three items listed. The wine-cup (*koso*) symbolizes what an individual does and says when under the influence of alcohol; the purse (*kiso*), represents one's honesty in business; and anger (*kaaso*) refers to how the person comports himself when angry. The passage continues, "and some say, from his laughter."

Many sages were known for their ability to laugh and enjoy the permissible pleasures of this world. Some even felt that it was sinful not to partake of permitted pleasures. Nonetheless, one important issue the Talmud addresses is whether an individual is permitted to be overly happy. This became a serious *halachic* question since many of the Talmudists felt that after the destruction of the Temple the Jewish people were forbidden to be too cheerful, and that only when the Messiah comes will the Jewish people be allowed to be joyous. Some sages felt an individual should be serious because, without the Temple, the Jewish people had no right to be filled with happiness. Indeed, four fast days were established to commemorate misfortunes associated with the destruction of both temples. Till this very day, observant Jews in good health fast a full day on Tisha B'Av (the ninth day of Av) to commemorate the destruction of both Temples.

Furthermore, too much levity leads to frivolity and light-mindedness, and that can lead a person to forsake the Torah way of life and instead pursue a hedonistic life dedicated to the pursuit of pleasure. Thus, some of the Talmudic sages were opposed to frivolity. The Talmud describes a scholar as one "who does not eat while standing, lick his fingers after

107

eating, move food around his mouth from side to side. He talks little, jokes little, sleeps little, has few luxuries, and rarely says 'yes, yes' or 'no, no.'"[19] The last are ancient forms of an oath.

It should also be noted that if a Babylonian sage would come up with an unusual explanation, the Talmud might state that "they laughed at this in the West" (i.e., in the academies of Israel which is to the west of Babylon). Apparently, some scholars in Israel had no problem laughing at explanations which they felt were ridiculous.[20]

Rabbi Zera was one scholar who was very strict about not laughing because he concurred with the opinion of Rabbi Yochanan who stated in the name of Rabbi Shimon b. Yochai: "It is forbidden for a person to fill his mouth with levity in this world."[21] Rabbi Zera's disciple, Rabbi Yirmiyah, who apparently did not agree with his teacher, was well known in the Talmud as one who asked humorous questions in order to get his teacher to laugh. It should be noted that Rabbi Shimon b. Yochai was concerned with excessive levity *in this world*. The verse he cites to prove his point is: "Then will our mouth be filled with laughter and our tongue with joyous song. Then will they say among the nations: 'The Lord has done great things for them' (i.e., bringing the exiles back to Zion)."[22] Prior to the coming of the Messiah, one is not permitted to be excessively joyous. However, after the redemption, Rabbi Shimon b. Yochai admits that excessive joy will be permitted, either because there will be no more need for mourning of the Temple since it will be rebuilt and/or because all of humanity will be at a high spiritual level and laughter and song will not lead to wrongdoing.

The Talmud relates that it was said regarding Rabbi Shimon b. Lakish (Resh Lakish) that never again was his mouth filled with levity in this world after hearing the above saying from his teacher, Rabbi Yochanan.[23] The one time we know of that Resh Lakish made a sarcastic, flippant remark to Rabbi Yochanan, it did not go well. Rabbi Yochanan and Resh Lakish were arguing about the ritual defilement of various weapons such as swords, knives, and spears. Rabbi Yochanan said to Resh Lakish, who had been a brigand before becoming a scholar:

> A robber understands the tools of his trade. Resh Lakish replied: "How have you benefited me (by making me give up my former life)? There I was called master and here I am called master. Rabbi Yochanan replied: I benefited you by bringing you under the wings of the Divine Presence.[24]

It is obvious that Resh Lakish did not regret changing his life. Unfortunately, neither he nor his teacher believed in humor in this world. Thus, when Resh Lakish tried for a witty comeback, it is easy to see why Rabbi Yochanan made the mistake of thinking that Resh Lakish was serious about there being no difference between a pious and dissolute life. His remark hurt Rabbi Yochanan terribly and, as a result of this Resh Lakish became ill (by divine punishment) and died.[25]

Rebbi (Rabbi Yehuda the *Nasi*, that is, the President of the Sanhedrin) was another of the Talmudists who did not wish to laugh. The Talmud states that when Rebbi laughed, punishment came to the world.[26] Rebbi even advised his children not to live in the town of Shekhanzib because the residents of that town were known as mocking sorts and might influence them to do the same.[27]

Bar Kappara, who had no such problem, frequently tried to make Rebbi laugh. The following story demonstrates how Bar Kappara tried to make Rebbi laugh by wearing an outlandish "hat."

> *Rebbi told Bar Kappara: Do not make me laugh and I will give you forty measures of wheat. Bar Kappara replied: Let the master see to it that I may take any measure that I wish. Bar Kappara took a large basket and tarred it on the outside (so that it could hold wheat), tilted it over his head, and said to Rebbi: Measure for me the forty grivas (a measure) of wheat that you owe me. Rebbi laughed and said: Did I not warn you not to make me laugh. Bar Kappara replied: I am merely asking you for the wheat you owe me.[28]*

Rebbi was reluctant to invite Bar Kappara to his son's wedding because he did not want Bar Kappara to make him laugh. The following passage indicates what happened.

> *Rebbi made a wedding feast for his son Shimon and did not invite Bar Kappara. Bar Kappara wrote on the wall of the wedding hall: Twenty-four thousand myriads of dinars were spent on this feast, yet Bar Kappara was not invited. Bar Kappara then told Rebbi: If for those who transgress His will, so much is granted, how much more so for those who obey His will. Rebbi then invited Bar Kappara. Bar Kappara said: If for those who obey His will, so much is granted in this world, how much more so will be granted to them in the next world.[29]*

Rebbi finally got upset with Bar Kappara for one of his riddles and said that he would not recognize Bar Kappara as a scholar, that is, he would not allow him to be ordained. And, indeed, Bar Kappara did not receive ordination as long as Rebbi was alive.[30]

Rabbah was able to compromise, using both humor and seriousness in his lectures:

> *Rabbah would say something humorous before starting to lecture to the scholars, and they would laugh; after that, he would sit in awe and begin his lecture.*[31]

Rabbi Meir, one of the great lecturers, was known for dividing his lecture into three parts: one third consisted of legal discourse, one third *aggada*, and one third parables. It is said that Rabbi Meir knew three hundred fox fables.[32] Apparently, Rabbi Meir worked hard at keeping his audience interested in the lecture; a lecture consisting solely of legal matters can be quite dull. Bar Kappara also knew three hundred fox parables and once so enthralled Rebbi's dinner guests with his fables that they did not eat their dinner.[33]

Rabbi Akiva was an individual who could find something to be happy about under the most adverse of conditions. Indeed, he was wont to say that "One should always accustom himself to say that everything the Lord does is for the good."[34] One story in the Talmud describes how Rabbi Akiva's colleagues wept when they heard the sound of the Roman crowds obviously enjoying life. Rabbi Akiva, on the other hand, was smiling. He told his puzzled friends: "If this is the reward for those who transgress His will, then, for those who obey His will, the reward will have to be all that much greater."[35]

Another story told in the Talmud illustrates Rabbi Akiva's renowned optimism. Rabbi Akiva and his colleagues were traveling in Jerusalem and noticed a fox emerging from where the Holy of Holies had been when the Temple stood. They began to cry and Rabbi Akiva smiled. He explained his behavior in the following manner. Now that he sees that the gloomy and morbid prophecy of Uriah has come to pass and Zion has become desolate, he believes that the optimistic prophecies of the later prophets such as Zecharia will come to pass. Thus, one day the redemption will come, the Lord will return to Jerusalem, it will be filled with healthy and happy people, and "Old men and old women will sit in the streets of Jerusalem."[36] The others said to Rabbi Akiva: "Akiva, you have comforted us. Akiva, you have comforted us."[37]

When Rabbi Eliezer became sick, his disciples, Rabbi Akiva among them, came to visit him. The others cried upon seeing their afflicted teacher, but Rabbi Akiva smiled. He explained his actions thus: As long as everything went well for Rabbi Eliezer, he was afraid that his teacher was receiving all of his reward in this world and leaving little for the next world. Now that he sees that Rabbi Eliezer is lying in pain he is glad knowing that there will be a great reward waiting for him in the afterlife.[38] Even while being tortured to death by the Romans, Rabbi Akiva was able to laugh. Rabbi Akiva was happy that he finally had the opportunity of fulfilling the verse[39] about loving the Lord with all your soul.[40] Despite Rabbi Akiva's optimistic approach to life, he recognized the danger of frivolity. Rabbi Akiva stated that: "Jesting and light-headedness lead a person to immorality."[41]

It is clear that some of the Talmudists felt very strongly that one should not manifest happiness in this world while others believed that there was nothing wrong with mirth. Nevertheless, when it came to teaching, most, if not all, felt that humorous parables, anecdotes, or riddles were probably an admirable way to both inspire the public and teach what might otherwise be rather dry material.

Even those sages who were very much in favor of humor were opposed to humor that mocked and was, therefore, hurtful. It should be noted, however, that they all agreed that being a scorner (*leitz*) is definitely a despicable trait. A scorner is an individual who mocks and derides others. His humor is not productive and is usually intended to belittle the weak and helpless, or make fun of positive values. Regarding those kinds of people, the Talmud says that they are one of the four groups of people who will not receive the divine presence in the afterlife, that is, God will have nothing to do with them.[42] The Psalmist notes the dangers of joining those who mock and sneer and do not elevate mankind.[43] The Psalmist praises the person who avoids a gathering of these types.[44] Clearly, humor that revels in the misfortunes of the infirm and weak, or that mocks religion or other positive societal values, is condemned by the Talmud.

The humor the Talmud approves of is beneficial and has a higher purpose: makes people enjoy God's world, pokes fun at sin, helps to bring peace to an altercation, etc.

At least one passage in the Talmud teaches that humor can pave our way into Paradise:

> *Rabbi Beroka Hozaah asked Elijah the Prophet: Is there any person in this market who is destined for Paradise? He replied, no. . . . While they were conversing, two people passed by. Elijah said: These two are destined for the world to come. Rabbi Beroka approached them and*

*asked them what they did. They replied: We are merry-makers, and
we cheer up people who are depressed . . .*[45]

Is humor permissible? We can imagine the Talmudic sages arguing
about it, well into the night . . .

Q: *How many* baalei teshuva[46] *does it take to screw in a lightbulb?*
A: *Are we allowed to do that?*

7

Recurring Characters and Themes

Two Jews with a long-running feud brought it to the Rabbi for adjudication. The first gave a long recitation of the wrongs his one-time friend had done to him. The Rabbi considered this and said "You're right."

Protesting, the second man presented his side of the dispute. Once again, the Rabbi thought about it long and hard and then said to the second man, "You're right."

The rebbetzin, overhearing, came over and whispered in her husband's ear, "But, they can't both be right!"

The Rabbi considered that. "You know what?" he said to her. "You're right too!"

The stories of the Talmud are a rich source of folklore, history, and culture, and contain many of the character types and themes we have come to expect. Much like the diverse group of characters and archetypes that populate modern Jewish humor—the impudent beggar, the snide waiter, the anti-Semite, the matchmaker, the schlemiel, the rich-like-Rothschild, the impoverished prankster Hershel Ostropoler, and more—the Talmudic literature has its own list of familiar characters. We will see in the chapters that follow—whether employed in the service of sarcasm, satire, parables, aphorisms, or wordplay—a number of recurring themes as well as character types in recurring roles. These include: students and their mentors, heretics, Athenians, pious fools, royalty, alcoholics, prostitutes, patience, poverty, arrogance and more.

Alcohol and Alcoholics

Yehuda and Chizkiyah, the children of Rabbi Chiya, were once eating a meal with Rebbi (the Nasi) and did not say anything. Rebbi said: Give the boys some strong wine so that they will say something. After they had drunk some wine, they said: The son of David (the Messiah) cannot come until the two patriarchal houses of Israel are no more, namely, the head of the captivity in Babylon (the exilarch) and the Nasi in Israel; for it is written,[1] "And he shall be for a sanctuary, and for a stone on which to dash oneself and for a rock on which to stumble for both houses of Israel." Rebbi said to them: My children, you are thrusting thorns into my eyes. Rabbi Chiya said to Rebbi: Do not be upset with them. The numerical value of the word yayin *(wine) is 70 and the numerical value of the word* sod *(secret) is 70. This teaches us that as wine enters, secrets escape.[2]*

In Hebrew, the letters of the alphabet have numerical values, for example, the first letter of the Hebrew alphabet, *aleph* is one; *bet*, the second letter is two, etc. The *gematria*, the sum of the numerical values of the letters, of both *yayin* and *sod* equal seventy.

Rabbi Acha said: There once was an individual who would sell household belongings and use the proceeds to drink wine. His sons said: Our father will not leave anything for us. So they gave him wine to drink, got him drunk, and took him out and placed him in a cemetery . . .

Their hope was that upon waking he would be frightened and not know how he got there and then give up drinking.

. . . Wine merchants passed by the gate of the cemetery. They heard that a seizure for public service was to take place in the province. They unloaded their wine and hid it in the cemetery and went to witness the cause of the clamor in the town. The man woke up from his sleep and saw a wineskin above his head. He untied it and placed the bottle in his mouth. Three days later his sons said: Let us go see what our father is doing. They went and found him with the bottle in his mouth. They exclaimed: Even here your Creator does not forsake you. Since He provides for you, there is nothing we can do to thwart His will. They agreed among themselves that they should alternate and each son should provide wine for him for one day.[3]

Sometimes one has to honor parents even when they are squandering their wealth and will thereby diminish the estate.

There once was a man who used to drink twelve measures of wine each day. One day he only drank eleven measures. He lay down to go to sleep but could not sleep. He got up in the middle of the night and went to the storekeeper and said to him: Sell me one measure. The storekeeper replied: I will not open for you because it is dark and I am afraid of the nightwatchmen. The man raised his eyes and saw a hole in the door and said: Give me wine through the hole. You pour the wine from within and I will drink it from outside. The storekeeper did it for him. The man drank and fell asleep in front of the door. The watchmen passed by and thought him to be a thief and beat him and wounded him.[4]

This story was used to explain the verses: "Who has wounds without cause? Those that tarry long over wine."[5] The sages frowned on overindulgence in wine. Indeed, the Midrash notes that the ten tribes were exiled on account of wine.[6] And years later, the tribes of Judah and Benjamin were exiled on account of wine.

The Midrash uses the following story to illustrate that the drunkard while drunk feels like he is in Paradise.

There was a pious student that had a father that drank too much wine. Every time that he collapsed in the street in a drunken stupor the youths would come and would pelt him with rocks and pebbles and scream: Look at the drunkard! When his righteous son saw this he was mortified and wanted to die. Every day he would tell his father: Father, I will get and bring to your house all the wine they sell in this country. But do not go to the tavern to drink because you are humiliating both me and yourself. The son would say this to his father every day and night until finally his father agreed not to go to the tavern. The pious son would then bring his father food and drink every day and every night and he would put him to sleep and leave.

One time, it was raining and the pious son was in the street going to the house of prayer when he saw a drunkard lying in the gutter with water running all over him. Youths were pelting him with rocks and pebbles and throwing clay in his face and into his mouth. When the pious person saw this he thought: I will go to my father and bring him here and show him this drunkard and how he is being humiliated by the youths. Perhaps this will convince my father never to drink at a tavern and get inebriated. He brought his father there and showed him the drunk. What did the elderly father do? He went to the drunk and asked him: Where did you get such good wine to drink?[7]

The story concludes with the father telling his pious son that he only has pleasure and the joy of Paradise from drinking.

Heretics and Other Sinners

Once Rabbi Shimon b. Yochai was visiting the sick and encountered a man who was swollen, afflicted with a disease of the bowels, and was blaspheming the Holy One. Rabbi Shimon said to him: Empty one, you should be praying for yourself, but instead you express blas-

phemies. He said: The Holy One should take away my ailment and give it to you. Rabbi Shimon said: The Holy One dealt with me appropriately, since I forsook the study of Torah and occupied myself with nonsense.[8]

That is, visiting undeserving sick people like you. Not everyone is suited for visiting the sick. Rabbi Shimon b. Yochai does not come across as exceptionally compassionate here.

Bringing this story up to date, we have the following:

A few weeks before his death, noted philosopher Sidney Morgenbesser, asked a fellow philosopher this about God:

"Why is God making me suffer so much?" he asked. "Just because I don't believe in him?"

And yet, lest we think Professor Morgenbesser had anything against God or His people, he once chastised a faculty member for hiding his Jewishness in this way: "Oh, I see your model is: *Incognito, ergo sum.*"

The next story follows a complex discussion regarding the law if a debtor hands money over to an agent and tells the agent to transfer the money to a creditor. The major question is whether the debtor may change his mind about repaying the debt once the money is in the hands of the agent and ask the agent to return the money. Another question concerns which party has liability if the money is lost in transit, before it reaches the hand of the creditor. Shmuel is of the opinion that since the sender (the debtor) is responsible for the debt until the money reaches the hand of the creditor, he therefore has the right to change his mind and ask the agent to return the money. The "custodians" in this story have their own way of resolving the dispute.

Rabbi Achi b. Yoshiyah had a silver vessel with custodians in Nehardea. He said to Rabbi Dostai b. Yannai and Rabbi Yosi b. Kipar, who were going to Nehardea: When you return from Nehardea, bring it with you. They went to Nehardea and received the vessel from the custodians. The custodians then said to the rabbis: We want you to give us a release from liability for any losses that may occur on the return trip. The rabbis said, "no." The custodians then told them to give back the silver vessel. Rabbi Dostai agreed but Rabbi Yosi refused. The custodians started to hurt Rabbi Yosi, and said to Rabbi Dostai: See what your friend is doing. Rabbi Dostai replied (out of fear): Give him a good beating.

When they returned to Rabbi Achi, Rabbi Yosi said to Rabbi Achi: Look, master, not only did Rabbi Dostai not assist me, but he even told them to give me a good beating. Rabbi Achi said to Rabbi Dostai: Why did you do this? He said: Those people are many cubits tall, their hats are a cubit, they speak from their navel (they have deep voices), and their names are terrifying . . . If they give the order to have someone tied up, he is tied up; if they give the order to have someone killed, he is killed. If they had killed Dostai, who would have given Yannai, my father, a son like me.[9]

This may not be the most chivalrous of responses, but it is certainly practical and definitely understandable – and has the ring of a modern punchline

The emperor once said to Rabbi Tanchum: Come, let us all become one people. He said: Very well. But we who are circumcised cannot become like you. You should circumcise yourselves and become like us.

The emperor said: You have spoken well. Nonetheless, anyone who bests the emperor must be thrown into an arena filled with wild beasts. He was thrown into the arena, but the animals did not eat him.

A heretic said to the emperor: The reason they did not eat him was because they were not hungry. They threw in the heretic and he was eaten.[10]

As this story illustrates, sometimes, a person has to know when to keep his mouth shut.

Rabbi Yehoshua b. Chananiah was once at the emperor's court. A heretic showed him, using pantomime, that Rabbi Yehoshua was part of a people whose Lord turned his face away from them. He showed the heretic via pantomime, that the Lord's hand is stretched out over us (to protect us). The emperor asked Rabbi Yehoshua: What did he show you? He said: A people whose Lord has turned His face away from them; I showed him that the Lord's hand is stretched out over us. They then asked the heretic: What did you show him. He replied: A people whose Lord has turned His face away from them. They asked: What did Rabbi Yehoshua show you? The heretic said he did not know. They said: A man who does not understand what he is being shown converses in pantomime in front of the emperor! They took him out and had him executed.[11]

As noted elsewhere, Rabbi Yehoshua was an expert at dealing with all types of people – heretics, Sadducees, Athenian sages, and the emperor, to name some – and few could best him in a debate.

In a small town in Italy during the medieval period, a local priest who hated Jews declared that there would be a disputation between himself, representing Catholicism, and a Jew. If the Jews lost, they were to be banished from the town. The debate, in one week's time, would be conducted only and entirely in sign language. All knew that this was a lost cause and no one wanted to speak for the Jews. No one, that is, except the town fool, Yankel. As there was no one else to come forward, Yankel appeared in the appointed place at the appointed time.

The priest began by drawing a large circle in the air. Yankel replied by stamping his foot on the ground. The priest, looking worried, held three fingers in the air. Yankel held up one finger. The priest grabbed a chalice of wine and a loaf of bread, drank a bit of wine and ate a bit of bread, and smiled complacently. Yankel took an apple out of the pocket of his work pants and took a big bite. Whereupon the priest threw his hands up in the air in despair. "I give up!" he said. "The Jews may remain in this town."

Amidst the post-disputation chaos, two groups of people crowded about, one around the priest and the Jews around Yankel, each clamoring for an explanation.

The priest said to his flock: "I began by drawing an arc reminding the Jew that God is everywhere. The Jew stamped on the ground responding that God was not in hell. Then I raised three fingers to indicate the Holy Trinity; he raised one finger to show that God was One and indivisible. Finally, I took out the holy bread and wine representing the body and the blood of our Savior. But then the Jew brought out the apple, reminding me of original sin, and then I knew that the debate was at an end."

The Jewish mob was at the same time listening to Yankel's explanation of the event: "First the priest pointed far away, meaning that the Jews had to leave town. No, I replied, stepping on the ground, we are staying right here! Then he tried to tell me that we had three days in which to leave; I held up one finger, meaning that not a single one of us was leaving. Finally, I guess he gave up because he took out his lunch, so I took out mine." [12]

The next two stories follow a discussion of the law that when one is traveling and is asked by an idolater, who would have little compunction about robbing innocent travelers, where he is heading, he should always name a place that is further than where he is actually going. For example, if one is traveling to a place that is one mile away he should tell the idolater that he is traveling to a place five miles away. Thus, if the pagan plans on robbing him, he might decide to rob him after they have traveled a mile, when it will be too late.

Once the students of Rabbi Akiva were going to Chezib (in Northern Israel). They were approached by highwaymen who asked them where they were going. They said: We are going to Acco. When they arrived at Chezib, they departed from them. The highwaymen asked them: Whose disciples are you? They answered: We are the disciples of Rabbi Akiva. The highwaymen said: Happy are Rabbi Akiva and his disciples for no wicked people will ever be able to harm them.

Rabbi Menashe was once traveling to the town of Be Torata (in Babylon). Some highwaymen approached him and asked him where he was going. He said that he was going to the town of Pumbedita. When they reached Be Torata, he departed from them. The highwaymen said to Rabbi Menashe: You are the disciple of Yehuda the deceiver. He said to them: You know him as a deceiver? May you all be excommunicated. They continued to steal for twenty-two more years but met with no success. When they saw what was happening, they all came and asked that the excommunication be rescinded . . . Come and note how different the thieves of Babylon are from the robbers of Israel.[13]

The Babylonian thieves were disrespectful of Rabbi Yehuda, whereas the Israeli thieves were respectful of Rabbi Akiva. They highwaymen in both stories were Jewish. According to the Talmud, this trick was originally used in the Torah, by Jacob. Jacob told his brother Esau to go ahead and that he would follow him later to Seir. There is, however, no record of Jacob going to Seir.[14]

Idolaters

The next story follows a Talmudic discussion regarding what types of idol worship are punishable by death. Normally, defecating before an idol would not be considered a form of idolatry, but the idol Baal Peor was actually worshipped by exposing one's self and then defecating before this Moabite deity—this practice all by itself may be worthy of a treatise on ancient humor. Incidentally, the Talmud condones and even encourages sneering and making fun of idols. Rabbi Nachman states: "All sneering is forbidden except the mocking of idols."[15] The Talmud often ridicules idols by distorting their names. For example, the Roman deity, Mercurius (Hermes, to the Greeks) is referred to in the Talmud as Markulis.

Sabta of Allas once rented his donkey to a heathen woman. When they reached the idol Baal Peor, she said to Sabta: Wait until I enter and come out. When she returned, he told her to wait until he had a chance to enter and leave. She said to Sabta: But are you not a Jew?

He replied: What does it matter to you. He entered, defecated on the idol's face, and wiped himself on the idol's nose. The idol's attendants seeing this praised him saying: No man has ever served this idol in such a manner.[16]

The Talmud concludes that even if one's intention is to disgrace Baal Peor by defecating before it, he has actually worshipped it. Thus, Sabta, who was trying to ridicule the idol inadvertently ended up "worshipping" it.

Terach, Abraham's father was an idol manufacturer. One day he went to town and left Abraham in charge of the idols. A person entered the establishment and wished to purchase an idol. Abraham asked him how old he was. He answered: About sixty years of age. Abraham said to him: Woe to this person who is sixty years old and desires to worship a one-day-old idol. The man became embarrassed and left.

One time a woman came with a plate of fine meal and said to Abraham: Take this and offer it to the idols. Abraham rose and took a stick in his hand and broke all of the idols except for one. He then placed the stick in the hand of the largest idol, the one that remained. When his father returned, he asked Abraham: Who did this to the idols? Abraham responded: I cannot hide what happened from you. A woman brought a plate of fine meal and asked me to offer it to the idols. I placed it before them and each one said: I will eat first. The big one among them rose, took the stick and broke the rest of them. Terach said to Abraham: Why are you mocking me? Do they have any intelligence? Abraham then said to his father: Should your ears not hear what you have just said?

Terach then took him and gave him over to Nimrod (the ruler). Nimrod said to Abraham: If you do not wish to worship these, then go and worship fire. Abraham replied: Should I not worship water which extinguishes fire? Nimrod said: Then go and worship water. Abraham said: Should I not worship the clouds that carry water? Nimrod said: Then go and worship the clouds. Abraham said: Should I not worship the wind which disperses the clouds? Nimrod said: Then go and worship the wind. Abraham said: Should I not worship human beings who endure the wind? Nimrod said: You are speaking empty words[17]

This story depicts Abraham as a young man proving to his father and to King Nimrod that idolatry is ludicrous. It is interesting to note that a similar legend appears in the Koran.

About Laban meeting with Jacob, his nephew and future son-in-law twice over, the Talmud has this to say:

When Laban saw Jacob he considered that Eliezer had been an insignificant member of the household and yet[18] "The servant took ten of his master's camels, and departed, bringing with him the best things his master owned." Jacob, who is the beloved of his household, should all the more so be bringing great wealth. When Laban did not see any property,[19] "he embraced Jacob," thinking that perhaps he has money hidden on his person. On not finding any money there, "he kissed him," thinking that perhaps he may have precious gems in his mouth. When he did not find anything, Jacob said to him: Did you think that I have come bearing wealth. All I have come bearing are words.[20]

The Talmudic sages did not trust Laban. He was too much of a trickster to be trusted even when hugging his nephew. Later on in Genesis, Laban accused Jacob of stealing his gods. The Talmud comments on this:

It is written: "Why have you stolen my gods?"[21] Rabbi Aibu said: When the children of Jacob heard this, they said (to Laban): We are ashamed of you, father of our mother, that at your old age you can say your gods have been stolen.[22]

How can you believe in the efficacy of idols if they don't even have the power to prevent *themselves* from being stolen?

When Bad Things Happen to Bad People

In the next two stories we see what happens to vicious practical jokers who mistreat newly arrived immigrants from Babylon.

Rabbi Zera came to Israel and he went to a bloodletter to be bled. Afterwards, he went to a butcher to purchase a litra *(approximately a pound) of meat. He asked the butcher: How much for the* litra *of meat? The butcher said: Fifty coins and one blow from an iron bar. Rabbi Zera said: Take sixty coins and do not strike me. The butcher refused. Rabbi Zera said: Take seventy and do not strike me. He still refused. Take eighty, Take ninety, until Rabbi Zera reached one hundred, but the butcher continued to refuse. Finally, Rabbi Zera said: Do what is your custom.*

That evening, Rabbi Zera went to the academy. He said to the rabbis: What an evil custom you have here in Israel that you do not let a person eat a litra *of meat until you strike him one blow. They said to him: What are you talking about? Who told you this? He said: so-and-so the butcher. They sent for the butcher and were going to punish him, but found that his coffin was already being taken out with the butcher's corpse inside. The rabbis said to Rabbi Zera: Did you get so angry at*

him that you caused him to be punished so severely (by God)? Rabbi
Zera said: May the same fate befall me if I asked for his punishment.
I was not even angry at him. I thought that this was actually your
custom here in Israel.[23]

Rabbi Zera was a very unattractive person and originally came from
Babylonia. This butcher apparently did not like Babylonians and wanted
to play a nasty joke on Rabbi Zera.

When Rabbi Yassa came to Israel, he went to the barber. Afterwards,
He went to the baths of Tiberias, when a scorner approached him
and gave him a blow on the neck saying: Your neck is loose and
has to be tightened. An official happened to be nearby and was
interrogating a robber and asking him who was his accomplice.
He looked up and noticed that the scorner was laughing at him.
The robber said: This one, who is laughing at me was my accomplice.
The scorner was taken and interrogated. He confessed to having once
killed someone. The two were taken away to be hung and each of
them was carrying a beam (that was going to be used to hang them).
Meanwhile, Rabbi Yassa emerged from the bathhouse. The scorner
said to Rabbi Yassa: My neck which was loose will now become tight-
ened. Rabbi Yassa said to him: Your luck is bad. Did you not know
that it is written:[24] *"And now do not scorn, lest your bonds become*
strong."[25]

This story illustrates the dangers of being a nasty joker and also how
one's own words can come back and haunt one.

The next story is of Titus who, according to the Talmud, had the
audacity to bring a harlot into the Temple and then committed a sin
with her while lying on a Torah scroll. Titus then took the sacred vessels
of the Temple and sailed with them to Rome. While at sea, a big storm
threatened to sink the ship.

Titus said: It seems that the God of these people only has power in
water. When Pharaoh came, he drowned him in water. When Sisero
came, he drowned him in water. He is also trying to drown me in
water. If he is so mighty, let Him go ashore and wage war with me.
A Heavenly voice rang out and said: Wicked one, son of a wicked one,
grandson of Esau the wicked, I have a tiny creature in my world, the
gnat, go ashore and fight it. When Titus landed, a gnat entered his
nose and fed on his brain for seven years. One day, he was passing a
blacksmith, when the gnat heard the noise of the smith's hammer, it
stopped gnawing at Titus' brain. Titus said: It appears that I have
found a remedy. Every day they brought a blacksmith to hammer
for him. If the blacksmith was a gentile, he was paid four zuzim *and*

if he was a Jew, Titus would say: It is payment enough for you to see your enemy suffer. For thirty days, this worked. But after that, the gnat became accustomed to the hammering. Rabbi Pinchas b. Aruba stated: I was there among the Roman nobility when Titus died. They opened his brain and found a gnat as big as a free bird (a swallow) weighing two selas.[26]

This story was supposed to mollify the people for the loss of the Temple. Titus gets punished for destroying the Temple and is put in his proper place by God.

Scholarship and Pedagogy

Rabbi Yosi lectured in Sepphoris that the Sodomites were envious of people of wealth. They gave wealthy people balsamum to safeguard and they would secret it in their storehouse. During the evening, the Sodomites would come and sniff it out like dogs and then they would dig down, break in, and steal the money.

That night, there were 300 break-ins in Sepphoris. The people of Sepphoris tormented Rabbi Yosi and said to him: You have provided a method for thieves to steal. He responded: Did I know that thieves would come?[27]

This is also a modern dilemma: Teach people about fraudulent behaviors that are against the law and you might actually encourage them to use these techniques.

The next selection shows the great lengths that the students of the Talmudists would go to in order to learn everyday manners from their teachers. The humor is incidental.

Rabbi Akiva said: Once I followed Rabbi Yehoshua into the bathroom and learned three things from him . . .

The Talmud here discusses personal hygiene mores.

. . . Ben Azzai told him: Is that how much effrontery you displayed towards your teacher?

He answered: It is all Torah! And Torah I need to learn!

. . . Ben Azzai said: Once I followed Rabbi Akiva into the bathroom and learned three things from him . . .

Rabbi Yehuda told him: Is that how much effrontery you displayed towards your teacher?

He answered: It is all Torah! And Torah I need to learn!

... Rabbi Kahana once hid under Rav's bed. He heard him chitchatting and bantering with his wife and then engaging in sexual intercourse, and said to him: It would seem that the mouth of Abba (Rav's real name) has not sipped of this broth before ...

Meaning, Rav is acting like one who is having intercourse for the first time.

... Rav responded: Kahana is that you? Get out, this is not the proper way.

Rabbi Kahana replied: It is all Torah! And Torah I need to learn![28]

There are numerous laws in the Talmud dealing with conjugal manners and personal hygiene. The Rabbis of the Talmud felt that one could learn a great deal from observing one's mentor and listening to a teacher's small talk.

Patience

The following story is used to illustrate the importance of being kind and patient.

Once there were two people who made a bet with each other saying that whoever is able to make Hillel lose his temper would receive 400 zuz. One of them said, I will make Hillel lose his temper.

It was Friday afternoon, before the Sabbath, and Hillel was washing his head. He went and passed the door of Hillel's house and exclaimed: Who here is Hillel? Who here is Hillel? Hillel put on his robe and went out towards him saying: My son, what do you wish? He said: I have a question to ask. Hillel replied: Ask my son, ask. He asked: Why are the heads of the Babylonians round (Hillel was originally from Babylonia)? Hillel answered: My son, you have asked a great question. The answer is because they do not have prudent midwives.

He left, waited awhile, returned, and exclaimed: Who here is Hillel? Who here is Hillel? Hillel put on his robe and went out towards him saying: My son, what do you wish? He said: I have a question to ask. Hillel replied: Ask my son, ask. He asked: Why are the eyes of the Tarmodians tender? Hillel said: My son, you have asked a great question. The answer is because they live in a sandy region.

He left, waited awhile, returned, and exclaimed: Who here is Hillel? Who here is Hillel? Hillel put on his robe and went out towards him saying: My son, what do you wish? He said: I have a question to ask. Hillel replied: Ask my son, ask. He asked: Why are the feet of the Africans wide? Hillel said: My son, you have asked a great question. The answer is because they live in swampy areas. He then said: I have many questions to ask, but I am afraid that you might become angry with me. Hillel put on his garment, sat before the man, and said: Ask all the questions that you wish to ask.

He said: Are you the Hillel that is called the Leader of Israel? Hillel answered: Yes. If you are him, may there not be more like you amongst Israel. Hillel asked him: My son, why? He replied: Because you made me lose four hundred zuz.

Hillel responded: One should be careful with his disposition. It is far better that you should lose 400 zuz, and 400 zuz more, than Hillel should lose his temper.[29]

The Talmud contrasts the patience and gentleness of Hillel with the strictness of Shammai. Hillel and Shammai were leaders of two major academies. The School of Hillel was generally more lenient in ritual law. According to the Talmud, after three years of disputes as to which view was correct, a Heavenly voice proclaimed that both views were the "words of the living God, but the law is in agreement with the School of Hillel."[30] The Talmud provides the reason that the Hillel view prevailed. The Hillelites were kinder and more patient than the Shammaites. They also studied both their own views and those of the Shammaites, and even mentioned the opposing views of the Shammai School before mentioning their own opinions.

A gentile once came before Shammai and asked him: Convert me on condition that you teach me the whole Torah while I am standing on one foot. Shammai chased him away with the builder's measuring rod which he held in his hand. He came before Hillel and made the same request. Hillel converted him and said to him: What is hateful to you, do not do to your fellow man. That is the whole Torah, and the rest is commentary. Go and learn it.[31]

Hillel's negative version of the Golden Rule is a great deal easier to obey than the positive version. Few individuals are capable of loving and treating their fellow human beings the way they treat themselves.

A gentile once came before Shammai and asked him: How many Torahs do you have? Shammai answered: Two, a written Torah and an oral Torah. The gentile replied: I believe in the written Torah, but I do not believe in the oral Torah. Convert me on condition that you only teach me the written Torah. Shammai rebuked and sent him away in anger. He went to Hillel and made the same request. Hillel converted him. On the first day he taught him aleph, bet, gimmel, dalet (the first four letters of the Hebrew alphabet), and the next day he reversed the

125

order of these letters. The convert said: Did you not teach me thus yesterday? Hillel said to him: Do you not rely on me as to what the letters are? Rely on me also with respect to the fact that there is an oral Torah.[32]

This story illustrates that Hillel was more tolerant and patient than Shammai. These different approaches to dealing with people also affected the academies that the two founded.

A Persian came to Rav and asked him to teach him Torah. Rav said to him (showing him the first letter of the Hebrew alphabet): Say aleph. The Persian said: Who says that this is an aleph? Perhaps there are others who say that it is not so. Rav said (showing him the second letter of the alphabet): Say bet. The Persian said: Who says that this is a bet? Rav scolded him and drove him out in anger. The Persian then came to Shmuel and asked him to teach him Torah. Shmuel said to him: Say aleph. The Persian said: Who says that this is an aleph? Shmuel said: Say bet. The Persian said: Who says that this is a bet? Shmuel grabbed and twisted his ear. The Persian said: My ear! my ear! Shmuel said to him: Who says that this is your ear? He replied: Everyone knows that this is an ear. Shmuel said to him: So too does everyone know that this is an aleph and this is a bet. Immediately, the Persian was silent and accepted the lessons.[33]

This story is used to illustrate that "patience is better than pride."[34]

Scholars and Scholarship

Rabbi Shimon b. Yochai said:

If a man plows in the plowing season, plants in the planting season, reaps in the reaping season, threshes in the threshing season, winnows in the wind season, what will become of the Torah? But when Israel performs the will of God, their work is performed by others.

Rabbi Shimon disagreed with Rabbi Yishmael who said that a man is obligated to combine working for a living with studying Torah.[35]

Ilfa suspended himself from the mast of a ship and said: If anyone comes and asks me to elucidate a baraita of Rabbi Chiya and Rabbi Oshiyah and I cannot clarify it by finding a basis to it in a Mishna, I will throw myself from the mast and drown.[36]

Ilfa was trying to prove that even though he left the academy to embark on a career in business, his knowledge was still intact. Needless to say, even knowing the possibly dire consequence of a too tough question—or, perhaps, *especially* knowing this—people still came and asked him questions. As noted, the *Mishna* was redacted by Rebbi and is more authoritative. The *baraitot*, also the statements of *Tannaim*, were redacted by Rabbi Chiya and Rabbi Oshiyah.

When the Leadership Is Criticized

"Can you please tell me where Reb Yankel, the shul gabbai, lives?" asked the stranger.

"You probably mean Reb Yankel 'Stutterer' whose father is Reb Avremel 'Eczema.' He lives down near the church."

When the stranger reached the church, he asked a passerby, "Can you please tell me where I can find Reb Yankel, the gabbai?"

"You mean Reb Yankel with the hernia, the wife beater? He buried three wives already. You'll find him two blocks over."

The stranger went a bit further and asked a shopkeeper, "Can you please tell me where Reb Yankel lives?"

"You mean Reb Yankel the goniff, who goes into bankruptcy every other year? There he is!"

The stranger introduced himself to Reb Yankel and said to him, "Reb Yankel, you must be paid a lot to be gabbai in this town."

"Nothing! Not even a penny!"

"Then why do you do it?"

"What a question!" said the gabbai. "Is honor nothing?"[37]

> *Yosi of Maon interpreted, in the synagogue of Maon, the verse: "Hear this, O priests, hearken, O House of Israel, and give ear, O royal house,"*[38] *saying. In the future, the Holy One will take the priests and make them stand in judgment and will say to them: Why did you not toil in the Torah? Did you not benefit from the twenty-four priestly gifts?*
>
> *The priests will say: They did not give us anything.*
>
> *Then the "House of Israel" will be asked: Why did you not give the priests the twenty-four gifts as I commanded in the Torah.*
>
> *They will say: Because the members of the house of the Nasi took everything.*
>
> *God will then say: "Give ear O ye house of the king, for yours is the judgment." Were these priestly gifts yours? Does it not say:*[39] *"And this shall be the priests due from the people." Therefore the judgment will be turned against you (i.e., the house of the Nasi).*
>
> *Rebbi (the Nasi) heard of this and became angry. Towards evening, Resh Lakish came to visit Rebbi and mollify him regarding what Yosi*

had said. Resh Lakish said: We should be grateful to the nations of the world, for they bring mimes to their theaters and circuses so that people should be entertained and should not fight with each other when they are idle. Yet, Yosi of Maon speaks words of Torah and you are angry with him . . .

That is, do you want us to be like the heathens that require entertainment rather than expressing serious ideas?

. . . Rebbi asked Resh Lakish: Does he know anything of the Torah? He answered, "yes." Rebbi asked: Has his learning been transmitted to him by reliable teachers? He answered, "yes." Rebbi asked: If I ask him a question, can he provide an answer? He answered, "yes." Rebbi said: If so, let him come here. When Yosi came, Rebbi asked him what is the meaning of the verse:[40] "Behold, all that use proverbs will use this proverb against you, saying: As the mother, so her daughter." Yosi said: Like the daughter, so is the mother; like the generation, so is the leader; like the altar, so are the priests. Here we say: As the garden, so is the gardener (i.e., as is the people, so is the leader). Resh Lakish said to Yosi: You have not yet finished mollifying Rebbi for the first affront and you are bringing another.[41]

A similar story can be found in the Jerusalem Talmud.[42] It is not clear why Rabbi Yosi was so hard on Rebbi who was known for his great humility.

Resh Lakish was once guarding an orchard and a person came along and began to eat some figs. Resh Lakish began to shout at him but was ignored. Resh Lakish said: Let that person be excommunicated. He replied: On the contrary, let the other person (i.e., Resh Lakish) be excommunicated. If I incurred a financial obligation to you (for eating the figs), does this mean that I also incurred excommunication? Resh Lakish went to the academy and told them what happened. They said to him: His excommunication is valid and yours is not.[43]

Resh Lakish actually had to go to the Nasi and have the excommunication absolved since he did not know who the fellow was that excommunicated him in order to ask him for absolution.

There was once a person from the town of Nehardea who entered a butcher shop in Pumbedita. He asked for some meat and was told to wait until the attendant of Rabbi Yehuda b. Yechezkel was served and then he would be served. He said: Who is Rabbi Yehuda b. Sheviskel . . .

Purposely mispronouncing the name so that it now means Yehuda the Glutton.

> *... that he should be ahead of me and be served before me. Rabbi Yehuda was told of the incident and excommunicated the Nehardean man. Rabbi Yehuda was then told that the man often called people slaves ...*

That is, he questioned their authentic Jewish lineage and claimed that they were descendants of slaves.

> *... Rabbi Yehuda then had him declared a descendent of slaves. Thereupon, the Nehardean went and summoned Rabbi Yehuda to a lawsuit before Rabbi Nachman. When the summons arrived, Rabbi Yehuda asked Rabbi Huna whether or not he should go. Rabbi Huna told him that he was not obligated to go because he was a great man ...*

And more knowledgeable than Rabbi Nachman.

> *... but should go out of respect for the Nasi's house ...*

Rabbi Nachman was the son-in-law of the exilarch, the leader of Babylonian Jewry.

> *... Rabbi Yehuda came to Rabbi Nachman's house and found him building a fence. He said: Do you not agree with the opinion of Rabbi Huna b. Idi in the name of Shmuel that once a person has been appointed a community leader, he is prohibited from doing menial labor in the presence of three people? ...*

This, because of the dignity of his position.

> *... Rabbi Nachman answered: I am simply making a small* gundrita. *Rabbi Yehuda said: Is the word* maakeh *used in the Bible or the word* mechitzah *used by the Rabbis repugnant to you? ...*

All three words mean fence, but Rabbi Nachman was using the more pretentious word.

> *Rabbi Nachman then asked Rabbi Yehuda to sit on the* karpita. *He replied: Is the word* safsal *used by the Rabbis or the word* itztaba *used by the people repugnant to you? ...*

All three mean bench or couch.

> . . . *Rabbi Nachman then asked Rabbi Yehuda to eat some* ethronga *(citron). He replied: This is what Shmuel stated: Whoever says* ethronga *is one-third supercilious. Either call it* ethrog, *the word used by the Rabbis or* ethroga, *the word used by the people.*

> *Rabbi Nachman then asked Rabbi Yehuda to drink some* anbaga. *He replied: Is the word* isparagus *used by the Rabbis or the word* anpak *used by the people repugnant to you? . . .*

All three mean a small cup of wine.

> . . . *Rabbi Nachman then said: Let my daughter, Donag, come and serve us some wine. He replied: Thus stated Shmuel: One should not be waited on by a woman . . .*

To serve men as it may encourage the mingling of the sexes, especially when wine is served.

> . . . *Rabbi Nachman said: But she is a minor. He replied: Shmuel stated explicitly that,whether she is an adult or a minor, one should not be waited on by a woman.*

> *Rabbi Nachman then said: Do you wish to send a greeting to my wife, Yalta? He replied: Thus stated Shmuel: Hearing the voice of a woman is indecency, he replied . . .*

In their society, greeting a woman directly was immodest.

> . . . *Rabbi Nachman said: You can send a greeting to her through a messenger. He replied: Thus stated Shmuel: One should not send a greeting to a woman. Rabbi Nachman said: You can send a greeting to her through her husband (i.e., himself). He replied: Thus stated Shmuel: One should not send a greeting to a woman at all.*

> *Rabbi Nachman's wife, who overheard the whole conversation, sent a message to her husband: Resolve this dispute expeditiously. Otherwise, he will make you appear to be like just another ignoramus.*[44]

The above story was used in the Talmud to support the opinion of the great scholar Shmuel who stated: Whatever genealogical blemish one accuses others of having, he himself has. It is a long story, but— remember the name-calling about slaves at the beginning? The story continues and at the end it was discovered that the Nehardean was indeed a descendent of slaves.

Outsmarted in Jerusalem

The Talmud tells us that: "Ten measures of wisdom descended to the world; nine were taken by the land of Israel and one by the rest of the world."[45] Many Talmudic stories demonstrate that those living in Israel, especially Jerusalem, were extremely intelligent. In our discussion of riddles, we note that the Talmud describes a debate between Rabbi Yehoshua and the Athenian sages, who were known to be very smart.[46] The Midrash Rabbah on Lamentations relates numerous stories that demonstrate the superiority of Jerusalemites over Athenians. Here, it turns out, even a child gets the better of the Athenian.

> *Once an Athenian came to Jerusalem where he met a child. He gave him some money and said: Go and bring both of us some figs and grapes. The child replied: Your might should be strengthened (i.e., well spoken). You earn your share with your money and I earn my share with my feet. When the child returned, he placed the lower quality fruit before himself and the better quality fruit before the Athenian. The Athenian said: People are right when they say that Jerusalem-ites are very wise. Since you realized that you did not supply any of the money, you took the worse fruits for yourself and the better ones you placed before me. The Athenian said: Let us cast lots for the better fruit. The child said: If I win, then I get your share, and if you win, you get my share. They cast the lot, and the child got the better fruit.[47]*

The child could not lose since he had the inferior fruits in front of him. His "heads I win, tails you lose" proposal was somehow accepted by the Athenian sage.

> *Once an Athenian came to Jerusalem where he met a child. He gave him some money and said: Go find and bring me something of which I can satiate myself and have something left over to take on the road. The child went and brought him some salt. The Athenian said: Did I ask you to bring me salt? The child replied: Did you not tell me to bring you something of which you could satiate yourself, and have something left over to take on the road? By your life, you now have something of which you can satiate yourself and have something left for the road.[48]*

Even the Athenians known for their wisdom could not outsmart the children of Jerusalem.

> *Once an Athenian came to Jerusalem where he met a child. He gave him some money and said: Go and bring me some eggs and cheese.*

When the child returned, he said to him: Tell me which cheese is from a white goat and which cheese is from a black goat? The child replied: You are the adult. You tell me, which egg is from a white chicken and which egg is from a black chicken?[49]

Another story demonstrating the superiority of Jerusalem children over Athenians. These stories might also hint at the superiority of Judaism over Hellenism, which was an important issue for many years,

Once an Athenian came to Jerusalem to learn wisdom. He studied for three and a half years without success. After the three and a half years, he bought a (Jewish) slave who was blind in one eye.

He exclaimed in disgust: After toiling for three and a half years to acquire wisdom, I buy one slave and he turns out to be blind. Said the seller: By your life, he is very wise and can see at a great distance with his wisdom.

When they came out of the gate, the slave said: Hurry so that we may overtake the caravan in front of us. The Athenian asked: Is there a caravan ahead of us? The slave replied: Yes. And there is a female camel in it which is blind in one eye. She is pregnant with twins and is carrying two wineskin bottles, one containing wine and the other vinegar. The caravan is four miles ahead of us and the camel driver is a gentile.

The Athenian said to the slave: Oh you who are from a stiff-necked people and only have one eye. How do you know that the camel is blind in one eye? The slave replied: I noticed that one side of the road has been grazed, but not the other side.

The Athenian asked: And how do you know that she is carrying twins in her womb? He replied: The camel laid down in the dust and I see the impression of the two of them.

The Athenian asked: And how do you know that she is carrying two skin bottles, one of wine and one of vinegar? He replied: From the drippings. Wine gets absorbed into the ground and vinegar bubbles.

The Athenian asked: And how do you know that the camel driver is a gentile? He replied: Because he urinated in the middle of the road, and a Jew does not urinate in the middle of the road only in a corner.

The Athenian asked: And how do you know that caravan is four miles in front of us? He replied: Up to four miles the camel's hoofprints are discernible, but not beyond that distance (after four miles, the sand covers the hoofprints).[50]

This is reminiscent of the Sherlock Holmes stories. The Jewish slave's powers of observation were remarkable.

An Athenian came to Jerusalem and made fun of the residents of Jerusalem. They said: Which one of us will go and bring him back here? One of them said: I will bring him back here with his head shaved. The Jerusalemite went to Athens and stayed in the house of this Athenian. In the morning, the two went for a walk in the marketplace. The Jerusalemite's sandal broke. He gave a tremis *(a very valuable Roman coin) to a shoemaker and asked him to make him another sandal. The shoemaker made him another sandal. The next day the two went for a walk in the marketplace and the other sandal broke. He said to the shoemaker: Take a* tremis *and make me another sandal. The Athenian said to the Jerusalemite? Are sandals so expensive in Jerusalem? The Jerusalemite answered in the affirmative. The Athenian asked: How much does a pair of sandals go for in Jerusalem? The Jerusalemite said: For about nine or ten* dinarim *(a ridiculously high price), and when they are cheap they go for about seven or eight* dinarim. *The Athenian said: If I come to Jerusalem with a cargo of sandals could you sell them for me. The Jerusalemite answered: Yes. However, do not come to Jerusalem without first notifying me. When the Athenian had completed his work, he purchased sandals and went to Jerusalem. He came to the gate of Jerusalem and sent for the Jerusalemite. When the Jerusalemite came, he said to the Athenian: We Jerusalemites have an agreement that any merchant who wishes to sell his merchandise must shave his head and blacken his face. The Athenian said: What do I care if I shave my head as long as I can sell my merchandise. He shaved his head and the Jerusalemite brought him to the center of the marketplace. A person came to him and asked him: How much for a pair of sandals? The Athenian answered: There are some for ten* dinarim, *some for nine, but none for less than eight. When the shopper heard this (the price was incredibly high), he hit the Athenian on the head with the sandal and did not buy anything. The Athenian (realized that he was tricked) said to the Jerusalemite: Did I treat you so badly when you were in my place? The Jerusalemite replied: In the future do not ridicule the people of Jerusalem.*[51]

An important part of humor is for those who are oppressed or on the bottom of the social ladder to be able to use humor to show their superiority over the oppressor. If they are not superior militarily or economically, at least they are smarter than those that rule over them. Judaism has battled with the Babylonians, the Persians, Greeks (Hellenists), Romans, Nazis, Communists, and so on. One way they never defeat us is in humor. In Jewish jokes, the winner is always the Jew, and it is always because of his wit that he prevails. This is universal in humor of the oppressed. The modern version of these anecdotes may be the jokes that begin, "A rabbi, a priest, and a minister . . ." or

"A Jew, a German, a Frenchman . . ." These are not necessarily truly *Jewish* jokes in that they can work well—and often do—for any ethnic group. Still funny, though.

A Frenchman, an Englishman, a German, and a Jew are on an airplane. The pilot announces that they're losing fuel and will crash unless the plane is lightened, namely someone will have to jump to his death to save the others.

The Frenchman cries, "Vive la France!" and jumps from the plane.

But the plane continues losing fuel, and another sacrifice must be made.

The Englishman cries, "God save the Queen!" and jumps.

Again the pilot announces more weight must be jettisoned.

So the Jew shouts, "Am Yisroel chai!"[52] *and throws the German out.*[53]

8

Satire, Irony, and Self-Deprecating Humor

Moscow, early 1970s. It's a cold winter day, and a long line has already formed in front of the butcher shop on the rumor that fresh meat will soon be delivered there.

After the eager citizens have stood in line for hours, the butcher sticks his head out the door and says, "Comrades, I've just had a call from the Party Central Committee. I regret to say that the shipment has been delayed, and at any rate there will not be enough meat for everyone. All Jewish citizens are required to leave the queue!"

The Jews obediently leave the line and go home.

Several hours later, as night falls, the butcher emerges one more time: "Comrades, I've just had another call from Central Committee. It turns out there will be no meat at all, so you should all go home."

The crowd finally, disperses, grumbling: "Those damned Jews get all the breaks!"

Satire, used to humorously point out an individual's vice or folly, may make use of wit, sarcasm, irony. The main distinguishing feature of satire is that it has a goal: reform of an individual or, more likely, of society.

In one Talmudic anecdote, Rabbi Gamliel (the Second) and his sister, Imma Shalom, try to expose a corrupt judge who lives in their neighborhood. The judge, called a philosopher, had a reputation as one who did not take bribes. This reputation, they knew, was undeserved:

> *Imma Shalom was the wife of Rabbi Eliezer and the sister of Rabbi Gamliel. There was a philosopher who lived in their neighborhood who had a reputation for not taking bribes. They wished to deride him. Imma Shalom brought him a golden lamp as a bribe and then appeared before him stating that she wished to inherit a share in her father's estate. He told Imma Shalom and Rabbi Gamliel to split the assets. Rabbi Gamliel said: But it is written in our laws that when*

*there is a son, the daughters do not inherit. The philosopher respond-
ed: Since the day you people were exiled from your land, the Torah
of Moses was superseded and replaced with a new book which states
that sons and daughters may inherit equally. The next day, Rabbi
Gamliel brought him a Libyan donkey (as a bribe). The philosopher
said to them: Look at the end of the book and it states: I have not come
to subtract or add to Mosaic law, and it is written in the Mosaic code
that where there is a son a daughter does not inherit. Imma Shalom
then said: May the Lord make your light shine as bright as a lamp
(hinting at her bribe). Rabbi Gamliel then responded: A donkey came
and knocked over the lamp.*[1]

This has the flavor of a sting with the brother and sister working
smoothly together to bring down the corrupt judge. The reader who
feels sorry for the poor heretical judge should know that the book of law
that the philosopher referred to which states that "sons and daughters
may inherit equally" does not exist. The second verse quoted by the
judge, "I have not come to subtract or add to Mosaic law . . .," is similar
to the verse from the Christian Bible: "Do not think that I have come
to abolish the Law or the Prophets; I have not come to abolish them
but to fulfill them."[2] Therefore, some scholars believe that the above
story derides the early Jewish Christians.[3] This story involving Gamliel
II and his sister must have taken place about 80 C.E., give or take a
few years. Christianity was at that time a Jewish sect that did not have
a wide following.

THE JUSTICE OF SODOM: Sodom was known as an evil place that
did everything to discourage strangers from living there. The following
humorous stories illustrate how depraved and corrupt a xenophobic
country can become.

*There were four judges in Sodom and their names were Liar, Falsifi-
er, Forger, and Justice Perverter. In Sodom, if one struck his friend's
wife and caused her to miscarry, the husband was told to give her
to the perpetrator so that he could make her pregnant again. If one
cut off the ear of his friend's donkey, the donkey's owner was told to
give the donkey to the perpetrator until the ear grew back. If one
struck another, the victim was told to pay the assaulter a fee for
bloodletting. One who crossed the river into Sodom by using the bridge
had to pay a toll of four zuz; one who crossed through the water, paid
eight zuz.*

*A fuller once came to Sodom and was asked to pay the four zuz toll.
He claimed that he crossed through the water. He was then asked to
pay eight zuz. He refused to pay so he was assaulted. He went to the*

judge and was required to pay the fee for bloodletting in addition to the eight zuz toll.

In the following Talmudic stories, the servant of Abraham, Eliezer, a smart man in his own right, easily outwits the xenophobic Sodomites, demonstrating that even the servant of a good person can outsmart wicked people.

Eliezer, the servant of Abraham, came to Sodom and was assaulted. He went to the judge and was told to pay the bloodletting fee. He took a stone and struck the judge. The judge asked: Why did you do this? Eliezer responded: Take the money you now owe me for bloodletting and pay the plaintiff and my money will stay with me.

The following is about the infamous bed of Sodom which, as depicted in the Talmud, is similar to the bedroom furniture of Procrustes in Greek legend.

In Sodom, there was a bed on which guests had to sleep. If one was too tall, his legs were cut, and if one was too short, he was stretched out. Eliezer, Abraham's servant, happened to go there. They invited him to lie down on the bed. Eliezer said: Since the day my mother died, I vowed not to sleep on a bed.

Finally,

When a poor person came to Sodom, every one gave him a dinar but wrote his name on it. However, no one would give or sell the poor person any food. When he died of starvation, each of the Sodomites would come and take back his money. The Sodomites had an agreement: Whoever invites a guest to a wedding, must be stripped of his clothes. There was a wedding and Eliezer happened to go there, but they did not serve him any food. When Eliezer wanted to eat, he sat at the very end of the bench. When he was asked who invited him, Eliezer would say to the individual sitting next to him, you invited me. This individual became afraid that if the others would believe that he invited someone to the feast, that he would be stripped of his clothes, so he ran outside. Eliezer kept doing this until eventually all the guests ran out and he ate the feast.[4]

Sodom and Gomorrah were destroyed because they did not believe in charity and helping the poor. These anecdotes use humor to illustrate how depraved a society can become when it cares only for its own citizens and is indifferent to justice.

Irony

Rabbi Altmann and his secretary were sitting in a coffeehouse in Berlin in 1935. "Herr Altmann," said his secretary, "I notice you're reading Der Stürmer! I can't understand why. A Nazi libel sheet! Are you some kind of masochist, or, God forbid, a self-hating Jew?"

"On the contrary, Frau Epstein. When I used to read the Jewish papers, all I learned about were pogroms, riots in Palestine, and assimilation in America. But now that I read Der Stürmer, I see so much more: that the Jews control all the banks, that we dominate in the arts, and that we're on the verge of taking over the entire world. You know—it makes me feel a whole lot better!"[5]

When an outcome is the opposite of what one expects, when there is a discrepancy between appearances and reality, when there exists an incongruity between what an individual expects to happen and what really does happen, the result is irony. It stands to reason, then, that documents, whose primary goal is commentary on other works, will point up such incongruities where they appear. For instance, we are reminded:

> *This is Ahasuerus who killed his wife because of his friend, and his friend because of his wife.*[6]

Early in the *Book of Esther*, King Ahasuerus had Queen Vashti killed on the advice of his friend and advisor, Memuchan, who is identified as Haman in the Midrash. At the end of the Book, the same king has his friend Haman killed because of his new wife, Queen Esther.

Benaiah, one of King Solomon's captains, captured Asmodeus, the King of demons, and brought him to the King in Jerusalem. Along the way, these two individuals held some interesting conversations:

> *Benaiah asked Asmodeus why he laughed when they overheard a man tell a shoemaker to make him shoes that would last for seven years. He replied: That man does not have seven days and he wants shoes that will last for seven years.*

> *He then asked him why he laughed when they passed a soothsayer who was divining. He replied: He was sitting on a king's treasure and he should have divined what was directly beneath him.*[7]

This story not-so-indirectly pokes fun at soothsayers. The idea that a fortune-teller purports to know that which is hidden to others and yet is unknowingly sitting on top of a treasure is a clever way of mocking magic and divination, which are prohibited to Jews.

Measure for Measure

Mrs. Horowitz was at the butcher shop. She insisted on examining the chicken before she agreed to purchase it. The butcher acquiesced, and Mrs. Horowitz put on her reading glasses, examined the chicken from every angle. Top, bottom, sideways, upside down, inside and out.

Finally, when the butcher could contain himself no longer, he said "Lady, could you pass that test?"

We have already seen that the motif of measure for measure runs all through the Bible. For example, the episode of Joseph and his brothers has many instances of irony. Dreams figure prominently in the life of Joseph. Joseph is sold as a slave by his brothers because of his dreams and becomes a Grand Vizier because of a dream. The words of Joseph's brothers to Joseph upon arriving in Egypt are quite ironic: "We are *all* the sons of the same man"[8] (emphasis added). They did not recognize Joseph since he was the Egyptian Grand Vizier. The Midrash points out the irony in their saying "we are all" of the same father.[9]

The Talmud derives the principle that the Lord punishes measure for measure, that is, the punishment fits the crime, from an incident described in Kings II.[10] There was a major famine in Samaria while the city was being besieged by the Arameans. Elisha the prophet declared that the next day the famine would not only be over but that the price of barley would become absurdly low. An officer of the king scoffed and said "Even if the Lord were to make windows in the sky," that is, for the grain to rain down, "will this come to be?" Elisha responded: "Behold, you will see it with your eyes but you shall not eat thereof." This is indeed what happened: A miracle occurred and the Aramean camp heard the sound of a great army so they fled. When the Jews found out that the Arameans left, they plundered the Aramean camp and the price of flour plummeted. The king's officer who scoffed was trampled to death.[11]

This sort of tit-for-tat punishment often results in a great deal of irony. The *sotah*, a wife suspected of infidelity, is one example provided by the Talmud to demonstrate this:

> *She stood at the doorway of her house to display herself to him (her lover), therefore the priest stands her by the Nicanor gate to show her humiliation to all.*
>
> *She spread beautiful kerchiefs on her head for him, therefore the priest removes her scarf from her head and places it under her feet.*
>
> *She adorned her face for him, therefore her face turns green.*

This occurs, if she is guilty, after partaking of the bitter water. Also:

> *She painted her eyes with eye-shadow for him, therefore her eyes extrude.*
>
> *She braided her hair for him, therefore a priest dishevels her hair.*
>
> *She beckoned him with her finger, therefore her fingernails fall off.*
>
> *She cinched herself with a belt, therefore a priest takes a common rope and ties it above the breasts.*
>
> *She stretched out her thighs to him, therefore her thighs fall off.*
>
> *She received him on her belly, therefore her belly blows up.*
>
> *She fed him the delicacies of the world, therefore her sacrifice consists of animal fodder (barley).*
>
> *She provided him with superior wine in exquisite cups, therefore a priest gives her to drink the bitter water from a vessel of earthenware . . .*
>
> *She acted in secret, therefore the Omnipresent publicizes it.*[12]

Other examples provided include Samson, who "sinned with his eyes," by straying after unsuitable women, and therefore had his eyes gouged out by the Philistines; and Absalom, who was arrogant about his hair and therefore he was hanged by his hair.[13] The Talmud also presents numerous such stories that contain irony. For example, here the Talmud depicts the conversation that might well have taken place between Jacob and Leah, the morning after their wedding, when Jacob realizes that he has been duped by Laban and married Leah instead of Rachel:

> *Jacob said to Leah: What is this! You are a deceiver, the daughter of a deceiver! Did I not call you "Rachel" last night and you answered me! Leah responded: Is there a teacher without students? I learned from you. Did your father not shout "Esau" and you answered him.*[14]

Jacob pretended to be Esau in order to receive the blessings that Isaac was planning to bestow on Esau. Leah told Jacob that she treated him the way he had treated his own father. This is not only a clever, sarcastic remark but is an important theme in Genesis: Those who deceive others are, in turn, deceived themselves.

> It says:[15] "Judah sent the young kid." Yehuda b. Nachman said in the name of Resh Lakish, it says:[16] "laughing in the habitable world of His earth, laughing before Him at all times." The Torah laughs at people. The Holy One said to Judah: You deceived your father with a kid of the goats; by your life! Tamar will deceive you with a kid of the goats.[17]

Joseph's coat of many colors was dipped in goat's blood in order to deceive Jacob[18] and make him think Joseph was devoured. Similarly, Judah was deceived by Tamar, his daughter-in-law, by means of a kid of goats.[19] The laughter refers to the fact that the Lord punishes measure for measure.

According to the Midrash, Caleb married Bityah, who was the daughter of Pharaoh as well as the woman who rescued Moses from the Nile as a baby and raised him. The Midrash's comment on this is as follows:

> Rabbi Abba b. Kahana and Rabbi Yehuda b. Simone had a difference of opinion: One said: Caleb rebelled against the counsel of the spies and Pharaoh's daughter rebelled against her father. Let therefore one rebel marry the other rebel. The other said: One rescued the sheep and the other rescued the shepherd.[20]

Israel is often compared to sheep and, of course, Moses was a shepherd, both literally and also as a leader of his people. Bityah's father, the Pharaoh, ordered the death of the Israelite boys and she saved Moses from this fate. The above Midrash illustrates the positive side of measure for measure, which may be used for rewards as well as punishments. Caleb, who rebelled against the evil spies, is rewarded with a wife who rebelled against the evil decree of her father.

The Midrash explains the somewhat harsh words that God spoke to Moses by drawing a parallel towards Moses's harsh words earlier to the Levites.

> The verse states:[21] "Rav lachem (you have taken too much upon you) sons of Levi." The Holy One said to Moses: You have struck them with a staff and you yourself will be struck with that same staff. You said "rav lachem" and in the future you will hear "rav lach."[22]

In Deuteronomy it says: "And the Lord said to me, let it suffice you (*rav lach*)."[23] God did not want Moses to speak to Him anymore about letting him enter the Promised Land. Note the symmetry of words.

As if the *Book of Esther* were not already chock full of measure-for-measure payback and punishment, the Midrash has God applying an appropriate punishment to Haman for all eternity. Here, Haman criticizes the Jewish people for wasting the resources of society by having too many holidays centered around lavish feasts.

> *Haman criticizes the Jewish people to King Ahasuerus: Once every seven days they have a Sabbath; every thirty days* Rosh Chodesh[24]; *in the month of Nissan they have Passover; in the month of Sivan, they have Shevuout; in the month of Tishri, they have Rosh Hashanah and Yom Kippur, and Sukkot . . . The Holy One said: Wicked one, you cast an evil eye on their festivals. I will topple you before them and they will celebrate an additional festival to commemorate your downfall, namely the days of Purim. This is what is meant by the verse:[25] "A fool's mouth is his ruin."[26]*

Again we see a measure-for-measure punishment. Haman complained that the Jewish people celebrated too many holidays so he became the cause of yet another Jewish holiday, Purim.

When Individuals Inadvertently Bring About Their Own Destinies

In the following passage, a royal princess attempts to belittle God using the words of the Holy Scriptures. In a turnabout, she is instead foiled by her own words:

> *The daughter of the emperor once said to Rabbi Yehoshua b. Chananiah: Your god is a carpenter since it is written,[27] "He lays the beams of His upper chambers with water." Tell Him to make me a spool. Rabbi Yehoshua said: Very well. He prayed on her behalf and she was afflicted with leprosy. She was taken to the open square of Rome and given a spool, since their custom was that anyone afflicted with leprosy was given a spool and removed to the open square and given skeins to wind and unwind so that passersby would see the victim and pray for their recovery. One day, Rabbi Yehoshua passed by and saw her sitting and winding and unwinding skeins on the spool in the square. He said to her: Are you satisfied with the spool my God gave you. She said: Tell your God to take back what he has given me. He replied: My God gives but does not take back.[28]*

This story uses irony to illustrate the danger of mocking God and Jewish Scripture and, incidentally, cautions us to be careful what we ask for.

The following story explains how a precious reward came into the hands of the aptly named Joseph-who-honors-the-Sabbath (*Yosef makir Shabbat*), and is also an example of a type of story depicting an individual who tries to escape his fate, but instead merely serves to carry out that fate:

> Joseph-who-honors-the-Sabbath had a certain gentile in his neighborhood who owned much property. A soothsayer told this neighbor that all his wealth would eventually be consumed by Joseph-who-honors-the-Sabbath. He went and sold all of his assets and purchased a large diamond, which he set in his headdress. Once, while he was crossing a bridge, the wind blew his headdress into the water and a fish swallowed it. Subsequently, the fish was caught and brought to the marketplace late on a late Friday afternoon. The fishermen asked: Who will buy the fish now? They were told to take it to Joseph-who-honors-the-Sabbath who is accustomed to buying fish in honor of the Sabbath. They brought him the fish and he bought it. When he cut open the fish, he discovered the diamond and sold it for thirteen roomfuls of gold dinarim. [29]

The "thirteen roomfuls" is Talmudic hyperbole. The moral lesson of this story is that one who spends lavishly in honoring the Sabbath will be repaid by the Sabbath. In this story, we see once again that the principle of measure for measure works for reward as well as punishment.

In another example of an individual who sealed his own fate with his own words, Rava visits Bar Sheshak, a highly placed gentile officer whom he took to be his friend:

> Rava sent a present to Bar Sheshak on a pagan festival, saying: I know that he does not worship idols. He visited him and found him sitting up to his neck in a bath of rose water with naked prostitutes standing by him. Bar Sheshak said: Do you Jews have anything that compares to this in the world to come (Paradise)? Rava answered: Ours is better than this. He said: What can be better than this? Rava responded: You have the fear of the state on you, we will not have the fear of the state upon us. Bar Sheshak said: What fear have I of the state? While they were sitting, a messenger of the king arrived saying: Rise, the king wants you. When Bar Sheshak was leaving, he exclaimed to Rava: May the eye of anyone who wishes you evil burst. Rava responded amen and the eye of Bar Sheshak burst. [30]

This incident illustrates that the only true rewards for living a spiritual life are in the after-world, not this world and that, furthermore, heathens cannot be trusted. This is not surprising given that Judaism is diametrically opposed to paganism and hedonism.

Self-Deprecating Humor

The Rabbi was praying fervently, raising his voice to the heavens. "Oh Lord, I know I am nothing!"

The Cantor joined him "I, too, Lord, am nothing."

Not to be outdone, the Shammes[31] *cried heavenward, "Lord, I am nothing!"*

Whereupon the Cantor rolled his eyes, nudged the Rabbi and, in a stage whisper, exclaimed, "Look who says he's nothing!"

The rabbis of the Talmud were not only sarcastic when dealing with heretics and nonbelievers - and each other - but they could also mock themselves. In the next selection we see that the sages could even refer to themselves as donkeys when compared with the scholars of the past.

> *If the ancient scholars were sons of angels, then we are sons of men; if they are sons of men, then we are sons of donkeys—and not the donkeys of Rabbi Chaninah b. Dosa and Rabbi Pinchas b. Yair, but ordinary donkeys.*[32]

Rabbi Chaninah's donkey was once stolen and refused to eat from the fodder provided by the robbers. The donkey of Rabbi Pinchas b. Yair would not eat untithed produce. This saying is similar to the statement of Rabbi Yishmael b. Yosi:

> *Just as there is a difference between gold and dirt, so too is the difference between our generation and the generation of my father.*[33]

Rabbi Yannai's last request of his sons is quite funny.

> *My sons, do not bury me in white shrouds or black shrouds. White, because I may not merit being with the righteous in Paradise and I will be as a groom among mourners. Black, because I may merit and I will be as a mourner among grooms. Rather, bury me in olayrin.*[34]

Olayrin is a gray robe. Rabbi Yannai not only had a great sense of humor, but was quite humble too.

> *Rabbi Yishmael b. Yosi once visited the home of Rabbi Shimon b. Yosi b. Lakunia. He was given a cup of wine. He took it and drank it in one shot. They said to him: Do you not agree with the statement, "One who drinks his cup in one shot is a glutton?" He responded: This was not said when your goblet is small, your wine is sweet, and my stomach is immense.*[35]

Rabbi Yishmael b. Yosi did have a huge stomach and he had no problem making fun of himself.

The following is a piece of advice from Rabbi Akiva:

> *Do not dwell in a town whose leaders are scholars.*[36]

Scholars are not good at running a town. Rabbi Akiva was himself a great scholar. His greatest blunder was in believing that Bar Kochba was the Messiah.

> *Our Rabbis taught: There are three types whose life is not a life, they are: the overly compassionate, the hot tempered, and the overly delicate. Rabbi Yosef stated: All of the above can be found in me.*[37]

Rabbi Yosef seemed to have the ability to make fun of himself and exaggerate his weaknesses.

The Babylonian scholars were known for getting into heated debates when arguing points of Jewish law. They also could make fun of themselves.

> *Three hate each other: Dogs, roosters, and sorcerers. Some say, also prostitutes and some say also the scholars of Babylon.*[38]

Community service is often considered to be a thankless endeavor, as confirmed in the following:

> *Rabbi Elazar was the charity administrator. Once he came home and asked his family: What did you do today? They said: A group of people came and they ate, drank, and offered prayers on your behalf. Rabbi Elazar said: This is not the proper thanks for me. On another occasion, he came to the house and asked: What did you do today? They said: A group of people came and they ate, drank, and cursed you out. He said: This is the proper thanks for me.*[39]

One should not expect to be thanked for community work; on the contrary, one should expect to be insulted.

The following episode follows a discussion of the importance of asking the pardon of individuals that one has wronged, especially before the Day of Atonement.

> *Rabbi Abba was upset with Rabbi Yirmiyah, so Rabbi Yirmiyah decided to go and placate him. He sat by Rabbi Abba's door and when the maid went to throw out the waste water some of it spilled on his head. Rabbi Yirmiyah declared: I have been made into a dung-heap. He applied the following verse[40] to himself: "From the dunghills He lifts up the needy." Rabbi Abba heard him and came out and said: Now I have to go and appease you, as it is written,[41] "Go humble yourself and importune your friend."[42]*

Rabbi Yirmiyah does not seem to have lost his sense of humor even in the most degrading of situations.

The next story illustrates Ulla's principle that one should not allow someone who can teach the four orders of the Mishna to serve him.

> *Resh Lakish was once travelling on the road and came to a pool of water. A man came, carried him on his shoulders, and started to cross with him. Resh Lakish asked him: Did you read the Bible? He replied: I did. Resh Lakish said: Did you learn Mishna? He replied: I can teach the four orders of Mishna. Resh Lakish said to him: You have sculpted out four mountains and you carry Resh Lakish on your shoulders? Throw the son of Lakisha into the water.[43]*

Despite the fact that Resh Lakish was one of the great scholars of his generation, he did not want any learned person to demean himself by serving him.

> *Rava stated: Three things I prayed for from Heaven, two were granted to me and one was not. The wisdom of Rabbi Huna and the wealth of Rabbi Chisda were granted to me, but the modesty of Rabbah b. Huna was not.[44]*

Apparently not.

Definitely Not Self-Deprecating

A *Tanna*[45] stated:

> *With the death of Ben Azzai, the trait of diligence disappeared. With the death of Ben Zoma, the art of lecturing disappeared ... With the death of Rebbi, the traits of humility and fear of Heaven disappeared.*

> *Rabbi Yosef said to the* Tanna: *Do not include humility, because there is still me.*[46]

It is not clear whether or not Rabbi Yosef was joking. In actuality, he was quite modest and was not afraid of publicly admitting that "my former statement was incorrect" when he made a mistake.[47]

> *Ben Azzai said: All the sages of Israel compared to me are like the peel of garlic except for this bald one.*[48]

Ben Azzai, known for his brilliance and diligence, was jokingly saying that the only sage of superior wisdom was Rabbi Akiva, who was bald.

A poor man came to America from the old country to find—to his great dismay—that the streets were not paved with gold. Like many of his ilk he became a peddler. When he heard about an opening for a shammes[49] in a small synagogue on Attorney Street, he immediately applied for the position.

"Can you read and write English?" asked the shul president.

"No," replied the peddler.

The president stood up in a huff. "In America, a shammes must be able to read and write. New York is not Boiberik, you know."

So the poor man sighed and went sadly away.

Over the course of time, the peddler began to prosper. He got into real estate and amassed a fortune. One day he needed a large loan to finance a real estate venture; the bank manager was very accommodating. "No problem," he said. "Just fill out this application and the money is yours."

"I—I can't write," stammered the realtor.

"Wow," said the bank manager. "If you have accomplished so much without knowing how to read or write, imagine what you would be today if you did know how!"

"Sure," muttered the former peddler. "I'd be the shammes of the Attorney Street Synagogue!"[50]

9

Sarcasm

It's Sunday, and two beggars are sitting on the pavement on either side of a large church. One holds a large cross while the other wears large Magen David (the Jewish star of David) on a chain around his neck. The churchgoers pass by, generally ignoring the beggar with the star of David, dropping some coins into the cup held by the other beggar.

A kindly priest approaches and, trying to be helpful, he turns to the guy with the star of David and says, "Don't you realize that this is a Christian house of worship? If you want to raise some money you should probably either hide that star of David or go collect elsewhere."

The beggar with the Magen David *turns to the one holding the cross, shrugs, and says, "Hey, Izzy! Look who's trying to teach us business."*

Many Jewish jokes make use of sarcasm. Rabbis can be sarcastic, as can schnorrers. Jewish mothers are always sarcastic. But the quintessential character to populate this type of humor is probably the Jewish waiter.

Customer: Excuse me, do you have a menu?
Waiter: Menu? You want to read, go to the library.

The Jewish waiter in these jokes is snide, sarcastic, and often puts the customer in his place. The Jewish waiter does not believe that, just because he serves his customers, they are superior to him. Superiority in Judaism is derived more from intelligence and wit than from social status. *Schnorrer* jokes have some of this element as well.

Sarcasm, humor that takes on a mocking, contemptuous tone is often a form of heavy verbal irony, that is, saying one thing and meaning another. Sarcasm is a powerful tool that can be used to devastate one's religious opponents, heretics, or just plain smart alecks. Sarcastic retorts can also be directed at friends who might enjoy a good quip or even, reflexively, towards the speaker himself when it becomes a self-mocking, self-deprecating type of humor. Even the Bible, as noted in an earlier chapter, has several good examples of sarcasm, as in the complaint of Dathan and Aviram to Moses[1]: "Is it but a small thing that you have brought us up out of (Egypt), a land flowing with milk and honey, to kill us in the wilderness, but you also have to lord it over us?"

If the Torah can employ sarcasm, the Talmud can certainly use this device. For example:

> The verse states[2]: "Hear this word, Oh cows of Bashan that are on the mountain of Samaria, who oppress the poor, that crush the needy, and that say to their lords, Bring that we may drink." Rava said: Such are the women of Machuza who eat without working.[3]

The prophet Amos sarcastically referred to the Israelite women of his time as "cows of Bashan," meaning they were as fat and beautiful as the cows that grazed on the rich pastureland of Bashan. He was angry particularly at the married women because he felt that their extravagant demands caused their husbands to become dishonest. Rava felt the same about the women of his town, Machuza. Rava felt that the women's extremely lavish lifestyle, without working themselves, encouraged their husbands to become dishonest.

It is interesting to note that in the Talmud some of the sharpest minds had the most mundane occupations, ranging from blacksmith to shoemaker. Work was never looked down upon. Regarding Rabbi Gamliel, who himself served the guests at his son's wedding, Rabbi Yehoshua said:

> We find even a greater man than Rabbi Gamliel that served. Abraham was the greatest of his generation, and it is written[4]: "And he stood over them . . ."[5]

In the Talmudic and Midrashic literature, we find numerous examples of sarcasm, and only relatively few selections are cited here. There are, for example, a large number of instances of sarcastic retorts directed at nonbelievers, heretics and other enemies of the Jewish people, boors, the ill mannered, and those who ask silly questions. The Babylonian sages were known for their sarcasm towards each other, and the Jerusalem sages had some sarcastic remarks to make about their Babylonian counterparts.

One Midrash examines the conversation between Balaam and his donkey. Apparently, even animals could come up with sarcastic retorts. This conversation took place when Balaam, who had a reputation for possessing supernatural powers, was hired by Balak, King of Moab, to curse the Jewish people. In the Torah verses, Balaam's donkey refused to budge when she saw an angel with a drawn sword blocking their path. Balaam got angry and started beating his donkey with a stick. God gave the donkey the power to speak and it asked Balaam: "What have I done to you that you have beat me these three times?" Balaam replied to his donkey: "Because you have mocked me. Had I a sword in my hand just now, I would have killed you." Whereupon the donkey said to Balaam: "Am I not your donkey upon which you have been riding all your life. Was I ever in the habit of doing this to you?"[6] In the Midrash, this conversation continues thus:

> This is what the donkey said to Balaam: You cannot kill me unless you have a sword in your hand. How then do you intend to eradicate an entire nation (with your curse)? Balaam was silent and unable to answer her.

> The Holy One had consideration for the dignity of mankind and knows what is best for them. He therefore muted the mouth of the beast. For had animals been able to speak, man would have been unable to work them or to stand up to them. Here was the dumbest of all animals, and Balaam was the wisest of all wise men, and yet as soon as the donkey began to speak he could not stand up to her.[7]

Balaam, a prophet with the gift of speaking to God, is made to look like a fool before his donkey who suddenly becomes superior to his master in intellect and supernatural powers. The reason for this is that God was displeased with Balaam's decision to accompany Balak's Moabite emissaries without notifying them that he was instructed by God not to curse the Israelites. It is also quite likely that Balaam had intentions to curse the Israelites, despite God's instructions to only speak what he was told by the Almighty.

In another reference to a Biblical conversation, the Midrash has Pharaoh sarcastically likening Moses and Aaron to those who, to use a modern cliché, might bring sand into the Sahara. Moses and Aaron did not impress Pharaoh with the sign that God told them to use; namely, turning the staff into a serpent.[8]

> At that moment, Pharaoh began to laugh at Moses and Aaron and cackle like a chicken at them saying: Are these the signs of your God. Normally, people bring merchandise into an area which has a shortage of them. Does one import fish brine into Apamea or fish into Acco? Do you not know that all types of magic are within my territory?[9]

151

Apamea and Acco were known as places replete with fish. Similarly, Egypt was the center of magic in the ancient world and, so, bringing magic into ancient Egypt was indeed equivalent to bringing sand to the Sahara.

Toward Heretics and Nonbelievers

Two friends, one a Jew and one Catholic, Are engaged in a discussion.

The Jew asks his friend: "A priest who gets a promotion, what is he now, a Bishop?"

Catholic: "Yep."

"And then?"

"If he's already a Bishop? Then he might become a Cardinal."

"And after that, what? Pope?"

"Um, yeah."

"And then?"

"Whaddaya mean then? There is no then."

"After Pope, then what?"

"What? So you want him to become God?"

"Why not?" says the Jew. "One of our boys made it!"

The Talmudic sages were frequently harassed by heretics and other nonbelievers who would try to best them. A sharp, biting sarcastic retort was often the outcome. The sages needed to know how to deal effectively with all types of disbelievers, especially those that went out of their way to mock Jewish beliefs.

Bruriah, the renowned scholarly wife of Rabbi Meir, could be quite sarcastic, especially when asked to answer a foolish question posed by a Sadducee. The Sadducees were a sect of Jews who only believed in the written law expressly stated in the Torah and refused to accept the oral law. They would, for example, literally sit in the dark all through the Sabbath, rather than leaving a lamp on, because of the verse, "You shall kindle no fire . . ."[10]

> *A certain Sadducee said to Bruriah: It is written,[11] "Sing you barren woman that has not borne." Because she did not give birth, should she rejoice? She replied: Fool, look at the end of the verse, where it is written, "For the children of the desolate one shall be more than the children of the married wife, says the Lord." What then is the meaning of "Sing you barren woman that has not borne?" Rejoice, Jewish people, who*

are compared to a barren woman, for not having borne children like you who are destined for Hell.[12]

In answering the Sadducee, Bruriah instructed him to continue to the end of the verse in question. At first, Isaiah compared Jerusalem to a barren woman, its inhabitants having been sent into exile. However, after the Jewish people return, Jerusalem will no longer be barren and she will be able to rejoice once again. Bruriah added the sarcastic remark that women who are barren rejoice when they do not have to give birth to a wicked son who is destined for Hell, to show her displeasure with the Sadducees.

In the next selection we see Rabbi Yehoshua ben Karchah verbally sparring with a eunuch, who was clearly an opponent of the Talmudic sages. Rabbi Yehoshua was bald and his family name, Karchah, also meant baldness. Here Rabbi Yehoshua engages in sarcastic repartee to respond to the nasty remarks of a heretical eunuch.

> *A certain eunuch asked Rabbi Yehoshua b. Karchah: How far is it from here to Baldtown? He responded: As far as it is from here to Eunuchtown.*
>
> *The eunuch said: A bald goat is worth four (dinars). Rabbi Yehoshua responded: A castrated lamb is worth eight.*
>
> *The eunuch, noticing that Rabbi Yehoshua was not wearing shoes, said: One who is on a horse is a king, on a donkey a free man, and one with shoes on his feet is human. As for one who has none of these things, a dead and buried person is better off than he. Rabbi Yehoshua replied: Eunuch, Eunuch, you told me three things and now you will hear three things. The majesty of the face is the beard, the happiness of one's heart is a woman, and "The heritage of the Lord is children."*[13] *Blessed be the Lord who has cut you off from all of these.*[14]

Rabbi Yehoshua b. Chananiah was known as a sage who could communicate effectively with all types of people. He himself once pointed out that in his entire life only three got the best of him: a woman, a little boy, and a little girl.[15]

> *A certain Sadducee once said to Rabbi Yehoshua b. Chananiah: You are a thorn, since it is written,*[16] *"The best of them is like a thorn." Rabbi Yehoshua responded: Fool, look at the end of the verse where it is written: ". . . the most upright is more than a thorn hedge . . ." Just as a thorn protects a gap (in a fence), so too the good ones among us protect us.*[17]

Similarly, here is how Rabbi Abuhu hoisted a heretic by his own petard.

> *A certain heretic whose name was Sasson said to Rabbi Abuhu: In the future, in the world-to-come (the Messianic age), you will draw water for me since it is written*[18]: *"You shall draw water for joy (sasson)..."*

The verse in question actually says *be-sasson*, in joy, as Rabbi Abuhu correctly points out, along with a pointed remark he just couldn't resist, as follows.

> *...Rabbi Abuhu responded: If it had been written "for joy" (le-sasson), it would be as you say. But since it is written "in joy" (be-sasson), this means that your skin will be made into a canteen which we will fill with water.*[19]

Clearly, the heretic knew that the verse did not refer to himself. Rabbi Abuhu demonstrated that he too could distort the verse, but to make fun of the heretic.

Certainly, Rabbi Gamliel, as *Nasi*, the President of the Sanhedrin, had to be sharp enough to respond to many different types of individuals. The next four stories demonstrate how Rabbi Gamliel dealt with heretics and nonbelievers. Apparently, the heretics caused the Jewish people a great deal of trouble because Rabbi Gamliel assigned the task of adding to the *Amidah* prayer a nineteenth benediction relating to heretics (*minim*) and slanderers to Rabbi Samuel the Lesser (*Shmuel Hakaton*). This benediction is still said today: "May the slanderers have no hope; and may all the heretics perish instantly..."[20]

> *A heretic once said to Rabbi Gamliel: I know what your God is doing. Rabbi Gamliel became faint and sighed. The heretic said to him: Why are you so upset? He said: I have a son overseas and I long for him. Please describe to me what he is doing. He replied: Do I know where he is? Rabbi Gamliel retorted: You do not know what is happening on the earth, and yet claim to know what is happening in Heaven!*

Similarly

> *A heretic once said to Rabbi Gamliel: I know the number of stars. Rabbi Gamliel said to him: How many teeth do you have? The heretic put his hand to his mouth and started counting. Rabbi Gamliel said: You do not even know what is in your mouth. Do you know what is in Heaven?*[21]

The sect to which the heretic or heretics in the above two stories belonged is impossible to determine. They do not appear to have been early Christians or Sadducees since they seem to be mocking the idea of a God residing in Heaven, a belief shared by Jews and Christians.

> *A heretic once said to Rabbi Gamliel: You Jews claim that the Divine Presence rests on every gathering of ten people. How many Divine Presences are there then? Rabbi Gamliel summoned the heretic's servant, tapped him on the neck and said: Why did you allow the sunlight to enter into your master's house? The heretic said: But the sun shines upon the whole world! Rabbi Gamliel then said: If the sun, which is but only one of thousands upon thousand upon myriads of the Holy One's servants, shines on the whole world, how much more so should the Divine Presence of the Holy One Himself be able to rest on many places simultaneously.*[22]

The idea of a *minyan* (ten Jewish males older than the age of thirteen, the minimum number required for congregational prayer) is Jewish, and based on oral tradition. This heretic could have been a Sadducee or pagan mocking this concept.

Rabbi Gamliel even had wiseacres challenging him in the bathhouse.

> *Proclos, son of Philosophos, asked Rabbi Gamliel in Acco, while he was bathing in the bathhouse of Aphrodite, the following: It is written in your Torah,*[23] *"Nothing that has been declared taboo should cleave to your hands . . ."*

In other words, one is not permitted to benefit from idols or, in this case, as Proclos continues, from the bathhouses dedicated to them.

> *. . . Why are you then bathing in the bathhouse of Aphrodite? Rabbi Gamliel replied: It is forbidden to answer Torah questions in a bathhouse. When Rabbi Gamliel came out he answered: I did not come into Aphrodite's boundary, she came into my boundary. People do not say let us make a bathhouse as an adornment for Aphrodite but say let us make Aphrodite as an adornment for the bathhouse. Furthermore, even if you were given a great deal of money you would not appear before your idol naked and after having experienced a nocturnal emission; neither would you urinate before it. This one stands by a gutter and all urinate before it. It says in the Torah "their gods"—one is not permitted to benefit from that which is treated as a god, that which is not treated as a god is permitted.*[24]

Proclos seems to have read the Torah and even knew a bit of the oral law. Rabbi Gamliel's clever response was serious and quite to the point.

Here is how the sage Amemar used humor to refute a Zoroastrian priest who believed in the concept of two deities—Hormiz, the Good Spirit and Ahriman, the Evil Spirit—constantly at war.

> *A Magus once said to Amemar: The top half of my body belongs to Hormiz and the bottom half of my body belongs to Ahriman. Amemar asked: Why then does Ahriman allow Hormiz to pass water through his territory?*[25]

Turnus Rufus, a Roman governor of Judea, once asked Rabbi Akiva:

> *Why is the day of Sabbath different from the other days of the week? Rabbi Akiva replied: Why is a person like you different than others (i.e., commoners)? Because my Lord desires it so, Turnus Rufus replied. The Sabbath likewise is distinguished because my Lord desires it so, Rabbi Akiva responded. He then said, this is what I meant to ask: How do you know this day is indeed the Sabbath. Rabbi Akiva answered: This can be proven from: the River Sabbateon; the necromancer; and your father's grave from which no smoke ascends on the Sabbath. Turnus Rufus said to Rabbi Akiva: You have disgraced, humiliated, and vilified him.*[26]

The River Sabbateon is said to be turbulent all week and quiet on the Sabbath. The necromancer could not work his magic on the Sabbath. Hell rests on the Sabbath and therefore, according to Rabbi Akiva, no smoke came from Turnus Rufus's father's grave on the Sabbath. During the rest of the week, however, he was being punished in the fires of Hell, hence the smoke. Turnus Rufus's wife tried to get even with Rabbi Akiva by seducing him. Her plot boomeranged. Not only did she not succeed in seducing him but she converted to Judaism and eventually married Rabbi Akiva.[27]

Another example is the case of Geviha b. Pesisa, who was a hunchback. When his deformity became the object of a verbal sally, he was ready with a fast retort.

> *A heretic once said to Geviha b. Pesisa: Woe to you wicked ones that say that the dead will be resurrected. If even the living die, then can one expect the dead to live? Geviha said: Woe to you wicked ones that say the dead will not be resurrected. If those that never existed now live, those that once lived will surely live again.*

The heretic exclaimed: You have called me wicked. If I get up and kick you I could straighten out your hunchback. Geviha replied: If you could do that you would be called a great physician and could command huge fees.[28]

The concept of resurrection was obviously important to Judaism. The Talmud declared that one who did not believe that the doctrine of resurrection was Biblical had no share in the world to come.[29] Note that belief in resurrection was not sufficient. One also had to believe that it was implied in the Torah. The Sadducees and the Samaritans were two heretical groups that did not believe in resurrection.

Geviha's retort could be considered to be the forerunner of the following classic Jewish joke.

An old Jew from a small Polish town was on his way to Warsaw. Opposite him in the train sat a Jew-hating "Pilsudski Colonel" with his dog. The officer openly showed his contempt for the old Jew. Whenever he spoke to his dog he called him "Yankel." At first the Jew said nothing but, finally, it got under his skin.

"What a pity that the poor dog has a Jewish name!" he muttered.

"How so?" asked the Colonel.

"With such a name as 'Yankel' he just has no chance!" replied the Jew. "It's a real handicap. Without it—who knows? He could even become a colonel in Pilsudski's army!"[30]

In the following, the philosopher challenging Rabbi Hosaiah was clearly a heretic. He was basically asking, why was Adam, the first man, not *born* circumcised?

A philosopher asked Rabbi Hosaiah: If circumcision is so precious to your Lord, why was it not given to Adam? Rabbi Hosaiah answered: According to your reasoning, why do you shave the hair of the corners of your head (with which you were born) but leave your beard intact? The philosopher said: Because the hair on my head has grown with me since the days of my foolish youth. Rabbi Hosaiah said: If so, you should blind your eyes, cut off your hands, and break your legs since they have also grown along with you since the days of your foolish youth. The philosopher exclaimed: To such a ridiculous rejoinder must you resort? Rabbi Hosaiah replied: I cannot dismiss you without a proper answer. The answer is that whatever was created during the first six days of creation needs further preparation: mustard needs sweetening, lupines need sweetening, wheat needs grinding, and even man needs improvement.[31]

Abraham, who was born 1,948 years after Adam, was the first person given the commandment of circumcision.

The next selection deals with an evil butcher who pretended to be observant but deceptively served his customers unkosher meats.

> There is a story of a butcher who lived in Sepphoris who caused his Jewish customers to eat unkosher meat. One Friday he drank wine, went up to his roof, fell off and died. The dogs began to lap up his blood. Rabbi Chaninah was asked: Are we allowed to remove the body (since the Sabbath had already started)? He responded: Leave it. It is written "Do not eat flesh that is torn by predators in the field. You shall cast it to the dogs. . . ."[32] He was stealing from the dogs and feeding it to the Jewish people. Therefore, leave the dogs alone since they are only eating what is rightfully theirs.[33]

It should be noted that Jewish law requires that the body of the deceased be treated with the greatest of dignity. For instance, the corpse must be watched in order to ensure that mice do not mutilate the body. Jewish law also prohibits taking part of a corpse and turning it into a vessel. This passage also has strong elements of irony, in addition to the obvious sarcasm. It is interesting to note that the verse in question, "You shall cast it to the dogs" plays a major role in a classic Jewish joke, included in Chapter 14 that ends with the punchline, "The dog is a machmir."

Toward Ignoramuses, Boors, and the Ill-Mannered

The sages could be sarcastic and humorous with the ignoramuses. In their society, someone considered to be an ignoramus—an *am ha'aretz*—was not merely uneducated but actually hated knowledge and was often quite dangerous. The term *am ha'aretz* referred to a totally immoral person who despises Torah and ethical values.

> Rabbi Elazar stated: It is permitted to stab an am haaretz *even on Yom Kippur that falls on the Sabbath. His students said to him: Rabbi, say to slaughter him (ritually). He replied: Ritual slaughtering (of animals) requires a benediction, whereas this does not require a benediction.*[34]

This was obviously a sarcastic remark and was not meant to be taken seriously or literally.

To understand the next selection one must know a bit about the history of Rabbi Kahana. Rabbi Kahana left Babylonia for Israel after he killed an informer who refused to listen to Rabbi Kahana's teacher, Rav—who had ruled that he should not become an informer—and was about to put someone's life in danger. Rabbi Kahana was instructed by Rav not to dispute Jewish law with Rabbi Yochanan at the academy in Israel for seven years. When Rabbi Kahana arrived he was seated at the front of the academy because they expected great wisdom from him. When they saw that he did not say anything, they moved him all the way to the back, seven rows back. Rabbi Kahana decided to consider the seven rows as seven years and began to debate Rabbi Yochanan. After a while, it became clear that he was brilliant and perhaps even more knowledgeable than the elderly Rabbi Yochanan, and Rabbi Kahana was moved back to the front and the cushions that Rabbi Yochanan was sitting on were pulled out from under him until he was sitting on the floor—probably, a symbolic way of indicating that someone else was more worthy of occupying the elevated seat of the grand teacher. Rabbi Kahana had a lip deformity from an old wound and when Rabbi Yochanan looked at Rabbi Kahana, he thought that he was impudently laughing at him. Rabbi Yochanan was deeply hurt and Rabbi Kahana immediately died. When Rabbi Yochanan found out that Rabbi Kahana had not been laughing at him but had a deformity, he went to the cave where they had placed the body of Rabbi Kahana and brought him back to life.[35]

> *Rabbi Kahana was a bright young person when he came to Israel. A boor saw him and snippily said: What is new in Heaven? He replied: I heard that your fate has been sealed. The boor died.*

> *Another boor encountered him and asked: What is new in Heaven? He replied: I heard that your fate has been sealed. The boor died.*

> *Rabbi Kahana thought to himself: I came to Israel for good purposes and I seem to be sinning. Did I come here to cause the death of Israelis? I must leave Israel and return to where I came from.*

> *He went to Rabbi Yochanan and asked him: A person whose mother humiliates him and his stepmother respects him, to which one should he go? Rabbi Yochanan said: He should go to the one that respects him.*

> *Rabbi Kahana then went and returned to Babylonia.*[36]

Israel is symbolized by the "mother" and Babylonia by the "stepmother." Rabbi Kahana realized that Rabbi Yochanan would not let him leave Israel if he had asked him a direct question.

> *Rava said: How foolish are some people who rise in deference to Torah scroll but do not rise out of respect for a great personage (that is, Torah scholar). In the Torah it is written "forty lashes," but the Rabbis came and decreased it by one.*[37]

The Talmudic sages interpreted the "forty lashes," mentioned in the Torah as a punishment for certain offenses, as "up to forty," that is, thirty-nine lashes. The full verse is: "Forty stripes he may give him, he shall not exceed."[38]

In the next selection, Rabbi Yehoshua makes a playful remark to someone who asks him a question which has no practical relevance to himself. The widow's son, who had no father, asked a seemingly serious question about how to honor both his parents. His questions were answered in kind.

> *A widow's son asked Rabbi Eliezer: If my father and mother both ask me for a glass of water at the same time, which one should I serve first? Rabbi Eliezer answered: Leave the honor due your mother and perform your obligation to your father first, since both you and your mother are obligated to honor your father. He then went to Rabbi Yehoshua who answered him the same. The widow's son then asked: Rabbi, if my parents are divorced what is the law? Rabbi Yehoshua responded: From your eyelids it can be seen that you are a widow's son. Pour water into a bowl for them and cackle to them as if they were chickens.*[39]

The orphan's crying had thinned out his eyelids. Rabbi Yehoshua was obviously trying to be humorous.

In ancient times, a scholar appointed as a judge and teacher would be assigned an individual to serve as an interpreter/announcer, an ancient (if literal) *loud*speaker. The sage would speak to his interpreter in a low voice with much or all of his lecture in Hebrew. The interpreter would expound to the audience in the language of the region (Aramaic). Here is how one such interpreter dealt with an incompetent judge and teacher.

An inept, but wealthy enough, man was appointed as a judge and teacher, and he was assigned Yehuda b. Nachmani as an interpreter. Yehuda bent down to hear what the new judge had to say to the public. The judge, however, did not know anything so he did not say anything to Yehuda. Yehuda then stood up and said to the public quoting the prophet Habbakuk[40]: "Woe unto him who says to wood, Awake! To the dumb stone, Arise! Can it teach? Behold it is overlaid with gold and silver and there no breath is within it."[41]

This verse is talking about idols made of wood and stone and covered with gold and silver. Yehuda used the verse to refer to an incompetent judge who got the job using a bribe of "gold and silver." Was he speaking in his own voice or acting as if he were simply transmitting the words of the so-called scholar? It is unclear. Either way, he got the job done.

A Scotsman and a Jew had a few drinks and hors d' oeuvres *in a rather expensive restaurant and the waiter presented them with a bill for $180.*

"I'll pay that," offered the Scotsman.

Newspaper headlines the next day read: "JEWISH VENTRILOQUIST FOUND DEAD IN ALLEY."[42]

This joke has virtually disappeared from recent collections of Jewish humor, possibly because the stereotype of Scots as stingy has virtually disappeared as well from popular culture. Today's youngsters do not even understand this joke without the added explanation that Scots were once upon a time subject to that bigoted ethnic slur. In a wonderful article, Christie Davies (1986) analyzes this and other examples of cross-ethnic humor. In the world of the Internet, this joke is famous for (very briefly) bringing down an Internet usenet, rec.humor.funny, on which it was posted on November 9, 1988 which, unfortunately, coincided with the 50th anniversary of Kristallnacht.[43] Interestingly, no one in that politically correct brouhaha seemed bothered by the ethnic bigotry against Scots in this joke, which to our sensibilities seems more egregious here. But, to continue:

Rabbi Akiva believed that good table manners were important. In the next selection we see that Rabbi Akiva could be sarcastic with individuals who displayed bad manners while eating. The Talmud believes that bread is a life-sustaining gift from God and must be treated with respect.

> *Rabbi Akiva was once staying with someone. The person took a piece of bread and leaned his plate against it. Rabbi Akiva snatched the bread and ate it. He said: Rabbi, you have no other piece of bread to eat except for the bread on which I am leaning my plate? Rabbi Akiva said: At first, I thought that you might be burned by tepid water, but now I realize that you are not even burned by boiling water.*[44]

At first Rabbi Akiva thought that a small hint would suffice that it is improper to treat bread in this manner but, apparently, that was too subtle—this individual could not take a hint.

And speaking of subtlety, something Jewish mothers think they excel at, we present the following:

A Jewish man phones his mother in Florida: "Mom, how are you?"

Mom: "Not so good. I'm very weak."

Son: "Why are you so weak?"

Mom: "Because I haven't eaten in 17 days."

Son: "Mom! Why haven't you eaten in 17 days!?"

Mom: "I didn't want my mouth to be full of food when you called."

This is somewhat similar to another well-worn joke in which a guest compliments his hostess "Your strudel is wonderful! It's so good, I just couldn't control myself; I ate two pieces." The hostess, nothing if not a template for a Jewish mother, replies, "You ate four, but who's counting?"

Toward Babylon and Babylonians

The sages living in Israel were wont to lambaste the Babylonians. Even the Babylonian scholars admitted that the "air of Israel makes one wise." The Talmud also notes that the "The scholars of Israel treated each other pleasantly and respectfully when debating law; the Babylonian scholars hurt each others feelings when debating."[45] The next two selections will show the disdain Rabbi Yirmiyah had for the scholarship of the Babylonians. He referred to Babylonia as a "dark land" either because of its low altitude[46] or because the Zoroastrians (fire-worshippers) did not allow the Jews to have any light during their festivals.[47]

> *Rabbi Yirmiyah remarked: The Babylonian fools, because they dwell in a dark land they express dark legal opinions.*[48]

Rabbi Yirmiyah felt that the Babylonian scholars would provide dubious explanations for various laws if they did not know the real reason. Furthermore:

> *It is written*[49]: *"He made me dwell in darkness like the eternally dead." Rabbi Yirmiyah said: This refers to the learning of the Babylonians.*[50]

The Babylonians were not pleasant to each other when debating, and Rabbi Yirmiyah preferred the Israeli style of argumentation. Rabbi Yirmiyah felt that all this bickering and competitiveness meant that the Babylonian opinions were not as well thought out and conclusive ("in darkness") as the Israeli ones.

It seems that the scholars of Babylon agreed with Rabbi Yirmiyah's assessment of them. Indeed, Abaye remarked to Rava that one Israeli scholar was equal to two Babylonian scholars. Rava replied:

> When one of us goes to Israel he is better than two of the Israeli scholars. After all, when Rabbi Yirmiyah was here he did not know what the rabbis were talking about, but after he went up to Israel he called us Babylonian fools.[51]

Rabbi Yirmiyah's teacher, Rabbi Zera, also referred to the Babylonians as fools when discussing their diet.

> Those Babylonians are fools, they eat bread together with bread.[52]

The Babylonians ate bread with their *daisa*, a dish made of pounded grain, similar to grits. This might be analogous to someone today who liked to eat pizza with bread.

Rabbi Shimon b. Yochai was also not impressed with Babylonia as the following passage suggests.

> It is written[53]: And I lifted up mine eyes and saw, behold, two women were coming forth and the wind was in their wings, for they had wings like the wings of a stork. And they lifted up the measure between the earth and heaven. And then I said to the angel that spoke with me, "where are they taking the measure?" And he said to me, "to build her a house in the land of Shinar (Babylonia)." Rabbi Yochanan said in the name of Rabbi Shimon b. Yochai: These two women symbolize hypocrisy and superciliousness that settled down in Babylonia.[54]

Apparently, Rabbi Shimon b. Yochai, who lived in Israel, believed that many phonies and egotistical individuals lived in Babylonia. His interpretation of the above verses is a bit sensational and surprising.

Normally, kissing and escorting a traveler on the road would be considered a good thing. But not, apparently, in Babylonia.

> Rabbi Gidal said in the name of Rav: If a Narshean kisses you, count your teeth. If a Nehar Pekodean escorts you it is because of the nice garment you are wearing (that he is looking to steal). If a Pumbedisean escorts you, change your inn.[55]

The people from the above Babylonian towns were known for their dishonesty.

> *Ulla visited Babylonia and noticed clouds. He exclaimed: Remove the clothing since it is going to rain. When it did not rain he said: Just as the Babylonians are false so too is their rain.*[56]

Ulla was a scholar who traveled frequently between Israel and Babylon, possibly to collect funds to help the poor of Israel. He was quite sarcastic at times and did not appreciate the Babylonian ways, as the next selections show.

> *Ulla visited Babylonia and noticed that one could purchase a basketful of dates for one zuz. He remarked: A basketful of dates for a zuz and the Babylonians still do not occupy themselves with Torah.*
>
> *That night he was in great pain from the dates and declared: A basketful of knives for a zuz, and the Babylonians still occupy themselves with Torah?*[57]

Ulla seemed to have the same opinion of Babylonians as did Rabbi Shimon b. Yochai that many of them were hypocrites. In the next selection, for example, Ulla was also not impressed with the way mourners were comforted in Babylonia. However, it is debatable whether he did much better in that regard.

> *When Rabbi Shmuel b. Yehuda's daughter died, the Rabbis said to Ulla: Let us go and comfort him. Ulla replied: What have I to do with Babylonian consolation which is blasphemous, since you Babylonians say, "What could have been done?" This suggests that if you could have done something, you would have done it . . .*

Meaning, even if it is not the will of the Lord. The Talmud continues . . .

> *. . . Ulla went on his own to Rabbi Shmuel and said to him: It says,*[58] *"Distress not the Moabites and do not provoke them to fight." Why would Moses decide to start a war without the Lord's permission? The answer is that Moses, on his own, deduced the following a fortiori. If in the case of the Midianites who only came to help the Moabites, the Torah says*[59]: *"Distress the Midianites and smite them." In the case of the Moabites themselves, all the more so. However, the Holy One told Moses: What you are thinking is not what I am thinking. Two fine doves do I expect to bring forth from these nations, Ruth the Moabite and Naamah the Ammonite (therefore Moses was commanded not to harm these nations). Now, if for two fine doves the Lord had mercy on two large nations and did not destroy them—so the Rabbi's daughter, if she had been virtuous and worthy*

of having righteous offspring, all the more so would she have been spared.[60]

Somehow, it seems doubtful that Ulla was ever again invited to console mourners.

Sarcastic Retorts, One Sage to Another

The Talmudic sages, being sharp and quick-witted, often engaged in verbal sparring and one-upmanship with one another. Often, this repartee was good-natured teasing; sometimes, not so much.

Ulla, though quite adept with verbal repartee here gets a good tongue-lashing from Yalta, the brilliant wife of Rabbi Nachman.

> *Ulla happened to visit the house of Rabbi Nachman. They had a meal and Ulla said the grace after the meal. He handed the cup of benediction to Rabbi Nachman. Rabbi Nachman said to Ulla: Send the cup of benediction to my wife, Yalta. Ulla replied: Thus taught Rabbi Yochanan; the fruit of a woman's body is blessed only from the fruit of a man's body, since it says, "He will bless the fruit of thy body."*[61] *It does not state the "fruit of her body" but the "fruit of thy body . . ."*

Therefore, it would not be necessary to send the cup of benediction to the wife too if it has been given to the husband.

> *. . . Meanwhile, Yalta heard that Ulla did not wish to send her the cup of benediction. She rose in anger, went to the wine store, and broke four hundred barrels of wine. Rabbi Nachman said to Ulla: Send her another cup. Ulla sent her the cup with following message: All the wine from the jug can be used for the cup of benediction . . .*

Ulla, speaking of *halacha*, Jewish law, thought he could mollify Yalta by saying that another cup of wine from the jug can also be used as a cup of benediction if the original cup has already been drunk. Ulla's strategy was a bit off the mark.

> *. . . She sent back the following message to Ulla: Gossip comes from peddlers and lice from rags.*[62]

Yalta was referring to the fact that Ulla continually traveled between Israel and Babylon. She was implying that words that come from a vagabond such as Ulla are as the lice in old clothing, that is, worse than useless. Perhaps, she was also making fun of his clothing.

The next selection will show how sarcastic Ulla was to a fellow sage who was somewhat obsessed with ensuring that his son would marry a woman of proper lineage. In Judaism, there are various genealogical classes. For example, the priests are the highest class and foundlings and bastards among the lowest.

> *Ulla visited the house of Rabbi Yehuda in Pumbedita. He noticed that Rabbi Yitzchak the son of Rabbi Yehuda was unmarried. Ulla asked Rabbi Yehuda, Why did you not find a wife for your son? He answered, Who knows where I can find a genealogically suitable wife for my son? Ulla said: Do you know from whom you are descended? Perhaps, from those regarding whom it is written[63]: "They ravished women in Zion, maidens in the cities of Judah." And even if you wish to say that if an idolater or a slave rapes a Jewish woman, the resulting offspring are legitimate. Then, perhaps we are descended from those regarding whom it is written[64]: "Those who lie upon ivory beds and stretch out on their couches . . ." This verse was interpreted by Rabbi Abuhu as referring to the people (living in Israel prior to the Temple's destruction) who ate and drank together, attached their beds, swapped wives, and fouled their beds with semen that was not theirs.[65]*

In Jewish law, an unmarried woman having an affair will not produce a bastard; a bastard is produced when a married woman commits adultery. Ulla was essentially telling Rabbi Yehuda not to overdo it in trying to find a woman of proper lineage for his son, since he has no way of knowing whether he himself (or indeed anyone) may be a descendent of wife-swappers and he is thus a bastard.

At the end of his life, Ulla, so quick with a biting, pointed remark, waxed downright poetic when speaking of the land of Israel. He died in Babylonia, very upset that he did not merit to die in Israel. Those who were with him when he died tried to comfort him by assuring him that his body would be brought to Israel. Ulla was not consoled, exclaiming:

> *"How does this benefit me If I lose my precious jewel in this unclean land. There is no comparison between one who delivers up his soul in the bosom of his mother to one who delivers up his soul in the bosom of a stranger."[66]*

The following well-known sarcastic remark is used in the Talmud when scholars try to prove their argument by citing a case involving the behavior of someone acting abnormally.

> *One cannot adduce proof from a fool.[67]*

For instance, Rabbi Eliezer tried to prove his argument that writing by means of making scratches or incisions on one's body is considered writing. (This makes a difference with regard to the Sabbath.) His proof was that an individual by the name of Ben Stada smuggled witchcraft secrets out of Egypt by writing them on his body. The others did not accept this argument since one does not bring proof from fools.

Rebbi's equally terse comment regarding a question he was asked:

> *It seems to me that he has no brains in his head.*[68]

The next selection describes what happened when Karna was sent to examine Rav who was coming from Israel to settle in Babylonia. Rav apparently felt that Karna was being disrespectful by asking him so many different questions—for example, how do we know that circumcision must be performed on the male organ and not, say, the heart or ear? The word *karna* means "horn."

> *Rav asked him: What is your name? He answered: Karna. Rav said: May it be His will that a horn grows out of your eye. Eventually, a horn (probably a sty) grew out of Karna's eye.*[69]

Bruriah, the wife of Rabbi Meir, was one of the great scholars of the Talmud.

> *Rabbi Yosi of Galile was once going on the road and met Bruriah. He asked her: Which road do I take to the city of Lod. She responded: Foolish Galilean, did our sages not state*[70] *that "one should not gossip excessively with a woman." You should have asked: Which way to Lod?*[71]

It appears that Bruriah was teasing Rabbi Yosi.

Not all sages of the Talmud were experts in both homiletics (*aggada* and law (*halacha*). Some of the Talmudists were mainly experts in homiletics, and some in law.

> *Rabbi Simlai came to Rabbi Yonason and said to him: Teach me homiletics. He said to him (probably jokingly): I have a tradition from my ancestors that we should not teach homiletics to either a Babylonian or someone from the South (of Israel) since they are haughty in spirit and lacking in their knowledge of Torah; you are from Nehardea (in Babylonia) and live in the South.*[72]

The next story follows a discussion as to whether a group of people that have agreed to join together and share a meal have the right to change their minds and send away an individual who eats very quickly and more than his fair share. This is analogous to a modern dilemma when a group decides to split the dinner bill and one individual orders caviar and champagne.

> *Rabbi Pappa and Rabbi Huna b. Yehoshua decided to join and share their bread. However, by the time Rabbi Huna b. Yehoshua ate one piece, Rabbi Pappa ate four. Rabbi Huna said to Rabbi Pappa: Divide what's left with me . . .*

Meaning, I do not like this deal and want out.

> *. . . Rabbi Pappa said: You accepted me already . . .*

Meaning, it is too late and you cannot back out anymore. By the way, this is indeed Jewish law.

> *. . . Ultimately, Rabbi Huna was able to prove his point and they divided the remainder of the bread.*
>
> *Rabbi Huna then went to share his bread with Ravina. By the time Rabbi Huna b. Yehoshua ate one piece, Ravina ate eight pieces.*
>
> *Rabbi Huna then said: Rather a hundred Pappas but not one Ravina.*[73]

Sometimes you just cannot win.

There is a dispute in the Talmud as to whether a *sukkah* that is erected on the deck of a ship is valid or not. Rabbi Akiva allows it, but Rabbi Gamliel is of the opinion that it is not valid since the *sukkah*, a temporary structure, cannot stand up to the typically forceful sea winds. It happened that the two were traveling on a ship during the holiday of *Sukkoth* and Rabbi Akiva erected his *sukkah* on the deck. The next morning, the wind blew away the *sukkah*. Rabbi Gamliel, in a masterful stroke of subtlety, remarked:

> *Akiva! Where is your* sukkah?[74]

When it comes to verbal repartee, modern Jewish humor often seems to have learned from the sages of old. For example:

For twenty years the same customer visited a certain Jewish restaurant and, without fail, always ordered the chicken soup. In all that time he never once complained about the food or service.

One evening, when the waiter had served the soup, the customer called him back to the table.

"Waiter, taste this soup."

"Why, what's the matter with it?"

"Just taste it!"

"Listen, if it's too cold, it doesn't taste right, whatever—I'll just take it back and bring you another serving."

"Taste the soup!"

"Why should I taste it? You don't want it you don't want it. So I'll bring you a change. Why should I argue with a good customer?"

The customer, his face dark with fury, stood up. "For the last time," he shouted, "TASTE THE SOUP!"

Intimidated, the waiter sat down. "All right, if you insist." He looked around. "Where's the spoon?"

"Ah-HAH!" exploded the customer.[75]

We note that this is definitely not of the "Jewish waiter" genre of humor. The waiter here, anything but sarcastic, is trying to be accommodating. It is the customer who engages in sarcastic, almost Talmudic, one-upmanship.

> *Rabbi Nachman and Rabbi Yitzchak were sitting and eating a meal together. Rabbi Nachman said to Rabbi Yitzchak: Will the master please expound upon something. He replied to him: Thus stated Rabbi Yochanan, "One should not speak during a meal lest the trachea act before the esophagus and thereby put the person's life in jeopardy." After they concluded the meal, Rabbi Yitzchak said: Thus stated Rabbi Yochanan, "Jacob, our forefather, did not die." He said to him: Was it for nothing that the lamenters lamented, the embalmers embalmed, and the gravediggers dug?*[76]

In the original Aramaic, the rhyme of the words makes it clear that Rabbi Yitzchak is being teased.

> vechi bachdi safdu saftanya
>
> vachantu chantaya
>
> vakavru kavraya?

Rabbi Akiva's view that Shimon bar Kochba, here referred to as Bar Kozba, was the Messiah was not universally accepted as we see from the following.

When Rabbi Akiva saw Bar Kozba, he said that this is the King Messiah. Rabbi Yochanan b. Torasa told him: Akiva, there will be grass growing out of your jaw and the son of David will not yet have arrived.[77]

Unfortunately, Rabbi Akiva was wrong; Bar Kochba was not the Messiah and he was defeated by the Romans. Bar Kochba's revolt lasted from the year 132 to 135 CE.

Daisa, as noted earlier, was a dish made of pounded grain, similar to grits.

Rabbi Yosi and Rabbi Yehuda were both eating daisa *out of one plate. One ate it with his fingers and the other ate it with a thorn.*

The one who was eating with the thorn said to the other: How long will you feed me your filth . . .

Meaning, the dirt that collects under the fingernails.

. . . The one who was eating with his fingers said: How long will you feed me your saliva.[78]

Looks like they both could have used some cutlery.

Dosa b. Harkinas was upset with his brother for siding with the School of Shammai in a case dealing with levirate marriage. Dosa was a member of the Hillel School and ruled in accordance with them. He said, in verse:

I have a younger brother (ach katan*)*

who is the first born of Satan (bechor Satan*).*

*His name is Jonathan (*Yonatan*)*

and he is one of the disciples of Shammai.[79]

The Hebrew words for younger brother (*ach katan*), first born of Satan (*bechor Satan*), and Jonathan (*Yonatan*) rhyme.

Regarding one who does not engage in procreation, Ben Azzai stated: It is as though he sheds blood and diminishes the Divine image. They told Ben Azzai: Some preach well and act well; some act well but do not preach well; you, however preach well and do not act well. Ben Azzai told them: But what shall I do, my soul loves the Torah.[80]

Ben Azzai was either a bachelor or was very briefly married to Rabbi Akiva's daughter but divorced her. He was too busy with his studies and felt he could not dedicate enough time for marriage.

In the following, the *ketubah* in question is the amount specified in a prenuptial certificate which is to be paid to the bride in case of death or divorce.

> *Rav stated: If a husband says that he will not feed or support his wife he must divorce her and pay her* ketubah. *Rabbi Elazar went and reported this statement to Shmuel who exclaimed: Give Elazar barley to chew. Rather than forcing the husband to divorce her, we should compel him to feed her.*[81]

Barley was livestock feed in Babylon. Shmuel's statement is equivalent to telling someone to eat straw, that is, Elazar is a fool for accepting this opinion. Rav and Shmuel were prominent first generation *amoraim* (*see* Appendices B and C) and were born around 175–180 CE. They were close friends. The Talmud records many of their disputes regarding civil and ritual laws.

The next selection shows a somewhat sarcastic remark made by Rabbi Sheshet. The argument in the Talmud deals with the situation in which a man is taken captive and, thus, may or may not be dead, and whether or not the next of kin may enter the estate and take temporary possession. Rabbi Sheshet finds support for his opinion from a *baraita*[82] that states, "the children will desire to enter their (captive) father's estate and will not be allowed."

> *Rabbi Amram said to Rabbi Sheshet: Perhaps what is meant is that the children will not be allowed to enter and* sell *their captive father's estate? Rabbi Sheshet replied: Perhaps you are from Pumbedita where they thread an elephant through the eye of a needle?*[83]

The academy in Pumbedita was known as a place where they used much *pilpul* (dialectics) and hair-splitting logic, as opposed to the academy in Sura where they had a different approach to scholarship. Incidentally, Rabbi Amram was Rabbi Sheshet's pupil so this question was clearly rhetorical, as he was very well acquainted with Rabbi Amram.

If a judge makes an error in a law which is cited in a Mishna, the most authoritative aggregation of laws, the ruling is revoked. Ravina asked Rabbi Ashi:

Is this also true if a judge made an error regarding a ruling of Rabbi Chiya and Rabbi Oshaiah? . . .

That would be in the *tosefta*, a collection of Jewish laws which is less authoritative than the *Mishna*. Rabbi Ashi answered:

. . . Yes!

Even a ruling of Rav and Shmuel? . . .

That would be even less authoritative than a *tosefta* which is the opinion of *tannaim*. Rabbi Ashi answered:

. . . Yes!

Even a ruling of ours?

Rabbi Ashi said: Are we then but reed cutters in a swamp?[84]

Reed cutting must have been a job performed by those of the lowest socioeconomic groups in Babylonia. Today we might say: what are we, chopped liver?

Regarding the plague of the frogs,

Rabbi Akiva stated that there was one frog that multiplied and filled all of Egypt. Rabbi Elazar b. Azariah told him: Akiva, what are you doing near homiletics? Cease your homiletic interpretations and go concentrate on the laws of leprosy and tents.[85]

Rabbi Elazar was saying in a warm and witty way that Rabbi Akiva's method of study was not suitable for homiletics (*aggada*), and his method of analysis would result in incorrect conclusions. His brilliance would be better suited for the considerably more difficult areas of law (*halacha*) dealing with ritual impurity of corpses in tents and leprosy. The verse in Exodus states: "and the frogs emerged."[86] In this verse the Hebrew word for frogs is singular, referring collectively to a huge mass of frogs.

The ten tribes will never return to Israel . . . This is the opinion of Rabbi Akiva. Rabbah b. Bar Chana said in the name of Rabbi Yochanan: Rabbi Akiva has forsaken his love of the Jewish people.[87]

Rabbi Akiva was known for his great love of the Jewish people. Rabbi Akiva, however, did believe that the ten tribes that were driven out of Israel by the Assyrians would never return. They were driven out of

Israel approximately 2,600 years ago and were replaced by foreigners brought from other Assyrian territories. No one is sure what became of the ten lost tribes.[88]

The punishment for certain offenses is flogging, as noted above. There are other infractions for which the punishment is *karet* (spiritual excision). Most commentators believe that this Divine punishment involves premature death, death of children, and/or torment of the soul in the next world. There are a number of negative commandments in which the punishment is flogging if the crime was committed in front of witnesses; but if no witnesses were present, the punishment is *karet*, the Divine punishment. There is an argument on the Talmud as to whether one who commits a transgression in front of witnesses and receives a flogging is thereby exempted from the Divine punishment of *karet*. Rabbi Chananiah b. Gamliel's opinion is that if one receives a flogging (by the court), then he is absolved from *karet*.

> *Rabbi Adda b. Ahava said in the name of Rav that the* halacha *follows the opinion of Rabbi Chananiah b. Gamliel. Rabbi Yosef said: Who went up to Heaven and came back with this information?*[89]

Rabbi Yosef was annoyed by the fact that Rabbi Adda was so certain of his opinion that he used the word "*halacha.*" Indeed, it is inappropriate to use this word which refers to Jewish ritual law, not to how the world is run by the Lord.

> *Ben Damah, the son of Rabbi Yishmael's sister, asked Rabbi Yishmael: A person such as I, who has learned the whole Torah, am I allowed to study Greek wisdom? Rabbi Yishmael read to him the verse*[90]*: "This book of the Torah should not leave your mouth, but you should meditate in it day and night." Go and find a time that is neither day or night and study Greek wisdom.*[91]

Incidentally, it is not entirely clear what is meant by "Greek wisdom." It either refers to a certain elitist way of speaking Greek which the masses could not comprehend[92] or Greek philosophy. Ben Damah met an unfortunate end. He was bitten by a snake and Yaakov of Kefar Sekania, an early Christian-Jew, came to cure him but Rabbi Yishmael did not allow it. He died and Rabbi Yishmael said about him: "Happy are you Ben Damah, for your body is pure and your soul has also departed in purity, and you have not transgressed the words of your colleagues . . ."[93]

In the following, the *amora* of Rabbi Yochanan was the person whose job it was to stand at the side of the lecturer and expound and interpret what was said.

> The verse states[94]: *"And the eyes of Leah were* rakkot." *The* amora *of Rabbi Yochanan translated this before Rabbi Yochanan: And the eyes of Leah were weak . . .*

The *amora* interpreted the verse to mean that Leah's eyes were naturally weak. In what is probably—believe it or not—the earliest known example of "the dozens," Rabbi Yochanan retorts:

> *. . . Your mother's eyes were weak! . . .*

And explains:

> *. . . What does* rakkot *mean? Her eyes became weak from crying.*[95]

Rabbi Yochanan's interpretation was that Leah's eyes were not naturally weak but, rather, that Leah wept because people used to say that the eldest son of Rebecca—Esau—would marry the eldest daughter of Laban—Leah.

Sometimes, later sages have employed sarcastic humor in their commentaries. The most notable in this regard is probably Abraham Ibn Ezra, a major, medieval commentary on the Hebrew Bible. In his commentary on the verse "Leah's eyes were tender (*rakkot*), while Rachel was shapely and beautiful,"[96] Ibn Ezra cites the opinion of Ben Ephraim, who claims that the Hebrew word *rakkot* (tender) is simply missing the letter *aleph*, in which case the word would read *arukhot* (long). Ibn Ezra then succinctly states "*Af hu khaser aleph*," that the name Ben Ephraim is also missing an *aleph*. Take away the *aleph* from Ben Ephraim's name and you are left with Ben Parim, meaning son of oxen.

On the verse, "If the ox of a person strikes the ox of his friend . . ."[97] Ibn Ezra notes the explanation of Ben Zuta who says that the "friend" in the above verse refers to another ox. Ibn Ezra felt (correctly) that "friend" in the verse refers to a person, not an ox, and comments that the only friend an ox ever had is Ben Zuta.

Genesis states that Esau "ran towards Jacob, hugged him, fell on his neck, and kissed him."[98] In the Torah, there are dots on the Hebrew word meaning "and kissed him" (*vayeshakehu*). Ibn Ezra notes that the explanation offered to explain the dots—that Esau really had bad intentions and tried to bite Jacob's neck—is a good explanation "for someone who has just been weaned from the breast." Ibn Ezra generally goes with a more direct interpretation of the Torah text and saw no reason to interpret this verse as if Esau had intended to hurt Jacob. For someone who insisted on keeping his commentaries brief, supposedly for lack of ink, still he seems to find value in using wit to enhance his commentary.

Against Sarcasm

Although sarcasm was considered an appropriate response when dealing with a heretic or a boor, and even a standard mode of repartee between colleagues, the sages of the Talmud recognized that a cutting remark is sometimes uncalled for and could be quite hurtful.

In the next passage, King David is mocked and taunted by scholars in study for his sin with Bathsheba and for having her husband Uriah the Hittite sent to the front to be killed.[99] He takes his complaint to the Almighty, describing how he has gone ashen (blood would not flow) from repeated humiliations.

> Rava lectured: What is meant by the verse,[100] "But in my infirmity they rejoiced and gathered together—against me the crippled, and even those I knew not; they tore me, and did not desist." King David exclaimed before the Lord: Creator of the Universe, you know very well that had they torn my flesh, my blood would not flow. Moreover, when they are engaged in studying the laws regarding the four deaths carried out by the courts, they interrupt their studies and say to me: David, one who commits adultery, what type of death is he punished with? I told them: If one commits adultery the punishment is death by strangulation, but he has a share in the world to come (Paradise). However, one who humiliates another in public has no share in the world to come.[101]

So King David has a ready retort for them as well.

The Talmud teaches that a nasty remark made to an undeserving person is a great sin. Here, Rabbi Shimon is taught the importance of being nice to all and not to allow his superior knowledge and intellect to result in arrogant behavior.

> Once Rabbi Shimon b. Elazar was coming from the house of his teacher in Migdal Gedor. He was leisurely riding on his donkey by the shore and felt very jubilant and proud because he had studied much Torah.

He encountered a person who was exceptionally ugly, who said to him: Peace on you Rabbi.

Rabbi Shimon did not return the greeting and said: Empty one, how ugly you are. Are all the people of your town as ugly as you? He responded: I do not know, but go tell the Craftsman who created me, "How ugly is the vessel that You have made." Immediately, Rabbi Shimon realized that he sinned. He descended from the donkey and prostrated himself before the person saying I beg your pardon, please forgive me . . .[102]

Rabbi Shimon eventually did convince the man to forgive him. He used this experience to lecture on the importance of being "gentle as a reed and not as tough as a cedar tree."

Question: How many Jewish mothers does it take to change a lightbulb?
Answer: Zero. "(Sigh!) I'll just sit in the dark."

10

Exaggerated Imagery and Other Hyperbole

More Yiddish Curses

May the dybbuks of all King Solomon's mothers-in-law settle in your mother-in-law and may they all nag you at the same time.

May you fall into the outhouse just as a regiment of Ukrainians is finishing a prune stew and twelve barrels of beer.[1]

Exaggeration and hyperbole do not have a big place in Jewish humor today. We don't have tall stories about, say, a Jewish Paul Bunyan with his blue ox, Babe. There are, however, hyperbolic characters in Jewish humor, for example, the Jewish mother, the snide and arrogant waiter, the self-confident *schnorrer*, etc. As we will see in this chapter, exaggeration does figure prominently in Talmudic and Midrashic literature.

The Talmud often speaks in exaggerated terms in order to make a point.

> *The curtain in the Temple was so large that it took three hundred priests to ritually immerse the curtain when it became unclean.*[2]

And, according to the Talmud, there was a golden vine that stood at the Temple's entrance that was suspended on poles. Whoever donated a branch or cluster of gold would bring it and hang it on the vine. Rabbi Elazar b. Zadok said regarding this vine that it once happened that three hundred priests were assigned to clear it off.[3]

The number three hundred is again used in the following Talmudic excerpt. Is it an exaggeration? Well, it might help to know that 300 *kor* of ashes is approximately 2,100 bushels!

> *There was a place in the middle of the altar where the ashes of the sacrifices piled up. There were times that 300 kor of ashes collected therein. Rava said this is an exaggeration.*

The sacrificial animal to be used for the daily burnt-offering was given water to drink in a cup of gold. Rava said this is an exaggeration.

Rabbi Ammi stated: The Torah, the prophets, and the sages use hyperbolic language . . . The Torah uses hyperbole as it says,[4] "the cities are great and fortified up to the heaven." The prophets speak in hyperbole as it is written[5] "and the earth was split by their sound."[6]

The point made here is that since the Torah uses hyperbole, it is an acceptable device that may also be used by the sages.

Mar Zutra stated: Between Azel and Azel there are four hundred camel-loads worth of interpretations.[7]

"Between Azel and Azel" refers to the verses in Chronicles I, beginning with "And Azel had six sons"[8] and ending with "these were the sons of Azel."[9] There may, indeed, be many interpretations of these verses, but 400 camel-loads—truckloads, in modern parlance—worth? Between "Azel and Azel" there are only a total of forty-seven verses!

It is written[10]: "The Lord has swallowed up without pity all the dwellings of Jacob." When Ravin came he said in the name of Rabbi Yochanan that the above verse refers to the 600,000 cities that Yannai the King had on the King's mountain; each containing a population equal to the number of people leaving Egypt (600,000), except for three which had twice as many . . . Ulla said I have personally seen that place and it could not hold even 600,000 reeds.[11]

The above is a typical Talmudic exaggeration, the purpose of which was to make the public realize the immensity of the tragedy of the Temple's destruction. The number 600,000 is often used in the Talmud metaphorically. Ulla is, of course, being sarcastic once again.

The next passage, about Og, the giant, is another wonderful example of Talmudic exaggeration and hyperbolic language.

Og said: How large is the Israelite encampment (in the Desert)? Three parsangs. I will go and uproot a mountain that is three parsangs wide and throw it on them and kill them all. He went and uprooted a mountain of three parsangs and placed it on his head. However, the Holy One sent ants which gnawed holes in the mountain and caused it to fall around Og's neck. Og attempted to remove the mountain but his teeth stretched out on each side so he could not remove the mountain . . .

> *Moses was ten cubits tall, he took an ax that was ten cubits long, and he jumped ten cubits and struck Og on his ankle and killed him.*[12]

Most commentaries consider this story a parable and the mountain—according to some—represents the Evil Inclination. Regardless, this is a funny story—the image of a giant with a mountain stuck on his head is quite humorous. The story of Og is mentioned in the Bible[13] and his bed is described in the Bible as being about nine cubits (approximately 13.5 feet) long.[14]

> *Og is actually Eliezer, Abraham's servant. Og was so huge that he was able to hide Abraham's feet in the palm of his hand. Once Abraham yelled at him and from fear Og's tooth fell out. Abraham took it and turned it into an ivory bed, and he slept there. Some say Abraham made the tooth into a chair in which he sat and used for the rest of his life . . .*

> *Og went and built sixty cities, the smallest of which was sixty* mil *high . . .*

> *What did Og eat? One thousand oxen and the same number of other species of animals. His drink consisted of one thousand measures. One drop of his semen was thirty-six* litras.[15]

More exaggeration of the size of Og. A *mil* is approximately one kilometer, and one *litra* is equal to 450 grams, which is almost one pound. By exaggerating Og's size, Moses's feat of killing him was made even more spectacular.

Sexual Imagery

Triebwasser, a twine merchant from New York, was trying desperately to sell some of his goods in Louisiana. But wherever he went, he kept encountering anti-Semitism. In one particular department store, the buyer taunted him: "All right, Jake, I'll buy some of your twine. As much as reaches from the top of your Jewish nose to the tip of your Jewish prick."

Two weeks later, the buyer was startled to receive a shipment containing eight hundred cartons of Grade A twine. Attached was a note: "Many thanks for your generous offer. Invoice to follow. (signed) Jacob Triebwasser—residing in New York, circumcised in Kiev." [16]

There is a Talmudic principle that evil men are always evil and, indeed, do the worst kind of evil deeds. Conversely, good people always do the best deeds. This principle itself is a form of hyperbole. According to the Talmud, King Nebuchadnezzar of Babylonia, who destroyed the First Temple and ruled over most of the world, committed sodomy with each of the kings he captured. However, something quite unusual occurred when it was King Zedekiah's turn to be sexually abused. In the following, the "righteous person" referred to is King Zedekiah.

> *Rabbi Yehuda said in the name of Rav: When that wicked man, King Nebuchadnezzar, wished to commit sodomy with that righteous person, his penis stretched out three hundred cubits and it went around to each (captive) king . . .*[17]

Talk about strange imagery! And, anyone who thinks the Talmudists were uninterested in sex should go back to yeshiva and study any of the passages that follow.

Pharaoh's image did not fare too well in the Talmud

> *Abitol the scribe said in the name of Rav: The Pharaoh that lived in the time of Moses was one cubit tall, his beard was one cubit long, and his penis was one cubit and a span long.*[18]

And a *span*. One would hope that Pharaoh did not trip over his beard—or anything else. It appears that the point Rav was making here was that Pharaoh was unusually libidinous. This obvious exaggeration is somewhat similar to the Americanism one might use to describe an obese person: "He is as wide as he is tall." Pharaoh's beard may have been as long as he was tall, but his penis was even a little longer—apparently, by exactly one span, a measure which is equal to the spread of the fingers of one hand.

Rachav was the prostitute who saved two of Joshua's spies by hiding them in her home when the Jewish people first entered the Promised Land.[19] Rabbi Yitzchak described Rachav's beauty in a very unusual way.

> *Rabbi Yitzchak: Anyone who says "Rachav, Rachav" will immediately have a seminal emission.*
>
> *Rabbi Nachman: I can say it and I am not affected.*
>
> *Rabbi Yitzchak: I am speaking of individuals who knew her and were familiar with her.*[20]

The following Midrash explains homiletically why the verse in Genesis says that "Sarah would be nursing *children*."[21] Sarah was ninety when she gave birth to Isaac, her *only child.*

Our mother Sarah was extremely modest. Abraham, our father, said to her: This is not the time for modesty. Uncover your breasts so that everyone will know that the Holy One has begun to perform miracles. She uncovered her breasts and they gushed forth milk like two springs. The matrons came and had their children nursed by her. They said: We are not worthy that our children should be nursed with milk from that righteous woman.[22]

This is also an obvious exaggeration. A related Midrash explains why the Bible had to state that Isaac was weaned.[23] This was necessary because, according to the Midrash, the neighbors were saying that Abraham and Sarah were passing off a foundling they brought in from the street as their own child.

Rabbi Yishmael b. Yosi and Rabbi Elazar b. Shimon were known to be very fat, with huge bellies, and so . . .

When Rabbi Yishmael b. Yosi and Rabbi Elazar b. Shimon came together, one could pass a yoke of oxen beneath their stomachs without touching them.

A Roman matron said to them: Your children are not yours. They responded: Our wives' stomachs are even bigger than ours. She said: All the more so this proves my assertion. Some say they responded: "For as the man is, so is his strength."[24] *Others say they responded: Love squeezes the flesh.*

The Talmud asks: Why did they answer her? After all, it says[25]*: "Do not answer a fool according to his folly." They responded to her in order that their children not be slandered.*

Rabbi Yochanan stated: The sexual organ of Rabbi Yishmael was like a wineskin of nine kav's capacity. Rabbi Pappa said: Rabbi Yochanan's organ was as a wineskin of five kav's capacity; some say three kav's capacity. Rabbi Pappa's own was as the baskets of Harpunia.[26]

Hmm. Not only was Rabbi Yishmael big bellied, but . . . And just in case the imagery of two big bellied folks like Rabbi Yishmael and his wife engaging in sexual intercourse is not enough . . .

A *kav* is a measure equal to twenty-four eggs, meaning, approximately 40 fluid ounces or 1.4 liters, and the baskets of Harpunia had a capacity of six *kavs*. Needless to say, the comments regarding the organs of the Talmudists seem very inappropriate, albeit humorous. The commentaries on the Talmud attempt to explain the reason these strange remarks were included in the Talmud. Tosafot, a major commentary on the Talmud, believes that the purpose of this passage was to discourage individuals from slandering people (and their children) who look like this, that is, have colossal stomachs. Other commentaries feel that the purpose for including it was to show that many of the sages had great sexual appetites but were able to control themselves. The size of the organ is a Talmudic way of saying that the sage had incredibly powerful sexual urges that he was nonetheless able to control. Indeed, the Talmud points out that the "the greater the man, the greater are his lusts."[27]

> *That evil person, Zimri, had sexual intercourse with Cozbi 424 times that day and Pinchas waited for Zimri's strength to diminish (before killing him) . . . We learned in a* baraita *that Zimri copulated with Cozbi 60 times until his testicles were like addled eggs and Cozbi was like a furrow filled with water. Rabbi Kahana said her backside was as wide as a* beit seah. *Rabbi Joseph taught that her vagina was a cubit wide.*[28]

This is clearly an incredible exaggeration. It appears that the Talmudic sages are trying to portray Zimri as an individual who, once he started giving in to his sexual desire for the Midianite temptress, Cozbi,[29] lost all control. In a clear case of Talmudic hyperbole, Cozbi's backside is said to be as wide as a *beit seah*, a measure equal to 2,500 square cubits or approximately 689 square yards. The Talmud also exaggerates the size of Cozbi's private parts, a humorous way to indicate how voluptuous and seductive she was.

It Was So Big That . . .

Absalom, the son of King David, rebelled against his father.[30] Absalom not only wanted the kingdom, but also slept with his father's concubines.

> *Abba Saul stated: I used to be a gravedigger and one time a cave opened up under me and I found myself standing in a corpse's eyeball up to my nose. When I returned, I was told that it was the eye of Absalom.*[31]

This story, a metaphor, describes in a humorous way how great was Absalom's desire. The super large eye is obviously a metaphor for great desire.

King Nebuchadnezzar had Chananiah, Mishael, and Azariah thrown into a blazing furnace for refusing to worship idols.[32] According to the

Talmud, the nations of the world spat at the Jews for forsaking such an incredible God and worshipping idols. This is how they put it:

> Where did Chananiah, Mishael, and Azariah go after they miraculously emerged unscathed from the fiery furnace Nebuchadnezzar had them thrown into?
>
> Shmuel said: They drowned in saliva.[33]

Chanania, Mishael, and Azariah were saved in this case but other Jews had succumbed. The saliva was the result of the people of other nations spitting in disgust at Jews who did not appreciate what they had. Clearly this was not meant to be taken literally, but illustrates the shame that the Jews have felt for worshipping foreign deities when they had the One God who could rescue his people from fire.

> Abba Saul was the tallest man in his generation and Rabbi Tarfon reached his shoulder.
>
> Rabbi Tarfon was the tallest man in his generation and Rabbi Meir reached his shoulder.
>
> Rabbi Meir was the tallest man in his generation and Rebbi reached his shoulder.
>
> Rebbi was the tallest man in his generation and Rabbi Chiya reached his shoulder.
>
> Rabbi Chiya was the tallest man in his generation and Rav reached his shoulder.
>
> Rav was the tallest man in his generation and Rabbi Yehuda reached his shoulder.
>
> Rabbi Yehuda was the tallest man in his generation and Adda his attendant reached his shoulder.
>
> Parshtabina of Pumbedita reached to half the height of Adda.[34]

Parshtabina of Pumbedita was known as a very tall man. This beautiful, metaphorical description cannot be taken literally or Abba Saul would have been several feet taller than Rabbi Yehuda, an Amorai who lived several generations before him.

> Rabbi Simlai came before Rabbi Yochanan and said to him: Please teach me the Book of Genealogies.[35] Rabbi Yochanan asked: Where do you come from? He said: From Lod. Rabbi Yochanan then asked: Where is your dwelling? He replied: Nehardea. He said to him: We do not teach it to people from Lod or Nehardea; and certainly not to you who is from Lod and dwells in Nehardea. He urged him until he

*finally was willing. He then said to Rabbi Yochanan: Teach it to me
in three months. Rabbi Yochanan took a clod and threw it at him,
saying: Bruriah, the wife of Rabbi Meir and the daughter of Rabbi
Chaninah b. Teradyon, who (was so brilliant that she) studied three
hundred laws from three hundred teachers in one day, but still could
not do it justice in three years of study, and you say you want to study
it in three months.*[36]

Rashi says that Rabbi Yochanan was trying to put him off, so he therefore used the excuse that he came from Lod and dwelled in Nehardea.

Here a woman is trying to compliment Rabbi Yehuda b. Illayi on his
healthy appearance.

*A matron once said to Rabbi Yehuda b. Illayi: Your face resembles that
of either a swine-breeder or a usurer. He answered: On my faith, both of
these occupations are forbidden to me. However, there are twenty-four
outhouses between my lodging place and the academy, and when I go
to the academy, I test myself in every one of them.*[37]

Rabbi Yehuda explained that his good health was due not to his
occupation but to his regular habits; he believed that the key to good
health and a robust complexion was to purge oneself thoroughly of all
excreta. He may have been exaggerating a bit.

Rabbah b. Bar Chana relates many tales describing incredible sights
that he saw on his travels. These tales are generally thought to be parables or allegories. Rabbah b. Bar Chana relates that sailors told him
of waves that lifted their ship so high that they saw the resting place of
a small star, and had the wave lifted them any higher, they would have
been burnt by the star's heat. He describes seeing an antelope as tall as
Mount Tabor and when it defecated, its excreta temporarily dammed
up the whole Jordan River. He describes a fish that looked like an island
and was covered with grass. Thinking that it was dry land, they started
a fire on its back in order to cook. The fish turned over and they almost
drowned. He describes a fish so long that the ship sailed for three days
and nights to go from one fin to the other. And the ship itself was sailing
at a speed faster than an arrow. An Arab showed him the Jews that died
in the desert during the forty years of wandering. They were lying dead
on their backs and one of them had his knee raised. The Arab was able
to pass under his knee on a camel with a raised spear and not touch
him. Rabbah was also shown the opening in the earth where Korach
and his group was swallowed up. He was able to hear them saying:
"Moses and his Torah are true, and we are liars."[38]

Hyperbole Involving Animals

Rabbah b. Bar Chana said: I saw a frog as big as the Fort of Hagronia. How big is the Fort of Hagronia? Sixty houses. A crocodile came and swallowed the frog, a raven came and swallowed the crocodile. Then the raven perched itself on a tree. Imagine how great was the strength of that tree. Rabbi Pappa b. Shmuel said: If I had not been there, I would not have believed it.[39]

Many interpret this story as symbolizing all the great empires that have devoured each other, but the Jewish people (represented by the tree) live on.

Once the egg of the Bar Yokanai bird fell and sixty cities were submerged (from the contents) and three hundred cedar trees were destroyed.[40]

It is not clear what this metaphor means.

Rabbah b. Bar Chana said: Once we were traveling in a ship and we saw a fish with a small parasite that had settled in its nostril. The fish died and the water cast it out and threw it onto the shore. Sixty towns were destroyed by the fish when it landed on them. Sixty towns ate from the fish and an additional sixty towns salted its remains. They filled three hundred barrels of oil from one of its eyeballs. When we returned after twelve months, we saw that they were cutting beams from the fish's skeleton and they settled down to rebuild those towns.[41]

This is another of the strange stories told by Rabbah b. Bar Chana. As noted above, these stories use a great deal of hyperbole and are parables, though not everyone agrees as to the meaning of these stories.

Rabbah b. Bar Chana said: The Arab merchant said to me, Come, and I will show you Mount Sinai. I went and saw that it was surrounded by scorpions and they stood like white donkeys. I heard a Heavenly voice declare: Woe is to me that I have sworn to send the Jewish people into exile. And now that I have sworn who can nullify the oath for me. When I returned, I came before the Rabbis and told them the story. They said to me: Every Abba is a donkey and every Bar Bar Chanah is an imbecile. You should have said: It is annulled for You.[42]

A rabbi has a right to annul vows in certain situations. Rabbah's name was actually Abba. The above story must also be a parable.

The emperor said to Rabbi Yehoshua b. Chananiah: Your God is likened to a lion since it is written,[43] "The lion has roared, who will not fear? The Lord has spoken . . ." What is so special about this? A horseman can kill a lion. Rabbi Yehoshua replied: He is not likened to an ordinary lion, but to the lion of heaven. The emperor said: I want you to show it to me. He said: You will be unable to look at it. The emperor insisted on seeing it. Rabbi Yehoshua prayed and it was removed from its place in heaven and brought to earth. When it was four hundred parsangs distance from Rome, it roared once and caused all the pregnant women to miscarry and the walls of Rome collapsed. When it was three hundred parsangs distance, it roared once and caused the teeth of every person to fall out, and the emperor himself fell from his throne to the ground. The emperor said to Rabbi Yehoshua: I beg of you to pray that the lion should return to its place. Rabbi Yehoshua prayed and it was returned to its place.[44]

This story might have been told to comfort the Jews who were being persecuted by the Romans. Rabbi Yehoshua traveled often to Rome on behalf of his brethren. The Talmud records many of his conversations with Hadrian.

And Other Unusual Imagery

The verse states[45]: "But Queen Vashti refused to come." We know that Vashti was shameless, as was stated previously that both Vashti and Ahasuerus had an immoral intent for making their feasts. So why did Vashti refuse to come? Rabbi Yosi b. Chaninah stated: It teaches us that she became leprous. We learned in a matnita *(collection of mishnas not redacted by Rebbi) that the angel Gabriel came and made her a tail.[46]*

According to the Midrash, King Ahasuerus's request that Vashti be brought wearing the royal crown meant wearing only the crown and nothing else, to show off her beauty. Since many of the Talmudists believed that Vashti was immoral and immodest they had to come up with an explanation as to why she refused to come and show off her beauty.

Some of the images conjured up by the descriptions given in the Talmud and Midrash can only be characterized as hyperbolic. In Talmudic times they believed that when one had a strong need to urinate, it was dangerous to hold it in. Thus, they even allowed one to urinate in public, when necessary. This, despite the fact that doing anything that is immodest or disgusting is generally prohibited.

> *Mar b. Ashi was walking on a bridge when he needed to urinate.*
> *They said to Mar: Your mother-in-law is coming.*
> *Mar responded: Even in her ear.*[47]

Meaning, I would urinate anywhere rather than holding it in and thereby endangering my health. Could this possibly be one of the earliest mother-in-law jokes?

> *The verse states*[48]: *"And Esau said to Jacob: Let me swallow, I pray of you, some of that red, red stuff." Rabbi Yitzchak b. Zeira said: That wicked person (Esau) opened his mouth wide like a camel and said to Jacob, "I will open my mouth and you just keep pouring it in."*[49]

Rabbi Yitzchak bases his explanation on the fact that the Hebrew word for swallow (*haliteni*) used in the verse is similar to the word used in the Talmud (*maleatin*) when it discusses the permissible way of feeding a camel on the Sabbath. There the word means to feed an animal by putting food in its mouth. Actually, the word *haliteni* is only used this one time in the Scriptures.

> *The verse states*[50] *"And Esau ran to meet him (Jacob), and hugged him, and fell on his neck, and kissed him, and they wept." Rabbi Yannai said why are there dots on the word "kissed him"? The verse teaches us that Esau did not come to kiss him but tried to bite Jacob on the neck. However, Jacob, our patriarch, his neck turned to marble and that evil man, Esau, his teeth were blunted. Why does it state that "they wept"? One wept because of his neck, and the other wept because of his teeth.*[51]

Certain words and phrases in the Torah have marks above them – dots. This may be similar to the way we make a word bold or underline it to emphasize something. Many of the sages could not believe that Esau, who came to meet Jacob with four hundred people, would actually hug and kiss him with love.

> *Rabbi Shimon taught: How skillful are the Jewish people in knowing how to get their way with their Creator? Rabbi Yudan said: They are like those Cutheans who are smart when they go begging. One of them goes to a woman and says to her: Do you have an onion to give me? After he gets the onion, he says: Can one eat an onion without some bread. After getting some bread, he says: Can one eat without having something to drink? In this manner, the Cuthean gets both food and drink.*[52]

So too, the Jews pray for a little and keep asking for more and more. Is this an early *schnorrer* joke?

> *Rabbi Shimon b. Chalafta was an obese man. One day he felt very hot, so he climbed up and sat on a mountain peak and told his daughter: My daughter, fan me with your fan and I will give you bundles of nard (a fragrant herb). Just then, a breeze began to blow. He said: How many bundles of nard do I owe the Master of this breeze.*[53]

Not much is known about Rabbi Shimon except that he was extremely poor.

> *Rabbi Gidal was accustomed to sit at the gates of the place used by the women for ritual immersion. He would say to them: Immerse yourself thus, immerse yourself thus. The rabbis said to him: Are you not afraid of the Evil Inclination (i.e., temptation). He replied: They appear to me like so many white geese.*[54]

Normally, it is prohibited to gaze at a woman that is not dressed modestly. While he had the best of intentions, Rabbi Gidal's behavior was definitely unusual.

> *The verses state*[55]: *"And there was a thick darkness in all the land of Egypt lasting for three days. They saw not one another and no one rose from his place." Our Rabbis said: There were a total of seven days of darkness . . . During the last three days of darkness, one who was sitting, could not get up; one who was standing, could not sit down; and one who was lying down, could not straighten up.*[56]

The darkness was so thick that the Egyptians were literally frozen in place. This is an example of humorous imagery used by the rabbis.

One Russian Jew speaks to another, "Let me tell you about winters in Moscow. You can't imagine the cold we have. One day I walked out to the street. The cold was unbearable. I had to clear my throat, but before the spittle reached the ground, it was frozen into a small stone." His friend smiled, but remained unimpressed. "You call that cold! Let me tell you about winter in Siberia. I was in Irkutsk. I met a man in the market and we began to converse. As the words came out of my mouth, they turned to ice. We were able to read them before they hit the ground."[57]

11

Wordplay: Puns, Acrostics, and Riddles

In modern Jewish humor, jokes involving wordplay often play upon the clash of the languages used by a people required to be multilingual. These languages include the traditional language of the Jewish people, Hebrew—and, sometimes, Yiddish—and the language of the host country of the current diaspora. For example:

A prominent British Jew is about to be knighted. At the ceremony, as the Queen dubs his shoulders with the sword, he is supposed to recite an ancient Latin oath.

However, the Jew can't seem to remember the difficult phrase. As he kneels before the Queen, and she touches his shoulders with the sword, the nervous man substitutes the first foreign words that pop into his head: "Ma nishtana halaila hazeh mikol haleilot,"[1] and hopes the Queen won't notice his error.

The Queen turns to her chamberlain, and says, "Why is this Knight different from all the other Knights?"

As we saw in Chapter 4, wordplay is evident throughout the Biblical canon. The Talmudists certainly continued this tradition. They enjoyed plays on words and often used this device to instill important moral lessons in their students. The Talmud often asks the question: "Why is it called . . .?" or "Why was he called . . .?" and responds with a pun or play on words. Words that sound like other words were employed as puns. Plays on people's names were used frequently. A particular acrostic type of wordplay took one word and split it into two or more pieces, with each piece a separate word. Riddles were used outright—in question and answer form—and also in an opaque, enigmatic way of speaking that required complex interpretation and explanation.

Hebrew was the language of the Bible and, in the days of the Talmud, Aramaic was the language of the people. When sharp-witted scholars speak two languages, and both are written without vowels, that presents many opportunities for wordplay, including puns, acrostics, plays on people's names, riddles, and enigmatic speech. There are many, many more examples in the Talmud than what we have here. These are but a small sampling of these types of frequently used Talmudic intellectual linguistic witticisms.

Bruriah, a wise and learned woman referred to in the Talmud, was the daughter of the great sage Rabbi Chaninah ben Teradyon and the wife of Rabbi Meir. Here is how she used wordplay to prove a point.

> *There were some highwaymen in Rabbi Meir's neighborhood that were harassing him terribly. Rabbi Meir prayed that they should die. Bruriah, his wife, told him: How do you justify saying such a prayer? Perhaps, you justify it because it is written*[2]*: "Sins will terminate from the earth." The verse does not say* "chottim" *(sinners) but* "chattaim" *(sins). Furthermore, look at the end of the verse, "and the wicked will be no more." If the sins will terminate, there will be no more wicked people. Therefore, pray that the highwaymen repent, and then the "wicked will be no more." He prayed for them and they repented.*[3]

Bruriah believed that it is better to eradicate the sin rather than the sinner, and employed wordplay to interpret the verse. Her opinion, according to many scholars, is that sin can be eradicated if the environmental conditions that cause it are removed.

> *Rabbi Elazar went to the privy and a Roman came and pushed him away. Rabbi Elazar got up and left, and a snake came and tore off the Roman's rectum. Rabbi Elazar quoted the following verse*[4]*: "Therefore I will give man in your stead." Do not read it as* adam *(man) but* Edom.[5]

The verse, quoted from Isaiah, says that when the Jewish people are good, God will see to it that other nations are destroyed instead of Israel. The Romans are considered to be moral descendants of Esau, who was also known as Edom.

The Hebrew word *sinah*, hatred, is very close to the name of the mountain, *Sinai*, where the Israelites received the Torah from God. According to the Midrash, God offered the Torah to other nations but they rejected it. And yet, the nations of the world hate the Jewish people for accepting the Torah and bringing monotheism into the world.

> *Why is it called Mount Sinai? It is the mountain where* sinah *came down to the nations of the world. What was its real name? Its name*

was Chorev. *Rabbi Abuhu disagreed: Its real name was Mount Sinai. Why was it called* Chorev? *Because* churbah *(ruin) descended on the idolaters because of it.*[6]

Rabbi Abuhu's opinion is that after revealing Himself on Mount Sinai and giving the Ten Commandments, God began to punish the idolaters.

In Hebrew, the word *asser*, to tithe, is similar to the word for becoming wealthy, *ashar*. And so we see:

It is written[7]: *"Asser te'asser" (You should surely tithe). This means give tithes in order that you should become wealthy.*[8]

Meaning, if you tithe, God will bless you and you will become wealthy. And, while we are on the subject of becoming wealthy:

Rabbah b. Bar Chana said in Rabbi Yochanan's name who stated in the name of Rabbi Yehuda b. Illai: Eat bazel *and dwell* bezel *(in the shadow) of your house.*[9]

In other words, eat simple foods like onions (*bazel*) and you will be able to afford a house. This is a play on the similarity of the words that mean onions and "in the shadow." Regarding eating simple foods, here is what Ulla has to say:

Ulla stated: They have a saying about it in the West (Israel): One who eats allita *(the fat tail) will have to hide himself in the* alita *(loft), but one who eats* kakule *(vegetables) may rest quietly by the* kikle *(marketplaces) of the town.*[10]

Allita means the "fat tail," — that is, the most expensive piece of meat. Today we might say "Champagne and caviar," if we could think of an alliterative play on words for it. Ulla meant to say that someone who eats expensive foods—like the fat tail—will have to hide from creditors. Eat simple foods like vegetables and you can go out anywhere, even in the public marketplace.

In Hebrew, wine is either *yayin* or *tirosh*.

Wine is called yayin *because it brings lamentation into the world; it is called* tirosh *because he who overindulges becomes poor.*[11]

There is a Hebrew word that is similar to *yayin* that means lamentation; that *tirosh* is similar to *rush*, a word meaning poverty.

Rabbi Abba said to Rabbi Ashi, we learn that "any scholar who is not as strong as iron is no scholar" from the verse[12]: "A land whose stones are iron," do not read the word as "avaneha" (stones) but "boneha" (builders).[13]

Scholars are known as builders because they help build society by teaching values. A scholar must have determination and be resolute or, in other words, as "strong as iron."

Rabbi Elazar stated: What is the meaning of the verse[14]: "I will make a help meet (ezer kenegdo) for him." If he is worthy, she will be a help to him; if not, she will be against him.[15]

In the Bible, God declares that he will create a help meet, a helpful partner, for Adam. The terminology used, *ezer kenegdo*, means someone to help him at his side, that is, a help meet. If you pick apart the phrase, the Hebrew word *ezer* means "help" and the word *kenegdo* means "against him."

For the next excerpt, it helps to know that *hain*, "yes" in Aramaic, is written exactly the same as *hin*, a Hebrew word meaning a measure, but pronounced differently.

What is taught by the verse[16]: "A just hin *you shall have." After all,* hin *is certainly included in* ephah. *The purpose is to teach you that your "yes" should be honest and your "no" should be honest.[17]*

The full verse reads, "Just balances, just weights, a just *ephah*, and a just *hin* you shall have." *Ephah* and *hin* are dry and liquid measures, respectively. The question asked is, why use two words for measure? "A just *ephah*" would have been enough to let us know that measures must be honest. Rabbi Yosi b. Yehuda is exploiting the similarity of the Hebrew word *hin* with the Aramaic word *hain* to teach a moral lesson.

The Torah says that Isaac loved Esau because he was "*tzayid bapiv*."[18] This literally means that Esau, the hunter (*tzayid*), provided his father with game for his mouth (*piv*). The Midrash has another meaning based on the fact that the Hebrew word "*tzayid*" can mean hunting or trapping, that is, Esau was a phony who knew how to fool his father. He used his mouth (*piv*) to trap or deceive his father.

What is the meaning of "tzayid bapiv"? Esau used to trap Isaac the pious with his mouth . . . When Esau came in from outside, he would ask his father: Does salt have to be tithed? Isaac would be surprised and say: See how meticulous my son is with the precepts. Isaac would say to Esau: My son, where were you this day? Esau would respond: At the house of study—Is this not the law? Is this not prohibited? Is this permitted? Using these words Esau would ensnare Isaac with his mouth.[19]

The Torah describes how Jacob fell asleep and had his vision of the angels ascending and descending a ladder. Rabbi Yochanan plays with the words of the verse:

It is written[20]*: "And Jacob awakened* mi-shenato." *Rabbi Yochanan interpreted it as* mi-mishnato.[21]

Mi-shenato translates as "from his sleep;" *mi-mishnato* means "out of his studies." Does Rabbi Yochanan's playful interpretation have Jacob falling asleep while studying?

The verse states[22]*: "Moses looked all around and when he saw that there was no man" he killed the Egyptian (who had beaten the Hebrew). Rabbi Yehuda said: He saw that there was no one man enough to be a zealot for the Holy One and kill the taskmaster.*[23]

This is a clever play of words on the expression "there was no man" which actually means that there was no one around to report him.

Nadav and Avihu were the sons of Aaron the High Priest. The Torah states that Nadav and Avihu were consumed by a heavenly fire for offering an unauthorized fire before God.[24]

Rabbi Levi stated: Nadav and Avihu were conceited. Many women remained unmarried waiting for them. What did they say? The brother of our father (Moses) is a king, the brother of our mother (Nachshon) is a prince, our father is a High Priest, and we are both deputies to the High Priest. What woman is then worthy of us?

Rabbi Menachma in the name of Rabbi Yehoshua b. Nechemiah quoted the following verse[25]*: "His young men were consumed by fire, and His virgins had no marriage song." Why were the young men (Nadav and Avihu) consumed by fire? Because the virgins had no marriage song.*[26]

Actually, the verse in Psalms has nothing to do with Nadav and Avihu; it poetically describes the battle with the Philistines. This is an example of a clever homiletic interpretation of a verse in order to make a point. Namely, that single men should not be too choosy.

> *The verse states[27]: "And it came to pass, in the days when the judges judged." Woe on the generation which judges its judges and woe on the generation whose judges are in need of being judged.[28]*

The verse in Ruth continues with "there was a famine in the land." The Midrash is suggesting that the phrase "judges judged" implies that the judges themselves were less than perfect and, therefore, a famine occurred.

> *The verse states[29]: "And Rebecca had an* ach *(brother) and his name was Laban." Why does it say* ach? *Rabbi Eliezer stated: Everyone who mentioned Laban's name said,* Ach![30]

Ach means brother and is also an exclamation of sorrow, namely – woe! Laban was so evil that even mention of his name caused people aggravation.

> *All the festivals will eventually be abolished, but Purim will never be abolished . . . Rabbi Elazar stated: Even Yom Kippurim will never be abolished.[31]*

Yom Kippur, sometimes called Yom Kippurim, is the Day of Atonement. The names of the festivals of Purim and Yom Kippurim sound alike. Rabbi Elazar may be engaging in wordplay. Yom Kippurim is the most holy of holidays and Purim is probably the least significant of the holidays. Yom Kippurim is a solemn fast day whereas Purim is a day of merriment.

Acrostic Wordplay—*Nutrikon*

Nutrikon is a commonly used device in Talmud and Midrash. It involves taking a Hebrew word and treating it as an acrostic or breaking up a word into several words. In the Bible itself, this device is used quite frequently. Thus, Abraham, whose Hebrew name was originally *Avram*, has his name changed to *Avraham* because he is now "*Av hamon goyim*."[32] *Av* means father, *hamon goyim* means multitude of nations, that is, *Avraham* has now become the father of a multitude of nations, whereas originally, he was only the *av* of *Aram*, that is, the father of the country of *Aram*.

The following Talmudic passages take place at the wedding of Rebbi's son, Rabbi Shimon. In addition to some clever wordplay, this episode contains some very humorous imagery as it demonstrates how far Rebbi was willing to go for intellectual satisfaction.

At the wedding of Rabbi Shimon b. Rebbi, Bar Kappara asked Rebbi: What is the meaning of the word "toevah"?...

This word, *toevah*, is used in the Torah, for example[33]: "And if a man lies with another man in the same manner as with a woman, both of them have committed a *toevah* (abomination)."

...Every interpretation offered by Rebbi was rejected by Bar Kappara, so Rebbi said: You interpret it. Bar Kappara replied: First let your wife come and pour me a small cup of wine. She came and poured him a cup. He then said to Rebbi: Get up and dance for me and then I will explain it to you. This is what the Torah means: toevah—toeh atta bah...

Toeh means "gone astray," *atta* means "you," and *bah* means "in it." Bar Kappara's meaning was: you have gone astray in it by leaving permitted intercourse with your wife for prohibited intercourse with a male.

...After his second cup, Bar Kappara asked Rebbi: What is meant by the word "tevel"?...

This word *tevel* is used in the Torah[34]: "A woman should not stand in front of an animal to have intercourse with it, it is *tevel* (a disgusting perversion)." Again, Rebbi's responses were not accepted as correct by Bar Kappara.

...Bar Kappara said: Do what I ask and then I will tell you. Rebbi complied, and Bar Kappara said: tevel hu means is there tavlin (spice) in it? Does this intercourse with an animal have more relish than normal intercourse? He then asked Rebbi: What is meant by the word zimah?...

This word is used in the Torah[35]: "Profane not your daughter to make her a harlot, lest the land fall into harlotry and the land become filled with *zimah* (lewdness)."

...Bar Kappara said: Do what I ask and then I will tell you. Rebbi complied, and Bar Kappara said: zimmah means zu mah he (who is she)...

In other words, if people become promiscuous then women will not know from whom they have become pregnant and men will not know whether women they marry are actually offspring or relatives of women they have slept with. The passage ends saying that Ben Elasah, Rebbi's son-in-law, could not stand watching his father-in-law degrading himself in this way, and he and his wife left.[36]

As noted earlier, Bar Kappara often tried to make Rebbi laugh—and Rebbi was a sage who did not believe in laughing. This is certainly an example of wordplay, but it also contains very humorous imagery. Just imagining the very serious Rebbi, the President of the Sanhedrin, dancing at Bar Kappara's behest—because he absolutely needed to know the answer to the riddle posed—is incredibly funny. Singing for one's supper? Here we see Rebbi willing to dance like a fool for intellectual satisfaction.

A particular type of *nutrikon* shows how an Aramaic word could have been derived as contraction of Hebrew words. Thus, for example, the Aramaic for door is *dasha*, which could be a contraction of the Hebrew words *derech sham*, literally, the way is there.[37]

> *Rabbi Shimon b. Abba stated: It should not be called* pikkadon *but* puk don.[38]

A *pikkadon* is an object one watches for another either as a favor or for a fee; *puk don* means "go out of this," that is, avoid this. Rabbi Shimon was playing on the word *pikkadon* by breaking it up into two other words having a different meaning. Watching an object for someone else can often lead to problems.

> *The verse states*[39]: *"The Egyptians made the children of Israel work with* pharech.*" Rabbi Elazar said: With a* peh rach.[40]

Rabbi Elazar plays on the word *pharech*, which actually means harsh, crushing, back-breaking labor, and the similar-sounding *peh rach*, which means gentle mouth. He is of the opinion that the Egyptians first smooth-talked the Hebrews into working for them for pay and then ultimately made them into slaves.

This following is a play on the Hebrew words for male, *zachar*, and female, *nekevah*.

> *Rabbi Yitzchak in the name of Rabbi Ammi stated: When a man comes into the world, he comes with his bread in his hand. The word for male,* zachar *means* zeh kar, kar *to be understood as it is written,*[41] *"And he prepared for them* keyra gedolah*"(a large feast). A female*

brings nothing with her. The word for female, nekevah, *means* nekiah ba'ah *(she comes clean).*[42]

Unlike a woman (in those days, certainly), a man comes into the world with his livelihood. The word kar is similar in written Hebrew to the word keyra as used in Kings II where it means feast. Women in the ancient world had to rely on men for their support.

It is written[43]*: "And Esau hated Jacob." Rabbi Elazar b. Yosi says: He harbored hatred toward Jacob and became his enemy, retaliator, and grudge bearer, and therefore they are even now referred to as the senators of Rome.*[44]

Senator is a *nutrikon* of the Hebrew words *soneh* (enemy), *nokem* (retaliator), and *noter* (one who bears a grudge). Rome, as noted, is believed to be the moral descendent of Esau.

The verse states[45]*: "Vayehi when Pharaoh let the people leave." As soon as Pharaoh let the Israelites leave he began to cry:* Vay! Vay! Hoy!*[46]

This is a clever play on the word *"vayehi"* which means and it came to pass. The Hebrew word *vayehi* sounds like the combination of two Hebrew words (*vay* and *hoi*) which mean "woe" and "alas." According to the Midrash, Pharaoh was upset that he let his slaves leave Egypt and said "*Vay! Vay! Hoy!*"—or "Woe! Woe! Alas!"—after the Israelites left.

It says[47]*: "The words of the wise are as* kaddarbanot." *Just as a* kaddur shel banot *(girls' ball) is thrown here and there, so too were the commandments flung far from Sinai.*[48]

Kaddarbanot are the prods used to goad animals. This is a word that sounds exactly like the words, *kaddur banot*, meaning, girls' ball. The commandments bounced all over the world. This is another example of a clever use of a pun.

Why is money called mamon? *It is a contraction of* mah attah moneh. *It is nothing.*[49]

Mah attah moneh translates to "what are you counting?" Meaning, why are you obsessing over money? Why waste your life on this nothing. Money is of little value compared to the good deeds you take with you to the next world.

Plays on People's Names

Four salesmen who had met in a train began to play cards. "Let's introduce ourselves," said one man. "My name's Cole."

"I'm Kent," said the second salesman.

"Carleton," said the third.

"Also Cohen," added the fourth.[50]

The Talmud believes that some names in the Hebrew Bible are not real names. For example, the Talmud has a tradition that the names of the spies are not their real names but they were named in the Bible after their (bad) deeds.[51] Also, there is an argument in the Talmud over whether Nimrod's real name was Amraphel or Nimrod. One opinion is that his real name was Amraphel but he was called Nimrod because he led the whole world in rebellion against God.[52] The Hebrew word for rebel is *morod* which sounds like Nimrod.

In the same vein, it is quite possible that many other names in the Hebrew Bible are not real but describe attributes of the individual. Yehuda Radday takes this view and claims that the Bible often distorts an individual's name in order to ridicule it.[53] The Talmud and Midrash occasionally take the approach that the Biblical name is not real, as noted above, but more often work with the assumption that the name is real but quite fitting. This concept may have its roots in the Books of Prophets. Abigail saw that David wanted to kill her husband for insulting him and his men when he was on the run from King Saul. Abigail told David: "Let not my lord take heed of this base fellow, of Nabal, for like his name so is he."[54] The Hebrew word *nabal* means wickedness, disgrace, or folly.

Indeed, in the Talmudic and Midrashic literature, a very common device is to show how someone truly deserved his or her name because of some action performed. For example, Balaam signifies *balah am* (he destroyed the people) because Balaam's advice[55] resulted in the plague that killed thousands of Israelites.[56]

A young couple were proud to be having their first child in America. At the hospital, when he found out his wife had just given birth to twins, the new father promptly fainted. His brother, newly arrived from the Old Country, came rushing in to help name the newborns.

When the new father came to, he was horrified. "My brother named the babies? But hardly speaks any English!" After a moment, he said,

"All right, I might as well hear it. What did he name the girl?"

"Denise."

"Denise? Well, that's not so bad. I like it. And what did he name the boy?"

"Denephew."

The Talmud states that the name Ahasuerus signified the fact that everyone who knew him said *ach la-rosho* (woe for my head). Similar to the play on the word *ach* (brother) for Laban, Rachel's brother, noted earlier in this chapter, the Talmud plays on the name Ahasuerus. With evildoers, the Talmud spares no one in their witticisms.

> *Why was he called Ahasuerus? Shmuel said because he blackened the face of Israel in his days like the sides of a pot. Rabbi Yochanan said because all that remembered him said woe for my head.*[57]

The name Ahasuerus is written *achashverosh* in Hebrew. The word for blackened is *hishchir*, meaning, King Ahasuerus blackened the face of Israel with her misery. Similarly, the Hebrew for "woe for my head" is *ach la-roshi*. In the same vein, a passage in the Midrash quotes Rabbi Berachiah saying, "Because he made the head of Israel ache (*hikchish rosh*) with fasts." And Rabbi Levi said, "Because he made Israel drink gall (*hishkah rosh*) and wormwood."[58]

Delilah's name[59] was very befitting according to the Talmud. The Hebrew word *dildul* means to weaken or deplete . . .

> *Rebbi stated: Even if her name would not have been called Delilah, it would have been appropriate to call her Delilah. She weakened (dilda-lah) Samson's strength, weakened his heart and weakened his deeds.*[60]

. . . and sounds like Delilah.

The Talmud asks:

> *Why was he called Korach? Because he created baldness in Israel.*[61]

The name Korach is very similar to the Hebrew word *karchah* which means baldness or, in this case, defoliation. Korach and his rebels were swallowed up by the earth after they rebelled against Moses.[62]

Orpah, Naomi's other daughter-in-law, turned her back on her mother-in-law when she left her after her husband died. Ruth, on the other hand, stayed with her mother-in-law and traveled with her back to Israel.[63] The word *oreph* means the nape of the neck. One Midrash states that she was called Orpah because she turned the nape of her neck (i.e., turned her back) on her mother-in-law.[64] Also:

> *Why was she called Orpah? Because everyone copulated with her from behind (like an animal).*[65]

Unlike Ruth, Orpah forsook her mother-in-law (see the *Book of Ruth*).

The Talmudists were extremely fond of employing wordplay with people's names. Those included here are just a very small sample of this commonly used device.

> *His name was not Mephiboshet . . . Why then was he called Mephiboshet? Because he embarrassed (King) David in* halacha.[66]

Mephiboshet, whose name literally means, "out of my mouth embarrassment,"—*mepi* (from my mouth) *boshet* (embarrassment)—corrected King David when he was mistaken regarding Jewish law. Mephiboshet was the son of Jonathan who was the son of King Saul.

> *Rabbi Adda b. Ahava saw a gentile woman wearing a red cloak (considered to be very improper for Jewish women) in the street. Mistakenly believing that she was a Jewish woman, he went over and tore it from her. After it was revealed that she was non-Jewish, he was fined 400 zuzim. He asked her for her name. She replied Matun. He told her: Matun, Matun is worth 400* zuzim.[67]

Rabbi Adda b. Ahava seemed to enjoy a good pun. The Aramaic word for two hundred is *matan*. Also, the word *matun* means to be slow and careful. Rabbi Adda's clever pun based on the woman's name made fun of his impulsivity.

Rabbi Shalmon came up with a compromise solution that enables people to satisfy the views of different authorities.

> *Rabbi Nachman b. Yitzchak asked him: What is your name? He replied: Shalman. He said to him: You are* shalom *(peace), and your learning is* shelemah *(impeccable). You made peace between the scholars.*[68]

> *The verse states*[69]*: "The Lord said to Hosea: Go take for yourself a wife of harlotry and children of harlotry . . . And Hosea went and took Gomer the daughter of Diblaim." Rav stated: "Gomer" means that everyone*

consummated their lust on her. "Diblaim" means that she was an
ill-reputed woman daughter of an ill-reputed woman.

Gomer is a Hebrew word meaning to finish or complete. The Hebrew word dibah means an evil report or an ill-reputed woman. *"Diblaim"* seems like a plural form of this word.

Shmuel said that Gomer was sweet in everyone's mouth as a cake of
pressed figs.

Develeh means a cake of pressed figs. The passage concludes with Rabbi Yochanan adding that everyone trampled on her like a cake of pressed figs, in other words they had intercourse with her.[70] Many scholars take this figuratively since it is difficult to imagine God telling Hosea to marry a prostitute. Others, however, take this story literally. Either way, the purpose of this was to show Hosea how difficult it was for God to abandon His people, even an unfaithful people who worshipped idols. Hosea would subsequently also have difficulty leaving his unfaithful wife.

Three sages arrive at an inn shortly before the Sabbath. Before asking the innkeeper to watch their valuables over the Sabbath they question him about himself.

Rabbi Meir, Rabbi Yehuda, and Rabbi Yosi went on a trip. When they
arrived at a certain place, they looked for an inn. They were provided
with one. They said to the innkeeper: What is your name? He replied:
Kidor. Rabbi Meir said: This indicates that he is a wicked person, for
it says[71]*: "Ki dor tahpukhot."*[72]

The innkeeper's name, Kidor, sounds like the first two words of the phrase, from Deuteronomy, *ki dor tahpukhot,* "for they are a perverse generation." Rabbi Meir did not deposit his money with the innkeeper but the other two did. After the Sabbath, the two tried to get their money back but the innkeeper denied ever having received anything from them.

Why was Caleb's daughter called Achsah? Because everyone who saw
her became angry with his wife.[73]

She was so beautiful that everyone became angry with his own wife. This is based on the similarity of the word *Achsah* with the Hebrew word *ka-as* (anger).

Four kings, led by Chedorlaomer, King of Elam, waged war against five kings, who rebelled against him.

> *The verse states*[74]: *"They waged a war against Berah king of Sodom, and with Birsha king of Gomorrah, Shinav king of Admah, and Shemever king of Zeboiim and the king of Bela."*
>
> *Rabbi Meir and Rabbi Yehoshua b. Karchah used to expound on names.*
>
> *He was called Berah because he was an evil son . . .*

Ben rah means evil son in Hebrew.

> *. . . Birsha because he was a wicked son . . .*

Ben rashah means wicked son.

> *. . . Shinav because he siphoned off money . . .*

Shoev mammon means to draw money.

> *. . . and Shemever because he would place wings on himself to fly (magically?) and bring money.*[75]

Sam ever means he placed wings. The implication is that the wings were brought about with magic. These were kings of evil empires so they were probably also quite evil. By playing on their names in this way, Rabbi Meir and Rabbi Yehoshua b. Karchah emphasized their evil natures.

Kemach is ordinary flour and *solet* is the finest and purest flour; *kimchaya* is the plural of *kemach*.

> *All* kimchaya *are* kemach, *but the* kemach *of Kimchit is* solet.[76]

Kimchit was the mother of seven sons who served as High Priests. She was asked what she had done to merit this unusual honor. Her answer was that the beams of her home had never seen the hair of her head or the hem of her undergarment, that is, she was very modest.

Amalek was the name of Esau's grandson and was also the name of a people that was the first to attack the Israelites when they left Egypt.[77] Here, the Talmudists discuss the "derivation" of the name Amalek. The Hebrew *am* means a people or nation.

Amalek means am yelek *(a people of locusts) quick as the* zahal *(another species of locust). Another opinion: Amalek means* am lak, *a people (*am*) that came to lap up (*laloke*) the blood of the Israelites.*[78]

Why was Miriam called Azuvah? Because all men forsook her.[79]

She was so unattractive that no one wanted to marry her. The Hebrew word *azav* means to forsake or to abandon. Caleb, however, married her because of her and her brothers' (Moses and Aaron) spiritual greatness. The Talmud teaches us the importance of marrying for more than physical appearance.

It is often said that human beings have two names: the name they are born with and the name they make for themselves. The Talmud often shows that these two names are the same. Indeed, Rabbi Meir was known as one who judged a person's character by his name. Because names often reflect one's deeds, it was not considered unusual for an individual to have several names. The Midrash lists several individuals with multiple names. For instance, Moses had ten names,[80] Moses's father-in-law, Jethro, had seven names,[81] and Solomon had seven names.[82] God, too, is known to His people by many names.

Riddles and Enigmatic Speech

Mendel Kravitz, eighty-four years old, was hit by a car and lay bleeding on the sidewalk. A policeman arrived on the scene and, glancing at the victim, immediately called for an ambulance and a priest.

The priest arrived first, and bending over Kravitz, he asked, "Do you believe in the Father, the Son, and the Holy Ghost?"

Kravitz lifted up his head, opened his eyes wide, and turned to the crowd that had gathered round him. "I'm laying here dying and he's asking me riddles!"[83]

Riddles were popular even in the time of the Judges. Samson challenged his companions at his wedding feast to solve the following riddle: "From the eater came out food, and from the strong came out sweetness."[84] God Himself could be enigmatic and in the middle of Belshazzar's feast a hand sent from above wrote the cryptic phrase: "*Mene mene, tekel upharsin.*" The king's wise men could not interpret the phrase and only Daniel could decipher it.[85]

The sages of the Talmud also loved to speak in riddles.

> *Rabbi Elazar stated: Why are the prayers of the righteous compared to a shovel? To tell us that just as the shovel overturns the grain in the silo and moves it from one place to another, so too does the prayer of the righteous overturn the mind of the Holy One from the attribute of mercilessness to the attribute of mercifulness.*[86]

A riddle and a wordplay. The Hebrew word for shovel is *eter* and is similar to the word which means entreaty or prayer, *atirah*.

> *The emperor asked Rabbi Yehoshua b. Chananiah: Why do you not attend the disputations at Be Avidan? He replied: The mountain has become covered with snow and surrounded by ice, the dog no longer barks, and the grinders do not grind.*[87]

There were disputations between the Jews and various heretical groups at the Be Avidan. Rabbi Yehoshua's answer for not attending these disputations was that he was too old: The hair on my head has become white, my beard is white, my voice is feeble, and my teeth do not chew.

> *An elderly Jew in Berlin finds himself surrounded by a group of raucous Nazis, who knock him to the ground and ask him, derisively, "Jew, who is responsible for the war?"*
>
> *The little Jew is no fool. "The Jews," he replies, "and the bicycle riders."*
>
> *"Why the bicycle riders?" ask the Nazis.*
>
> *"Why the Jews?" counters the old man.*[88]

Rabbi Yehoshua was an expert with riddles and used them to demonstrate his superiority over the Athenian wise men. The next selection describes part of a debate between Rabbi Yehoshua and the Athenian sages.

> *The Athenians asked Rabbi Yehoshua: When salt has lost its flavor, what should it be salted with? He answered: With the after-birth of a mule. They asked: Does a mule have an after-birth? He replied: Does salt lose its flavor?*
>
> *They asked him: Where is the center of the earth? He straightened out his finger and said, "here." They said: How can you prove it? He said: Bring rope and measure.*
>
> *They said to him: We have a pit in the middle of the field, bring it to town? He said to them: Make me a rope from bran and I will then do as you request.*

They said to him: We have a broken millstone, sew it up for us. He said: Pull the threads out of the pieces for me and I will then sew it up for you.

They asked: A garden bed of knives, how can it be reaped? He said: With the horns of an ass. They asked: Does an ass have horns? He said: Is there a garden bed of knives?

They brought him two eggs and asked: Which is from the white chicken and which from the black chicken? He brought them two cheeses and asked: Which is from the black goat and which is from the white goat?

They asked him: A chick that dies while in the shell, where did its spirit go? He said: From where it came, there it went.

They said: Show us an article whose value is not worth the damage it causes. He brought a mat and spread it out. It was too big to get through the door, so he said to them: Go get a pick-ax and tear down the door. This is an example of an article that is not worth the damage it causes.[89]

Rabbi Yehoshua did indeed prevail over the Athenian sages.

Many of the Talmudists enjoyed using enigmatic speech, often employing *nutrikon* toward this end. Sometimes, even their servants indulged.

When the maid of Rebbi used enigmatic speech she used to say: The ladle hits against the barrel, let the eagles fly to their nest . . .

This was a clever way of telling the students that the wine barrel was empty therefore the ladle knocks against the bottom and the students should finish their meals and go home.

. . . When she wanted them to remain at the table, she would say to them: The crown of her friend shall be removed from her and the ladle will float in the barrel like a ship that floats in the sea.[90]

The stopper of the barrel resembles a crown and so let us remove the stopper of another barrel that is full of wine. Rebbi's maid was quite knowledgeable in many areas. The Talmud relates that the rabbis did not know the meaning of various words (e.g., *haluglugot, salselehah*) until they heard her use them.[91] Apparently, Rebbi's maid was a language expert. Rebbi's maid was held in such esteem that when she excommunicated someone it was taken seriously.[92]

When Rabbi Yosi b. Assyan spoke enigmatically, he used to say: Prepare for me an ox in judgment on a poor mountain.[93]

What he wanted was beets with mustard. The word for beets, *tiradin*, can be broken up into two words *tur* (ox) and *din* (judgment); *chardull* which means mustard can be broken up into the two words *har* (mountain) and *dull* (poor).

> *When Rabbi Yosi b. Assyan made inquiries about an innkeeper, he would say: The man of this raw mouth what is this good that there is?*[94]

In other words, how good is his inn? The word for innkeeper, *ushpizakna*, can be broken up into four words *ush* similar to *ish* (man), *pi* (mouth), *zeh* (this), *nah* (raw).

> *The Rabbis said to Rabbi Abuhu: Show us where Rabbi Elai is hiding. Rabbi Abuhu said to them: He amused himself with a young woman, an* Aharonit *(i.e., of the family of Aaron),* acharonit *(the latest one),* aironit *(a lively one),* vahiniratu *(and she kept him awake last night)...*

Rabbi Elai's second wife was from the tribe of Aaron, and she was vivacious and kept him awake at night. Either his first wife had died or he had a second wife since polygamy was then permitted.

> *... Some say this referred to a woman. Others say this referred to a tractate.*[95]

Rabbi Elai's studies of the tractate dealing with priestly laws, his latest area of study, were stimulating and kept him awake at night. Rabbi Abuhu was being cute by using four similar words to take a roundabout way of saying that Rabbi Elai was sleeping.

The next selection is a blessing given to the son of Rabbi Shimon b. Yochai.

> *May it be His will that you sow but not reap; you should bring in but should not bring out; you should bring out but not bring in; your house should be desolate and your inn be lived in; your table (meals) should be in turmoil; you should not see a new year.*[96]

When the son returned to his father he was greatly disturbed saying: "Not enough that they did not bless me but they caused me much aggravation." He then explained to his son that these are all indeed blessings. "Sow but not reap" means that you should have children and they should not die. "You should bring in but not bring out" means that your sons should bring home daughters-in-law and that they should not become widows and thus have to leave. "You should bring out but not bring in" means that your daughters should marry and not have to return home because their husbands have died. "Your house should be desolate and your inn be lived in" means that you should live a very long life so that your grave (that is one's permanent "house") should be empty and desolate for a long time. This world, which is temporary, is an inn. "Your table (meals) should be in turmoil" by lots of children. "You should not see a new year" means that your wife should not die so that you do not need to find a new wife. "New year" alludes to a wife because in the Torah there is a special law for a groom in the first year with a new wife.[97]

> *A certain person said while dying: I leave a barrel of earth to one son, a barrel of bones to another, and a barrel of cotton stuffings to another. They did not understand what he meant. The sons went before Rabbi Banaah. He said: Do you have land? They said, "yes." Do you have cattle? They said, "yes." Do you have cushions? They said, "yes." Rabbi Banaah said: If so, that is what your father meant.*[98]

Rabbi Banaah was an expert at deciphering riddles. He was appointed a judge by the authorities because of his unique abilities.

> *It once happened that an individual wrote out his will saying: My son shall not inherit me until he becomes a fool . . .*

When Rabbi Yosi b. Yehuda and another individual went to ask Rabbi Yehoshua b. Karchah's opinion on this unusual will . . .

> *. . . they looked in from the outside and saw him crawling on his hands and feet, a reed stuck in his mouth, and following his (baby) son. When they saw Rabbi Yehoshua, they hid themselves. Later, they went in to Rabbi Yehoshua's house to ask him about this will. He began to laugh and said: As you live, this matter you are asking about just occurred to me. He then said to them: When a person has children, he acts as though he were a fool.*[99]

The fact that an individual would make such an enigmatic will indicates that people were quite positive that the sages would be able to interpret their puzzling statements.

> *Rabbi Akiva was sitting and lecturing and noticed that his audience was drowsy. He desired to rouse them he so he asked the following: Why was it befitting that Esther should rule over 127 provinces? The*

reason is as follows: Let Esther, a descendant of Sarah who lived 127 years, come and rule over 127 provinces.[100]

Unusual questions or surprising information has a tendency to wake up an inattentive audience. In fact, many of the wordplays in the Talmud may have been similarly motivated. For example:

Rebbi was sitting and lecturing and noticed that his audience was drowsy. He desired to rouse them so he said the following: One woman in Egypt gave birth to 600,000 at one time. There was a student there and his name was Rabbi Yishmael b. Yosi who asked him: Who was it? Rebbi told him: It was Yochevet, who gave birth to Moses who was equal to the 600,000 of Israel.[101]

Approximately 600,000 adult males left Egypt.[102]

Rabbi Yosi b. Kisma said: Two are better than three and woe for the one thing that goes but does not return. What is it? Rabbi Chisda said: It is one's youth.[103]

The two feet of youth are better than the two feet plus a cane of old age.

Rebbi asked Rabbi Shimon b. Chalafta: Why have we not received you on the festival the way my ancestors used to receive your ancestors? He replied: The rocks have become higher, what is near has become far, two have turned into three, and the peace-maker of the home has ceased to be.[104]

Meaning, he was old and small steps have become high, it was hard to walk a short distance, and he needs a cane. In addition, he was impotent—that's what he meant when he said that his "peace-maker" doesn't work anymore.

The following riddle was presented by Jewish schoolchildren to an Athenian visiting Jerusalem. What are the following: Nine go out but eight come in; two give drink, one drinks, and twenty-four serve?[105]

The answer to the above riddle was nine months of pregnancy results in eight days of circumcision (if a boy is born). The "two which give drink" are the mother's breasts, which one child drinks from for twenty-four months until the child is weaned.

In the next selection, Rabbi Mattenah answers some difficult riddles and shows that the birth of Moses is hinted at in Genesis and that the obviously Persian names of Haman, Mordechai, and Esther can be found in the Bible.

> *The Pappunians asked Rabbi Mattenah: How do we know about Moses from the Torah (i.e., where in Genesis, before Moses was born, is Moses hinted at)? He replied, because it says[106]: "Bashagam (since man is nothing) but flesh; therefore shall his days be 120 years."*
>
> *How do we know about Haman from the Torah? He replied, Because it says[107]: "Hamin haetz . . ." (Did you eat from the tree which I commanded you not to eat from?)*
>
> *How do we know about Esther from the Torah? He replied, Because it says[108]: "And I will utterly hide (asthir) My face."*
>
> *How do we know about Mordechai from the Torah? Because it says[109]: "flowing myrrh" which is translated by the Targum (Aramaic translation of the Bible written by Onkelos) as meira dachia.[110]*

The numerical value (gematria) of the letters of the word "bashagam" is 345, the same as Moshe (Moses), and Moses lived to the age of 120 years. The Hebrew word Hamin (is it from the) is similar to the name Haman, astir (to hide) is similar to Esther, and meira dachia (flowing myrrh) is similar to Mordechai. The Purim story took place about 1,000 years after the Torah was given to the Jewish people.

"What is the proof that a good piece of kugel is critical to the enjoyment of the Sabbath? That the gematria of kugel is that of Shabbat."

"Um, Rabbi. But the gematria of kugel is NOT Shabbat."

"It's not? So, eat a little more kugel!"

12

Humorous Sayings and Remarks

God couldn't be everywhere, so He created mothers.

The Talmud had a great deal of respect for aphorisms used by the people and even tried to demonstrate that many common sayings had a basis in Scriptures. Each of the sayings and aphorisms quoted in the Talmud are intended to reflect a general truth about the world and about life. They are nuggets of advice based on experience, either personal or collective. Once again, the categorization here is not intended to be exhaustive, but rather, to make it easier on the reader and to indicate the topics that seemed to be important to the Talmudic sages. As one can see, many of the sayings can easily fit into multiple overlapping categories.

Counting and Measuring: Classifying the World

The Talmud loves aphorisms that count and measure. These are intended as an aid to understanding a confusing and complex world by classifying the elements in it.

Counting

Where there are two Jews, there are three opinions.

> *Rabbi Yochanan stated: Concerning three, the Holy One personally makes a public announcement (declaring their praise) every day: a bachelor who lives in a large city and does not sin (sexually), a poor person who returns a lost object to its owner, and a rich person who tithes his produce in secret.*[1]

The rich person who tithes his produce in secret does not wish to flaunt how much he gives to the poor. Today it is probably more difficult to find older singles living in the city who are celibate. The more things change, the more they remain the same. Oh, wait—that's an aphorism too!

Three kinds of people do not go to hell, because they have suffered sufficiently in this world.

> *Three do not see the face of* Gehinnom *(hell). They are: one who suffers from crushing poverty, one who suffers from bowel sickness, and one who is hounded by creditors. Some say, also one who has a bad wife.*[2]

Interestingly, bowel sickness was considered one of the most painful illnesses. Today, one might use, say, lung cancer as a very painful illness.

Only the Talmud would come up with the following as a way to describe the exquisite pleasure of the world to come (Paradise).

> *Three things in this world hint at the pleasure of the world to come: The Sabbath, sunshine, and* tashmish. *What kind of* tashmish? *If it means* tashmish hamittah, *sexual intercourse, this weakens the body. It must mean* tashmish nekavim, *the pleasure of relieving oneself.*[3]

The word *tashmish*, which literally means "service," is used in several phrases, like, for example, *tashmish hamittah*, sexual intercourse and *tashmish nekavim*, relieving oneself. Only the Talmud would dare to compare the pleasure of Paradise to the pleasure of relieving oneself. People who suffer from constipation will have a better understanding of this passage.

> *Four people the mind cannot tolerate: An arrogant pauper, a rich man who is a cheat, a lecherous old man, and a leader who lords over the public but does not help them in times of difficulty.*[4]

This is somewhat similar to Ben Sira's saying: "But three kinds of men my soul hates, and I am greatly angered at their existence: A poor man who is arrogant, a rich man who is deceitful, and an old man who is a philanderer."[5]

> *Rabbi Shimon b. Yochai stated: There are four types that the Holy One hates, and I do not like. They are: The man who enters his house suddenly, and it goes without saying his friend's house; the man who holds his penis while urinating; a person who urinates naked before his bed and one who has intercourse in the presence of any living creature.*[6]

The man who holds his penis while urinating is presumably doing so in such a way that he arouses himself. The one who urinates near his bed is just too lazy to go outside to the outhouse. In ancient times, it was not unusual for people to have intercourse in the presence of slaves. It is unclear why Rabbi Shimon adds "and I do not like," but presumably the Lord appreciates the vote of confidence.

> *There are four types of students.*
> *One who is quick to learn and quick to forget, his gain is offset by his loss . . .*

That is, his loss is greater than his gain and he will not know very much.

> *. . . One who is slow to learn and slow to forget, his loss is offset by his gain . . .*

That is, his gain is greater than his loss and he will eventually know a great deal.

> *. . . One who is quick to learn and slow to forget, he is wise.*
> *One who is slow to learn and quick to forget, this is a bad portion.*[7]

Apparently, they did not know about the fifth type of student, the one who doesn't come to class. In a similar vein:

> *There are four types among those that sit before the scholars: A sponge, funnel, strainer, and a sieve. A sponge absorbs everything. A funnel lets in at one end and out the other end. A strainer lets out the wine and retains the sediment. A sieve lets out the flour dust and retains the fine flour.*[8]

A humorous way to describe four types of students a teacher must deal with. A good student (the sieve) knows how to distinguish between valuable information and trivial, unimportant information.

> *Five things did Canaan command his children: love each other, love robbery, love licentiousness, hate your masters, and never speak the truth.*[9]

Canaan was the son of Ham. The Canaanites, that is, children of Canaan, were evil, and they were driven out of the land of Israel by the Jewish people.

Seven have no share in the world to come: A scribe, a teacher of young children, the best of doctors, a town judge, a shopkeeper, a law officer, and a butcher.[10]

Why the town judge? This is the one who sits alone as a judge without consulting others. Individuals working in the above professions have to be especially scrupulous to be honest and careful in their work. For instance, scribes who are careless when writing the Holy Scriptures can cause the public to miscomprehend important religious precepts. Doctors who do not heal the poor or are too arrogant to consult with other professionals when uncertain of a diagnosis might cause the death of others.

There are seven types of Pharisees (including) . . .

The bruised Pharisee, who walks without lifting his feet from the ground in exaggerated piety and thereby knocks his feet against stones.

The bloodletting Pharisee, who is afraid to look at women and walks with his eyes shut and thereby bangs his head against the wall.

The pestle Pharisee, who walks so bent over, because of exaggerated humility, that he looks like a pestle.[11]

In other words, he walks with his head perpendicular to his body so that he looks like a hammer-shaped pestle. The scholars of the Talmud were Pharisees but they hated Pharisees who were phonies or demonstrated overdone piety. Note that the Talmud uses the imagery of an exaggerated walk to depict the essence of the religious hypocrite. This brings to mind some modern Jewish humor making appearances on blogs and YouTube, for example, the work of *FrumSatire* about the different ways of "shuckling" (shaking) during prayer.[12]

Measuring

Too great a modesty is half conceit.[13]

Another way of making sense of a complex world is to describe the elements in relation to each other in terms of measures. This is a "how much" approach as opposed to the "how many," or counting, approach of the previous section.

Ten measures of wisdom descended to the world; nine were taken by the land of Israel and one by the rest of the world.

Ten measures of beauty descended to the world; nine were taken by Jerusalem and one by the rest of the world.

Ten measures of wealth descended to the world; nine were taken by the early Romans and one by the rest of the world.

Ten measures of poverty descended to the world; nine were taken by Babylon and one by the rest of the world.

Ten measures of arrogance descended to the world; nine were taken by Elam and one by the rest of the world.

Ten measures of strength descended to the world; nine were taken by Persia and one by the rest of the world.

Ten measures of vermin descended to the world; nine were taken by the land of Medea and one by the rest of the world.

Ten measures of sorcery descended to the world; nine were taken by Egypt and one by the rest of the world.

Ten measures of plagues descended to the world; nine were taken by swine and one by the rest of the world.

Ten measures of licentiousness descended to the world; nine were taken by Arabia and one by the rest of the world.

Ten measures of impudence (bastardship—Rashi) descended to the world; nine were taken by Mesene and one by the rest of the world.

Ten measures of talk descended to the world; nine were taken by women and one by the rest of the world.

Ten measures of drunkenness descended to the world; nine were taken by Kush and one by the rest of the world.

Ten measures of sleep descended to the world; nine were taken by slaves and one by the rest of the world.[14]

The Talmudists were obviously referring to conditions that existed in their times. The Talmud uses the word *kav* (an ancient measure equal to about 1.4 liters) to signify measures. The above must have been quite humorous to those familiar with the mentioned places.

> *The world is one-sixtieth of the Garden, the Garden is one-sixtieth of Eden, Eden is one-sixtieth of Gehinnom (hell). Thus, the whole world is like a pot cover in relation to Gehinnom.*[15]

This is a cute way of saying that Hell is enormous in size—216,000 times greater than the world—because so many people end up there.

Making a Living

Nine Rabbis cannot make a minyan; but ten cobblers, yes.[16]

> *Rabbi Shimon b. Elazar stated:*
>
> *Did you ever see a wild beast or bird with a trade? I have never in all my life seen a deer drying fruits in the field, a lion carrying heavy burdens, or a fox who kept a shop, and yet none of them die of hunger.*
>
> *Now, if these, who have been created to serve my needs are able to support themselves without difficulty, how much more reasonable is it to expect that I, who have been created to serve my Master (God), should be able to support myself easily, without trouble. However, my deeds were evil and I have thereby ruined my livelihood.*[17]

Rabbi Shimon b. Elazar laments in an emotional and poetic way the need to work rather than engage solely in spiritual undertakings. The image of a lion serving as a porter is quite humorous.

Occupations

> *The best of doctors is destined for Hell.*[18]

Many doctors refuse to treat sick people who are poor. Some are too arrogant to consult with others when they are unsure of a diagnosis and thereby may actually contribute to sickness and death.

> *The world cannot do without either a spice-dealer or a tanner. Happy is he whose occupation is that of a spice-dealer and woe to him whose occupation is that of a tanner.*[19]

This is another way of expressing the view that "Great is labor for it honors the worker."[20] The Talmudists had a great deal of respect for a laborer and many of them worked in occupations ranging from grave-digging to shoemaking.

> *A doctor who heals for nothing is worth nothing.*[21]

An unpaid physician's advice will not be taken seriously.

> *One who rents one garden eats birds; one who rents many gardens, the birds eat him.*[22]

One who rents too many gardens to work as a sharecropper and overextends himself will lose everything and die of poverty.

> *Rav told Rabbi Kahana: Skin a carcass in the street and receive wages and do not say I am an important person and this type of work is beneath my dignity.*[23]

Rav's advice to Rabbi Kahana is a bit colorful but also demonstrates the importance of working for a living.

How to Squander Money

> *Rabbi Yochanan stated: One whose father left him money and desires to squander it should wear clothing of expensive linen, use vessels made of glass, and should hire workers and not sit and watch them.*[24]

The Talmudists frowned on ostentation and believed that a person should be careful with his or her money.

Poverty

Poor people were provided with additional and better food on Sabbaths and the festivals, and yet . . .

> *It is written in the book of Ben Sira:*[25] *All the days of the poor are wretched. What about the Sabbaths and the festivals? The answer supports the opinion of Shmuel, for Shmuel said: A change of diet is the beginning of intestinal disorders. Ben Sira also added that the nights of the poor are also wretched. Why? The poor person's roof is lower than the other roofs and his vineyard is on the highest hills. Thus, the rain from other roofs pours onto his roof, and the earth from his vineyard is washed down into others' vineyards.*[26]

Many of the Talmudic sages were extremely poor. Shmuel was a sage and doctor.

Holding Office

Remarks of Rabbi Yehoshua b. Perachiah on his office as President of the Sanhedrin:

> *Rabbi Yehoshua b. Perachiah stated: Formerly, if a person were to say to me "accept this office," I would have tied him up and placed him in front of a lion. But now if one were to say to me "give up the office," I would pour a kettle of boiling water over him.*[27]

Here, Rabbi Yehoshua is showing how one is affected by power. He also proves this from the Scriptures by showing that at first Saul fled from high office but after becoming King of Israel, he tried to kill David.

> *Whoever runs after office, office runs away from him; whoever runs away from office, office runs after him.*[28]

People are afraid of someone who seeks power. They are much more likely to trust one who tries to avoid it since the latter is less likely to become a tyrant than the former.

A Hasid consulted with his Rabbi. "Rebbe," he asked. "The Talmud states that if you run away from power and honor, honor will chase you."

"That's correct," said the Rabbi.

"In that case," continued the Hasid, "I have run away from honor all my life. Why has it not run after me?"

"That's simple," said the Rabbi. "While you were running away from honor, you were continually looking back over your shoulder to see if it was following."

People

Scholars and Students

> *Rabbi Yochanan b. Zakkai stated: If all the heavens were sheets of parchment, all the trees pens, and all the seas ink, they would be inadequate to describe the wisdom I acquired from my teacher. However, the wisdom I acquired from my teacher is as much as the amount of water a fly immersing in the Mediterranean Sea removes—a minuscule drop.*[29]

Rabbi Yochanan b. Zakkai was Hillel's disciple. He is saying that whatever he learned, it was still a tiny amount compared to what his teachers had to offer. When the Romans were besieging Jerusalem, Rabbi Yochanan b. Zakkai pretended to be dead and was taken out of the city by his students. The zealots did not allow any living person to leave Jerusalem because they wanted to fight the Romans. Rabbi Yochanan had an audience with Emperor Vespasian and convinced him to spare Yavneh and its sages, spare Rabbi Gamliel and his family, and to provide a doctor to heal Rabbi Zadok.[30]

> *Even prostitutes preen each other, how much more so should scholars.*[31]

Prostitutes help each other by preening, that is, they do each other's hair and makeup. The excerpt above is a witty way of saying that scholars should be supportive and respectful of each other.

> *Rabbah b. Huna stated: Every person who possesses Torah but does not have the fear of Heaven in him is like a treasurer who was given the inner keys but not the outer keys. How is he going to enter?*[32]

Another saying indicating how much the sages hated religious hypocrisy.

> *Any scholar who lacks common sense, a carcass is better than he.*[33]

Being an "ivory tower" scholar is not sufficient. One has to understand the psychology and needs of the people.

> *If you wish to be strangled, hang yourself from a tall tree.*[34]

This is a clever way of saying that if you must decide on a controversial matter, ask a great sage and rely on his authority.

Guests

> *Ben Zoma said: What does a good guest say? How much trouble did my host trouble himself for me! How much meat did he bring for me! How many loaves of bread did he bring for me! All the trouble that he troubled himself was only for my sake. However, the bad guest says: What trouble did the host trouble himself for me? I ate one piece of bread, one piece of meat, and drank one cup of wine. All the trouble which the host troubled himself with was only for the sake of his own wife and children.*[35]

Ben Zoma is pointing out that it is only a difference of perception. It is just as easy to see the good in people as the bad.

> *Whatever your host tells you, do* (aseh)*; except leave* (tzey)*.*[36]

This saying rhymes in the original language, Hebrew: *Kol ma shetomar lach baal habayit, aseh.Chutz me-tsey.* It probably means

219

that one should not act in such a manner that the host asks him to leave.

> All people should be in your eyes as robbers, but respect them like Rabbi Gamliel.[37]

If you do not know somebody, be careful, especially if you are inviting him into your home. Rabbi Gamliel was the Nasi, the President of the Sanhedrin.

Sinners

> Rabbi Yosef said to Abaye: It is not the mouse that is the thief but the hole.[38]

If the mouse had no hole to hide in, he would be unable to steal. Using this reasoning, one who fences stolen property should be punished more severely than the thief.

> Rabbi Adda b. Ahava stated: A person that has sinned and confesses his sin, but does not make restitution to what can he be likened? To a person that is holding an unclean (dead) sheretz in his hand; even if he ritually immerses himself in all the waters of the world, the immersion will be of no avail. If, however, he throws the sheretz away, as soon as he immerses himself in forty seahs of water, the immersion becomes effective immediately.[39]

In ancient Jewish law, one who comes into contact with a dead person or dead sheretz (impure crawling creature) becomes ritually unclean and cannot eat of sacrifices or enter the Temple. Unclean people were required to ritually immerse themselves in a mikveh (ritual bath) consisting of a minimum of forty seah (about 87 gallons) of water. Immersing with a dead reptile is similar to apologizing to someone for mocking him by saying: "Fatso, I am sorry that I made fun of your weight."

Who Is Blessed

> Rabbi Yochanan stated: "Blessed shall you be in the city"[40] means that your bathroom will be near your table.[41]

Rabbi Yochanan considers it a blessing not to have to walk too far to the outhouse.

Hypocrites

Better a Jew without a beard than a beard without a Jew.[42]

As we saw earlier, the Talmud castigated and mocked religious hypocrites.

> *Rabbi Tarfon stated: I wonder if there is anyone in this generation that is able to admonish others. If one says to a person, "remove the splinter from between your teeth" he would be told, "remove the beam from between your eyes."*[43]

A hypocrite who has committed many misdeeds cannot admonish others.

> *King Yannai said to his wife: Do not be afraid of either the Pharisees or the non-Pharisees, but fear the hypocrites who appear to be Pharisees. For their deeds are the deeds of Zimri and they seek to be rewarded like Pinchas.*[44]

King Alexander Yannai was a Sadduccee who ruled over the Jews from 102 to 78 B.C.E. The story of Pinchas and Zimri is told in the book of Numbers.[45]

> *The verse states:*[46] *"If the anointed priest sins . . ." Rabbi Levi taught: Shame on a town whose physician suffers from gout, whose eye doctor is missing an eye (to disease), and whose defense attorney in capital cases acts as the prosecutor.*[47]

The High Priest, that is, the anointed priest, is supposed to help atone for the sins of the people, not commit them. During certain time periods, for example, when the Romans controlled Israel, the position of High Priest was often purchased rather than obtained through merit and thus High Priests were often not of the best character. Prior to the revolt of the Maccabees, many of the High Priests were Hellenists who were antagonistic to Judaism.

Pious Fools

Piety is generally considered to be a virtue, however, when it comes to fools, particularly those who don't understand the nature of true piety, there really is such a thing as being too pious. Pious fools were hated by the sages of the Talmud and considered a menace to society.

> *What is an example of a pious fool? One who sees a woman drowning in the river and says "It is improper that I should gaze at her and rescue her," and thereby lets her drown.*[48]

221

What is an example of a pious fool? One who sees a child drowning in the river and says: "After I remove my phylacteries, I will rescue him."[49]

The Talmudic sages realized that foolish people who believe themselves to be pious can cause a great deal of harm. Think of how many people were killed in the name of religion for the most trivial of reasons. Even great scholars can cause great tragedies when they are overly pious and do not consider all possible consequences of their decisions. The Talmud is critical of Rabbi Zecharia b. Abkulas for his extreme piousness. He was so concerned with the prohibition of sacrificing an animal with a blemish in the Temple that he was even willing to offend the Roman emperor. This caused the emperor to send an army against Israel and resulted in the destruction of the Temple.[50]

Ignorant Ones

One coin in a bottle cries "kish, kish."[51]

A single coin jingles loudly. A bottle full of coins, however, makes no noise. Similarly, one scholar in a family of ignorant people stands out. Another explanation for this saying is that the more ignorant the person – that is, the more empty – the more noise he makes. A truly wealthy individual is much less likely to brag about his wealth. This was a popular proverbial saying.

Women

Eliezer Berkovits demonstrates that many of the derisive opinions regarding women found in the Talmud and Midrash are not authentically Jewish, and parallel beliefs and practices found among the Greeks and in the various other societies in which Jews lived.[52] Some, but by no means all, of the Talmudists had negative opinions regarding women. Others had very favorable attitudes toward women and believed women had superior intelligence, were modest, and merciful. Rabbi Levi, quoted below, was clearly of the former group.

Rabbi Yehoshua of Sichnin said in the name of Rabbi Levi . . . the Lord considered from which organ to create Eve. He said:

I should not create her from Adam's head lest she become swell-headed

nor from the eye, lest she become too inquisitive and prying

222

nor from the ear, lest she become an eavesdropper

nor from the mouth, lest she become garrulous

nor from the heart, lest she become envious

nor from the hand, lest she become one who must touch everything

nor from the foot, lest she become a run-around.

I will, however, create her from a modest place in the man, a place that is covered even when a person is standing naked (i.e., the rib). As he created each of her organs, He said: Let the woman be modest, let her be modest.

Despite all this, "You ignored all my counsel." [53]

I did not create her from the head, and she is swell-headed, as it is written: [54] *"They walk with a stretched-forth neck."*

And not from the eyes, yet she is inquisitive and prying, as it is written: [55] *"And wanton eyes."*

And not from the ears, yet she is an eavesdropper, as it is written: [56] *"And Sarah was listening behind the tent door."*

And not from the mouth, yet she is garrulous, as it is written: [57] *"Miriam and Aaron spoke against Moses."*

And not from the heart, yet she is envious, as it is written: [58] *"And Rachel envied her sister."*

And not from the hand, yet she is one who must touch everything, as it is written: [59] *"And Rachel stole the teraphim that belonged to her father."*

And not from the foot, yet she is a run-around, as it is written: [60] *"And Dinah went out."* [61]

The above is among the most negative remarks about women. It should be noted that Rabbi Levi gets into trouble for another of his interpretations (that Abraham examined himself and found that he was circumcised) and is called a liar and a prevaricator by Rabbi Abba b. Kahana.[62]

God says to Adam in the Garden of Eden, "Adam, I can see that you are lonely. I'm going to make a companion for you. She will cook for you and clean for you and never contradict you. She will help you in all your endeavors, and she will never get a headache."

Adam: "What will she cost me?"

God: "An arm and a leg."

(Pause.) Adam: "What do I get for a rib?"

A woman is only envious of the thigh of another woman.[63]

The Talmud believed that King Ahasuerus slept with other women to make Esther jealous so that she would reveal the secret of her nationality.

> *One cup of wine is right for a woman, two are repulsive, three cause her to overtly proposition men, and after four, she can proposition a donkey in the street and not care.*[64]

The above is an exaggerated and humorous way of describing the danger of overindulgence in wine.

> *When a woman sleeps, the wicker basket (in which women carried objects such as yarn) on her head falls.*[65]

This saying teaches us that when a woman is loafing around, no one notices the work she has done.

> *A woman grows her hair long like Lilith (a long-haired demon), sits when urinating like an animal, and is used as a pillow by her husband.*[66]

In a Talmudic discussion of the ten curses with which Eve was cursed, two of the above are considered—urinating sitting down, like an animal, and being used as a pillow by her husband, during sexual intercourse. There is a disagreement as to whether these two are to be considered curses.

The Torah describes three different deaths for the idolaters who sinned during the incident of the golden calf: the sword, plague, and dropsy.

> *A wise woman asked Rabbi Eliezer: Since with regard to the incident of the golden calf, they were all equal (that is, all equally guilty), why then did they not all die in the same manner? He answered her: There is no wisdom for women except at their spindle.*[67]

Rabbi Eliezer, a member of the Shammai School, was against teaching the Torah to women and therefore answered the woman sarcastically. His strong opinions ultimately lead to his excommunication.[68]

The name Deborah (Devorah, in Hebrew) means bee and Chuldah means weasel.

Rabbi Nachman stated: Pride is unbefitting of women. There were two proud women and their names are disgusting. The name of one is bee and the name of the other is weasel. Regarding the bee it is written:[69] "And she sent and called Barak," whereas she should have gone to him. Regarding the weasel it is written:[70] "Tell the man," and she should have said, Tell the king.[71]

Deborah was one of the Judges who ruled Israel before Saul became the King of Israel; Chuldah was a prophetess.

Rava said in the name of Rabbi Yitzchak: Just as a donkey, the moment it has no food in its trough, immediately cries out, so too a woman cries out the moment when there is no wheat in the house.[72]

Even today, financial problems are a major reason for strife in a marriage.

Human Behavior

If you can't say something nice, say it in Yiddish.

Rabbi Yochanan stated: If the Torah had not been given, we would have learned modesty from a cat...

The cat performs its bodily functions in private and covers up its excreta.

... not stealing from an ant...

Ants prepare diligently for the winter.

... sexual conduct from a dove...

A dove is faithful to its mate.

... and conjugal manners from a rooster which appeases its mate and then has intercourse.[73]

To "appease" his mate, the rooster first walks around its mate and spreads his wings before mating. Many laws of the Torah can be derived from common sense. Unfortunately, one might learn from the wrong animals, for example, how to conduct business from a shark.

Gossip

> Rabbi Elazar stated: Why are the fingers of a person pointed like pegs? So that if a person hears things that are not proper, he should place his fingers in his ears.[74]

In the same discussion, the Talmud notes that the ear lobe is soft and the rest of the ear is hard so that if one hears something improper (e.g., gossip), he could tuck his lobe inside his ear.

Silence

> Silence is good for the wise, and how much more for fools. As it is written[75]: "Even a fool when he keeps silent is considered wise."[76]

The Talmudists also said "the best medicine of all is silence,"[77] and "A word is worth one *selah* (ancient coin), silence is worth two."[78]

> If there was a hanging in someone's family, one should not say to him, "Hang this fish up."[79]

This is another popular proverbial saying discussed in the Talmud. Be extremely careful not to remind someone of an incident that caused his family much embarrassment, even to the extent of not using an insensitive word in a completely different context.

Modesty

> The goose bends its head down while walking but its eyes look afar.[80]

This popular expression was used to describe the farsightedness of Abigail who, after convincing David to spare her husband, told David to remember her. Apparently, Abigail, who the Talmud counts as one of the seven prophetesses of Israel, gazed into the future and realized that her husband would die for his sins shortly and was hinting to David that she might become available. This is indeed what happened. Nabal died and David married Abigail.[81]

Cleanliness

> Once, Hillel the Elder had concluded his studies with his disciples and was walking with them. His disciples asked him: Rabbi, where are you going? He replied: To perform a religious obligation. They asked: What religious obligation? Hillel replied: I am going to bathe

in the bathhouse. The disciples asked: Is this then a religious obligation? He said to them: Yes! If somebody who is appointed to scour and clean the statues of kings that are erected in theaters and circuses obtains his sustenance from this work and, not only this, but even associates with the nobility of the kingdom, how much more so should I, who was created in the image and likeness of God—as it is written:[82] "For God made man in His own image"—clean my body.[83]

Hillel using witty *a fortiori* reasoning to prove the importance of personal hygiene.

Arrogance

If now, man who excretes from his bowels filth, prides himself over other creatures; all the more so, were his bowels to excrete spikenard oil, balsamum, or any other type of spice, he would certainly pride himself over other creatures.[84]

The sages loathed arrogant individuals. As they pointed out: "The end of man is maggots."[85]

If your friend calls you a donkey put a saddle on your back.[86]

This proverbial saying discussed in the Talmud teaches us that sometimes one is better off accepting what others say about them rather than arguing. Similarly:

If one person tells you that you have the ears of a donkey, pay him no mind; if two tell it to you, order a bridle for yourself.[87]

If several people give you the same criticism, it is very likely to be true.

Sex and Marriage

A woman gets married hoping he'll change; the man hopes she won't.

Rabbi Yochanan stated: There is a small organ in a person: When it is hungry, it is satisfied; when it is satisfied, it is hungry.[88]

In case you haven't figured it out, the "small organ" Rabbi Yochanan is referring to here is the sex organ. Rabbi Yochanan believed that the best way to avoid licentiousness is through self-control and restraint.

A woman is a wineskin full of excrement and her mouth is full of blood, yet all run after her.[89]

This remark indicates amazement that men should ever be attracted to women. Obviously, it follows that the innate desire that men have for women must be of divine origin.

Rabbi Yochanan stated: Rather walk behind a lion but not behind a woman; behind a woman but not behind an idol.[90]

Rabbi Yochanan is describing in a cute way the danger of walking after a married woman as it may lead to impure thoughts or worse. Following an idol might tempt one to join the pagans who worship the idol.

Rabbi Yochanan stated: Whoever philanders, his wife also philanders . . . And this is similar to what the proverb states: He is among the big pumpkins and his wife is among the small pumpkins.[91]

Rabbi Yochanan says that if the husband is not faithful to his wife, then wife will also not be faithful.

When a divorced man marries a divorced woman, there are four minds in the bed.[92]

This implies that the husband is thinking of his ex-wife, and the wife is thinking of her ex-husband.

Rava asked Rabbi Rabbah b. Mari: From where is derived the popular proverbial saying that, "Sixty pains befall the teeth of a person who hears the noise made by his neighbor's eating while he himself does not eat?" . . . Rava said: I derive it from here: It is written,[93] "Isaac brought her into his mother Sarah's tent, and took Rebecca for his wife and he loved her. Isaac was then comforted for the loss of his mother." This verse is then immediately followed by: "And Abraham took another wife whose name was Keturah."[94]

Abraham saw how Isaac was comforted by his wife, so he missed having a wife. The verse stating that Abraham took another wife (Keturah) immediately follows the verse describing how Isaac took Rebeccah as a wife and loved her.[95]

Rabbi Chiya said to Rav: May the Lord save you from something worse than death.[96]

Rav did not know what Rabbi Chiya meant by this until he found the verse "And I have discovered something more bitter than death, the woman whose heart is snares and nets."[97] Rabbi Chiya had apparently meant may the Lord save you from an evil wife. The blessing did not help, for Rav had a bad wife.

Lovers in love do not require a lot of room, but . . .

> When our love was strong, we lay down upon the edge of a sword; but now that our love is not strong, a bed that is sixty cubits wide is not large enough for us.[98]

When people are in love they do not notice many big problems; when they are not, even the smallest of problems seem insurmountable.

The next selection describes what it was like in ancient Jerusalem on the fifteenth day of the month of Av and on Yom Kippur when the unmarried girls went out and danced before the single men. All the girls wore borrowed, simple, white clothing so as not to embarrass the girls from poor homes who could not afford fancy clothing.

> The pretty ones would say: Look for beauty because a woman is only for beauty. Those who came from a distinguished family would say: Look for a good family because a woman is only for providing children. The rich girls would say: Look for wealth. The unattractive girls would say: Make your selection for the sake of Heaven.[99]

Interestingly, this sort of "singles function" took place on Yom Kippur, a day set aside for atonement of sins, as well as on the 15th of Av. Apparently, the sages considered marriage to be so important that this holy day was used for the purpose of encouraging young people to marry. The sages also stated that a couple's sins are forgiven on their wedding day.

> It was taught, Rabbi Meir used to say: Just as people differ with respect to food so too do they differ in how they treat their wives.
>
> There is a person who, when a fly falls into his cup, throws it out and does not drink from it. This is the way of Pappus b. Yehuda who used to lock his wife in before leaving the house (he did not trust her and did not let her talk to anyone).
>
> There is a person, who when a fly falls into his cup, will throw the fly out and then drink from the cup. This is the way of most men who do not mind if their wives talk with their brothers and relatives.

There is the person who when a fly falls into his dish will crush it and eat it. This is the way of an evil person who sees his wife go out with her hair uncovered, spin cloth in the street with her arms exposed, bathe in the same place where men bathe[100] and does nothing. It is a precept from the Torah to divorce this type of woman.[101]

As with most traits, it is best to be in the middle. Demanding extreme modesty from a wife can be as bad as allowing extreme immodesty.

What happens when a fly falls into a coffee cup?

The Italian tosses the cup away in a fit of rage.

The Frenchman delicately removes the fly, and drinks the coffee.

The Asian man eats the fly, throws out the coffee, and asks for tea.

The Russian drinks the coffee with the fly. After all, it was an extra, included at no charge.

The Israeli sells the coffee to the Frenchman and the fly to the Asian man, and with the profits invents a device that keeps flies from falling into coffee.

Rabbi Dostai b. Yannai believed that the differences between the sexes could be explained by studying the creation of Adam and Eve.

> *Rabbi Dostai b. Yannai's disciples asked Rabbi Dostai: Why does a man search for a woman and a woman does not search for a man? He answered: This is analogous to the case where one lost something. Who goes in search of whom? The one who lost the object searches for that which he lost . . .*

Man is searching for woman who was created from his missing rib.

> *. . . They asked: Why does a man face downward and a woman face upward toward the man during sexual intercourse? He answered: Man faces the substance from which he was created (the earth) and woman faces the substance from which she was created.*
>
> *They asked: Why is it easy to placate a man and difficult to placate a woman? He answered: Man takes after the substance from which he was created and woman takes after the substance from which she was created . . .*

Man was created from earth, and everyone steps on it; woman was created from flesh and bones, which are sensitive.

> *. . . They asked: Why is a woman's voice sweet and a man's voice not sweet? Man takes after the substance from which he was created and woman takes after the substance from which she was created.*[102]

A high pitched sound is made when beating on a bone but virtually no sound is made when beating on the earth.

Living Life to the Fullest

> *Shmuel said to Rabbi Yehuda:* Shinena, *hurry up and eat, hurry up and drink, for the world from which we must depart is like a wedding feast.*[103]

This is similar to the expression, "eat, drink, and be merry for tomorrow we die." Shmuel called Rabbi Yehuda *Shinena*, meaning, sharp or keen one. Or, this might refer to the fact that Rabbi Yehuda had big teeth (*shinayim* is translated as teeth, in Hebrew). The next saying is similar to this one. Shmuel and Rav were close friends.

> *Rav said to Rabbi Hamnuna: My son, If you possess (wealth), do good for yourself, for there is no pleasure in the grave and death does not tarry.*
>
> *And if you should say: I will leave a share for my children, who will tell you in the grave (whether they are spending your money wisely).*
>
> *The children of man are like the grass of the field, some effloresce and some wither.*[104]

Parents usually do not know which of their children are likely to need their money after they are gone.

What do you do to get rid of someone?

If he's rich you ask him for a loan; if he's poor you give him a loan.[105]

13

Allegories, Parables, and Fables

There once was poor wagon driver in the Old Country who bemoaned how much money he had to spend feeding his horse. Suddenly, he had a brainstorm: All he had to do was gradually reduce the horse's feed so that the animal would become accustomed to eat less. So that's what he did.

Over the course of months, the wagon driver gave his horse less and less to eat. At first, the animal appeared to be acclimating to the new budgetary realities, but then one day he just upped and died.

Whereupon, the poor man exclaimed: "This had to happen—just as I was getting the beast used to eating almost nothing at all!"

The sages of the Talmud were intellectuals. Many were also gifted educators. Like good teachers everywhere, they used allegories, parables, and fables to make their lectures more entertaining and, at the same time, to teach their students important moral lessons.

Many of the allegories, parables, and fables in the Talmud use the form of the *mashal*, with its associated *nimshal*. The *mashal* illustrates a moral lesson using a fictional tale which may be variously considered to be a parable, fable, metaphor, or allegory. The *mashal* is explicitly or by implication paired with its *nimshal*, which is the application of the *mashal* to reality. For a discussion of the use of the *mashal* in Talmudic and Midrashic literature, and the distinction of the mashal form from that of parable, fable, and allegory as they are generally used, the interested reader is directed to the book by David Stern.[1]

Allegories

The Talmud, and especially the Midrash, is replete with allegories. In attempting to explain a difficult concept, the Midrash often begins with *mashal lemah hadavar domeh*—meaning, allegorically, to what can this

233

be compared—and then follows with an allegorical tale or example. Frequently, these are humorous, which helps to make the point.

> *Rabbi Abuhu and Rabbi Chiya b. Abba once came to a place. Rabbi Abuhu taught* aggada *(homiletics) and Rabbi Chiya b. Abba taught* halacha *(ritual law). Everyone left Rabbi Chiya to hear Rabbi Abuhu's lecture. Rabbi Chiya felt hurt.*
>
> *Rabbi Abuhu said to him: I will give you a parable to describe what this situation is like. There were two salespeople: One was selling precious stones and the other was selling trinkets. To whom will the public flock? Obviously, to the seller of the trinkets.*[2]

Rabbi Abuhu was known for his great humility. He attempted to mollify Rabbi Chiya by comparing his own lectures to mere "trinkets."

> *Rabbi Ammi and Rabbi Assi sat before Rabbi Yitzchak Naphcha. One asked him to speak on* halacha *(ritual law) and the other asked him to speak on* aggada *(homiletics). When he started to discuss* halacha, *one did not let him continue and when he started to discuss* aggada, *the other did not let him continue.*
>
> *Rabbi Yitzchak Naphcha told them: I will give you a parable to describe what my situation is like. It is like that of the man with two wives: one young and one old. The young wife plucked out his gray hairs to make him look younger and the old wife plucked out his black hairs to make him look older. Eventually, the man was bald.*[3]

As noted earlier in this book, some of the sages preferred homiletics—*aggada*— and others Jewish law. It was obviously not easy for a teacher to satisfy everyone. The Talmud actually blends the two approaches together and has enough of both styles to satisfy everyone.

A philosopher once asked Rabbi Gamliel to answer the question as to why the Lord punishes the idolaters and not the idols themselves. He responded with a *mashal*.

> *A human king once had one son and this son raised a dog. He named the dog with his father's name. When the son would take an oath, he would say: By the life of this dog, my father. When the king heard, with whom should be enraged, the son or the dog?*[4]

On a personal note, as we read this parable, it is hard not to make the comparison to a certain academic colleague of the senior author who named his dog "Hershey," in this case, as a compliment—or, at least, so taken.

Agrippa, the general, asked Rabbi Gamliel why the Lord is "jealous" when one worships idols.[5] "Is not a wise man only jealous of another wise man, a warrior of another warrior, and a rich man of another rich man?" Rabbi Gamliel replied with a *mashal* involving polygamy, which was legal at the time.

> *This is similar to a married man who takes another wife. If the second wife is superior to the first, the first will not be incensed. But if the second wife is inferior to her, she will be incensed.*[6]

According to the Midrash, when Moses and Aaron approached Pharaoh and said to him, "This is what the God of the Hebrews says: Let My people go,"[7] Pharaoh's answer was that he did not know this God. The Midrash continues:

> *Pharaoh said to Moses and Aaron, "Wait while I search my archives." He then immediately went into his palace and investigated every nation and their gods. He started with the god of Moab, the god of Ammon, and the god of Sidon, and then told Moses and Aaron: I have searched His name in my archives and I have not found Him.*
>
> *Rabbi Levi said: To what can this be compared? To a priest who had a foolish slave. The priest left the country and the slave went to find his master in the cemetery. He began to shout at the people standing there: Did you not see my master here? They said to him: Is your master not a priest? He answered: Yes. They said: Fool! Who ever saw a priest in a cemetery? So too did Moses and Aaron say to Pharaoh: Fool! Is it normal to look for a dead person among the living or a living person among the dead? Our God is a living God, the others you mentioned are dead.*[8]

The *nimshal*: Just as priests are prohibited from going into a cemetery and will not be found there, in the same way, it is also ridiculous to look for the name of the Living and True God in a book filled with pagan deities.

In espousing on the idea that all Jews suffer when one Jew sins, Rabbi Shimon b. Yochai gave the following *mashal*:

> *This can be compared to people sitting in a boat. One passenger took a drill and started boring under his place. His fellow passengers said to him: What are you sitting and doing? He replied: What do you care? I am only boring underneath my own place. They said to him: The water will rise and flood the whole ship for us.*[9]

This parable is used to explain why Jews are obligated to rebuke others who are behaving improperly.

From the Torah we know that Moses and Aaron did not enter the land of Israel because of their sin regarding the "waters of strife," and not for the same reason that the rest of the Israelites had to die off in the desert over the course of forty years, for repeatedly angering and rebelling against God during their time in the wilderness. The following parable is used to explain why Moses wanted to make sure that the Torah explicitly states the reason that he could not enter the promised land.[10]

> *This is similar to two women who were going to be flogged by the court, one for sexual immorality and the other for having eaten unripe grapes of the Sabbatical year. The woman who ate the grapes told the members of the court: I beg of you to tell everyone why I am being flogged so that they should not say that I was also immoral. They therefore took grapes of the Sabbatical year and hung it on her saying: That woman has been sexually immoral and this woman has eaten of the grapes of the Sabbatical year.[11]*

The following parable defends God against a charge of stealing a piece of meat out of Adam's body in order to create Eve.

> *A heretic once said to Rabbi Gamliel: Your God is a thief, for it is written[12]: "And the Lord caused Adam to fall into a deep sleep and he slept, and He then took one of his ribs."*
>
> *Thereupon, the heretic's daughter said leave him be since I will answer his question. She turned to her father and said: Please contact the authorities. He asked her, why? She responded: Burglars broke in last night and robbed us of our silver pitcher and replaced it with a gold pitcher. He told her: I wish they would come every day. She then said: Well then, was it not better for Adam that they took a rib from him and gave him a handmaid to wait on him. He told her: This is what I mean. Why was the rib not taken openly from Adam.*
>
> *She said to him: Bring me some raw meat. She took it placed it under the ashes and then told him to eat it. He told her: I find it disgusting. She then exclaimed: Had Eve been taken from him openly, Adam would have found her repulsive.[13]*

It would be very difficult to eat a steak if we had to watch the cow being slaughtered, skinned, and cut up. So too, Adam would not have been able to live with Eve had he witnessed her creation from his side.

Rabbi Ulla explicated: What is the meaning of the verse,[14] "Be not overly wicked"? Does this mean "Overly wicked" is not permitted, but slightly wicked is? If one has eaten garlic and has bad breath, should he eat more garlic so that his breath should be foul-smelling even longer?[15]

Ulla uses a clever metaphor to indicate that people should not use the excuse that they have committed one misdeed to justify the continuance of doing evil.

Parables

The idea that God cannot be seen directly is mentioned in Exodus. God told Moses: "You cannot see My face, for man shall not see Me and live."[16] In the following parables, Rabbi Yehoshua tries to explain this concept to the "emperor." Talmudic parables often include references to royalty.

The emperor said to Rabbi Yehoshua: I wish to see your God. He said: You cannot see Him. The emperor insisted on seeing Him, so Rabbi Yehoshua had the emperor stand facing the sun during the summer solstice. He said to the emperor: Go and look at the sun. The emperor said that he was unable to do this. Rabbi Yehoshua said: If you say that you cannot gaze at the sun which is but one of the servants that minister to God, then how can you possibly see the Divine Presence itself?

The emperor said to Rabbi Yehoshua: I wish to prepare a banquet for your God. Rabbi Yehoshua replied: You cannot. The emperor asked: Why not? He replied: Because He has too many troops. The emperor insisted so Rabbi Yehoshua told him to prepare a banquet on the bank of the Rebita River where there was a great deal of room. The emperor toiled for six months during the summer preparing the banquet, but a strong wind came and swept everything into the sea. The emperor toiled another six months during the winter preparing the banquet, but a rain came and sank everything into the sea. The emperor asked: What is the meaning of this? Rabbi Yehoshua replied: These are only the attendants who sweep and sprinkle that come before Him. The emperor said: If so, I cannot possibly prepare a banquet for all His troops.[17]

In the second *mashal*, the wind represents the sweepers and the rain the sprinklers. In Talmudic times, the earthen floors were sprinkled with water to keep the dust down. This allegory has elements of both parable and of fable. Fables frequently make use of forces of nature in an anthropomorphic way.

In the next passage, body and soul are envisioned as arguing that each without the other would do no wrong. To prove this point each describes an innocent existence since they parted ways.

> *Antoninus said to Rebbi: The body and the soul can both exonerate themselves from the final judgment. How so?*
>
> *The body can say: The soul has sinned. Indeed, since the day the soul has departed from me, I lie in the grave like a silent stone. The soul can say: The body has sinned. Indeed, since the day that I have departed from the body, I fly in the air like a bird.*
>
> *Rebbi replied: I will tell you a parable to describe what this situation is like. A human king once had a beautiful orchard with exquisite fig trees in it. He set two gardeners to take care of it, one lame and the other blind. One day, the lame one said to the blind one: I see exquisite figs in the orchard. Come take me on your shoulders and we will pluck them and eat them. The lame one mounted the blind one's shoulders and they went and ate the figs. Several days later, the owner of the orchard came and asked: Where are my exquisite figs? The lame one said to him: Do I then have legs to walk with? The blind one said to him: Do I then have eyes with which to see? What did the owner do? He made the lame one mount the blind one and judged them as one. So too the Holy One will bring the soul and throw it back into the body and judge them together.[18]*

The "Antoninus" referred to in the Talmud has been variously identified with Marcus Aurelius, Severus, Caracalla, and others.[19]

The following parable illustrates the importance of building for future generations, rather than only considering our own needs.

> *Hadrian, may his bones be pulverized, was once passing through the paths of Tiberias and saw an old man standing and cutting through the ground to plant fig trees. He said to him: Old man, old man! If you had worked early (when young) you would not have to work late. He replied: I did work early, and do work late; what is pleasing to the Lord of Heaven, let Him do. Hadrian asked: By your life, how old are you this day? The old man replied: I am one hundred years old. Hadrian said: You are one hundred years old and you are standing and cutting through the ground and planting fig trees. He replied: If I merit it, I will eat of them; if not, just as my forefathers provided for me, so too will I provide for my children. Hadrian said to him: By your life, if you merit to eat from these figs, notify me . . .*

Hadrian persecuted the Jews and killed a large number of people, hence the expression "may his bones be pulverized" after the mention of his name. The morality tale takes interesting turn as it continues:

> . . . Eventually, the old man's trees produced figs and he brought them to Hadrian. He was shown great honor by Hadrian after he identified himself to Hadrian and was asked to sit in a chair of gold. In addition, Hadrian had the old man's basket of figs filled with gold coins.
>
> Now the wife of the old man's neighbor told her husband, a fool, that the emperor Hadrian loves figs and was exchanging them for gold. Her husband took a sack of figs and brought them to the palace. The emperor was told that a certain elderly person was standing at the gate of the palace and had brought him figs, because he had heard that the emperor liked figs and was exchanging them for gold dinarim. The emperor ordered that the elderly person should be placed before the gate to the palace and that everyone who passed by should throw a fig in his face. Toward evening, they let the elderly man go and he went home and said to his wife: I shall pay you back for the "honor" shown to me. She replied: Go and boast to your mother that it was figs and not citrons and that the figs were ripe and not hard.[20]

The following parable illustrates that the reward for living a good life is in the next world. As the Talmud notes: There is no reward for good deeds in this world.[21] All rewards are in the afterlife.

> Once the wife of Rabbi Chaninah b. Dosa told her husband: How long will we go on and suffer so much? He told her: What should we do? She replied: Go and pray that you should be given from the good that is reserved for the righteous in the world to come.
>
> He prayed and something that resembled the palm of a hand emerged (from Heaven) and gave him one leg of a golden table. Subsequently, his wife saw in a dream that in the future all the righteous will sit at a golden table of three legs but they would be eating at a golden table of two legs. He said to her: Is it acceptable to you that all the righteous will eat at a whole table and we at a defective table? She said to him: What should we do? Pray that the leg should be taken away from you. He prayed and it was taken away.[22]

Sometimes, the task of understanding the allusions in parables and fables is left largely to the reader, without providing an explicit *nimshal*.

> Alexander of Macedon paid a visit to the King of Katzia who showed him much silver and gold. Alexander said: I do not need your silver or gold. I have only come to observe your legal system and see how you dispense justice.

As Alexander and the king were conversing, two people came before the king for judgment. One said: I purchased a dunghill from this man and found a treasure in it. I said to him: I bought a dunghill, I did not buy a treasure. Therefore, the treasure is yours. The other party said: I sold you the dunghill and everything in it, therefore the treasure is yours.

While the two were arguing, the king asked one of them: Do you have a son? He answered in the affirmative. The king asked the other party: Do you have a daughter? He also answered in the affirmative. The king said to them: Marry your children to each other and give them the treasure.

Alexander started to laugh. The king asked Alexander: Why are you laughing. Did I not judge correctly? If this case had come before you, how would you have judged? Alexander replied: We would have killed both of them and the treasure would have gone to the king. The king said: Is that how much you love gold and silver?

The king ordered that a feast be prepared for Alexander consisting of meat of gold and chicken of gold. The meal was brought before Alexander. Alexander said: Do I then eat gold? The king retorted: Woe to thee! You do not eat gold, so why do you love gold so much? The king asked: Does the sun shine in your country? Alexander said "yes."

The king asked: Does rain fall in your country? Alexander said "yes." The king asked: Do you have small cattle in your country? Alexander said "yes." The king said: Woe to thee! It is not for your sake but for the sake of the cattle that the sun shines and the rain falls for you.[23]

The above is probably a parable demonstrating how an ideal world would function if everyone cared about justice. Alexander may be an archetype in the Talmud. The Hebrew word *ketz* means "end" and some translate Katzia—as in the King of Katzia—as end of the world.

Fables

Like parables, fables are fictional morality tales that allude or apply to the real world in some manner. They generally contain some anthropomorphic aspect and state a relatively simple general truth about the world. Fables use animals, plants, inanimate objects as characters.

The Midrash Rabbah uses the following parable to illustrate what happens when leaders do not lead and instead get their cues from their followers.

The tail of the snake complained to its head as to why it always leads; the tail wanted to go first. The head agreed and allowed the tail to lead. With the tail leading, the head was dragged into a ditch filled with water. The tail then encountered a fire and pulled the head into it. It then dragged the head through thorns.[24]

Some of the Talmudists, especially Rabbi Meir, the disciple of Rabbi Akiva, were known to be experts at "fox stories." Bar Kappara, at a wedding banquet for Rebbi's son, entertained the guests with three hundred fox fables at every course, and had them so enraptured that they did not touch their sumptuous food.[25] The fables that Bar Kappara related are not recorded in the Talmud. The next selection is one of the few fox parables in the Talmud.

Once the government issued a decree forbidding Jews from studying Torah. Pappus b. Yehuda found Rabbi Akiva publicly gathering crowds together and teaching them Torah. He said to him: Akiva, are you not afraid of the government?

Akiva replied: I will answer you with a mashal. *A fox was once walking by a riverbank and saw fish gathering together and going from one place to another. The fox said to them: From what are you fleeing? They said to the fox: We are fleeing from the nets which people have set to capture us. He said to them: Would you like to join me here on the dry land so we can live together the way my ancestors lived with your ancestors? They said to him: Are you the one they call the most cunning of all animals? You are not wise but foolish. For if we are afraid in the element where it is natural for us to live, how much more so in the element where we must die.*

So too is it with us Jews. If such is our condition while we study the Torah, regarding which it is written[26]: *"for this is your life and the length of your days," it will certainly be much worse for us if we go and neglect it.*[27]

A people cannot survive without their values. The Romans were trying to force the Jews to give up their religion. Rabbi Akiva was eventually tortured to death by the Romans.

Geniva said: It is like a fox who found a vineyard that was fenced in on all sides. There was one hole through which the fox wanted to enter but was unable. What did the fox do? He fasted for three days until he became emaciated and weak and was then able to fit through the hole. He then ate of the grapes and became fat. He wanted to leave but found that he could not fit through the hole. He fasted again for another three days until he became emaciated and weak, and returned to his former state, and went out. When he exited, he turned his face and looked at the vineyard and said: Vineyard, vineyard, what good are you and what good are your fruits! Everything that is inside is beautiful and praiseworthy, however what pleasure does one have from you? The way an individual enters you is the way one leaves.[28]

This fable is used by Geniva to illustrate the verse in Ecclesiastes: "As he came forth from his mother's womb, naked shall he return as he had come."[29] Geniva was not popular with the sages since he used to torment the *Resh Galuta* (Exilarch, i.e., the leader of the Babylonian Jews), Mar Ukva. Geniva was ultimately placed in chains by the Romans and executed.[30]

The following fable was used to explain why Noah[31] had to switch from a raven (a non-kosher bird) to a dove (a kosher one) in order to determine whether the waters of the flood had subsided.

The raven gave Noah an irrefutable response. It said: Your Master (God) hates me and you hate me. Your Master hates me since he commanded that, of the clean animals, you should select seven and of the unclean animals only two. You hate me, since you ignore the species of which you have seven to choose from and select from the species of which you have only two, to send from the ark.[32]

Some scholars use this passage to demonstrate the value of every species and show that it is not permissible to eradicate any species from our planet.

Rabbi Yehoshua b. Chananiah was a student of the legendary Rabbi Yochanan b. Zakkai. He was quite witty and dealt very often with heretics and even the Roman emperor. When the Romans gave permission to the Jews to rebuild the Temple and then effectively changed their minds (because the Samaritans badmouthed the Jews to the Romans) by telling the Jews that they could rebuild it but in a new location, there were Jews that favored starting a revolt. Rabbi Yehoshua told the people the following fable to calm them down.

A lion, after devouring its prey, had a bone lodged in its throat. The lion declared that any creature that removed the bone would be rewarded. An Egyptian heron (with a long beak) came and stuck its head in the lion's mouth and removed the bone and then demanded its reward. The lion said: Be glad that you can now brag and say that you were able to place your head in a lion's mouth and survive.

Let us be grateful that we entered into dealings with this people and emerged unscathed.[33]

It appears that Rabbi Yehoshua was familiar with *Aesop's Fables*. The above is a variation of "The Wolf and the Crane."

Once upon a time, in a small town, a husband and wife, very pious and modest folks, owned a general clothing store. Here's how modest they were:

When a male customer came in, the wife would turn her back and the husband attended. When a female customer entered the store, the husband would turn his back and the wife attended.

Until one day when a man and a woman came in together. Both husband and wife turned around and the couple cleaned them out!

Moral: Best not to be too damned pious.

14

Talmudic Tales

Yankel, with a wagon-load of candles, picked up Motl on the well-trod road between two shtetls. Along the way, Yankel went on about how wonderful his candles were. Motl, impressed, offered to buy the entire load of candles, figuring he could sell them in the next shtetl. They decided on a figure and the transaction was completed.

Yankel, reconsidering, offered to buy them back, giving Motl a small profit, and the deal was done. A while later, Motl made Yankel a slightly higher offer, which was also accepted. And so it went, as they traveled along the long, winding country road. Yankel and Motl kept selling that same load of candles back and forth, each to the other.

Night fell, and they camped by the side of the road. Motl took one candle from the topmost crate and tried to light it. That's when he realized that it had no wick. Quickly he examined the rest of the stock—no wicks!

"Yankel," he remarked to his friend and business companion, "your wonderful candles are useless. They have no wicks."

Yankel answered, "Motl, my friend. You are mistaken. These candles are not for lighting; they are for business." And the two continued to sell the wares back and forth each to the other all the way to the next shtetl.

As opposed to parables or fables, the many anecdotes, or "happenings," discussed in the Talmud are not presented as fictional narratives, and are not likened to any other reality. Both types of narratives, though, are intended to teach the audience a moral lesson. Avraham, the son of Maimonides, in his introduction to the *Ein Yaakov*, states that the stories of the Talmud can be classified into several types. Some stories are indeed true stories used to illustrate, prove, or refute a law or to teach us a moral lesson. Some stories of the Talmud, however, did not occur but are actually dreams or visions. Also, there are stories mentioned in the Talmud that occurred but the Talmud uses exaggeration or hyperbole in the writing of the story, since this was the literary style frequently used by the sages of the Talmud. In addition, there are stories that have actually happened but are in parable form. Unfortunately, when reading a story today there is no sure way of knowing into which category it falls and one must use his or her own judgment.

Animals

A respected rabbi of a town worked hard for his community, deciding on numerous questions of Jewish law that came up on a regular basis. After a few years of this, he needed a break and announced that he was going on an extended vacation. The townspeople had a bit of trouble finding a substitute rabbi of similar capabilities so they did the best they could. One member of the board of the synagogue wanted the position and claimed to be able to do the job. The board was skeptical but had few options.

When they asked him how he would be able to answer questions regarding whether food is kosher or not, he said, "I have a very smart dog. He knows that the Torah says that non-kosher meat should be thrown to a dog, for it is written[1]: 'You shall not eat the flesh of an animal that was torn (treife) in the field; throw it to a dog.' So for any questions regarding whether meat is kosher or not, I will simply throw it to the dog. If it is treife, he will eat it. If it is not treife, he will stay away from it and we will then know it is kosher."

When the rabbi returned several months later from his vacation, everyone in town was happy to see him. The rabbi, having heard about the plan, asked the substitute rabbi, "So, how did it work out with the dog?"

The answer: "It worked out pretty well. There was only one problem: The dog is a machmir."

This modern classic appears to be a direct descendent of the donkey stories we will look at shortly. A *machmir* is someone who is very strict in his interpretations of Jewish law. A *meikil*, on the other hand, is one who tries to find leniencies in Jewish law. For observant Jews there is a subtext to this joke: Any dog can be a *machmir*; it takes a real scholar to be *meikil*.

Fables are also stories involving animals, but the key here is that these stories actually happened (or are considered to have happened). Fables are, by definition, "fabulous" and are not meant to be taken literally. It is interesting to note that even the Biblical episode with Balaam's talking donkey is treated by some commentators (e.g., Saadia Gaon) as figurative, since donkeys do not talk. However, the Talmud does seem to take it literally.

Stories are told of the legendary donkey of Rabbi Pinchas b. Yair.

The donkey of Rabbi Pinchas b. Yair was stolen by robbers at night. It was hidden by them for three days and refused to eat anything. After the three days the robbers decided to send it back to its owner, since they were afraid that it would die and smell up their cave. They sent it away and it returned to its master's home. When it reached the gate, it began to bray.

Rabbi Pinchas said: Open the gate for this poor creature. It has not eaten anything for three days. They opened the gate and let her in. Rabbi Pinchas said: Give her something to eat. They gave her barley but she refused to eat it. They told Rabbi Pinchas that the donkey refused to eat. Rabbi Pinchas asked them whether they observed the laws of tithing. They responded affirmatively. He asked whether they had given the tithe that is due according to the law of demai. *They responded: Did you not teach us that one who purchases grain for cattle, flour for tanning hides, oil for lights, and oil for smearing vessels is exempt from the tithe of* demai? *Rabbi Pinchas said to them: What can we do for the poor creature given that she is so stringent for herself?*

They tithed the barley and the donkey ate.[2]

The word *demai* refers to produce purchased from ignorant people and thus there is a suspicion that the tithes may not have been given. Rabbi Pinchas's legendary donkey was a *machmir*, stringent with the tithing laws, even more stringent than most people. By the way, a similar story is told of the donkey of Rabbi Chaninah b. Dosa.[3] And here is another.

Rabbi Pinchas b. Yair was once going to ransom captives. He reached the Ginnai River and said to it: Ginnai, split your waters for me and I can cross you. It said to him: You are going to do the will of your Creator and I am doing the will of my Creator. You are uncertain whether or not you will be successful in ransoming the captives, but I am certainly doing what I am supposed to be doing. Rabbi Pinchas said: If you do not split your waters, I will decree that no water shall ever again flow through you. The river split for him.

There was with him a certain person who was bringing the wheat for the Passover matzot. *Pinchas said: Split for him, as well, since he is engaged in the performance of a precept. The Ginnai split.*

There was also an Arab merchant who was accompanying them. Rabbi Pinchas said: Split for him, as well, so that it should not be said, see how poorly they treat a fellow traveler. The river split for him . . .

They stopped at an inn and they placed barley before the donkey but the donkey refused to eat. They sifted the barley, but it still refused to eat. They cleaned it, but it still refused to eat. Rabbi Pinchas said to them: Perhaps you have not tithed it? They tithed it and the donkey ate it. Rabbi Pinchas said: This poor creature is going to do the will of its Creator and you are trying to feed it untithed produce.[4]

Some would consider these stories fables. In this case, not only is the donkey very religious, but the Ginnai River is anthropomorphized as well. These stories of legendary donkeys prompted the sages to say, as noted in an earlier chapter:

If the ancient scholars were sons of angels, then we are sons of men; if they are sons of men, then we are sons of donkeys—and not the donkeys of Rabbi Chaninah b. Dosa and Rabbi Pinchas b. Yair, but ordinary donkeys.[5]

Once, in a certain place, there was a lizard which used to harm people. They went and informed Rabbi Chaninah b. Dosa. He said to them: Show me its hole. They showed him its hole. He went and placed his heel over the hole's opening. It came out and bit Rabbi Chaninah and immediately died. He then placed it on his shoulder and brought it to the academy. He said to them: My children, see, it is not the scorpion that kills but the sins that kill.

On that occasion they said: Woe to a person that encounters the lizard, but woe to the lizard that encounters Rabbi Chaninah.[6]

Rabbi Chaninah b. Dosa was a disciple of Rabbi Yochanan b. Zakkai. He was extremely poor but never wanted to accept any gifts. The Talmud states that, "A heavenly voice emerged from Mount Horeb saying: The whole world is sustained because of Chaninah my son, but Chaninah my son is satisfied with a *kav* of carob from Friday to Friday."[7] A *kav* is approximately 1.4 liters.

The Spiritual and the Supernatural

Rabbah created a person and sent him to Rabbi Zera. Rabbi Zera spoke to it but it did not respond. He said to the creature: You are a creation of the magicians, return to the dust from which you came.

Rabbi Chaninah and Rabbi Oshiyah would sit and study The Book of Creation every Friday afternoon. They then created a young, choice calf and ate it.[8]

Could these stories be the basis of the legends of the Golem and Frankenstein's monster?

The next story describes an interesting lawsuit in which a barrel of wine, set down by weary porters under a drain pipe for the runoff from a roof, disturbed the demon lurking there who promptly destroyed the barrel. The porters sought restitution. According to one opinion in the Talmud, demons often lurk beneath drainpipes.

> *Once, there were porters who were carrying a barrel of wine. Wishing to rest, they set it down under a drain pipe and the barrel burst. They came before Rabbi Mar b. Ashi, who blew the shofar and excommunicated the demon.*
>
> *The demon then appeared. Rabbi Mar b. Ashi asked him: Why did you do this? He replied: What should I have done? They placed the barrel on my ear. He said to the demon: What are you doing in a public place? You did what is improper and therefore you are obliged to pay.*
>
> *The demon said: Will you please give me some time to make restitution? They set a deadline for repayment. When the day for repayment came, the demon did not show up. Some time later, the demon came to make restitution.*
>
> *Rabbi Mar b. Ashi asked him: Why did you not come before? He replied: We demons have no permission to take anything that is tied up, sealed, measured, or counted. I therefore had to wait until I could find things that are ownerless.*[9]

Even demons have to obey the law.

> *Rabbi Yochanan stated: The righteous man, Choni Hamagel, was troubled about the meaning of the following verse his whole life. It says*[10]: *"A song of ascents, when the Lord brings back the captivity of Zion, we will be like dreamers." He wondered: Is it possible for one to sleep and dream for seventy years straight? . . .*

This is a reference to the Babylonian exile, which lasted for seventy years.

> *. . . One day, as he was traveling along the road, he saw a man planting a carob tree. He said to him: How long will it take for this tree to bear fruit? The man replied: Seventy years. Choni said to him: Are you sure that you will be alive in seventy years? He replied: When I came into the world I found a carob tree; just as my forefathers planted for me, so too I am planting for my children.*

Choni sat to eat some bread and fell asleep. A grotto formed around him while he slept, and hid him from sight and he slept for seventy years. When he awoke, he saw someone gathering carob from the tree. Choni asked him: Are you the person that planted this tree? He said: No, the tree was planted by my grandfather. Choni said: Apparently, I have slept for seventy years. He noticed that his donkey had given birth to herds of donkeys. He went to his house and asked: Is the son of Choni Hamagel alive? He was told that the son was no longer living but the son's son was alive. He then said: I am Choni Hamagel but no one believed him. He went to the academy and heard the sages saying that the law is as clear to us as it was in the days of Choni Hamagel. In those days, whenever he came to the academy he clarified any difficulties that we had. Choni said: I am Choni. They did not believe him and they did not treat him with the proper respect. He was hurt and prayed for his death and died. Rava said: Accordingly, the proverbial saying, "Either friends or death." [11]

This story seems to be an early version of the Rip Van Winkle legend. Not everyone takes this story literally, but the lesson applies to all time.

Dreams and their Interpretations

Rebbi and Rabbi Yishmael both interpreted dreams but, as we see in the following passage, they each used a different approach.

Bar Kappara said to Rebbi: I saw in a dream that my nose fell off. Rebbi replied: This means that wrath has been removed from you . . .

The word "*af*" can be translated to mean either nose or wrath.

. . . He said: I saw in a dream that both of my hands were cut off. Rebbi said: You will not require the labor of your hands . . .

That is, you will become wealthy.

. . . He said: I saw in a dream that both my legs were cut off. Rebbi said: You will ride on a horse.

He said: I dreamed that they said to me: You will die in the month of Adar *and not see* Nissan. *Rebbi said: This means that you will die in distinction* (adruta) *and will not be tempted* (nisayon).

Now on to Rabbi Yishmael's approach.

A heretic once said to Rabbi Yishmael: I saw in a dream that I was providing olives with oil to drink. Rabbi Yishmael said: This means that he committed incest with his mother.

He said: I saw in a dream that I uprooted a star. Rabbi Yishmael said: You have kidnapped a Jew.

He said: I saw that I swallowed a star. Rabbi Yishmael said: You have kidnapped a Jew and spent the proceeds.

He said: I saw that my eyes were kissing each other. Rabbi Yishmael said: You have committed incest with your sister.

He said: I saw that I kissed the moon. Rabbi Yishmael said: You have committed adultery with a Jewish woman.[12]

As the passages above show, Rebbi and Rabbi Yishmael interpreted dreams in two completely different manners. In Rabbi Yishmael's interpretations, objects are symbols. For instance, providing an olive with oil to drink symbolizes committing incest with one's mother; their oil was olive oil, which issues from the olive. This approach is similar to Freud's approach to dream interpretation. Rebbi, on the other hand, believed that dreams foretell the future. For instance, his interpretation of a loss of hands meant that the dreamer would become wealthy.

Spirits of the Dead and the World to Come

Many stories of the Talmud involve the dead and the next world. The next two stories follow a discussion in the Talmud as to whether the dead are aware of the plight of the living.

Once, a certain pious person gave a poor person a dinar *on the eve of Rosh Hashonah during a famine year. His wife became angry and he went and spent the night in the cemetery. He overheard two spirits speaking to each other, one saying to the other: Let us fly about the world and listen from behind the Heavenly curtain what punishment will come to the world. The other spirit replied: I cannot because I am buried in a mat of reeds, but you go and tell me what you hear. The spirit left, flew away and returned. The other spirit said to her: My friend, what did you hear from behind the Heavenly curtain? She replied: I heard that anyone who plants at the first rainfall will have his crop destroyed by hail. The man went and planted his crop after the first rainfall. Everyone's crop was destroyed by hail except for his.*

The following year, he went and spent the night in the cemetery. He overheard the same two spirits speaking to each other, with one saying to the other: Let us fly about the world and listen from behind the Heavenly curtain what punishment will come to the world. The other spirit replied: I already told you that I cannot because I am buried in a mat of reeds, but you go and tell me what you hear. The spirit left, flew away and returned. The other spirit said to her: My friend, what did you hear from behind the Heavenly curtain? She replied:

I heard that anyone who plants by the second rainfall will have his crop destroyed by squall. The man went and planted his crop by the first rainfall. Everyone's crop was destroyed by squall except for his.

His wife said to him: How is that last year everyone's crop was destroyed by hail except for yours, and this year again everyone's crop was destroyed by squall and yours was not? He told her the whole story. It was said, that not much time elapsed when the wife had a dispute with the mother of the deceased girl and said to her: Come and I will show you that your daughter is buried in a mat of reeds.

The following year, he went and spent the night in the cemetery. He overheard the same two spirits speaking to each other, with one saying to the other: Let us fly about the world and listen from behind the Heavenly curtain what punishment will come to the world. The other spirit replied: Leave me be. Our conversation has been overheard by the living. [13]

Most of the commentaries (e.g., Maharsha) believe that the above story was a dream. Apparently, it is hard to imagine that a pious individual would spend Rosh Hashonah night in a cemetery.

Zeiri once deposited money with his landlady, and while he was away at the academy she died. He went after her to the cemetery and asked her: Where is the money? She said to him: Go and take it from under the doorpost at such and such a place. And tell my mother to send my comb and my eye makeup with so-and-so who will be coming here tomorrow. [14]

This is reminiscent of the joke in which the recently deceased friend appears to his living friend, a great lover of baseball, in a dream and tells him that he has good news and bad news for him. The good news is that there is baseball in the next world. The bad news is that he will be playing shortstop the following day.

The father of Shmuel was the custodian of money belonging to orphans. Shmuel was not with him when he died and he was called "the devourer of orphan's money . . ."

Because he died suddenly, and no one knew where the money was, the father of Shmuel was suspected of spending their money on himself.

. . . Shmuel went after his father to the courtyard of death (probably the cemetery) and said to the souls of the dead: I am looking for Abba. They said to him: There are many Abbas here. He said: I want Abba b. Abba. They said: There are also many Abbas b. Abba here. He

said: I want Abba b. Abba, the father of Shmuel; where is he? They said: He went up to the Heavenly academy. While this was going on, he noticed the soul of Levi sitting outside. He said to Levi: Why are you sitting on the outside? Why have you not gone up to the Heavenly academy? Levi said: Because they told me that for every year that I did not enter the academy of Rabbi Efes (when I was alive) and hurt his feelings, they will not allow me to enter the Heavenly academy.

Meanwhile, Shmuel's father arrived. Shmuel noticed that he was crying and laughing. He asked him: Why are you crying? He said: Because you will be here very soon. He asked him: Why are you laughing? He said: Because you are greatly respected in this world. He said to him: If I am respected, then let them allow Levi to enter the Heavenly academy. They allowed Levi to enter.

He then asked his father where he hid the orphan's money. He said: Go and take it from under the millstone. The money that is above and below it belongs to us, and the money in the middle belongs to the orphans. Shmuel asked his father why he did this. He replied: If thieves come they will take mine (seeing only the money on top) and if the earth ruins the money it will ruin mine (being on the bottom). [15]

Rabbi Efes became head of Rebbi's yeshiva after Rebbi died. Rebbi actually designated Rabbi Chaninah b. Chama but he refused the position since he was younger than Rabbi Efes. Rabbi Chaninah and Rabbi Levi sat together outside the lecture hall.[16] Whether this story is to be taken literally or not, it does provide some interesting lessons. One very important lesson is that even great individuals are punished in the afterlife for hurting people's feelings.

The following story illustrates that the next world does not work the same way as does this world.

Rabbi Yosef, the son of Rabbi Yehoshua b. Levi, once took ill and became unconscious. When he revived, his father asked him: What did you see when you were unconscious?

He replied: I saw a topsy-turvy world: the people who are on top here, are low there, and the people who are low here are high there.

Rabbi Yehoshua said: My son, you saw a clear world. And how are we there? He replied: Just as we are here, so are we there. Also, I heard them saying: Happy is he who comes here with his learning in his hand. [17]

In this world, people are respected for the wrong reasons. In the next world, the respect you get is based solely on merit.

> *Rabbi Zera said: Last night Rabbi Yosi b. Chaninah appeared to me in a dream. I asked him: Next to whom are you seated in the heavenly academy?*
>
> *He replied: Next to Rabbi Yochanan.*
>
> *I asked: Next to whom is Rabbi Yochanan seated.*
>
> *He said: Next to Rabbi Yannai.*
>
> *I asked: Next to whom is Rabbi Yannai seated.*
>
> *He said: Next to Rabbi Chaninah.*
>
> *I then asked: Next to whom is Rabbi Chaninah seated.*
>
> *He said: Next to Rabbi Chiya.*
>
> *I said to him: Why is Rabbi Yochanan not worthy to be seated next to Rabbi Chiya?*
>
> *He said: In a place of fiery sparks and flaming torches, who will allow* Bar Naphcha *(the smith's son) to enter?*[18]

Rabbi Yochanan was known as *Bar Naphcha* which means the son of a smith. It is not clear whether Rabbi Yochanan's father was a blacksmith or whether his name just happened to be *Naphcha*. This story confirms that a number of the Talmudic sages took their dreams seriously.

> *There was a magus who used to exhume the dead. When he came to Rabbi Tobi b. Mattenah's grave, Rabbi Tobi grabbed the magus's beard. Abaye came and said to Rabbi Tobi: I beg of you to let go of him. The following year, the magus came to the grave again and Rabbi Tobi grabbed his beard. Abaye came, but he did not let go of the beard. They had to bring scissors and cut off the beard of the magus.*[19]

The Zoroastrians did not believe in burying the dead, since this would defile the earth.

The next two stories deal with the three evil kings who have no share in the world to come: Jeroboam, Ahab, and Menashe.

> *Rabbi Abuhu was wont to lecture about the three evil Jewish kings. He became ill, so he decided to discontinue these lectures. When he recovered, he continued his lectures about the three kings. He was asked: Did you not decide not to lecture anymore about the three kings? He replied: Did they repent so that I should do likewise?*
>
> *Rabbi Ashi ended his lecture at the discussion of the three kings. He declared: Tomorrow we will begin the lecture about our colleagues . . .*

These kings were supposed to be great scholars and that is why he facetiously referred to them as "colleagues."

> *King Menashe appeared to Rabbi Ashi in his dream and said: You call us colleagues and your father's colleagues, do you know what part of the bread one is supposed to slice off when reciting the* Hamotzi *blessing? Rabbi Ashi told him that he did not know.*
>
> *Menashe declared: You do not know what part of the bread one is supposed to slice off when reciting the blessing and you call us colleagues? Rabbi Ashi said: Teach it to me and tomorrow I will lecture about it in your name.*
>
> *Menashe answered: Slice the bread where it is well-crusted and baked. Rabbi Ashi asked: Since you are so wise, why did you worship idols?*
>
> *Menashe responded: Had you been there, you would have lifted up the hem of your garment to run after idols to worship. On the following day, Rabbi Ashi told his colleagues: Let us begin our lecture about our teachers.*[20]

This story teaches one not to judge others too hastily. Indeed, Hillel stated: "Do not judge your fellow human being until you have been in his position."[21] Menashe was twelve years old when he became king and ruled in Jerusalem for fifty-five years. He "did what was evil in the eyes of the Lord" and erected altars to Baal and other false gods.[22] It only adds to the tragedy that his father was the saintly King Hezekiah who eradicated idolatry from Judea.

Elijah The Prophet

> *Rabbi Yehoshua b. Levi found Elijah the prophet standing by the entrance of Rabbi Shimon b. Yochai's burial cave and asked him: Will I be allowed to enter the world to come? Elijah replied: If this Master here desires it. Rabbi Yehoshua said: I saw two (Elijah and myself) but heard the voice of a third (the Divine Presence).*
>
> *Rabbi Yehoshua then asked Elijah: When will the Messiah come? He replied: Go ask him yourself. Rabbi Yehoshua asked: Where does he abide? He replied: At the entrance of Rome. Rabbi Yehoshua asked: By what sign will I be able to recognize him. He replied: He sits among the poor who suffer from various ailments; all of them untie and then retie all their bandages at once. He unties and ties his bandages one at a time, saying to himself: Should I be needed, I must not be delayed. Rabbi Yehoshua went to him and said: Peace on you, my master and teacher. The Messiah replied: Peace on you, son*

of Levi. Rabbi Yehoshua asked: When are you coming, master? He said: Today.

When Rabbi Yehoshua returned to Elijah, Elijah asked him what the Messiah said to him. Rabbi Yehoshua replied that he said, Peace on you, son of Levi. Elijah told him that this means that both Rabbi Yehoshua and his father are assured of a share in the world to come. Rabbi Yehoshua said to Elijah: He lied to me. He said he was going to come today and he did not come. Elijah replied: What he meant was,[23] "Today, if you will heed His voice."[24]

This is a somewhat humorous way of emphasizing that the Messiah will come when everyone is good. This passage figured prominently in the Disputation between Nachamanides and Fra Paulo Christiani. Nachamanides turned the tables on Paulo Christiani by showing that the above proves that the Messiah had not yet come. Rabbi Yehoshua b. Levi lived during the third century.

Rabbi Yosi lectured in Sepphoris that Elijah the Prophet was hot tempered. Elijah used to visit him regularly, but after this, he did not appear for three days. When he came, Rabbi Yosi asked him: Why did the master not appear? Elijah responded: Because you called me hot tempered. Rabbi Yosi said: Well, does this incident not prove that the master is hot tempered?[25]

Elijah was the prophet in the time of King Ahab and Queen Jezebel. He prayed for a major famine because of the evil deeds of the king and queen. According to legend, since Elijah never actually died, he visits the supremely righteous.

Miracles

A man is hiking down a steep trail, when he loses his footing and slides off the side of a cliff.

"God!" he exclaims. "Please make a miracle and save me!"

Moments later his shirt gets caught on a protruding branch, and as he is dangling hundreds of feet in the air, he shouts once again: "God! Please save me!"

Just then, a heavenly voice calls out: "Do you trust Me, My son?"

"Yes! Yes God, I trust you. Just please save me!"

"Let go of the branch and I'll catch you."

(Pause.) "Is anyone else out there?"

Once, a person's wife died and left him with a baby son that needed to be nursed and he could not afford to pay a wet nurse. A miracle occurred for him and his breasts opened up like the two breasts of a woman and he nursed his son.

Rabbi Yosef said: Come and see how great was this person that a miracle of this type should occur for him. Abaye said: On the contrary, how lowly was this person that the order of creation had to be changed for him.[26]

Rabbi Yosef believed that if the Lord had provided the father with wealth he would then have hired a wet nurse and the miracle would not have been obvious. It is a testimony to the man's greatness that such an obvious miracle was performed for him. Abaye, on the other hand, felt that with wealth, he could also have taken care of other needs. Since he was not such a great person, only one problem—feeding his baby—was solved for him.[27]

Sometimes, the consequences of getting drunk—even on the holiday of Purim—can be deadly. However,

Rava said: One should get so drunk on Purim that he cannot distinguish between "cursed is Haman" and "blessed is Mordechai."

Rabbah and Rabbi Zera once had the Purim feast together. They got drunk and Rabbah got up and slaughtered Rabbi Zera. The next morning, Rabbah prayed for him and Rabbi Zera came back to life.

The following year, Rabbah asked Rabbi Zera to join him again for the Purim feast. Rabbi Zera replied: Miracles do not happen every single time.[28]

Rabbi Avraham, the son of Maimonides, believes that this story is not to be taken literally. What actually happened, he says, was that Rabbah pummeled Rabbi Zera and the beating was so severe that the term "slaughtered" is used to describe it. This is not very different from our own idiom in which words such as kill and slaughter do not always connote death.

Nachum ish Gamzu was called gamzu *because no matter what happened to him he would say* gam zu latovah *(this too is for the best). One time the Jews desired to send a gift to the emperor. They decided that Nachum ish Gamzu should go because miracles often happened to him. They sent him with a chest full of precious stones and jewels. On the way, he spent the night in a certain inn. During the night the innkeepers emptied the chest and filled it with earth. In the morning, when Nachum discovered what had happened he exclaimed: This too is for the best.*

When he arrived at the palace and they saw that he had brought a chest filled with earth, the emperor wanted to have all the Jews killed. They are mocking me, he declared. Nachum exclaimed: This too is for the best.

Elijah appeared in the guise of one of the officers, and said: Perhaps, this earth is the miraculous earth used by their patriarch Abraham; when he threw earth at his enemies it changed into swords and when he threw straw it changed into arrows. Indeed, it is written[29]: "He made his sword like dust, his bow as the driven straw." Now, here was a country which they were unable to conquer but when they used this earth against it they prevailed. They took Rabbi Nachum to the treasury, filled his chest with precious stones and jewels and sent him home with great honor.

On his return journey, he spent the night in the same inn. The innkeepers asked Rabbi Nachum what he brought to the emperor that so much honor was shown to him. He replied: What I took from here, I brought there. They tore down their inn and brought the earth to the emperor and stated: The earth that was brought to you came from us. They tested the earth and found it to be ordinary earth and they executed the innkeepers.[30]

This story like many others involving Nachum ish Gamzu demonstrates the importance of having faith in God and being able to say, in the face of adversity, "this too is for the best," *gam zu latovah.*

Power of Blessing

Rabbi Huna once appeared before Rav wearing a belt made of reeds. Rav asked him: What is the meaning of this? He answered: I had no wine for Kiddush[31] so I pawned my belt to get some wine. Rav said: May it be His will that you should become covered with silken robes.

On the day that Rabbi Huna's son Rabbah got married, Rabbi Huna, who was a very short person, was slumbering on a bed. His daughters and daughters-in-law, not noticing him, removed and threw their silken robes on him until he was covered in silks. When Rav heard about this he became angry saying: Why did Rabbi Huna not say when I blessed him, The same to you.[32]

This story shows why the sages declared: "The blessing of an ordinary person should not be considered lightly in one's eyes."[33] And all the more so, the blessing of a great person.

Human Behavior

Prayer

The next story demonstrates that perception is indeed in the eyes of the beholder.

> *A certain student once went down to the reader's desk in the synagogue to lead everyone in prayer in the presence of Rabbi Elazar. He prolonged the prayer too much and the students complained to their teacher, Rabbi Elazar: Teacher, how great a lengthener is this student! Rabbi Elazar responded: Is he a greater lengthener than Moses, our teacher, of whom it is written[34]: "the forty days and the forty nights that I prostrated myself" (before the Lord).*
>
> *On another occasion, a certain student went down to the reader's desk in the synagogue to lead the congregation in prayer in the presence of Rabbi Elazar. He shortened the prayer too much and the students complained to their teacher, Rabbi Elazar: Teacher, how curt is this student! Rabbi Elazar responded: Is he curter than Moses, our teacher, of whom it is written[35]: "O Lord I beseech you, please heal her."[36]*

Moses's prayer for his sister, Miriam, who was punished with leprosy was a five-word prayer (in Hebrew), with four out of the five words consisting of only two letters each. This story illustrates that sincerity is more important than the length of the prayer. Of course, to this very day, Jews complain about the person leading the service, who is praying either too fast or too slow. Often, one is told by some to slow down and by others to speed up.

Manners

The next story follows a discussion of situations in which an elder may be exempt from certain obligations if they might be undignified for him.

> *Once, Rabbi Yishmael b. Yosi was traveling on the road when he met a certain man who was carrying a bundle of wood. The man put them down and rested. After resting, he said to Rabbi Yishmael: load the wood on me . . .*

This is in accordance with Jewish law which requires one to help load up even a donkey.[37]

> *. . . Rabbi Yishmael said to him: How much is the bundle worth? He replied: half a zuz. Rabbi Yishmael paid him half a zuz and declared the bundle ownerless . . .*

Rabbi Yishmael did not want anyone to be guilty of stealing so he made the bundle ownerless.

> . . . Thereupon the man took possession of the bundle for himself. Rabbi Yishmael gave him another half zuz and declared the bundle ownerless.
>
> Seeing that that man was going to take possession of the bundle again, Rabbi Yishmael declared: I have pronounced it ownerless for the whole world except for you.[38]

Besides being an elder, Rabbi Yishmael b. Yosi was known for his obesity.

The next passage follows a discussion of people who were very diligent in ensuring that others would not be embarrassed, even if it might result in shame to themselves.

> Rebbi was once sitting and lecturing and he smelled the odor of garlic. He said: Whoever has eaten the garlic, please leave. Rabbi Chiya got up and left. Seeing Rabbi Chiya leave, all of the other students rose and left. The next morning, Rabbi Shimon, the son of Rebbi, met Rabbi Chiya and asked him: Are you the one who caused my father grief by eating garlic? Rabbi Chiya responded: Heaven forbid! There should never be one like this in Israel. I did not eat the garlic but left in order not to embarrass the real culprit.[39]

The other students then followed Rabbi Chiya in order not to embarrass him. Shaming another person publicly is a great sin and is tantamount to murder, according to the Talmud.

> Rabbi Akiva once prepared a meal for his students. He prepared two dishes for them, one raw and one cooked. He first served them the raw dish. The wise students grabbed the stalk with one hand and attempted to break off a piece using their other hand, and when it did not come off, they gave up and just ate their bread. The foolish students grabbed the stalk with one hand and bit into it with their teeth. Rabbi Akiva said to them (sarcastically): Not like that my children, place your heel on it in the plate. Afterwards, he served them the cooked dish which they ate and were sated. He then said to them: My children, I only did this to test you to determine whether or not you had manners.[40]

Rabbi Akiva believed that manners were very important. As a teacher, he wanted his students to learn more than just Jewish law.

Speech and Speaking Clearly

> *Two advisors stood before Hadrian. One contended that speech is best and the other maintained that silence is best.*
>
> *One said: Master, there is nothing better than speech, for without speech how would brides be praised. How could there be any transactions in the world? How could ships set sail on the sea? Immediately, the king asked the one who claimed that silence is best: What do you have to say on behalf of silence?*
>
> *As soon as he started to speak, the other one struck him on the mouth. The king said to him: Why did you strike him? He replied: Master, I advocated on behalf of speech with speech; this one wishes to support his position with that which is mine.*[41]

That is, speech. This is certainly a clever way to win the argument.

> *Rabbi Shimon b. Gamliel once told Tabi his servant to go and buy him good food in the marketplace. He went and bought him tongue. He then said to Tabi: Go and buy me bad food in the marketplace. Tabi went and bought him tongue. Rabbi Shimon b. Gamliel said to him: What is the meaning of this? When I asked you for good food, you bought me tongue and when I asked you for bad food, you bought me tongue. Tabi replied: From a tongue can come good and from a tongue can come bad. When a tongue is good, there is nothing better; but when it is bad, there is nothing worse.*
>
> *Rebbi once made a meal for his students and served them tender tongues and hard tongues. They started picking the tender tongues and leaving the hard ones. Rebbi said to them: Understand what you are doing. Just as you pick the tender and leave over the hard, so too should your own tongues be tender to each other.*[42]

Both stories are used to illustrate the importance of heeding what one says, because "Death and life are in the hands of the tongue."[43]

The Talmud states that the Galileans were not clear in the way they spoke and therefore did not retain their knowledge.[44] The Talmud relates several stories of Galileans who did not speak precisely or clearly.

> *Once there was a Galilean who went about inquiring: Who has an amar? Who has an amar? (He did not speak clearly) They said to him: Foolish Galilean! Do you mean a* chamar *(donkey) to ride on, or* chamar *(wine) to drink, or* amar *(wool) for clothing, or an* imar *(lamb) to slaughter?*
>
> *... There was a woman who came before a judge and said to him (what sounded like): My master, slave, I had a beam and they stole you from*

me, and now it was so long that if they hanged you on it, your feet would not reach the ground.[45]

What the woman was actually trying to say was: I had a board and they stole it from me. It was so long that if they stretched you out on it, your feet would not touch the ground. In Aramaic, there are a number of words that sound alike yet have very different meanings. This is similar to *hair* and *here* in English which might sound alike if one does not enunciate properly. The purpose of these stories might have been to show the public the importance of speaking clearly.

Repentance

The great Rabbi Shimon b. Lakish, known as Resh Lakish, started out as a highwayman. Here is the tale of his first meeting with his future brother-in-law (spoiler alert).

> *One day, Rabbi Yochanan was bathing in the Jordan River, when Resh Lakish saw him and leaped into the Jordan River after him. Rabbi Yochanan said to him: Your strength should be used for Torah. Resh Lakish said: Your beauty should be for women. Rabbi Yochanan said to him: If you repent, I will give you my sister in marriage and she is even more beautiful than I. Resh Lakish accepted the offer. He then wanted to jump back across the river in order to retrieve his clothing, but did not have the strength.*[46]

The idea here is that, since studying weakens an individual, once Resh Lakish agreed to become a scholar rather than a brigand, he lost some of his immense strength. Resh Lakish became a great scholar known for his erudition and great piety.

Here is a story about envious Rabbis and the evil eye.

> *Rabbi Zera fasted one hundred fasts so that the fire of Gehinnom (Hell) should have no effect on him. Every thirty days he would test his body in the following manner to determine whether he was resistant to fire. He would heat up the oven and would go and sit inside of it, yet the fire would have no effect on him. One day the Rabbis fixed their eyes (they were envious and this is an example of the effect of an evil eye) upon him and his thighs became singed. From then on he was known as the "little one with the singed thighs."*[47]

This nickname stuck. Once, when Rabbi Zera became ill, Rabbi Abuhu said: "If the little one with the singed thighs recovers I will make a feast for the Rabbis."[48]

Also, in Rabbi Zera's neighborhood there were highwaymen that he befriended hoping that he might eventually get them to repent. However, his colleagues were annoyed with him for befriending such characters. When Rabbi Zera died the highwaymen said: Until now we had the little one with the singed thighs to pray for us. But now, who will pray for us? They then felt remorse in their hearts and repented.[49]

This philosophy is consistent with the approach used by Bruriah, the wife of Rabbi Meir who told her husband to pray that the highwaymen in their neighborhood repent, not die. He listened to her and the sinners gave up their wicked ways.[50]

It was said regarding Rabbi Elazar b. Durdia that he did not leave one prostitute in the world without having intercourse with her. One time he heard that there was a prostitute overseas who charged a purse of dinarim as her fee. He took a purse of dinarim, went and crossed seven rivers to be with her. While they were having intercourse, she passed wind. She said: Just as this wind will never return back to its place, so too, Elazar b. Durdia will never be accepted in repentance. . . .

He went and placed his head between his knees and cried aloud in penitence until his soul departed. A Heavenly voice proclaimed: Rabbi Elazar b. Durdia is destined for life in the World to Come. . . .

Rebbi, upon hearing this, cried and exclaimed: Some acquire Paradise after many years (of hard work), and others acquire Paradise in one moment. Rebbi also said: Not enough that penitents are accepted but they are even called "Rabbi."[51]

This story illustrates the power of sincere penitence based on remorse, even at the last moments of one's life. One of the prayers said on the High Holy Days emphasizes that, saying "Penitence, Prayer, and Charity cancel the stern decree."

Once, a man who was very scrupulous in observing the commandment of wearing zizit,[52] heard of a prostitute who lived overseas that charged four hundred gold dinarim as her fee. He sent her four hundred gold dinarim and made an appointment with her. On his appointed time, he came and sat by her door. Her servant came and informed her that that the person who sent her the four hundred dinarim had arrived and was waiting by the door. She told him to come in and he entered. She then prepared seven beds (one above the other), six of silver and one of gold. Between each bed there was a silver ladder and the ladder to the uppermost bed was of gold. She then went up to the top bed and sat on it naked. He also started to climb up in order to sit naked beside her, when his four zizit struck him in the face.

He slipped off and sat on the ground. She also then slipped off and sat on the ground. She said: By the Emperor of Rome, I will not leave you alone until you tell me what fault you saw in me. He responded: By the Temple Service, I assure you that I never saw a woman as beautiful as you. However, there is one precept that our Lord commanded us and it is called zizit . . . and now these zizit appeared to me as four witnesses. She told him: I will not leave you alone until you tell me your name, the name of your city, the name of your teacher, and the name of your academy in which you learned Torah. He wrote this down and then placed the note in her hand.

She got up and divided her estate into three parts: One-third she gave to the government,[53] one-third to the poor, and one-third she kept for herself. The bedding she also kept for herself. She came to the academy of Rabbi Chiya and said to him: Rabbi, please provide instructions so that I may be converted to Judaism. Rabbi Chiya said to her: My daughter, perhaps you have set your eyes on one of the students? She took out the note and gave it to him. He said to her: Go and have a good life with the husband you are going to acquire. Thus, the very bedding that she spread out for him for illicit purposes she was then able to spread out for him for licit purposes.[54]

This story shows how a precept guards one from sin. In particular, the *zizit* worn on the clothing are supposed to remind the wearer of the 613 Biblical precepts. For a fascinating interpretation of this story see the referenced article by Eliezer Berkovits.[55]

Sex and Marriage

A matron once made sexual demands on Rabbi Zadok. He said to her: My heart is weak (from hunger) and therefore I am not physically able; is there perhaps something to eat? She said: There is something unclean (i.e., unkosher). He said: What is the difference? If I do this sin, I may as well eat this. She fired up the oven and placed the meat inside. Rabbi Zadok went and sat in the oven. She said: Why are you doing this? He said: Whoever does this (sexual immorality), will fall into this (the fires of hell). She said to him: If I knew how serious a matter this was to you, I would not have bothered you.

Rabbi Kahana used to sell ladies' baskets. Once a matron made sexual demands upon him. He told her: Let me first go and adorn myself. He went to the roof and jumped from it, but Elijah (the prophet) came and caught him. Elijah said to Rabbi Kahana: You troubled me to come from four hundred parsangs away. Rabbi Kahana replied: What made me go into this (line of work), is it not my dire poverty? Elijah thereupon gave him a vessel full of dinarim.[56]

The matrons in the above stories were influential people and the sages were probably afraid of them.

The following story follows a discussion of the law that a man may not be alone with a woman.

There were these redeemed captives that were brought to the town of Nehardea. They were taken to the house of Rabbi Amram the Pious, lodged in the upper story of his house, and the ladder leading to it was taken away. As one of the women passed by, her face was illuminated by a light shining through the skylight. Rabbi Amram took the ladder, which ten could not lift, set it up single-handedly and started ascending it. When he reached the half-way point, he stemmed his feet. He raised his voice and started yelling: There is a fire in Amram's house. When the rabbis came and saw him on the ladder they said: You have shamed us. He told them: It is better that you be ashamed of Amram in this world than I be ashamed of Amram in the world to come.[57]

Even pious people can have weak moments. The Talmud does not whitewash the lives of the sages. Piety does not result from having no desires, but from the ability and willingness to overcome them.

Once, a man married a woman who was missing a hand and he did not realize it until the day of her death. Rebbi said: Come and see how modest was this woman that her husband did not know. Rabbi Chiya said to him: For a woman it is natural. Rather, how modest was the man for not noticing the defect in his wife.[58]

The sages believed very strongly in the importance of modesty, and that it would be natural for a woman to try to cover up such a deformity.

Rav was often tormented by his wife. When he asked for lentils, she would make him peas, and when he asked for peas, she would make him lentils. When his son Chiya grew up, he reversed his father's request. Rav said to Chiya: Your mother has improved. Chiya responded: I caused it by reversing your request. He said to him: This is what is meant by the proverbial saying, "Your own descendent will teach you reasoning." However, you should not do this, because it says,[59] *"They have taught their tongue to speak falsehood, they weary themselves committing iniquity."*[60]

The Talmud mentions this story in their discussion of the importance of being married. A sample[61] of The Talmud's philosophy regarding marriage includes the view that "Any person who has no wife lives without joy, without blessing, and without goodness" and "Any person who has no wife is not a person" (i.e., is not complete). The Talmud also discusses what a bad wife is like. "What is a bad wife? Abaye said: One who prepares a meal for her husband and also prepares her mouth," that is, to curse and castigate him.

> *Rebbi was occupied in the preparations for his son's marriage into the family of Yosi b. Zimra. It was agreed that Rebbi's son would study for twelve years at the academy and then get married.*
>
> *The girl was passed in front of the boy. He said: Let it be six years.*
>
> *They passed the girl in front of him again and he said: Let me be married first and then I will go and study.*
>
> *He felt ashamed in front of his father. Rebbi said to him: My son, you have the temperament of your Creator. First it says[62]: "You will bring them in and plant them." Then it says[63]: "They shall make Me a sanctuary and I will dwell among them."[64]*

Originally, the sanctuary was not going to be built until the Jewish people had conquered the Holy Land. God reconsidered and decided that it should be built in the wilderness.

The Mishna says that when Rabbi Yishmael died, the following was said at his funeral:

> *Daughters of Israel weep for Rabbi Yishmael who clothed you . . .*

He was known for prettying up the single women and even provided a young lady missing a tooth with a false gold tooth at his own expense.[65] And, here he argues that if a man makes a vow that he will not marry a woman because she is ugly, the vow is null and void if she is made attractive.

> *Once, a person vowed not to marry his sister's daughter because she was ugly. They brought her to the house of Rabbi Yishmael and he had her beautified (by having her dressed up and adorned). Rabbi Yishmael then summoned the man and asked him: My son, is this the woman regarding whom you made the vow? He replied: No. Rabbi Yishmael allowed him to marry her.*
>
> *At that time, Rabbi Yishmael cried and said: The daughters of Israel are beautiful but it is poverty that makes them homely.[66]*

The next story is used to illustrate the laws regarding how much maintenance is provided for a widow out of her late husband's estate. Abaye, also known as Nachmeni, had just died and his widow Chomah—thrice widowed, as we find out—was asking Rava to determine a proper amount for her support.

> *Chomah, Abaye's wife, came before Rava asking that the estate provide her an allowance for food. Rava granted it to her. She then said: Grant me an allowance for wine. Rava replied: I know that Nachmeni did not drink wine. Choma responded: By your life, master, he gave me to drink from goblets as long as my arm. As she was showing her arm, it became exposed and its beauty radiated through the courtroom. Rava rose, went home, and had intercourse with his wife, Rabbi Chisda's daughter. His wife asked him: Who was at court today? Rava answered: Chomah, the wife of Abaye. Rava's wife then chased after Chomah, hitting her with the straps of a chest and drove her out of the town of Machuza saying: You already killed three men and now you have come to kill another.[67]*

In their society, women's arms were covered completely. Rava's wife felt that Choma was flirting with her husband. Choma had first married Rachava of Pumbedita, and after his death she married Rabbi Yitzchak b. Rabbah, and after his death, Abaye.

> *A man once said to his wife: I vow that you are to receive no benefit from me until you show something beautiful in you to Rabbi Yishmael b. Yosi.*
>
> *Rabbi Yishmael said: Perhaps her head is beautiful? No, it is round.*
>
> *Perhaps her hair is beautiful? No, it is like flax stalks.*
>
> *Perhaps her eyes are beautiful? No, they are bleary.*
>
> *Perhaps her ears are beautiful? No, they are bent over.*
>
> *Perhaps her nose is beautiful? No, it is obstructed.*
>
> *Perhaps her lips are beautiful? No, they are thick.*
>
> *Perhaps her neck is beautiful? No, it is too short.*
>
> *Perhaps her abdomen is beautiful? No, it is swollen.*
>
> *Perhaps her feet are beautiful? No, they are broad like a duck's.*
>
> *Perhaps her name is beautiful? No, it is* Liklukit *(meaning soiled and befouled).*
>
> *He said to them: It is beautiful that she was named* Liklukit, *because she is soiled by her many defects. And he permitted her to her husband.*[68]

This story illustrates the lengths to which the Talmudic sages would go to annul a vow, especially when it came to bringing peace between husband and wife. The Talmud relates that a man vowed that he would not receive any benefit from his wife unless she made Rabbi Yehuda and Rabbi Shimon taste her cooking. Rabbi Yehuda felt that it was important for him to bring peace between husband and wife so he went to taste her cooking.[69] His reasoning was that since the Bible allows the name of the Lord to be erased (when making the bitter waters)[70] in order to bring peace between man and wife, all the more so should he do everything in his power to bring peace. Rabbi Meir used the same reasoning to allow a woman to spit on him, as we see in the next selection.

> *Rabbi Meir was accustomed to lecture in the synagogue of the town of Chamat every Friday evening. There was a woman who regularly went to hear his sermon. One time, the sermon took longer than usual. She hurried home but the candle was already extinguished. Her husband asked her where she had been. She replied: I went to hear the sermon. He said to her: I swear that such and such should happen to me if I let you back into my house before you spit in the lecturer's face.*

> *Rabbi Meir heard what happened through divine inspiration. He pretended that he had a serious eye ailment and proclaimed that any woman who knows how to cure an ailing eye by incantation, should come forth and charm for him (in those days, incantations were usually accompanied by spitting in front of the sick person). Her neighbors told her: Now you have an opportunity to go back home to your husband. Pretend that you know how to incantate and you will then be able to spit in his eye. She came before Rabbi Meir and Rabbi Meir asked: Do you know how to incantate? She was so in awe of Rabbi Meir that she answered negatively. Rabbi Meir said to her: Regardless, just spit seven times in my eye without the incantations and my eye will get better. After she finished spitting, he told her: Go home to your husband and tell your husband that he asked you to spit once and you spat seven times.*

> *His students said to him: Teacher, should the Torah be treated in such a humiliating way. If you would have told us what happened, would we not have had the husband brought here and flogged on the bench until he reconciled with his wife. Rabbi Meir said to them: Should the honor of Meir be more than the honor of his Creator? The Holy Name was written in holiness, yet the Torah allows it to be erased in water in order to bring peace between husband and wife. All the more so should the honor of Meir be disregarded.[71]*

Under certain circumstances, a woman who is suspected of being an adulteress (*sotah*) may be forced to drink of the bitter waters which contains an erased portion of the Torah.[72]

For centuries, Jews have derived difficulties, misunderstandings—and, sometimes, humor—out of the clash of languages and cultures in when we are immersed. There once was a Babylonian sage who married a woman from Israel, and the couple had some—uh—issues

> *There was a Babylonian who went to Israel and married a woman there. He told her to cook two talfi for him . . .*

In Babylonia this would mean preparing a small amount of lentils for him, but it translated a bit differently for the Israeli woman.

> *. . . She cooked exactly two lentils for him and he got angry at her. The next day he asked her to cook two griva . . .*

A *griva* is a large measure equal to 144 eggs. The Babylonian husband thought his wife would reduce the amount as she had done the day before.

> *. . . She cooked him two griva. He told her to go and bring two butzini . . .*

Meaning melons in Babylonia, but candles in Israel.

> *. . . so she brought him two candles. He told her: Go break them on resha d'baba . . .*

Meaning the top of the door in Babylonia, but the head of Baba in Israel.

> *. . . Now, just then Baba b. Buta was seated near the door and holding court. She went and broke the candles on his head. Baba asked her: Why did you do this to me? She replied: This is what my husband requested that I do. Baba said to her: You are performing your husband's will. May the Omnipresent One bring forth from you two children such as Baba b. Buta.*[73]

Baba b. Buta was a student of Shammai the Elder, and a very prominent judge (humble too). He was blinded by Herod, who eventually rebuilt the Temple at Baba's suggestion. This is another story that demonstrates how important peace between husband and wife was to the sages.

> *The daughter of Rabbi Chisda was sitting on her father's lap and Rava and Rami b. Chama were sitting before them. Rabbi Chisda asked his daughter: Which one of them would you want for a husband? She replied: Both.*
>
> *Rava said: And I want to be last.*[74]

This is indeed what happened. She was first married to Rami b. Chama and when he died she married Rava. This story is used to prove the saying of Rabbi Yochanan that "Since the day of the Temple's destruction, prophecy has been taken away from prophets and given to madmen and children."

> *Avishag said to King David: Let us get married. David responded: You are forbidden to me . . .*

Since he already had the maximum number of wives permitted to a king.

> *. . . She said to him: When the thief has lost his spirit, he then becomes virtuous . . .*

That is, you are old, have lost your virility, and are just giving me an excuse.

> *. . . David then said to his servants: Summon Bathsheba. And it is written*[75]*: "And Bathsheba went to the king, into the chamber." Rabbi Yehuda said in the name of Rav: On that occasion, Bathsheba had to be wiped off thirteen times.*[76]

David had relations with Bathsheba, one of his wives, the mother of Solomon, numerous times to prove to himself that he was still virile. King David was old and suffered from an illness which caused him to always be cold. Avishag was used as a warmer for the king but he did not have relations with her.

> *A matron once asked Rabbi Yosi b. Chalafta: In how many days did God create this world? He replied: In six days, as it is written*[77]*: "For in six days the Lord made Heaven and earth."*
>
> *She then asked: What has God been doing from then until now? He said: God sits and matches up people, the daughter of so-and-so for*

so-and-so, the wife of so-and-so for so-and-so, the wealth of so-and-so for so-and-so.

She said: Is that all He does? I can also do it. I have many servants and maids and I can match them up in a very short time. He said to her: It may seem easy for you, but it is as difficult for the Holy One as splitting the Red Sea. Rabbi Yosi b. Chalafta then left.

She went and took one thousand of her servants and one thousand of her maids and had them stand in a line. She then said you marry this one, you marry this one, etc., until they were all matched up in one night. The next morning, they came to her this one with a crushed head, this one with a detached eye, and this one with a broken leg. She said to them: What happened to you? One said, I do not want him, another said, I do not want her. She immediately sent for Rabbi Yosi b. Chalafta. She said to Rabbi Yosi: There is no god like your God. It is true that your Torah is pleasing and praiseworthy; you answered me beautifully.[78]

The sages believed that making a match was as difficult as splitting the Red Sea,[79] possibly because both require going against nature (with marriage, human nature). Rabbi Yosi referred to his wife as "my home," meaning that his wife was the cornerstone of his life and family.[80] There is a Jewish tradition that anyone who makes three matches is guaranteed a place in Paradise.

That making matches is important to the Jewish people is evidenced, perhaps, by the sub-genre of Jewish humor concerning matchmakers—who don't always have to be professionals

At a senior citizens' club in Miami Beach, the widow Birnbaum notices a new fellow sitting off to the side. He is tall and distinguished with a mane of white hair and a nice suit. She walks over and sits down.

"Are you new here?"

"Yes," he replies, "I just moved down to Florida."

"May I ask from where?" says Mrs. Birnbaum.

"Joliet, Illinois."

"And may I ask what you did there?" she persists.

"I was in prison."

"Really? For how long, if I may ask?"

"Twenty-five years," he replies.

"Twenty-five years? May I ask, if you won't take offense, for what crime?"

"I murdered and dismembered my wife," he replies.

"Ah," says Mrs. Birnbaum, "so you're single?"[81]

In Jewish law, if a couple has been married for ten years without any children they may get divorced. The following beautiful and moving Talmudic tale is about just such a couple.

> *Once, there was a woman in Sidon who lived with her husband for ten years and had no children. They went to Rabbi Shimon b. Yochai and told him that they desired to separate. He said to them: By your lives, just as when you married each other you had a feast, so too when you separate you should part with a feast. They went on their way and made a festival for themselves and prepared a huge feast and drank a great deal. When the husband became clear-minded, he said to his wife: My daughter, take any precious article that you see in the house and bring it to your father's house. What did she do? After he fell asleep, she ordered her servants and maids to carry him out in his bed and bring him to her father's house. In the middle of the night, he woke from his sleep. After the effects of the wine had dissipated, he asked his wife: My daughter, where am I? She said: In my father's house. He asked her: What am I doing in your father's house? She replied: Is this not what you said to me in the evening, that I could take any precious object and bring it to my father's house? There is no object more precious to me than you. Subsequently, they went back to Rabbi Shimon b. Yochai (and told him the story). He stood up and prayed for them to have children, and she became pregnant.*[82]

It's nice when true love overcomes all.

Judgment and Justice

> *There was a man who overheard his wife saying to her daughter: Why are you not more discreet in your sex life? I have ten sons and only one is from your father. When he was about to die he said: I leave all my property to one of my sons.*

> *They did not know which one he meant, so they went to Rabbi Banaah. He said to the children: Go and beat at your father's grave until he comes and reveals which one of you he made his heir. They all went to the grave, but the one who was the real son did not go. Rabbi Banaah said: All the property should be given to this one.*

> *The nine brothers went and slandered him to the authorities, saying: There is one among the Jews who extracts money from people without witnesses or proof. Rabbi Banaah was arrested and thrown into prison. His wife came to the authorities and said: I had one slave, they cut off his head, skinned him, ate his flesh, and filled the skin with water*

and provided drink with it for their friends, and they did not pay anything for it. They did not understand what she was saying to them, so they decided to bring the wise man of the Jews and ask him. They summoned Rabbi Banaah and he told them: She means a wineskin which has been made from the hide of the animal stolen from her. They said: Since he is so smart, let him sit at the gate and become a judge.[83]

As noted in an earlier chapter, Rabbi Banaah was an expert at deciphering riddles. Rabbi Banaah's student was the famous Rabbi Yochanan.

In the Old Country, marriages among Jews from different villages were sometimes arranged by mail. Bride and groom never met until the engagement was sealed.

One such groom travels from his village to the village of his intended. When he gets off the train, he sees—not one—but two young women with their mothers. There was a mix-up somewhere, and each claims him as her intended spouse.

The dispute escalates until all parties are brought before the Bet Din, the rabbinical court. The court hears the claims of both parties. The chief rabbi finally decrees, "We shall take the young man and cut him in half, and you can each have a part of him."

One of the mothers shrieks in horror.

The other says, "It seems like a fine solution."

The rabbi points at her and says, "That's the real mother-in-law."[84]

When the litigants come to court both sides must be treated the same. Thus, it is prohibited for, say, one of the parties to sit while the other must stand. Also, Jewish law mandates that one should rise for a scholar or the wife of a scholar which presented Rabbi Nachman with the following dilemma

> *The widow of Rabbi Huna had a case to adjudicate before Rabbi Nachman. Rabbi Nachman said: What should I do? If I rise when she enters my courtroom, then her opponent's ability to plead his case will become stopped up. If I do not rise, a scholar's wife is like a scholar and this would be disrespectful. He told his attendant: Make a goose fly and force him toward me so that I will get up.*[85]

This story shows the innovative way Rabbi Nachman solved the problem of how to rise for the widow of a great scholar and not intimidate the other litigant.

The next story follows a ruling that anyone who hits another person on the ear must pay a fine.

> *Chanan, the evil one, once struck another person on the ear. They went to Rabbi Huna. He said to Chanan: Go pay a fine of a half zuz. Chanan had a defaced zuz and wanted to use it to pay the fine. However, the defendant did not want to accept it (and have to give change). So Chanan hit him again and gave him the whole zuz.*[86]

Now we know that Chanan earned his title.

The next story illustrates the principle in Jewish law that two witnesses are required in order to punish a transgressor for violating Jewish law, for example, adultery or idolatry. Thus, if one comes alone to testify this only has the effect of slandering the alleged perpetrator. The sin referred to in the following is usually taken to be a sexual one.

> *Once, Tuvia sinned and Zigud came alone to the court to testify against him. Rabbi Pappa had Zigud flogged. Zigud said to Rabbi Pappa: Tuvia sinned and Zigud is flogged.*[87]

The above saying, "Tuvia sinned and Zigud was punished" is today an expression in modern Hebrew that is used whenever a person is punished for another's sins.

Cases of mistaken identity are frequent in Chelm.

Mendel the butcher is walking to his store one morning when a perfect stranger runs up and slaps him on the face. "That's for you, Yankel," the stranger calls out.

To which Mendel responds, after recovering from the shock, with a laugh.

"Why are you laughing?" asks the stranger. "Do you want me to hit you again?"

"No, please," comes the reply. "It's just that the joke's on you—I'm not Yankel!"[88]

15

Humorous Cases and Other Absurdities

A naïve young man, still studying in yeshiva, has been to the match-maker and is about to go out on his first real date. Naturally, he is quite anxious.

His father gives him this piece of advice to help him cope: "When one goes out with a woman on a date, one discusses three subjects: love, family, and philosophy."

Once on the date, the young man and the young woman, equally naïve, sit quietly in the park. Finally, the young man decides to speak up. Love, he thinks to himself. What do I love? I love noodles! Upon which, he turns to his date and asks, "Do you love noodles?" "No," comes the response.

Hmm. *He thinks,* Okay, family. *"Do you have a brother?" "No."*

This is harder than I thought. Philosophy. How do I bring philosophy into the conversation ? *"If you had a brother," he finally asks, "would he have loved noodles?"*

The major purpose of the Talmud was to elaborate on the written laws of the Hebrew Bible. Thus, the Talmud is replete with legal, ethical, and moral questions. Sometimes, Talmudic cases may seem quite farfetched, and even humorous, but they are actually being used to illustrate some fine legal points. There are three major reasons the Talmud considers so many unusual, even bizarre, cases: to derive legal principles; as a pedagogic device, to entertain while teaching; and as brainteasers to sharpen the mind.

To Derive Legal Principles

Whether a situation is possible or not is immaterial when the Talmud is trying to establish legal principles. Purely theoretical (at least in their days) cases are discussed because the sages felt that principles derived from these discussions would clarify the law and thus provide a more thorough understanding of it. Discussions of theoretical cases in the Talmud have allowed scholars of today to use Talmudic logic and principles to solve current legal questions. One example of this is the Talmudic discussion of a "tower flying in the air."

Rabbi Ammi said: Doeg and Achitophel asked three hundred questions concerning a tower flying in the air.[1]

The questions considered by Doeg and Achitophel deal with ritual impurity. Rashi, the major commentary on the Talmud, provides several explanations for what is meant by "the tower flying in the air." One explanation is that the tower flies through the air by way of magic. Obviously, in Talmudic times the idea of an airplane did not exist even in theory—Doeg and Achitophel lived even earlier, during the time of King David. This case, however imaginary in their day, could serve as a device to answer the question as to whether the ritual impurity of certain places like, say, a graveyard, only affects those walking on the ground directly—then it is the ground that is the problem—or whether those flying above these areas are affected because the impurity also hovers in the air above these places.

Or consider the argument in the Talmud regarding an individual who throws a knife into a wall and the flying knife inadvertently slaughters an animal in the legally correct manner.[2] *Shechitah*, the ritual method of slaughtering animals so as to make them kosher, consists of swiftly cutting through the majority of the animal's windpipe and esophagus. The purpose of *shechitah* was to ensure that the animal died in a quick and painless manner. This process is quite complicated and can be invalidated in several ways including, for example, pausing during the *shechitah*, pressing the knife down into the neck of the animal rather than cutting, or using a knife with a nick. It is therefore quite unlikely that proper *shechitah* can be accomplished by accident. Whether this case is physically possible or not is unimportant to the Talmudic sages. What matters are determining whether or not slaughtering requires intent. Interestingly, this case would be quite possible today with a machine that slaughters animals.

As a Pedagogic Device, to Make the Lecture More Entertaining

A second reason that the Talmudic sages discussed some rather bizarre and unusual cases might have been to entertain and to make the lectures more interesting and stimulating. One sage used humorous questions as a way of getting his teacher to laugh. Rabbah often started his lectures with something humorous to get his students to laugh.[3] Once they were in a good mood, then the lecture was conducted in an atmosphere of reverence.

The following passage, which shows that the sages were curious about everything and asked questions about any subject, was included in the Talmud even though it does not appear to explain or enhance any law or legal principle. It may have been included purely to entertain. One major commentary, the Maharsha, sees this passage as a metaphor, and the questions as dealing in actuality with the plight of the Jewish people. Whether or not it is not a metaphor, the passage indicates the great curiosity the Talmudic sages had about nature.

> *Rabbi Zera encountered Rabbi Yehuda standing by the door of his father-in-law's house. He observed that Rabbi Yehuda was in a very cheerful mood and understood that if he asked him the secrets of the universe, he would tell him.*
>
> *Rabbi Zera asked: Why do the goats go first at the head of the flock and then the sheep? Rabbi Yehuda replied: It is in accordance with the creation of the world. First there was darkness and then there was light . . .*

The goats are dark colored and the sheep are white. The next question notes that some animals have tails that appear to "dress" them modestly.

> *. . . Rabbi Zera asked: Why do sheep have thick tails which cover them, and the goats do not have tails which cover them? He answered: Those with whose material we cover ourselves are themselves covered, while those with whom we do not cover ourselves are themselves not covered. . . .*

Rabbi Zera notes that it is only fitting that sheep cover themselves modestly with their tails as we use their wool to dress ourselves.

> *. . . Rabbi Zera asked: Why does a camel have a short tail? He answered: Because the camel eats thorns. . . .*

A long tail would get entangled in the thorns.

> *. . . Rabbi Zera asked: Why does an ox have a long tail? He answered: Because it grazes in the marshland and has to chase away the gnats with its tail.*

> *Rabbi Zera asked: Why are the antennae of locust soft? He replied: Because it dwells among willows and if the antenna were hard it would be broken off when it bumped against trees and the locust would go blind. For Shmuel said: If one wishes to blind a locust, let him remove its antennae.*
>
> *Rabbi Zera asked: Why is the chicken's lower eyelid bent upwards? He answered: Because it lives on the rafters, and if smoke entered its eyes it would go blind.*[4]

To Sharpen the Mind

A third reason for outrageous questions and cases may have been as brainteasers. They sharpened the minds of both the students and teachers and often helped clarify the law. The sages of the Talmud enjoyed parables and riddles, so it is not surprising that many of the Talmudic legal questions are similar to riddles, that is, brainteasers. Many Talmudic questions are so scabrous that they do not have any answers, and the Talmud concludes, *taiku*—meaning, the question stands.

As we shall see from the examples in this chapter, these three reasons are by no means mutually exclusive. A brainteaser presented as an intellectual challenge can at the same time be an entertaining part of the lecture as well as a conduit to the development of abstract principles of law.

Strange Questions: What Is the Law if . . .

On the night before Passover, one is obligated to clean out one's home and rid it of all leavened products such as bread. In the following passages, Rava's original question—concerning a mouse carrying bread into a house that has already been cleaned and checked for Passover—is not so improbable but then it leads to a string of questions, one less probable than the other. These questions are not only legalistic brainteasers but also help establish legal principles. Unfortunately, the questions are so abstruse that they cannot be answered.

> *Rava asked: What is the law if a mouse enters a house with a piece of bread in its mouth and subsequently a mouse leaves with a piece of bread in its mouth? Do we say that the same mouse that entered left, or perhaps it is a different mouse? . . .*

This question is important because if we assume the same mouse goes in the house and out again carrying the bread in its mouth, the house is still ready for Passover; if it is a different mouse, the bread is probably different too and the house has to be searched all over again. Even today this is not an improbable scenario as children and toddlers have been known to scamper back and forth with food of all kinds. However, Rava continues and makes the question even more complex

> . . . Should you say that we assume that the same mouse that entered left, what is the law if a white mouse enters a house with a piece of bread in its mouth and then a black one leaves with a piece of bread in its mouth? This is definitely a different mouse. Perhaps one mouse snatched the bread from the other? . . .

If it is a different mouse then the house must be cleaned again—unless we can assume that one mouse snatched the bread from the other's mouth! Different mouse, but the same piece of bread. Just in case we are a little skeptical on this point, Rava continues

> . . . Should you say that mice do not snatch away food from each other, what is the law if a mouse enters a house with a piece of bread in its mouth and a weasel leaves with a piece of bread in its mouth? The weasel will certainly snatch food away from the mouse. . . .

If we assume that the weasel snatched the bread from the mouse's mouth, then the house does not have to be cleaned again.

> . . . or perhaps it is a different piece of bread, since if this bread was snatched from the mouse, then the mouse itself would have also been in the weasel's mouth. Should you say that had the weasel snatched the bread from the mouse, then the mouse itself should have been in the weasel's mouth, what then is the law if a mouse enters a house with a piece of bread and then a weasel leaves with both a mouse and a piece of bread in its mouth? Here, it is certainly the same. . . .

If the weasel has both the bread and the mouse in its mouth it must be the same piece of bread and, therefore, the house is still ready for Passover. Or is it?

> . . . or perhaps, if it were the same, then the bread should have been in the mouth of the mouse. But perhaps because of fear, the mouse dropped the piece of bread from its mouth? The question is left unresolved.[5]

One is not surprised that Rava's questions could not be answered. Rava was a pedagogue. This brainteaser was probably a way of both entertaining his students and challenging them at the same time.

279

We know that the high priest was only permitted to marry a virgin. The question was asked

May a high priest marry a virgin who has become pregnant?[6]

The conclusion, predicated on the belief that it was possible for a virgin to become pregnant if she bathed in water into which a man had discharged his semen, was yes. The question seems outlandish in and of itself, but is even more so when one considers that when it was asked, the Temple had already been destroyed; thus, there were no more high priests. The question, about a very practical-sounding, though strange, problem was actually an abstract, theoretical exercise.

The Biblical source for divorce is in Deuteronomy. The Scripture states: "he writes for her a document of severance and places it in her hand."[7] Thus, in Jewish law, divorce can only be performed via a document with a specific format that is written by the husband or his agent. This document is called a *get*, a bill of divorce. If a man gives his wife a *get*, and says that the paper on which the document is written is his, then the wife is not divorced. By retaining ownership of the paper, the husband has, in effect, not given anything to his wife. Rabbi Papa, a brilliant pedagogue who liked to challenge his students and colleagues, took this one step further into the realm of the outlandish when he asked

If one gives his wife a get and says "this is your divorce, but the paper between each line or each word is mine," what is the law?[8]

The Talmud's conclusion? The question stands.

The Bible prohibits plowing a field with an ox and a donkey working together.[9] The Talmud explains that this law applies to any kind of work and any two species of animal.[10] The reason probably had to do with the fact that pairing a large animal, such as an ox, with a smaller animal, such as a donkey, would cause unnecessary pain for both. It is much easier for animals of the same species and size to work in tandem. Rechaba, in a seemingly serious fashion, asked

What is the law if someone drives his wagon using a goat and a fish?[11]

More important than the possibility of this exact pairing above is that Rechaba was trying to establish the parameters of the law. Does the law only prohibit pairing two land-based animals?

The Talmud discusses situations in which townspeople have a right to prevent outsiders from competing with them in their local marketplace. Generally, the townspeople have priority in their own marketplace. However, in the case of scholars who have merchandise to sell, this rule is waived and they are given preference in the marketplace. This was done to provide them with sufficient time to study and teach. Of course this would necessarily bring up the question, who is a scholar? Anyone can answer a simple question; to be considered a scholar one must be able to answer an esoteric question. The Talmud relates the following incident, in which Rabbi Dimi wished to market produce in the town of the exilarch, the leader of the Babylonian Jews. The question used to test Rabbi Dimi's scholarship was rather strange.

> *Rabbi Dimi of Nehardea brought dried figs in a ship and wanted to sell them in the marketplace in the exilarch's town. The exilarch asked Rava to examine Rabbi Dimi and determine whether he was indeed a scholar and was thus entitled to special market privileges. Rava then said to Rabbi Adda b. Abba: Go and smell the vessel. . . .*

An expression meaning, go check him out, which Rabbi Adda did using a question about whether a basket was a basket or just plain dung.

> *. . . Rabbi Adda went and asked Rabbi Dimi the following question: If an elephant swallows a basket made of willow twigs and evacuates it through its rectum, can the basket become ritually unclean. He could not provide an answer.*
>
> *Rabbi Dimi asked Rabbi Adda: Are you Rava? Rabbi Adda struck him on his sandal and said: Between Rava and me there is a great difference. However, I am your teacher and Rava is the teacher of your teacher. Rabbi Dimi did not get special preference in selling his figs and his figs spoiled. He then went to Rabbi Yosef and said: See how they mistreated me. Rabbi Yosef said: The One who did not delay in avenging the wrong inflicted on the king of Edom will not delay avenging the wrong done to you. . . . Shortly thereafter, Rabbi Adda died.*[12]

The Talmud adds that everyone blamed himself for the death of Rabbi Adda. Rabbi Yosef was upset because he thought that his curse caused the untimely death of Rabbi Adda. Rabbi Dimi felt that Rabbi Adda died because he caused financial loss to him over the spoiled figs. Other rabbis found reasons to blame themselves. It would seem that Rabbi Adda could have asked a more relevant question. According to Tosafot, each of the rabbis was upset because the Talmud states: "Whoever is the cause of a fellow human being punished, is not permitted within the inner circle of the Holy One."[13]

> *Rabbi Achadboi b. Ami asked Rabbi Sheshet, What is the law if one commits intercourse with himself?*[14]

This would be a problem if it were considered sodomy, intercourse between two males. Rabbi Sheshet responded, "You annoy me by asking about something that is physically impossible." Of course, then the Talmud proceeds to discuss what the law would be if one somehow manages to accomplish this physical impossibility, say, in an unerect state.

Rabbi Zera did not believe in laughing in this world since he was of the opinion that one should not laugh until the Messiah comes and creates a world of peace and justice. He, therefore, must have been serious when asking the following question.

> *Rabbi Shimon b. Chalafta was walking on the path when he encountered lions. They roared at him. He quoted the verse,*[15] *"The young lions roar for their prey," and two pieces of meat miraculously fell from heaven. The lions ate one of the pieces and left over the other piece.*
>
> *Rabbi Shimon took the piece of meat to the academy and asked whether it was kosher or not. He was told: Nothing unkosher descends from heaven.*
>
> *Rabbi Zera asked Rabbi Abuhu: If a piece of meat resembling a donkey (an unkosher animal) falls from heaven, may it be eaten? Rabbi Abuhu replied: Foolish* yarod,[16] *they already told you that nothing unkosher descends from heaven.*[17]

It is good to know that if pork chops rain down from heaven observant Jews will be allowed to eat them. Have you ever heard the expression "raining cats and dogs"? Well, if this happens in the form of meat, they may be kosher.

Rabbi Eliezer was presented with a challenging question by one of the earliest Christians, at a time when Christianity was still a Jewish sect. He was once arrested by the Romans under suspicion of heresy; it may be that the Romans, who were pagans at that time, suspected him of being a Christian. After his release, he and the other sages tried to figure out what he had done that had prompted Heaven to punish him with such an ordeal.

When Rabbi Eliezer was arrested because of suspicion of heresy, they brought him to the basilica for trial. The judge said to him: How is it that an elderly man like you should engage in such absurdities? Rabbi Eliezer said: I consider the Judge to be truthful. The judge thought that Rabbi Eliezer was referring to him, but actually Rabbi Eliezer was referring to his Father in Heaven. The judge said to him: Because you consider me truthful, therefore I will pardon you.

When Rabbi Eliezer came home, his students came to comfort him but he would not accept consolation. Rabbi Akiva said to him: Rabbi, please allow me to say one thing that you have taught me. He said: Speak. He said to him: Rabbi, perhaps you heard some heresy and found it pleasing; and this is why you were arrested. He said to him: Akiva, you reminded me. Once, I was walking in the upper market of Sepphoris when I encountered someone by the name of Yaakov of Kefar Sekania. He said to me: It says in your Torah,[18] "Do not bring a prostitute's fee or the price of a dog into the house of your Lord." May one use such a donation for the purpose of building a toilet for the high priest? I did not answer him. He then said to me: This is what I was taught. It says[19]: "From the prostitute's fee it gathered and to the prostitute's fee shall they return," the money came from a filthy place so let it return to a filthy place.[20]

Yaakov of Kefar Sekania was a disciple of Jesus and has been identified with either James, son of Alphaeus, or James the Little.[21] It seems that early Christians also employed strange questions as a studying device.

If a ship carrying wheat was lifted by a storm and the wheat rained down subsequently from heaven elsewhere, may this wheat be used for the offering of two loaves for the holiday of Shavuot?[22]

The Torah requires that the offering of two loaves be brought "from your dwelling places."[23] Wheat falling from the sky may not qualify.

Not all strange questions were tolerated. Rebbi was of the opinion that one should not laugh in this world. As we have seen, some of his colleagues would try to make him laugh.[24] In the next passage, Plimo attempts to seriously ask Rebbi about the use of *tefillin* (phylacteries), which an adult male places daily on his head and arm, by a two-headed man.

Plimo asked Rebbi: If one has two heads, on which one should he place his phylacteries? Rebbi responded: Either go into exile or accept excommunication. Meanwhile, a man came to the academy saying that he just begotten a two-headed son and wanted to know how much must be given to the priest for the redemption of the first-born.[25]

This odd question may actually be important in establishing the parameters of the law regarding phylacteries. For example, is the requirement on the head or on the person? If it is on the head, then each head should have its own. Rebbi presumably thought that Plimo asked this question in order to deride him. It is doubtful, however, that Plimo would ask a question to taunt or annoy Rebbi. As we saw in the chapter on Satan, Plimo was extremely pious and caused Satan aggravation with his daily curse, "an arrow in Satan's eyes."

In Jewish law, the first-born cattle have special status and belong to the priests. The following is another example of "impossible" questions with possibly important repercussions for today.

> *What is the law if a weasel inserts its head into a pregnant animal's womb, takes the fetus into its mouth and pulls it out of the womb and then the weasel reinserts its head into the womb of another animal and spits out the fetus, who then emerges naturally (and is now the first-born)?*
>
> *What is the law if the wombs of two animals become attached and the fetus leaves one womb and enters the other womb, and then emerges from the latter womb?*[26]

Is it a first-born or not? The first question deals with a situation in which the first-born had emerged from the womb previously through unnatural means. The second case deals with a situation in which the fetus would have been a first-born had it stayed in its original womb. Today's technology actually enables the transfer of a fetus to a surrogate mother. A somewhat related issue would be: if an egg donated by one woman is fertilized in vitro and implanted in another woman, who is the mother?

The Bible does not allow an individual to take both the mother bird and the chicks from the nest.[27] The mother bird must first be chased away and then the the chicks may be taken. This rule only applies in the wild so, for example, a nest in one's own pigeon coop would be exempted. What if one finds a bird's nest in a very unusual place?

> *A Pappunian asked Rabbi Mattenah: What is the law if one finds a bird's nest on a person's head. Does he have to send away the mother bird before taking the chicks?*[28]

The Talmud concludes that the mother bird must indeed be chased away if one wishes to remove the chicks from a nest situated on the top of one's head.

The following is an example of one of the absurd questions asked by Rabbi Yirmiyah in his attempt to get his teacher to laugh. As noted above, Rabbi Zera was of the opinion that one should not laugh until the Messiah comes and creates a world of peace and justice.

> Rabbi Yirmiyah asked Rabbi Zera: According to Rabbi Meir, who says that if a woman aborts a fetus that looks like an animal it is considered a valid abortion . . .

Thus, the woman becomes ritually unclean just as if she had aborted a human fetus.

> . . . what is the law if the father receives for the "animal" born from a woman a token of betrothal. Is the person considered married to the "animal?"

> . . . To such an extent did Rabbi Yirmiyah try to make Rabbi Zera laugh. But he would not laugh.[29]

The Talmud states that this is clearly an absurd question because it is impossible for an animal-like fetus born to a human being to survive.

Even Rabbi Yirmiyah could go too far. He was once temporarily expelled from the academy for one of his questions. The following passage assumes that a pigeon found within fifty cubits of a coop came from that coop, rather than from the wild.

> A baby pigeon that is found within fifty cubits of a coop belongs to the coop's owner. If it is found outside the fifty cubits, then it belongs to the finder. Rabbi Yirmiyah asked: If one foot of the pigeon is within the fifty cubits and one foot is outside, to whom does it belong?

> . . . It was for this that they expelled Rabbi Yirmiyah from the academy.[30]

This sounds like a teenager cracking wise until you recall that these were all grown men with jobs and families. Rabbi Yirmiyah was reinstated to the academy when his colleagues became aware of his great humility after sending him a difficult question. Rabbi Yirmiyah was quite pious and was a fervent believer in the imminent arrival of the Messiah as his unusual death bed request indicates: "Dress me in a nice white garment, put socks and shoes on my feet and a staff in my hand. Place me on my side so that when the Messiah comes, I will be ready."[31]

Other Strange Questions

Even the strange questions of heretics may be discussed in the Talmud as the next selection, a piece of witty repartee between Rabbi Abuhu and an unnamed heretic, illustrates.

> A certain heretic said to Rabbi Abuhu: Your God is a priest, since it is written[32]: "And take for Me terumah" (the priestly tithe on produce). Now, when God buried Moses[33] in what did He immerse Himself?... If you wish to say that God immersed Himself in water, it is written[34]: "Who measured the waters with His fist."

That is, there is not enough water in the whole world to accommodate God. The heretic here alluded to the Jewish law requiring that a priest coming into contact with a corpse ritually purify himself by immersing in a *mikveh* (ritual bath).

> ... Rabbi Abuhu answered: He bathed in fire, for it is written[35]: "For behold, the Lord shall come in fire." The heretic asked: is then immersion in fire effective? Rabbi Abuhu replied: On the contrary, the primary method for purification is by fire as it is written[36]: "and all that cannot go through fire, you shall make go through water."[37]

Rabbi Abuhu was apparently teasing the questioner. The verse he cited in Numbers refers to vessels and not to individuals. To wit, vessels used for roasting nonkosher foods directly over fire must be purified in fire, that is, burned out; vessels used for cooking nonkosher foods in hot water are cleansed with boiling water.

The heretic is the prototype for many skeptics today, who present impossible questions—for example, Can God, who is omnipotent, kill Himself?—to show their own superiority to the believer. What this particular heretic did not count on was that Rabbi Abuhu, like the other Talmudic sages, was used to outlandish and challenging questions, and was quite capable of using his own razor sharp wit to respond to the seemingly serious question with a seemingly serious response.

What do you say when God sneezes? You bless You?
How about when an atheist sneezes?

> Queen Cleopatra asked Rabbi Meir: I know that the dead will be
> resurrected, as it is written,[38] "And they will blossom out of the city
> (Jerusalem) like grass of the earth." However, when they rise, will they
> be naked or clothed? He answered, this can be deduced a fortiori from
> a grain of wheat. If a grain of wheat, which is buried naked, sprouts
> forth with many coverings, how much more so the righteous, who are
> buried in their clothing.[39]

This is not the famous Cleopatra who lived in the time of Marc
Anthony, but may perhaps be a descendent. Apparently, this Cleopatra
was a very shallow individual. Of all things to worry about: whether or
not the resurrected will be naked or dressed.

> An emperor asked Rabbi Gamliel: You claim that the dead will come
> back to life. But they turn to dust, and can dust come back to life? His
> daughter said to Rabbi Gamliel: Let me answer him. There are two
> potters in our town: One makes his pots from liquid and the other
> from clay. Which is the more praiseworthy? The emperor replied: The
> one who fashions from liquid. His daughter then said: If he can create
> from liquid, He can certainly do so from clay.[40]

If God can create humans from liquid, that is, semen, He can certainly do so from clay or dust. As noted in an earlier chapter, Rabbi
Gamliel (the Second) was often involved in disputes with heretics.
The Roman emperor enjoyed asking him questions and the Talmud
describes several encounters with the Emperor. He was known for his
brilliance, and two Roman officials were sent to him to study. They
learned the Torah, Mishna, Talmud, Jewish law, and homiletics from
Rabbi Gamliel.[41]

> Rabbi Elazar's students asked him: Why does a dog know its owner,
> and a cat does not? He said to them: If one who eats from that which
> a mouse has eaten forgets his studies, that which eats the mouse itself
> should all the more so be forgetful.
>
> Rabbi Elazar's students asked him: Why do all animals rule over mice?
> He said to them: Because of their bad disposition. The students asked:
> What is it? Rava said: Because they even damage clothing. Rabbi Papa
> said: They even damage the handle of a hoe.[42]

The sages (and probably all of society during that time period)
believed that eating something from which a mouse has eaten is harmful
for one's memory. They also felt that mice gnaw at clothing even though
they derive no benefit from it.

Unusual Scenarios

Using scenarios to teach is a pedagogic approach used today as well. For instance, courses in business ethics are often taught using scenarios. Students are presented with scenarios consisting of ambiguous ethical situations and are asked to provide their opinions as to the proper response. Talmudic scenarios are also used for teaching. However, the scenarios may be totally improbable. Here, we present a small sample of some very unusual scenarios

Can someone vow to take on the life of a Nazirite conditionally? In the following unusual—and highly improbable—scenario, several individuals vow conditionally to become Nazirites. One who vows to become a Nazirite was prohibited from three basic things: cutting his hair; becoming ritually impure by coming into contact with the dead; and drinking wine (i.e., intoxicants) or even eating grapes. One could become a Nazirite for a period ranging from a minimum period of thirty days to a lifetime.[43] To understand the following rather humorous scenario, we also need to know that a *koy* is a species of deer and the rabbis of the Talmud were uncertain as to whether it falls into the category of domestic cattle (*behemah*) or wild beast (*chayah*).

> *If*
>
> *a person saw a* koy *and said: I am a Nazirite if that is a wild beast*
>
> *a second person said: I am a Nazirite if that is not a wild beast*
>
> *a third person said: I am a Nazirite if that is cattle*
>
> *a fourth person said: I am a Nazirite if that is not cattle*
>
> *a fifth person said: I am a Nazirite if that is both a wild beast and cattle*
>
> *a sixth person said: I am a Nazirite if that is neither wild beast or cattle*
>
> *a seventh person said: I am a Nazirite if one of you is a Nazirite*
>
> *an eighth person said: I am a Nazirite if none of you is a Nazirite*
>
> *a ninth person said: I am a Nazirite if all of you are Nazirites*
>
> *then they all are Nazirites.*[44]

This strange case illustrates in a rather colorful way that one can become a Nazirite even in a case where there is doubt.

Speaking of conditions, the Talmud states that if a husband gives his wife a *get* the divorce has to be a complete "severance" and there should not be any lifelong or impossible conditions. If a husband says,

> *This is your* get *on condition that you ascend up into heaven, on condition that you descend down into the depths, on condition that you swallow a reed four cubits long, on condition that you bring me a reed 100 cubits long, or on condition that you walk across the Great Sea (Mediterranean), this is not a valid* get. *Rabbi Yehuda b. Taima says that a* get *such as this is valid.*[45]

These are examples of impossible conditions. The Talmud also considers possible conditions that are in violation of Jewish law, such as if the condition is that the wife must eat pig meat, a nonkosher food prohibited to Jews.[46]

The next selection involves a rather unusual way of presenting one's wife with a *get*.

> *Rabbi Chisda stated: If a man gives his wife a* get *and the* get *is in her hand but the end of a string which is attached to the* get *is in the husband's hand, then the law is: If the string is so strong that the husband could pull the* get *and bring it to himself, then the* get *is not valid. If not, then the divorce is valid.*[47]

The reason for the above is that the Bible refers to the bill of divorce as a "document of severance." Therefore, the break must be complete, there should not be any lifelong conditions and the delivery of the get to the wife must be done is such a way that the husband does not have physical control of the bill of divorce.

Some of the funniest scenarios discussed in the Talmud involve the laws of indirect causality. For example, the Talmud attempts to determine who is guilty of murder in the following case.

> *If one throws a child from the top of the roof and someone else comes and kills the child with a sword there is a dispute between Rabbi Yehuda b. Batyra and the Rabbis.*[48]

The one with the sword killed the child after it was thrown from the roof and before he hit the ground. Therefore, the child actually dies from the sword, not from the impact with the ground. The dispute is whether only the person with the sword is guilty or whether no one can be punished for the crime. The one who threw the child from the roof is not considered the murderer because the child was actually killed by the sword.

Even in modern law, distinctions are made between first-degree murder, second-degree, etc. However, this case is probably not in any law books.

> *Rava said: If one shot an arrow at another and the target had a shield in his hand and someone else came along and took the shield away; or even if the shooter himself went and removed it (after shooting the arrow), he is not liable. Because at the moment he shot the arrow at his victim the shield would have stopped it.*[49]

Rava is of the opinion that one cannot be executed in certain cases of murder that involve indirect causation. Some commentaries have come up with a clever way of explaining how the shooter of the arrow can remove the target's shield after firing: There was a long rope attached to the shield and the shooter pulled on it immediately after firing the arrow. Rava discusses another case involving indirect causation. One throws another person into a pit and there is a ladder in the pit so that the victim can climb out of the pit. However, someone else comes along and takes away the ladder and the person in the pit dies.[50] This is also a case where both parties are not liable for execution.

The following is a case that actually happened but will probably never occur again.

> *Rabbi Yehuda in the name of Rav related that once a man lusted after a woman and his heart became seized with such a fervent passion that his life was in danger. They asked the doctors what to do.*
>
> *The doctors said: There is no remedy for him except for sexual intercourse with her.*
>
> *The sages said: Let him die rather than have intercourse with her.*
>
> *The doctors said: Let her stand naked before him.*
>
> *The sages said: Let him die rather than have her stand naked before him.*
>
> *The doctors said: Let her speak to him from behind a partition.*
>
> *The sages said: Let him die rather than have her speak to him from behind a partition.*[51]

There is an argument in the Talmud as to whether this was a married or single woman.

The following scenario may be viewed as the answer to a brainteaser: How can plowing a single furrow result in as many as eight transgressions? The Talmud comes up with a truly unusual scenario. For each transgression, the Biblical source for the relevant violation is given in the notes to this chapter.

> *An individual plows a furrow mingling seeds from diverse species such as wheat, barley, and grape...*

So, starting the countoff: Sin Number 1.[52]

> *... during a Festival...*

Sin Number 2.[53]

> *... occurring in a Sabbatical year...*

Sin Number 3.[54]

> *... using an ox and a donkey yoked together...*

Sin Number 4.[55]

> *... each of the animals in question is consecrated, set aside for the benefit of the Sanctuary, and is thus not permissible for ordinary labor...*

Sins Number 5 and 6.[56]

> *... the person plowing is both a priest and a Nazarite, and the furrow is being plowed in a cemetery, which is off limits to both priests...*

Sin Number 7.[57]

> *... and Nazarites.*[58]

And there you have it . . . drumroll . . . Sin Number 8![59]

Three Jews are having an argument about how progressive their respective synagogues are. One says, "On Yom Kippur we provide folks with ashtrays, so everyone can smoke during the services."

The second Jew says, "That's nothing. We give out sandwiches during Yom Kippur services. Ham sandwiches."

"We have you both beat," says the third. "One week before Rosh Hashana, we put up a big sign: "Closed for the Holy Days."

Water used for ritual purification must be "living" water and not water brought in pails from a spring. What about Miriam's spring? Is it considered ritually pure?

A moveable spring is clean and that is the spring of Miriam.[60]

The legendary Miriam's spring miraculously followed the Israelites during their forty years of wandering in the wilderness and provided them with water. This is a theoretical concept since springs do not move from place to place.

Rabbi Yitzchak b. Abdimi said: One may perform ritual immersion in the eye of a fish.[61]

One suspects that Rabbi Yitzchak never saw a fish that huge. Rabbi Yitzchak was an expert in Biblical exegesis and homiletics. Rava once said regarding Rabbi Yitzchak: "Every Biblical verse which Rabbi Yitzchak b. Abdimi did not explain . . . remains unexplained."[62]

Strange Proofs

Rabbi Tabi said in the name of Rabbi Yoshiah: What is the meaning of the verse,[63] "There are three that are never sated . . . the grave, the barren womb"? What is the connection between the grave and the womb? This is to teach you that just as the womb takes in and gives forth, so too does the grave take in and give forth.

Meaning at the resurrection of the dead. Here Rabbi Tabi wishes to connect the grave and the womb. The third thing mentioned in the verse as never sated, dry earth for which there is never enough rain, is not relevant to this discussion.

We can prove a fortiori that resurrection of the dead will take place. The womb is entered silently (the semen during intercourse), yet gives forth with loud noise (the crying infant); the grave which is entered with loud noise (the mourners) should all the more so give forth with loud noise. Here is an answer to those that say that resurrection of the dead is not from the Torah.[64]

This story is a clever proof but not entirely convincing. The concept of resurrection was very important to Judaism. The Sadducees and the Samaritans were two heretical groups that did not believe in resurrection and the Talmudists worked hard trying to prove that it had its basis in the Torah.

The Romans asked Rabbi Yehoshua b. Chananiah: How do we know that the Holy One will resurrect the dead and that He knows the future? He told them: Both are derived from the verse,[65] "And the Lord said to Moses, Behold you are about to lie with your ancestors and rise up; this nation will stray after the foreign gods of the land." They replied: Perhaps the verse means "and this nation will rise up." Rabbi Yehoshua replied: At least you hold half of the answer: He knows the future.[66]

There is no way that the verse can be interpreted so that the "rise up" refers to Moses. Rabbi Yehoshua, known for his wit, was being cute. The verse means: Behold you are about to lie with your ancestors and this nation will (then) rise up and stray after the foreign gods of the land. Indeed, idolatry was a problem almost immediately after the Israelites entered the promised land, especially within the tribe of Dan.

Rabbi Yosi b. Taddai used the following case to ridicule *a fortiori* reasoning.

This is the question which Rabbi Yosi b. Taddai of Tiberias asked Rabbi Gamliel: I am permitted to cohabit with my wife yet I am prohibited from marrying her daughter. All the more so, I should be forbidden from marrying the daughter of a married woman since I am prohibited from cohabiting with her . . .

According to this reasoning a man would only be permitted to marry the daughter of an unwed mother, divorcee, or widow.

. . . Rabbi Gamliel replied: Go and provide a wife for the High Priest regarding whom it is written,[67] *"Only a virgin of his own people shall he marry." A fortiori reasoning cannot be used to abolish something from the Torah. Rabbi Gamliel then excommunicated Rabbi Yosi b. Taddai.*[68]

The Torah states explicitly that the High Priest may marry. This was probably a short-term excommunication to punish Rabbi Yosi b. Taddai for ridiculing this type of reasoning which is used widely in the Talmud to derive numerous laws. This is the only time he is mentioned in the Talmud.

Humorous cases and brainteasers are excellent pedagogic tools for those studying law and even for other disciplines. They make the lectures more interesting and help clarify matters. Using improbable scenarios is somewhat reminiscent of the way computer programs are tested. Extreme data is used and if the program works with the unusual data it will presumably work with any kind of data. Examining far-fetched, and even impossible, cases enables one to determine what should be done in more routine cases. Talmudic scenarios and questions are as interesting today as they were almost 2,000 years ago and have ensured that the Talmud will continue to be used as a source to help solve new questions that arise as society becomes more and more complicated.

A Rabbi, in explaining Talmudic logic to a student, employed the following case.

"Two men come up out of a chimney. One is dirty, the other clean. Which one takes a bath?" The student answered: "That's easy. The dirty one takes the bath."

"Now think about it this way," said the Rabbi. "The dirty one looked at the clean one and saw a clean face. And the clean one saw that his partner's face was dirty."

"Oh, I get it Rabbi. The clean one takes the bath!" said the student.

"Still no," responded the Rabbi. "The Talmud would go on to ask: If two men come out of a chimney, how is one clean and the other dirty?"

Part IV
Conclusion

16

Is There a "Jewish" Sense of Humor?

Humor is the *lingua franca* of the Jewish people. Lenny Bruce had a routine in which he differentiated between things that are "Jewish" and those that are "goyish." In his estimation, Count Basie and anyone living in a big city would be considered Jewish. Kool-Aid, evaporated milk and Butte, Montana—goyish.[1] Similarly, Philip Roth, in *Portnoy's Complaint*, describes how the words tumult, bedlam, and spatula seemed so Jewish to him that as a first grader when presented with a photo of a spatula he could not for the life of him come up with the word in English.[2] In one episode of the television show *Seinfeld*, Jerry Seinfeld took umbrage that Tim Whatley, his dentist, converted to Judaism for the jokes. Jerry claimed that he resented it not as a Jew, but as a comedian. In an episode of the television show *Curb Your Enthusiasm*, the Larry David character (played, of course, by Larry David) comes to believe that his birth parents were gentiles, not Jews. In a hilarious montage, he adeptly engages in all the activities and behaviors he considers "goyish," for example, repairing a roof, tinkering with a car, and drinking in a bar. He has also somehow lost his "Jewish angst"—which promptly returns of course when he finds out that his genetic material is Jewish after all.

Even—or, especially—outside the world of the professional comic, we find ordinary folk answering a question with a question, employing a sarcastic retort, offering self-deprecating witticisms. For Jews, this special brand of humor has become a defining characteristic, marking their uniqueness among the peoples of the world.

Many have asked "Who are the Jews?" This, of course, is somewhat different from the perennial "Who is a Jew" question that repeatedly causes friction in Israel and which a colleague of the authors believes could be answered quite simply by invoking the infamous Nuremberg

Laws of 1935. A well-used expression is, "You're a Jew when a Gentile says you are a Jew." But we digress—slightly.

A Jewish convert to Christianity walks down the street with his good friend who happens to be a hunchback. They pass the local synagogue.

"You know," says the convert, "I used to be a Jew."

"Interesting," says the hunchback. "I used to be a hunchback."

Indeed there may not be another people so concerned with its own identity or character. Witness the many jokes which feature representatives of other groups—and a Jew. For example:

An Italian, a Scot, a Russian, a German, and a Jew are walking on a hot summer day.

After a while, the Italian says: "I am so thirsty. I must have wine."

The Scotsman says: "I am so thirsty. I must have whisky."

The Russian says "I am so thirsty. I must have vodka."

The German says "I am so thirsty. I must have beer."

The Jew says: "I am so thirsty. I must have diabetes."

The Jewish people—in fact, we are referred to as a people (*am*) in the Holy Scriptures—have variously been considered a race, a religion, an ethno-cultural group, and a nation. Are we a race? Certainly, up until the middle of the last century, many "others" were considered to be races by the "white" majority—for example, the Irish race, the Italian race, and, of course, the Hebrew or Jewish, race. Those were the days when a member of one of these "others" groups was expected to try to be a "credit" to one's race. People not of the majority—which was generally considered to be the White Anglo Saxon Protestants in the "civilized" West—were not "white," no matter what their skin color. However, today we tend to use the terminology of race a bit more scientifically, requiring involvement of some bit of biology or DNA. As with other antiquated terms that have outlived their usefulness, the term race is more confusing than edifying. If "black" and "white" imply race instead of, or in addition to, just skin color, why are bi- or multi-racial individuals considered "black" if their skin color is any shade darker than a brown paper bag?[3]

At any rate, it is exceedingly hard to justify calling the Jewish people a race—at least, that is, since the Nazis were vanquished in the last century. There is no DNA test for membership nor is common ancestry a requirement to be considered Jewish. On the other hand, it is interesting to note that some recent genetic studies show that Jews as a group do share a common ancestry, that is, that the so-called *"cohen* gene" (or, priest gene) is more prevalent in Jews than in the general population. Of course, over the centuries, Jews have intermarried and otherwise intermingled with whatever nation they happened to live among, producing white Jews, Asian Jews, black Jews, etc. Hence, today, there is no single skin color or racial template for the Jewish people. Even in Talmudic times, the sages contemplated this question.

> *Rabbi Yishmael states: "The Jewish people . . . are like the* eshkroa. *They are neither black nor white skinned but of an intermediate color."*[4]

Eshkroa is usually translated as wood from a boxwood tree. Apparently, the natural Jewish skin color was originally closer to the color of boxwood—a kind of yellow-brown—than Caucasian white, and thus probably closer to the skin color of many Sephardic Jews than that of most Ashkenazic Jews.

On the other hand, similar to membership in a race, you can't easily get out of being Jewish. According to traditional Jewish law, anyone born of a Jewish mother, whether observant or not, is a Jew—and good luck trying to get out of that!

Jacob had left the old country for America some years earlier. He has finally made enough money to send for his family.

"Yankele, where is your beard and payos*?" his mother asks upon seeing him.*

"Mama," he replies, "In America, nobody wears a beard"

"But at least you keep the Sabbath?" his mother asks.

"Um, no. Here, everybody works on the Sabbath."

"But kosher you still eat?"

"Mama, it is very difficult to keep kosher in the New World."

Pause. She leans over to him and whispers, "Tell me, Yankele, are you still circumcised?"

Many American Jewish "assimilation" jokes highlight this dilemma. For example,

Mrs. Horowitz attended a society event under an assumed name, pretending to be a Gentile. At the dinner, seated at a table with several

Gentile women, she was on her best behavior. "My dear," she asked the woman next to her in her most refined voice. "Would you please pass the butter?" The butter was passed, but it accidentally fell into her lap. "Oy vey!" She exclaimed. Catching herself, she quickly added: "Whatever that means."

A large portion of assimilation-related Jewish humor is especially meaningful, poignant, and, yes, humorous to the wandering Jew who periodically is forced to lay down roots in a new and alien land. For example, the following bit of humor from the Soviet era.

Telephone rings. "Hello."
"Hello. May I please speak to Moshe?"
"There is no Moshe here."
"Really? There is no one called Moshe there?"
"No Moshe here." Hangs up.
Ring. "Hello."
"Hello. Is Mischa there?"
"Just a moment." Calls out, "Moshe! It's for you!"

Are we a religion? Of course, *Judaism* is a religion; there is no question of that. But what kind of religious group tolerates so many secular members, and even those who don't believe in God? And lest one think that it is only in our so-called modern times that Judaism is factionalized and bisected and trisected into many different sects, one is reminded that over the course of Jewish history, there have been Sadducees, Pharisees, Essenes, the School of Hillel, the School of Shammai, the separate Kingdoms of Judah and Israel, idol worshippers (still considered Jewish—just sinners), and even a period of time when the High Priests themselves were hostile to Judaism or not Jewish at all.

The rescue ship finally comes and finds a lone Jew deserted on a desert island. He is so excited to see another human being, he can barely contain himself. He shows the rescue team how he has occupied his many months of loneliness. "Here is the shul I built for myself," he says proudly.

"And what is this other fine structure?" the captain asks admiringly.

"Oh that," the Jew sneers. "That's the shul I don't daven *in."*

Is this a cloistered, insulated religion that accepts neither the convert nor the sinner? Well, no. Not only does the Torah state no less than thirty-six times to accept the convert (i.e., "the stranger among you"[5]), but the Messiah—the savior of the Jewish people—is to be a scion of the House of David, thus claiming in his (or her) ancestry both Ruth the Moabite, a convert, and Tamar, a pseudo-harlot[6]—and indeed Moab, the product of an incestuous union.[7] It is worth noting that even when the Torah condemns Israelites who worshipped idols or other false gods, it never revokes the sinner's membership in God's people. There is a large body of Jewish jokes that gently poke fun at those of us whose level of observance is somewhat less than pristine. For example:

Rothman occasionally liked to partake of the forbidden meat. He went to a restaurant way at the other side of town where no one knew him, took a table near the kitchen, and placed his order. As it would happen, his Rabbi stopped in to use the pay phone, noticed him at his table, and came over to chat. Naturally, just as Rothman was trying to devise a good reason for being in a treife *restaurant, his order arrived, a whole roast suckling pig with an apple stuffed in its mouth. Rothman immediately exclaimed: "Funny way they have of serving fruit here!"*

Are we a cultural goup? It's a tempting characterization, but—nope. Just as Jews mingled DNA with whatever nations they lived among over the centuries, they also took on the culture of their host country and, not incidentally, were subsequently very surprised to be thrown out. Interestingly, according to opinions expressed in the Babylonian Talmud by Rabbi Eliezer and Rabbi Yochanan, the reason the Lord exiled the Jews among the nations was in order that proselytes should join them.[8] The Jerusalem Talmud goes even further and states: "When the Jewish people do the will of the Holy One, God goes all over the entire world and sees who is a righteous person among the nations and brings him and attaches him unto the Jewish people."[9] The Jewish people boast family heritages from a panoply of countries and cultures, including: Ethiopia, Western Europe, Eastern Europe, India, China, Africa, Turkey, Iran, Egypt, etc.

In a displaced persons camp after the end of World War II and the liberation of the remnants of European Jewry, an old Jewish man—the sole survivor of his entire family—is asked where he would like to be resettled.

"Australia," he answers.

"Australia?" the clerk asks. "Why so far?"

The old Jew answers: "Far from where?"

Perhaps, a nation? Today, even though Israel plays a big part in the cultural and religious lives of Jews all over the world, only those holding actual Israeli citizenship would really consider themselves to be Israelis. In terms of culture—language, food, attitudes and, yes, humor—Israel has been incorporated into the large number of cultures and nationalities represented. Granted, it is in a leadership position.

A Russian, a Pole, an American, and an Israeli are interviewed.

The interviewer asks each, in turn, "Excuse me, what is your opinion on the current meat shortage?"

The Russian replies, "What's an 'opinion'?"

The Pole replies, "What's 'meat'?"

The American replies, "What's a 'shortage'?"

And the Israeli replies, "What's 'excuse me'?"

So, perhaps Jews are not quite a defined race, not quite a cohesive religion, not quite a distinct culture, not quite a nationality. We are, however, an identifiable people (*am*)—certainly, to the anti-Semite. We are an extended family, a tribe. Our fathers are Abraham, Isaac, and Jacob; our mothers are Sarah, Rebecca, Rachel, and Leah.

During the Civil War—it was Passover—Myer Levy of Philadelphia, a Union soldier, was in a Virginia town when he saw a young boy sitting on his front steps eating a piece of matzah. According to historian Bertram Korn, when Levy asked the boy for a piece of matzah, the child ran into his house, shouting at the top of his lungs, "Mama! There's a damn Yankee Jew outside!" Naturally, the boy's mother invited Levy to join them for the seder that night.[10]

When one member of the extended family recognizes a fellow Jew, he can kick back and just be himself. No longer does he have to be on his best behavior—this is family, after all.

A Galician Jew, traveling on a train, finds himself in an empty compartment. He goes about making himself comfortable by unbuttoning his coat, opening a newspaper, and putting his feet up on one of the empty seats.

A few minutes later, the door opens and a gentleman in modern dress comes in and sits down. The Jew immediately pulls himself together, takes his feet off the seat, and assumes a proper pose. The stranger sits in silence, looking through his notebook and apparently making some calculation. "Excuse me," he says suddenly, "Do you know when Yom Kippur is this year?"

"Aha!" says the Jew, and puts his feet back up.[11]

There is something about being "one of us" that somehow matters to us. For example:

Three Jewish converts to Christianity are having drinks in an exclusive country club.

"I converted out of love," says one. Seeing the dubious looks on his friends' faces, he adds, "Not for Christianity but for a Christian girl. My wife insisted that I convert."

"And I converted in order to succeed in law," the second one says. "I would never have been appointed a federal judge if I hadn't become an Episcopalian."

The third says, "I converted because I think the teachings of Christianity are superior to those of Judaism."

To which the other two respond indignantly. "What do you take us for, a couple of goyim?*"*

In Chapter 1 we saw that humor is a bonding device. For a people that loves language and wit perhaps this, more than anything, is the bond that ties us together as a people. Somehow, we are connected to each other by some sort of *secret handshake*— be it recognized ritual, whether we all do these rituals or not, whether we all believe in what we're doing or not; be it shared history of oppression and otherness; be it a common literature—we are, after all, the people of the book; be it by a shared sense of humor dating all the way back to our very beginnings as a people.

Closing Thought

In examining what a people laugh at, we come close to learning what they value. The Jewish people—oppressed throughout history, dispersed to all parts of the globe, for most of its history a disenfranchised minority in a hostile host country, the People of the Book, always needing to live by their wit—drew upon its traditions from the Scriptures, the Talmud, and the Midrash. Jews, by and large, were not going to be strongmen, they would not win barfights; and neither were they going to be – uh - extraordinarily good looking.

> *The emperor's daughter said to Rabbi Yehoshua b. Chananiah: Such a magnificent Torah in an ugly vessel. He told her: Learn from your father's palace. Where is the wine stored? In earthen vessels, she replied. The whole world stores their wine in earthen vessels, and you also use earthen vessels. You should store your wine in vessels of silver and gold. She went and transferred the wine into silver and gold vessels and the wine spoiled. He then told her: The Torah is also like this. She stated: But there are good looking people who are scholars. Rabbi Yehoshua answered her: If they would be ugly they would be even more knowledgeable.[12]*

Rabbi Yehoshua b. Chananiah, was known to be quite unattractive and, rather than denying this, he embraced it. Clearly, he felt that very handsome people are often self-centered and spend more time on looking good than improving themselves. In classic nerd tradition, wit is more important than good looks and being funny is more important than being strong. Humor wields tremendous power. The pen, especially when crafting words with a bit of humor, can indeed be mightier than the sword. Rabbi Jonathan Sacks called humor "the weapon of the weak against the stong . . . What we can laugh at, we can rise above."[13]

While walking home one evening, two Jews notice a pair of hoodlums eyeing them from across the street.

One says to the other, "We'd better hurry it up. There are two of them and only two of us!"

What did Jews give the world? Monotheism and morality, certainly. But—we like to think—a love of humor, too. Humor, after all, is not only medicine for the body; it is good for the soul as well.

One smart aleck to another: Isn't one of the Commandments, "Humor thy father and thy mother" . . .?

Sociologist Peter Berger, a proponent of the redemptive power of humor[14] considers the human instinct for humor and playfulness a vehicle for salvation.[15] Many individuals look toward religion for salvation but, as we know, religion can just as easily be a force for evil as a force for good. One thing religious zealots all have in common is that they lack the ability to laugh at themselves. Religion is a wonderful thing, but even religion—when it takes itself too seriously—can be divisive. Perhaps, when all the world learns to laugh together we will truly be united.

We are reminded that when Elijah the prophet was asked by Rabbi Beroka Hozaah if any of the individuals around them in the marketplace were destined for Paradise (i.e., Heaven), he pointed out two people and said:

> *These two are destined for the world to come. Rabbi Beroka approached them and asked them what they did. They replied: We are merry-makers, and we cheer up people who are depressed . . .*[16]

So we know that jesters go to Heaven when they die. *That's* how important humor is to God.

Speaking of jesters, Joseph Boskin, professor at Boston University, once played an April Fools' (read, Purim) joke of magnificent proportions.

In 1983, an Associated Press article picked up by many newspapers[17] *provided the "scholarly" origin of April Fools' Day, quoting Joseph Boskin, professor of history at Boston University, who explained that the practice began during the reign of Constantine. Apparently, a group of court jesters and fools claimed they could do a better job of running the empire. According to Boskin, Constantine was amused, and allowed a jester named Kugel to be king for one day. Kugel passed an edict calling for absurdity on that day, and the custom became an annual event. "It was a very serious day. In those times fools were really wise men. It was the role of jesters to put things in perspective with humor."*

Kugel? *It took some time for the good folks at the Associated Press to figure out that they'd been victims of an April Fools' joke.*

Presumably, the newspapers that ran with this bogus story did not have Jewish editors or fact checkers. Anyone Jewish would have been quite skeptical that the Jester's name really was Kugel.

The Talmud tells us that every individual is asked several questions upon arrival in the world to come, in order to determine what is his due, and that the very first question is "Were you honest in business?"[18] With all due humility, we would like to believe that somewhere near the top of that list of questions is going to be, "Did you make people laugh?"

Appendixes

Appendix A: Important Dates in Jewish History

Abraham, Forefather of the Jewish people: 1813–1638 B.C.E.
Isaac, son of Abraham: 1713–1533 B.C.E.
Jacob, son of Isaac: 1653–1506 B.C.E.
Moses: 1393–1273 B.C.E.
Jewish people wander the wilderness for forty years: 1313–1273 B.C.E.
Jewish people cross the Jordan River and enter Israel: 1273 B.C.E.
Joshua, successor to Moses: 1355–1245 B.C.E.
Jewish people ruled by Judges: 1228 B.C.E.
Saul anointed first King of Israel by Samuel the Prophet: 879 B.C.E.
David: 907–837 B.C.E.
Solomon: 849–797 B.C.E.
First Temple completed by Solomon: 826 B.C.E.
First Temple destroyed by Babylonians under Nebuchadnezzar: 423 B.C.E.
Second Temple completed: 349 B.C.E.
Alexander the Great meets Shimon *HaTzadik* (the righteous): 313 B.C.E.
Yehuda HaMaccabi rules: 139 B.C.E.
Alexander Yannai: 126–78 B.C.E. (ruled from 102 B.C.E.)
Shammai starts his own academy: 46 B.C.E.
Hillel (the Elder) becomes leader of the sages: 32 B.C.E.
Herod finishes renovating the Second Temple: 11 B.C.E.
Hillel (the Elder) dies: 9 C.E.
Second Temple destroyed by Romans under Titus: 69 C.E. (some say 70 C.E.)
Rabbi Yochanan b. Zakkai: 47 B.C.E.–74 C.E. Rabbi Yochanan is the sage who escaped from the siege of Jerusalem shortly before the destruction of the Second Temple and convinced Vespasian to spare the family of the Nasi.
Sanhedrin led by Rabbi Gamliel II (Nasi), Rabbi Yehoshua (Av Bet Din), and Rabbi Eliezer b. Hyrkanos in Yavneh: 75 C.E.

Source: *The Jewish Time Line Encyclopedia* by Mattis Kantor (Northvale, NJ: Jason Aronson Inc. 1989)

Appendix B: The Time Periods of the Talmudic Sages

The date of birth and date of death is unknown for most of the Talmudic sages; at best, we only know in which generation they lived. The following classification of generations is somewhat arbitrary but is quite frequently used:

Pre-Tannaitic period, Zugot: 200 B.C.E.–40 C.E.

First-generation Tannaitic Period: 40–80 C.E.

Second-generation Tannaitic Period: 80–110 C.E.

Third-generation Tannaitic Period: 110–135 C.E.

Fourth-generation Tannaitic Period: 135–170 C.E.

Fifth-generation Tannaitic Period: 170–200 C.E.

Transition Period: 200–220 C.E.

First-generation Amoraic Period: 220–250 C.E.

Second-generation Amoraic Period: 250–290 C.E.

Third-generation Amoraic Period: 290–320 C.E.

Fourth-generation Amoraic Period: 320–350 C.E.

Fifth-generation Amoraic Period: 350–375 C.E.

Sixth-generation Amoraic Period: 375–425 C.E.

Seventh-generation Amoraic Period: 425–460 C.E.

Eighth-generation Amoraic Period: 460–500 C.E.

Appendix C: The Sages and Their Generations

Note: Tannaim are from Israel unless otherwise specified.

Abaye: Fourth-generation Babylonian Amora. There is a dispute as to whether his real name was Abaye or Nachmeni. He was an orphan and raised by Rabbah b. Nachmeni.

Abba: Second- and third-generation Amora. He was born in Babylonia but moved to Israel.

Abba b. Abba: Father of Shmuel. Lived at the beginning of the Amoraic period.

Abba b. Kahana: Third-generation Israeli Amora.

Abba Saul: Third- and fourth-generation Tanna.

Abiathar: Second-generation Israeli Amora.

Abitol: Second-generation Amora. He is the author of only three statements, all in the name of Rav (see Moed Katan 18a).

Abuhu: Third-generation Israeli Amora.

Acha: Fourth-generation Israeli Amora.

Acha b. Yaakov: Third- and fourth-generation Israeli Amora. Student of Rabbi Huna.

Achi b. Yoshiyah: Fifth-generation Babylonian Tanna.

Adda b. Abba: Fourth-generation Babylonian Amora.

Adda b. Ahava: First- and second-generation Babylonian Amora.

Aibu: Third-generation Israeli Amora.

Akiva b. Yosef: Third-generation Tanna, martyred about 136 C.E.

Amemar: Fifth- and sixth-generation Babylonian Amora.

Ammi: Third-generation Israeli Amora.

Amram: Second- and third-generation Babylonian Amora.

Amram the Pious: Second-generation Babylonian Amora.

Ashi: Sixth-generation Babylonian Amora. He was responsible for compilation of the Gemara (Babylonian Talmud), although some small changes were made until about 500 C.E. He died about 427 C.E.

Assi: Third-generation Israeli Amora. In the Jerusalem Talmud he is referred to as Rabbi Yassa. He was a colleague of Rabbi Ammi.

Baba b. Buta: Disciple of Shammai the elder. Lived during the generation before the destruction of the second Temple.

Banaah: Transition period between Tannaim and Amoraim.

Bar Kappara: Transition period between Tannaim and Amoraim. Lived in Israel.

Ben Azzai: (Shimon b. Azzai) Third-generation Tanna.

Ben Damah: Nephew of Rabbi Yishmael.

Ben Zoma: (Shimon b. Zoma) Third-generation Tanna.

Berachiah: Fourth-generation Israeli Amora.

Beroka of Hozaah: Not much known about him except that Elijah the Prophet revealed himself to him (see Taanit 22a).

Bruriah: Wife of Rabbi Meir and known for her incredible knowledge of Torah. Lived in the fourth generation of Tannaim.

Chananiah b. Gamliel: Fourth-generation Tanna.

Chaninah (b. Chama): First-generation Israeli Amora. Born in Babylonia but settled in Israel (Sepphoris).

Chaninah b. Dosa: First-generation Tanna.

Chaninah b. Papa: Third-generation Israeli Amora.

Chaninah b. Teradyon: Third-generation Tanna.

Chisda: Second- and third-generation Babylonian Amora.

Chiya: Transition period between Tannaim and Amoraim.

Chiya b. Abba: Third-generation Amora. Born in Babylonia but settled in Israel when young.

Chiya b. Ashi: Second-generation Babylonian Amora.

Chizkiyah b. Chiya: First-generation Amora. Born in Babylonia but settled in Israel. His twin was Yehuda b. Chiya.

Chomah: Wife of Abaye.

Choni Hamagel: He probably lived at the end of the Hasmonean period in the time of Salome Alexandra (139–67 B.C.E.). However, there may have been another individual with this name, a grandfather of the other. In the Jerusalem Talmud (Taanit 3:9), Choni slept for the seventy years of the Babylonian exile.

Derusai: Fifth-generation Israeli Amora.

Dimi: Third- and fourth-generation Babylonian Amora.

Dosa b. Harkinas: First-generation Tanna.

Dostai b. Yannai: Fifth-generation Tanna.

Efes: The scribe of Rebbi. He took over as head of Rebbi's yeshiva in Israel after Rebbi died. Rebbi actually designated Rabbi Chaninah b. Chama on his deathbed, but he refused the job because Rabbi Efes was older than him.

Elai: Third-generation Israeli Amora.

Elazar b. Pedat: Second-generation Amora. Born in Babylonia but settled in Israel.

Elazar b. Azariah: Third-generation Tanna.

Elazar b. Durdia: Not clear when he lived. He either lived at the same time or before Rebbi.

Elazar b. Shimon: Fifth-generation Tanna.

Elazar b. Yosi: Fifth-generation Tanna

Elazar b. Zadok: There were three Tannaim with this name. One Elazar b. Zadok was alive when the Temple was still extant.

Eliezer b. Hyrkanos: Second-generation Tanna.

Elisha b. Avuyah: Third-generation Tanna who became a heretic and was therefore known as *"Acher"* (the other).

Gamliel II (of Yavneh): Nasi. Second-generation Tanna. Husband of Imma Shalom and brother-in-law of Rabbi Eliezer b. Hyrkanos.

Geniva: First- and second-generation Babylonian scholar. He was a disciple of Rav but was involved in a serious feud with Mar Ukva and was therefore not respected by many scholars.

Geviha b. Pesisa: According to one story, he lived in the time of Alexander the Great.

Gidal: Second-generation Babylonian Amora.

Hamnuna: Second-generation Babylonian Amora.

Hillel (Hazaken): Zugot, contemporary of Shammai, died about 9 C.E.

Hosaiah: First-generation Israeli Amora.

Huna: Second-generation Babylonian Amora. He was a disciple of Rav.

Huna b. Yehoshua: Fifth-generation Babylonian Amora.

Ilfa: Second-generation Israeli Amora.

Imma Shalom: Wife of Eliezer b. Hyrkanos.

Kahana: Second-generation Babylonian Amora. Disciple of Rav. Four different sages had this name.

Karna: First-generation Babylonian Amora.

Levi b. Sisi: Transition period between Tannaim and Amoraim. Lived in Israel. He was a disciple of Rebbi and a friend of Abba b. Abba, the father of Shmuel, when he lived in Babylonia toward the end of his life.

Levi: Third-generation Israeli Amora. His major disciple was Yehoshua of Siknin.

Mar b. Ashi: Seventh-generation Babylonian Amora.

Mar Zutra: Sixth-generation Babylonian Amora.

Mattenah: First-generation Babylonian Amora. He lived in Pappunia, a town near Pumbedita.

Meir: Fourth-generation Tanna.

Menachma: Fifth-generation Israeli Amora.

Menashe: Third-generation Babylonian Amora.

Nachman: Second- and third-generation Babylonian Amora.

Nachman b. Yitzchak: Fourth-generation Babylonian Amora.

Nachum Ish Gamzu: Second-generation Tanna.

Oshiyah: Third-generation Amora born in Babylonia but moved with his brother (Rabbi Chaninah) to Israel.

Oshiyah: First-generation Amora. A student of Bar Kappara. The *baraitot* were redacted by Rabbi Chiya and Rabbi Oshiyah.

Pappa: Fifth-generation Babylonian Amora.

Pappa b. Shmuel: Third- and fourth-generation Babylonian Amora.

Pinchas b. Yair: Fifth-generation Tanna.

Plimo: Fifth-generation Tanna.

Rabbah bar bar Chana: Third-generation Amora. Born in Babylonia but studied in Israel. Known as a world traveler.

Rabbah b. Huna: Second- and third-generation Babylonian Amora.

Rabbah b. Nachmeni: Third-generation Babylonian Amora, known simply as "Rabbah."

Rabbah b. Mari: Third and fourth-generation Israeli Amora.

Rabbah b. Shila: Third- and fourth-generation Babylonian Amora.

Rami b. Chama: Fourth-generation Babylonian Amora.

Rav: First-generation Babylonian Amora. His real name was Abba b. Aibu.

Rava: Fourth-generation Babylonian Amora.

Ravin: Third- and fourth-generation Amora. Born in Babylonia but studied in Israel. He seems to have traveled quite frequently between Babylonia and Israel.

Ravina: Sixth-generation Babylonian Amora. Two Amoraim had this name.

Rebbi: see Rabbi Yehuda the Nasi.

Sabta of Allas: It is not known whether or not he was a sage and when he lived.

Sachorah: Third- and fourth-generation Babylonian Amora.

Shalmon: Fifth-generation Babylonian Amora.

Shammai (Hazaken): Zugot, contemporary of Hillel. Founder of Bet Shammai.

Sheshet: Second- and third-generation Babylonian Amora.

Shimon b. Abba: Third-generation Amora. Born in Babylonia but moved to Israel.

Shimon b. Chalafta: Fifth-generation Tanna.

Shimon b. Elazar: Fifth-generation Tanna.

Shimon b. Gamliel (the First): Fourth Nasi from the House of Hillel. He was the head of the Sanhedrin when the Second Temple was destroyed. His daughter, Imma Shalom, married Rabbi Eliezer b. Hyrkanos. He was one of the ten martyrs killed by the Romans.

Shimon b. Gamliel (the Second): Sixth Nasi from the House of Hillel. He was the head of the Sanhedrin during the fourth generation of Tannaim. His son was Rebbi.

Shimon b. Lakish also known as Resh Lakish: Second-generation Israeli Amora.

Shimon b. Menashia: Fifth-generation Tanna.

Shimon b. Rebbi: Youngest son of Rabbi Yehuda the Nasi. Transition period between Tannaim and Amoraim.

Shimon b. Yochai: Fourth-generation Tanna.

Shimon b. Yosi b. Lakunia: Fifth-generation Tanna.

Shmuel: First-generation Babylonian Amora. Also known as Mar Shmuel.

Shmuel b. Yehuda: Third-generation Babylonian Amora.

Simlai: Second-generation Amora. He was probably born in Babylonia but moved to Israel and settled in the South (Lod). Some, however, feel that he was born in Lod (southern part of Israel).

Tabi: Third- or fourth-generation Israeli Amora. Not to be confused with Tabi, the servant of Rabbi Gamliel.

Tanchum b. Chanilai: Second-generation Israeli Amora. A disciple of Rabbi Yehoshua b. Levi.

Tarfon: Second-generation Tanna.

Tobi b. Mattenah: Third-generation Babylonian Amora.

Ulla: Second- and third-genration Amora. Lived in Israel but spent a great deal of time in Babylonia.

Yalta: Wife of Rabbi Nachman.

Yannai: First-generation Israeli Amora.

Yehoshua of Sichnin: Fourth-generation Israeli Amora. A major disciple of Rabbi Levi.

Yehoshua b. Chananiah: Second-generation Tanna.

Yehoshua b. Karchah: Fourth-generation Tanna.

Yehoshua b. Levi: First-generation Israeli Amora.

Yehoshua b. Nechemiah: Fourth-generation Israeli Amora.

Yehoshua b. Perachiah: Became President of the Sanhedrin about two hundred years before the destruction of the Second Temple.

Yehuda b. Batyra: Third-generation Tanna.

Yehuda b. Chiya: First-generation Amora. Born in Babylonia but settled in Israel. Chizkiyah b. Chiya was his twin.

Yehuda b. Illayi: Fourth-generation Tanna.

Yehuda b. Nachmani: Second- and third-generation Israeli Amora.

Yehuda b. Simone: Third- and fourth-generation Israeli Amora.

Yehuda b. Yechezkel: Second-generation Babylonian Amora. He established the famous academy in Pumbedita.

Yehuda the Nasi, also referred to as Rebbi: Fifth-generation Tanna, redactor of the Mishna. Died about 219 C.E.

Yirmiyah: Israeli Amora of the third and fourth generations.

Yishmael b. Elisha: Third-generation Tanna.

Yishmael b. Elisha: First generation of Tannaim. He was a high priest who lived towards the end of the Second Temple.

Yishmael b. Yosi: Fifth-generation Tanna.

Yitzchak Naphcha: Second- and third-generation Israeli Amora. Later in his life, he moved to Babylonia.

Yitzchak b. Abdimi: Third-generation Babylonian Amora.

Yitzchak b. Zeira: Fourth-generation Israeli Amora.

Yochanan: Second-generation Israeli Amora. His full name was Yochanan b. Naphcha.

Yochanan b. Torasa: Third-generation Tanna.

Yochanan b. Zakkai: First-generation Tanna. One of Hillel's disciples.

Yonason b. Elazar: First-generation Israeli Amora.

Yosef: Third-generation Babylonian Amora.

Yosef b. Yehoshua b. Levi: Second-generation Israeli Amora.

Yoshiah: Third-generation Israeli Amora.

Yosi b. Assyan: Third-generation Israeli Amora.

Yosi b. Chalafta: Fourth-generation Tanna.

Yosi b. Chaninah: Second-generation Israeli Amora.

Yosi b. Kipar: Fifth-generation Tanna.

Yosi b. Kisma: Third-generation Tanna.

Yosi b. Yehuda: Fifth-generation Tanna.

Yosi b. Taddai: Tanna whose name is mentioned only one time in Derech Eretz Rabbah. He was excommunicated by Rabbi Gamliel.

Yosi b. Zimra: Transition period between Tannaim and Amoraim.

Yosi of Galile: Third-generation Tanna.

Yosi of Maon: Second-generation Israeli Amora.

Yudan: Fourth-generation Israeli Amora.

Zadok: Probably the son of Elazar b. Zadok who was a second-generation Tanna. There was another Rabbi Zadok who started to fast forty years before the destruction of the Temple in 70 C.E.

Zecharia b. Abkulas: Rabbi whose advice not to sacrifice a blemished animal sent by the Roman emperor resulted in the destruction of the Temple.

Zeiri: Second-generation Babylonian Amora

Zera: Third-generation Amora born in Babylonia but settled in Israel.

Source: *Encyclopedia of Talmudic and Geonic Literature* by Mordechai Margalioth (Editor) (Tel Aviv, Israel: Yavneh Publishing House, 2000).

Appendix D: Classic Commentators

ABRAHAM IBN EZRA (1089–1164): Spanish poet, philosopher, astronomer, and Biblical commentator born in Toledo, Spain.

MAIMONIDES (1135–1204) known by the acronym RAMBAM (Rabbi Moshe Ben Maimon). A codifier, philosopher, and physician. He wrote the *Yad Hachazaka* (Mishneh Torah), an important codification of Jewish Law. He was also the author of *Guide for the Perplexed,* a renowned philosophical work. He was born in Cordoba and lived in Egypt.

RASHBAM (c. 1085–c. 1174): An acronym for Rabbi Shmuel ben Meir, grandson of Rashi and a major Biblical commentator. He was born and lived in France.

RASHI (1040–1105) an acronym for Rabbi Shlomo ben Yitzchok, a major French Biblical and Talmudic commentator. He was born in Troyes, France.

SFORNO (1475–1550): Italian-Jewish Bible commentator. He was a physician and lived in Bologna.

SIFTE CHACHAMIM (1641–1718): A supercommentary on Rashi's commentary on the Pentateuch written by Rabbi Shabbetai Bass, a cantor in Prague.

TOSAFOT (twelfth and thirteenth centuries): The word means additions. A major commentary on the Talmud that was written by various scholars, mainly from France and Germany.

Appendix E: Mostly Punch Lines, an Index of Jokes

The Jewish humor of today used in this volume is listed here—mostly—by punch line. That so many Jewish jokes can be referenced by their punch lines is probably an indication of how popular humor is among Jews, that the jokes are repeated, reworked, and passed along from one individual to another, and from one generation to the next.

Notes

Preface
1. See Henry Spalding (1976, 306).

Chapter 1
1. See, e.g., Holden (1993), Goldin and Bordan (1999), Witkin (1999), Weinberger and Gulas (1992), Honeycutt and Brown (1998).
2. Berk (1998), Burkhart (1998).
3. Hyers (1969, 220).
4. Wikipedia.com, as of July 7, 2013.
5. Telushkin (1992, 19), Wisse (2013,12).
6. Berrin (2009).
7. Gordon (2012).
8. Philologos (2013).
9. Novak and Waldoks, (2006, xxxix–xlviii).
10. Whitfield (1986).
11. Whitfield (1986).
12. Most of the Jewish jokes in this book are classics—so well known that a definitive source is often not relevant. Where a source is not cited, the authors composed the narratives.
13. See, e.g., Novak and Waldoks (1981), Spalding (1985), Telushkin (1992). Also noteworthy is Ausubel (1948).
14. Novak and Waldoks (2006, 73).
15. Lipman (1991).
16. Personal communication.
17. Telushkin (1992, 109).
18. There are many versions of this joke circulating. Not necessarily a Jewish joke, it is easily adaptable to any two opposing groups, say, the Hatfields and the McCoys.
19. Telushkin (1992, 16–18).
20. Novak and Waldoks (1981, xlvi).
21. according to TV Guide in 2003.
22. Adapted from Mallow (2005, 142).
23. Guri (2004).
24. ibid.
25. Hecht (2004).
26. ibid.

27. Novak and Waldoks (2006, 153).
28. "The Man in the Street." *All in the Family*, season 2 episode 11. John Rich, Dir. Teleplay by: Don Nicholl and Paul Harrison & Lennie Weinrib. Aired December 4, 1971. The Yiddish curse, loosely translated into English, goes something like this: "May you live in a house with a thousand rooms. And may you have a bellyache in each one!"
29. Novak and Waldoks (2006, 153).
30. Winston-Macauley (2011).
31. Winston-Macauley (2009).
32. Ausubel (1948, 21).
33. Mallow (2005, 5).
34. Whitfield (1986).
35. Schachter (2008, xi–xii).
36. Rothstein (2013).
37. Novak and Waldoks (1981, xlvi–xlvii).
38. Wisse (2013, 33).
39. Freud (1905, 112).
40. One source of this well-known expression is Midrash Leviticus Rabbah 9:3.
41. Telushkin (1992, 97–98).
42. Keith-Speigel (1972).
43. Gerard (1759).
44. Beattie (1776).
45. Kant (1790).
46. Schopenhauer (1819).
47. Novak and Waldoks (2006, 95).
48. Spencer (1860).
49. Freud (1960).
50. Lipman (1991, 201).
51. Hobbes (1651).
52. Gruner (1997).
53. Keith-Spiegel (1972).
54. Novak and Waldoks (2006, 24).
55. Cohen (1999, 12).
56. Veatch (1998).
57. LaFollette and Shanks (1993).
58. Babylonian Talmud, Eruvin 65b.
59. Made famous in the West by John Godfrey Saxe (1816–1887) in his poem "The Blind Men and the Elephant."
60. Martineau (1972).
61. Gruner (1997, 101).
62. Grotjahn (1957, 23).
63. Davies (1993).
64. Novak and Waldoks (2006, 82).
65. Friedman and Friedman (2003b).
66. Cohen (1999, 12–32).
67. Holden (1993, 67).

68. Koller (1988, 11).
69. Ziv and Gadish (1989).
70. Two elephants are sitting in a bath. One asks, "Would you please pass the soap?" The other responds, "No soap, radio."
71. Telushkin (1992, 101).
72. Oring (1992, 116), Henkin (2006).
73. Price (1954).
74. Ziv (1998, 6–7).
75. Ben-Amos (1973).
76. Oring (2010).
77. Wisse (2013, 13).
78. Fishkoff (2011).
79. Wisse (2013, 22).
80. Genesis 17:17–19.
81. Sacks (2013).
82. Exodus 14:11.
83. Mallow (2005, 5), Telushkin (1992, 18), Brodsky (2011), Isbell (2011), Wisse (2013, 22), Brand (2013).
84. Frank (2004).
85. Friedman and Friedman (2012).
86. Feinsilver (1980).
87. Berger (1997).
88. Joseph Telushkin (1992, 18–19).
89. Spalding (1976, 18–26).
90. Novak and Waldoks (2006, 51–57).
91. *Fiddler on the Roof*, Prologue.
92. From Telushkin (1992, 83), citing Freud, *Jokes and Their Relation to the Unconscious*
93. Psalms (145, 15)
94. Babylonian Talmud, Ketubos 67b.
95. The jokes cited in this book are indexed in Appendix E—by punch line, of course.

Chapter 2

1. Babylonian Talmud, Sanhedrin 14b.
2. b. stands for either *ben* (Hebrew) or *bar* (Aramaic) and means "son of."
3. Chajes, (1960, 195).
4. Maimonides Commentary on the Mishna: Babylonian Talmud, Sanhedrin, Chapter 10.

Chapter 3

1. Novak and Waldoks (2006, 127)
2. Psalms 2:4.
3. Novak and Waldoks (2006, xlvii).
4. Hyers (1969, 220)
5. Buber, (1947, 258).
6. Babylonian Talmud, Berachot 6a.

7. I Chronicles 17:21.
8. Buber (1947, 222).
9. Aleichem (1956, 57).
10. Aleichem (1956, 50).
11. Aleichem (1956, 48).
12. Midrash Genesis Rabbah 68:4.
13. Genesis 18:12.
14. Genesis 18:13
15. Babylonian Talmud, Bava Metzia 87a.
16. Babylonian Talmud, Bava Metzia 87a.
17. Genesis 18:25.
18. Job 38: 4 and 12.
19. Genesis 18:23–33.
20. Novak and Waldoks (2006, 190).
21. Genesis 27:22.
22. Genesis 27:40.
23. Genesis 19:36.
24. Genesis 16:12.
25. Source: Sifre Deuteronomy 33:2.
26. Midrash Lamentations Rabbah 3:1.
27. Midrash Lamentations Rabbah 3:1.
28. Exodus 3 and 4.
29. Exodus 4:13–14.
30. Numbers 27:15–16.
31. Midrash Numbers Rabbah 21:15.
32. Babylonian Talmud, Berachot 9b.
33. Exodus 3:14.
34. Exodus 3:14.
35. Numbers 14:17.
36. Babylonian Talmud, Shabbat 89a.
37. Exodus 32:10.
38. Babylonian Talmud, Berachot 32a.
39. Babylonian Talmud, Berachot 32a.
40. Exodus 22:19.
41. Midrash Exodus Rabbah 43:4; also in Babylonian Talmud, Berachot 32a.
42. Exodus 20:3.
43. Exodus 32:32.
44. Midrash Exodus Rabbah 47:9.
45. Midrash Numbers Rabbah 2:15.
46. Exodus 32:11.
47. Midrash Exodus Rabbah 43:7.
48. Exodus 3:10.
49. Exodus 32:7.
50. Deuteronomy 9:29.
51. Piska D'Rav Kahana, Pesikta 16.
52. Numbers 14:16.
53. Babylonian Talmud, Berachot 32a.

54. see Numbers 13–14.
55. Psalms 26:2.
56. Babylonian Talmud, Sanhedrin 107a.
57. Babylonian Talmud, Sanhedrin 107a.
58. Babylonian Talmud, Sanhedrin 107a.
59. Babylonian Talmud, Berachot 7a.
60. Babylonian Talmud, Taanit 25a.
61. Novak and Waldoks (2006, 225).
62. Babylonian Talmud, Chagigah 15b.
63. Deuteronomy 30:12.
64. Exodus 23:2.
65. Babylonian Talmud, Bava Metzia 59b.
66. Babylonian Talmud, Bava Metzia 59b.
67. Both tractates deal with ritual impurity and are quite difficult.
68. One cannot die while studying Torah.
69. In response to the Heavenly question.
70. Babylonian Talmud, Bava Metzia 86a.
71. Mishneh Torah, Laws of Leprosy, 2:9.
72. Here the Talmud is citing Proverbs 22:29.
73. The Temple.
74. Here the Talmud is citing Job 34:33.
75. Babylonian Talmud, Sanhedrin 104b.
76. Kranc (2005).
77. Isaiah 43:9.
78. Exodus 15:3.
79. *Sukkah* is the temporary booth covered with twigs that Jews dine in during the holiday of Tabernacles.
80. Psalms 2:4.
81. Babylonian Talmud, Avodah Zarah 2b–3b.

Chapter 4

1. Novak and Waldoks (2006, 288).
2. Knox (1969).
3. Jemielty (1992).
4. Jonsson (1985, 41–50).
5. Whedbee (1998).
6. Bonham (1988, 38–51).
7. Good (1965).
8. Knox, (1969).
9. Klein (1989).
10. Novak and Waldoks (2006, 198).
11. Genesis 44:34.
12. Genesis 37:26.
13. Genesis 37:31.
14. Genesis 38:20.
15. Genesis Rabbah 85:9.
16. Genesis 31:30.

17. Midrash Genesis Rabbah 74:8.
18. Jonsson (1985, 44–45)
19. Genesis 37:25.
20. Genesis 43:11.
21. Genesis 30:1.
22. Genesis 45:18.
23. Exodus 12:36.
24. Exodus 15:17.
25. Midrash Yalkut Shimoni, Exodus 15:253.
26. Deuteronomy 30:12.
27. Numbers 16:12.
28. Midrash Numbers Rabbah 18:10.
29. Numbers 12.
30. Numbers 11.
31. Judges 5:30.
32. II Samuel 11:1–16.
33. II Samuel 12:1–5.
34. II Samuel 13:2.
35. II Samuel 13:5.
36. Good (1965, 182).
37. Esther 6:7–11.
38. Esther 3:5.
39. Esther 10:3.
40. Genesis Rabbah 19:11.
41. Genesis 3:11.
42. Genesis 4:9.
43. Numbers 22:9.
44. Isaiah 39:3–6.
45. Numbers 16:13.
46. Exodus 14:11.
47. Numbers 14:2.
48. Numbers 14:28–29.
49. I Samuel 21:15–16.
50. II Kings 18:23.
51. II Kings 18:27.
52. Judges 10:14.
53. I Kings 18:27.
54. Knox (1969).
55. II Kings 1:2–3.
56. Jeremiah 2:27–28.
57. Psalms 115:4–8.
58. Job 12:4.
59. Job 38:4.
60. Genesis 8:9.
61. Genesis 2:25.
62. Genesis 3:1.
63. Genesis 6:11–14.

64. Genesis 6:17.
65. Genesis 9:20.
66. see Midrash Rabbah Genesis 36:3.
67. Midrash Tanchuma Genesis Toldot 8.
68. Genesis 25:28.
69. Leviticus 19: 4.
70. see commentaries of Ibn Ezra and Rashi.
71. Job 13:4.
72. See, e.g., Psalms 106:36, 115:4, 135:15 and I Samuel 31:9.
73. Genesis 34:7, Genesis 45:5.
74. e.g., Leviticus 26:30, I Kings 15:12.
75. Leviticus 18:27.
76. Deuteronomy 25:16.
77. e.g., Exodus 8:22, Deuteronomy 7:26.
78. Genesis 19:8.
79. Genesis 22:14.
80. Genesis 25:23.
81. Genesis Rabbah 63:7.
82. Genesis 25:30.
83. Genesis 30:28.
84. Genesis 33:11.
85. see Genesis 40: 13,19, 20.
86. Genesis 41:51.
87. Genesis 48:22.
88. Genesis 49:9.
89. Genesis 37: 33.
90. Exodus 1:19.
91. see Sotah 11b.
92. Exodus 2:12.
93. see Midrash Exodus Rabbah 1:29.
94. Exodus 10:10.
95. Yalkut Shimoni Exodus 392.
96. Exodus 32:12.
97. see Yalkut Shimoni 392.
98. Exodus 12:36.
99. Leviticus 11:45.
100. Babylonian Talmud, Bava Metzia 61b.
101. Numbers 16:3–13.
102. Leibowitz (1980, 206).
103. Numbers 16:3.
104. Numbers 16:15.
105. Numbers 25:17.
106. Numbers 25:14–15.
107. Deuteronomy 8:3.
108. Novak and Waldoks (2006, 141).
109. Judges 15:16.
110. I Samuel 15:14.

111. Joshua 15:19.
112. Hosea 13:7.
113. see Hosea 12:2.
114. Hosea 14:4.
115. Ruth 1:20.
116. Ruth 2:12.
117. see Midrash Ruth Rabbah 5:4.
118. Genesis 17:19.
119. Genesis 16:11.
120. Genesis 32:29.
121. Genesis 9:27.
122. Genesis 25:26.
123. Genesis 27:36.
124. Genesis 30:23–24.
125. Genesis 49:8.
126. Genesis 49:16.
127. Genesis 49:19.
128. I Samuel 25:25.
129. II Samuel 3:33.
130. I Samuel 22:18.
131. Babylonian Talmud, Sanhedrin 106b.
132. Isaiah 7:6.
133. Good (1965, 158).
134. Jeremiah 20:3.
135. Genesis 31:42.
136. Genesis 31:53.
137. see Genesis 34.
138. II Kings 22:14.
139. used in II Chronicles.
140. II Chronicles 34:20.
141. Schachter (2008, 102).
142. Bonham (1988, 44–46).
143. Exodus 8:3.
144. see the commentary of Sifte Chachamim.
145. Currid (1997, 108–9).
146. Exodus 16:3.
147. Numbers 11:5.
148. Judges 3:20.
149. Hosea 13:2.
150. see the commentary of the Ibn Ezra.
151. The Song of Songs 1:9.
152. The Song of Songs 4:1–2.
153. The Song of Songs 7:5.
154. Proverbs 11:22.
155. Proverbs 21:19.
156. Proverbs 25:24.
157. Proverbs 27:15.

158. Proverbs 26:3.
159. Proverbs 26:3.
160. Proverbs 26:9.
161. Proverbs 26:11.
162. Proverbs 26:13.
163. Proverbs 26:14.
164. Proverbs 26:15.
165. Proverbs 26:16.
166. Esther 7:8.
167. Genesis 23:11-15.
168. Jeremiah 32:9.
169. Genesis 32:2.
170. Genesis 32:12.
171. Genesis 32:29.
172. Genesis 33:14.
173. Exodus 3:10.
174. Exodus 32:7. See Piska D'Rav Kahana, Pesikta 16.
175. Exodus 32:10.
176. Midrash Exodus Rabbah 42:9.
177. e.g., I Samuel 19:6, 20:3, 20:21, 25:26.
178. Numbers 14:21.
179. e.g., Isaiah 49:18, Jeremiah 22:24.
180. Numbers 24:16.
181. Numbers 22:29.
182. Midrash Numbers Rabbah 20:14.
183. Numbers 22:28.
184. Numbers 24:3.
185. I Samuel 9:11.
186. I Samuel 9:12–13.
187. Babylonian Talmud, Berachot 48b.
188. I Samuel 25:31.
189. Babylonian Talmud, Megillah 14b.
190. I Samuel 25:42.
191. e.g., see Miles (1990), Hyers (1987, 91–109).
192. Jonah 3:4.
193. Ruth 2:8–22.
194. Esther 1:22.
195. Midrash Esther Rabbah 4:12.
196. Psalms 2:4.

Chapter 5

1. An earlier version of the material in this chapter appeared in Friedman and Lipman (1999).
2. Zechariah 3:1.
3. I Chronicles 21:1.
4. Job 1:7.
5. see, e.g., Radin (1956), Hynes and Doty (1993), Hyde (1998).

6.   Babylonian Talmud, Bava Batra 16a.
7.   Babylonian Talmud, Avodah Zarah 20b.
8.   Babylonian Talmud, Sukkah 52a.
9.   Babylonian Talmud, Sukkah 52a.
10. Babylonian Talmud, Sukkah 52b.
11. Babylonian Talmud, Sukkah 52b.
12. Babylonian Talmud, Kiddushin 30b.
13. e.g., Sforno on Genesis 3:1.
14. Pirkei Rabbi Eliezer 13; Midrash Yalkut Shimoni Genesis 2:25.
15. Babylonian Talmud, Sanhedrin 107a.
16. II Samuel 11:2.
17. Babylonian Talmud, Kiddushin 81a.
18. Babylonian Talmud, Kiddushin 81a.
19. Babylonian Talmud, Kiddushin 81a–81b.
20. I Samuel 1.
21. Babylonian Talmud, Bava Batra 16a.
22. Midrash Tanchuma, Vayera 22.
23. Midrash Rabbah Genesis 66.
24. Midrash Tanchuma Genesis: Noah 13.
25. Genesis 9:20–28.
26. Babylonian Talmud, Avot D'Rabbi Natan 12:4.
27. Babylonian Talmud, Ketubot 77b.
28. Babylonian Talmud, Ketubot 77b.
29. Babylonian Talmud, Berachot 51a.
30. Babylonian Talmud, Avodah Zarah 20b.
31. Midrash Ecclesiastes Rabbah 3:2.
32. Babylonian Talmud, Sukkah 53a.
33. I Kings 3:12.
34. Proverbs 13:23.
35. Babylonian Talmud, Chagiga 4b.
36. Babylonian Talmud, Avodah Zarah 20b.
37. Babylonian Talmud, Moed Katan 28a.
38. Babylonian Talmud, Moed Katan 28a.

Chapter 6

1.   Novak and Waldoks (2006, 2).
2.   Babylonian Talmud, Sanhedrin 109b.
3.   Babylonian Talmud, Shabbat 119a.
4.   Babylonian Talmud, Bava Batra 158b.
5.   Babylonian Talmud, Gittin 57a.
6.   Babylonian Talmud, Berachot 54b.
7.   Babylonian Talmud, Bava Batra 73a–74a.
8.   Babylonian Talmud, Shabbat 119a.
9.   Babylonian Talmud, Sanhedrin 109b.
10. Babylonian Talmud, Pesachim 113b.
11. Babylonian Talmud, Sanhedrin 38b.
12. Midrash Leviticus Rabbah 4:6.

13. Babylonian Talmud, Menachot 44a.
14. Babylonian Talmud, Shabbat 30b–31a.
15. Babylonian Talmud, Niddah 23a.
16. Babylonian Talmud, Chagigah 15b.
17. Babylonian Talmud, Menachot 37a.
18. Babylonian Talmud, Eruvin 65b.
19. Babylonian Talmud, Derech Eretz Zuta 5.
20. see Babylonian Talmud, Nazir 42a; Babylonian Talmud, Sanhedrin 109a.
21. Babylonian Talmud, Berachot 31a.
22. Psalms 126:2.
23. Babylonian Talmud, Berachot 31a.
24. Babylonian Talmud Bava Metzia 84a.
25. Babylonian Talmud, Bava Metzia 84a.
26. Babylonian Talmud, Nedarim 50b.
27. Babylonian Talmud, Pesachim 112b.
28. Babylonian Talmud, Nedarim 50b–51a.
29. Babylonian Talmud, Nedarim 50b.
30. see Jerusalem Talmud, Moed Katan 3:1.
31. Babylonian Talmud, Shabbat 30b.
32. Babylonian Talmud, Sanhedrin 38b.
33. Midrash Leviticus Rabbah 28:2.
34. Babylonian Talmud, Berachot 60b.
35. Babylonian Talmud, Maakot 24a–24b.
36. Zecharia 8:4.
37. Babylonian Talmud, Maakot 24b.
38. Babylonian Talmud, Sanhedrin 101a.
39. Deuteronomy 6:5.
40. Jerusalem Talmud, Berachot 9:5.
41. Babylonian Talmud, Avot 3:17.
42. Babylonian Talmud, Sotah 42a.
43. Psalms 1.
44. Psalms 1:1.
45. Babylonian Talmud, Taanit 22a.
46. Literally, one who has returned to the faith.

Chapter 7

1. Isaiah 8:14.
2. Babylonian Talmud, Sanhedrin 38a.
3. Midrash Leviticus Rabbah 12:1.
4. Midrash Leviticus Rabbah 12:1.
5. Proverbs 23:29–30.
6. Genesis Rabbah 36:4.
7. Midrash Tanchuma Leviticus: Shmini 11.
8. Babylonian Talmud, Avot D'Rabbi Natan 41:1.
9. Babylonian Talmud, Gittin 14b.
10. Babylonian Talmud, Sanhedrin 39a.
11. Babylonian Talmud, Chagigah 5b.

12. Many versions of this joke can be found, The one here has been mostly adapted from Novak and Waldoks (2006, 88–89).
13. Babylonian Talmud, Avodah Zarah 25b–26a.
14. Genesis 33:14.
15. Megillah 25b.
16. Babylonian Talmud, Sanhedrin 64a.
17. Midrash Genesis Rabbah 38:13.
18. Genesis 24:10.
19. Genesis 29:13.
20. Midrash Genesis Rabbah 70:13.
21. Genesis 31:30.
22. Midrash Genesis Rabbah 74:8.
23. Jerusalem Talmud, Berachot 2:8.
24. Isaiah 28:22.
25. Jerusalem Talmud, Berachot 2:8.
26. Babylonian Talmud, Gittin 56b.
27. Babylonian Talmud, Sanhedrin 109a.
28. Babylonian Talmud, Berachot 62a.
29. Babylonian Talmud, Shabbat 30b–31a.
30. Babylonian Talmud, Eruvin 13b.
31. Babylonian Talmud, Shabbat 31a.
32. Babylonian Talmud, Shabbat 31a.
33. Midrash Ecclesiastes Rabbah 7:8.
34. Proverbs 7:8.
35. Babylonian Talmud, Berachot 35b.
36. Babylonian Talmud, Taanit 21a.
37. Adapted from Ausubel (1948, 10).
38. Hosea 5:1.
39. Deuteronomy 18:3.
40. Ezekiel 16:44.
41. Midrash Genesis Rabbah 80:1.
42. Sanhedrin, end of Chapter 2.
43. Babylonian Talmud, Moed Katan 17a.
44. Babylonian Talmud, Kiddushin 70a–70b.
45. Kiddushin 49b.
46. Babylonian Talmud, Bechorot 8b.
47. Midrash Lamentations Rabbah 1:6.
48. Midrash Lamentations Rabbah 1:7.
49. Midrash Lamentations Rabbah 1:9.
50. Midrash Lamentations Rabbah 1:12.
51. Midrash Lamentations Rabbah 1:13.
52. "The nation of Israel lives."
53. Mallow (2005, 163).

Chapter 8

1. Babylonian Talmud, Shabbat 116a–b.
2. Matthew 5:17.

3.   see Herford (1975, 146–55).
4.   Babylonian Talmud, Sanhedrin 109b.
5.   Source: Wikipedia entry on *Jewish Humour*.
6.   Midrash Esther Rabbah 1:1.
7.   Babylonian Talmud, Gittin 68b.
8.   Genesis 42:11.
9.   Midrash Genesis Rabbah 91:7.
10.   Kings II 7:1–20.
11.   Babylonian Talmud, Sanhedrin 90a.
12.   Babylonian Talmud, Sotah 8b–9a.
13.   Babylonian Talmud, Sotah 9b.
14.   Midrash Genesis Rabbah 70:19.
15.   Genesis 38:20.
16.   Proverbs 8: 30–31.
17.   Midrash Genesis Rabbah 85:9.
18.   see Genesis 37:31.
19.   see Genesis 38.
20.   Midrash Leviticus Rabbah 1:3.
21.   Numbers 16:7.
22.   Midrash Numbers Rabbah 18:18.
23.   Deuteronomy 3:26.
24.   first day of the Jewish lunar month.
25.   Proverbs 18:7.
26.   Midrash Esther Rabbah 7:12.
27.   Psalms 104:3.
28.   Babylonian Talmud, Chullin 60a.
29.   Babylonian Talmud, Shabbat 119a.
30.   Babylonian Talmud, Avodah Zarah 65a.
31.   Sexton.
32.   Babylonian Talmud, Shabbat 112b.
33.   Jerusalem Talmud, Gittin 6:7.
34.   Babylonian Talmud, Shabbat 114b.
35.   Babylonian Talmud, Pesachim 86b.
36.   Babylonian Talmud, Pesachim 112a.
37.   Babylonian Talmud, Pesachim 113b.
38.   Babylonian Talmud, Pesachim 113b.
39.   Jerusalem Talmud, Peah 8:6.
40.   Psalms 113:7.
41.   Proverbs 6: 3.
42.   Babylonian Talmud, Yuma 87a.
43.   Babylonian Talmud, Megilla 28b.
44.   Babylonian Talmud, Moed Katan 28a.
45.   An early sage; see Appendix B or C.
46.   Babylonian Talmud, Sotah 49b.
47.   e.g., Babylonian Talmud, Kiddushin 39a; Babylonian Talmud, Sanhedrin 61a.
48.   Babylonian Talmud, Bechorot 58a.

49. sexton.
50. Adapted from Ausubel (1948, 16).

Chapter 9

1. Numbers 16:3.
2. Amos 4:1.
3. Babylonian Talmud, Shabbat 32b–33a.
4. Genesis 18:8.
5. Babylonian Talmud, Kiddushin 32b.
6. Numbers 22.
7. Midrash Numbers Rabbah 20:14.
8. See Exodus 7:8–14.
9. Midrash Exodus Rabbah 9:6.
10. Exodus 35:3.
11. Isaiah 54:1.
12. Babylonian Talmud, Berachot 10a.
13. Psalms 127:3.
14. Babylonian Talmud, Shabbat 152a.
15. Babylonian Talmud, Eruvin 53b.
16. Micah 7:4.
17. Babylonian Talmud, Eruvin 101a.
18. Isaiah 12:3.
19. Babylonian Talmud, Sukkah 48b.
20. Babylonian Talmud, Berachot 28b.
21. Babylonian Talmud, Sanhedrin 39a.
22. Babylonian Talmud, Sanhedrin 39a.
23. Deuteronomy 13:18.
24. Babylonian Talmud, Avodah Zarah 44b.
25. Babylonian Talmud, Sanhedrin 39a.
26. Babylonian Talmud, Sanhedrin 65b.
27. Babylonian Talmud, Nedarim 50b, see commentary of Rashi.
28. Babylonian Talmud, Sanhedrin 91a.
29. Babylonian Talmud, Sanhedrin 90a.
30. Adapted from Ausubel (1948, 441).
31. Midrash Genesis Rabbah 11:6.
32. Exodus 22:30.
33. Jerusalem Talmud, Terumot 8:3.
34. Babylonian Talmud, Pesachim 49b.
35. see Babylonian Talmud, Bava Kama 117a–117b.
36. Jerusalem Talmud, Berachot 2:8.
37. Babylonian Talmud, Maakot 22b.
38. Deuteronomy 25:3.
39. Babylonian Talmud, Kiddushin 31a.
40. Habbakuk 2:19.
41. Babylonian Talmud, Sanhedrin 7b.
42. Adapted from Davies (1986).

43. See "The Rec.humor.funny Ban" at http://www.netfunny.com/rhf/rhfban. html
44. Babylonian Talmud, Derech Eretz Rabbah 9.
45. Babylonian Talmud, Sanhedrin 24a.
46. Rashi, Babylonian Talmud, Pesachim 34b.
47. Soncino Babylonian Talmud, Pesachim 34b, note 1b.
48. Babylonian Talmud, Pesachim 34b.
49. Lamentations 3:6.
50. Babylonian Talmud, Sanhedrin 24a.
51. Babylonian Talmud, Ketubot 75a.
52. Babylonian Talmud, Nedarim 49b.
53. Zecharia 5:9–11.
54. Babylonian Talmud, Sanhedrin 24a.
55. Babylonian Talmud, Chullin 127a.
56. Babylonian Talmud, Taanit 9b.
57. Babylonian Talmud, Taanit 9b.
58. Zecharia 5:9–11.
59. Numbers 25:17.
60. Babylonian Talmud, Bava Kama 38a–38b.
61. Deuteronomy 7:13.
62. Babylonian Talmud, Berachot 51b.
63. Lamentations 5:11.
64. Amos 6:4.
65. Babylonian Talmud, Kiddushin 71b.
66. Jerusalem Talmud, Kelaim 9:3.
67. Babylonian Talmud, Shabbat 104b.
68. Babylonian Talmud, Yevamot 9a.
69. Babylonian Talmud, Shabbat 108a.
70. Babylonian Talmud, Avot 1:5.
71. Babylonian Talmud, Eruvin 53b.
72. Jerusalem Talmud, Pesachim 5:3.
73. Babylonian Talmud, Pesachim 89b.
74. Babylonian Talmud, Sukkah 23a.
75. Adapted from Spalding (1985, 255).
76. Babylonian Talmud, Taanit 5b.
77. Jerusalem Talmud, Taanit 4:5.
78. Babylonian Talmud, Nedarim 49b.
79. Babylonian Talmud, Yevamot 16a.
80. Babylonian Talmud, Yevamot 63b.
81. Babylonian Talmud, Ketubot 77a.
82. Opinions expressed by Tannaim but not part of the Mishna edited by Rebbi.
83. Babylonian Talmud, Bava Metzia 38b.
84. Babylonian Talmud, Sanhedrin 33a.
85. Babylonian Talmud, Sanhedrin 67b.
86. Exodus 8:2.

87. Babylonian Talmud, Sanhedrin 110b.
88. However, see, e.g., E. Avichail, *The Tribes of Israel: The Lost and Dispersed* (Jerusalem, Israel: Amishav, 1990).
89. Babylonian Talmud, Maakot 23b.
90. Joshua 1:8.
91. Babylonian Talmud, Menachot 99b.
92. See Rashi on Babylonian Talmud, Sotah 49b.
93. Babylonian Talmud, Avodah Zarah 27b.
94. Genesis 29:17.
95. Midrash Genesis Rabbah 70:16.
96. Genesis 29:7.
97. Exodus 21:35.
98. Genesis 33:4.
99. See II Samuel 11–12.
100. Psalms 35:15.
101. Babylonian Talmud, Sanhedrin 107a.
102. Babylonian Talmud, Taanit 20a–20b.

Chapter 10

1. Novak and Waldoks (2006, 153).
2. Babylonian Talmud, Chullin 90b.
3. Ibid.
4. Deuteronomy 1:28.
5. I Kings 1:40.
6. Babylonian Talmud, Chullin 90b.
7. Babylonian Talmud, Pesachim 62b.
8. I Chronicles 8:38.
9. I Chronicles 9:44.
10. Lamentations 2:2.
11. Babylonian Talmud, Gittin 57a.
12. Babylonian Talmud, Berachot 54b.
13. Numbers 21:33–35.
14. Deuteronomy 3:11.
15. Babylonian Talmud, Soferim 21:9.
16. Novak and Waldoks (2006, 83).
17. Babylonian Talmud, Shabbat 149b.
18. Babylonian Talmud, Moed Katan 18a.
19. See Joshua 2.
20. Babylonian Talmud, Taanit 5b.
21. Genesis 21:7.
22. Midrash Genesis Rabbah 53:9.
23. Genesis 21:8.
24. Judges 8:21.
25. Proverbs 26:4.
26. Babylonian Talmud, Bava Metzia 84a.
27. See Babylonian Talmud, Sukkah 52a.
28. Babylonian Talmud, Sanhedrin 82b.

29. See Numbers (25:1–15) for a full description of the calamity that befell the Jewish people when they fornicated with the heathen and idolatrous women of Moab and Midian.
30. II Samuel 13–20.
31. Babylonian Talmud, Niddah 24b.
32. Daniel 3.
33. Babylonian Talmud, Sanhedrin 93a.
34. Babylonian Talmud, Niddah 24b–25a.
35. A commentary on Chronicles.
36. Babylonian Talmud, Pesachim 62b.
37. Babylonian Talmud, Berachot 55a.
38. Babylonian Talmud, Bava Batra 73a–74a.
39. Babylonian Talmud, Bava Batra 73b.
40. Babylonian Talmud, Bechorot 57b.
41. Babylonian Talmud, Bava Batra 73b.
42. Babylonian Talmud, Bava Batra 74a.
43. Amos 3:8.
44. Babylonian Talmud, Chullin 59b.
45. Esther 1:12.
46. Babylonian Talmud, Megilla 12b.
47. Babylonian Talmud, Bechorot 44b.
48. Genesis 25:30.
49. Midrash Genesis Rabbah 63:12.
50. Genesis 33:4.
51. Midrash Genesis Rabbah 78:9.
52. Midrash Leviticus Rabbah 5:8.
53. Babylonian Talmud, Bava Metzia 86a.
54. Babylonian Talmud, Berachot 20a.
55. Exodus 10:22–23.
56. Midrash Exodus Rabbah 14:3.
57. Schachter (2008, 111).

Chapter 11

1. From the Passover Haggadah, this translates to: Why is this night different from all other nights?
2. Psalms 104:35.
3. Babylonian Talmud, Berachot 10a.
4. Isaiah 43:4.
5. Babylonian Talmud, Berachot 62b.
6. Babylonian Talmud, Shabbat 89a.
7. Deuteronomy 14:22.
8. Babylonian Talmud, Shabbat 119a.
9. Babylonian Talmud, Pesachim 114a.
10. Babylonian Talmud, Pesachim 114a.
11. Babylonian Talmud, Yuma 76b.
12. Deuteronomy 8:9.
13. Babylonian Talmud, Taanit 4a.

14. Genesis 2:18.
15. Babylonian Talmud, Yevamot 63a.
16. Leviticus 19:36.
17. Babylonian Talmud, Bava Metzia 49a.
18. Genesis 25:28.
19. Midrash Tanchuma Genesis, Toldot 8.
20. Genesis 28:16.
21. Midrash Genesis Rabbah 69:7.
22. Exodus 2:12.
23. Midrash Exodus Rabbah 1:29.
24. Leviticus 10:1–2.
25. Psalms 78:63.
26. Midrash Leviticus Rabbah 20:10.
27. Ruth 1:1.
28. Midrash Ruth Rabbah 1:1.
29. Genesis 24:29.
30. Midrash Hagadol Genesis 24:29.
31. Yalkut Shimoni Proverbs 9.
32. Genesis 17:5.
33. Leviticus 20:13.
34. Leviticus 18:23.
35. Leviticus 19:29.
36. Babylonian Talmud, Nedarim 50b–51a.
37. Babylonian Talmud, Shabbat 77b.
38. Jerusalem Talmud, Yevamot 13:1.
39. Exodus 1:13.
40. Babylonian Talmud, Sotah 11a–11b.
41. II Kings 6:23.
42. Babylonian Talmud, Niddah 31b.
43. Genesis 27:41.
44. Midrash Genesis Rabbah 67:8.
45. Exodus 13:17.
46. Midrash Exodus Rabbah 20:1.
47. Ecclesiastes 12:11.
48. Midrash Numbers Rabbah 15:22.
49. Midrash Numbers Rabbah 22:8.
50. Novak and Waldoks (2006, 113).
51. Babylonian Talmud, Sotah 34a.
52. Eruvin 53a.
53. Radday (1990).
54. I Samuel 25:25.
55. Numbers 22.
56. Babylonian Talmud, Sanhedrin 105a.
57. Babylonian Talmud, Megillah 11a.
58. Midrash Esther Rabbah 1:1.
59. Judges 16.
60. Babylonian Talmud, Sotah 9b.

61. Babylonian Talmud, Sanhedrin 109b.
62. Numbers 16–17.
63. Ruth 1.
64. Midrash Ruth Rabbah 2:9.
65. Babylonian Talmud, Sotah 42b.
66. Babylonian Talmud, Berachot 4a.
67. Babylonian Talmud, Berachot 20a.
68. Babylonian Talmud, Berachot 39b.
69. Hosea 1:2–3.
70. Babylonian Talmud, Pesachim 87a–87b.
71. Deuteronomy 32:20.
72. Babylonian Talmud, Yuma 83b.
73. Babylonian Talmud, Temurah 16a.
74. Genesis 14:2.
75. Midrash Genesis Rabbah 42:5.
76. Midrash Leviticus Rabbah 20:11.
77. See Exodus 17:8–16.
78. Pesikta D'Rav Kahana, Piska 3.
79. Babylonian Talmud, Sotah 12a.
80. Midrash Leviticus Rabbah 1:3.
81. Midrash Exodus Rabbah 27:8.
82. Midrash Ecclesiastes Rabbah 1.
83. Novak and Waldoks (2006, 96).
84. Judges 14:12–14.
85. See Daniel 5.
86. Babylonian Talmud, Sukkah 14a.
87. Babylonian Talmud, Shabbat 152a.
88. Novak and Waldoks (2006, 82).
89. Babylonian Talmud, Bechorot 8b.
90. Babylonian Talmud, Eruvin 53b.
91. Babylonian Talmud, Rosh Hashanah 26b.
92. Babylonian Talmud, Moed Katan 17a.
93. Babylonian Talmud, Eruvin 53b.
94. Babylonian Talmud, Eruvin 53b.
95. Babylonian Talmud, Eruvin 53b.
96. Babylonian Talmud, Moed Katan 9b.
97. See Deuteronomy 24:5.
98. Babylonian Talmud, Bava Batra 58a.
99. Yalkut Shimoni Psalms 92.
100. Midrash Genesis Rabbah 58:3.
101. Midrash Song of Songs 1:15.
102. See Exodus 12:37.
103. Babylonian Talmud, Shabbat 152a.
104. Babylonian Talmud, Shabbat 152a.
105. Midrash Lamentations Rabbah 1:11.
106. Genesis 6:3.
107. Genesis 3:11.

108. Deuteronomy 31:18.
109. Exodus 30:23.
110. Babylonian Talmud, Chullin 139b.

Chapter 12

1. Babylonian Talmud, Pesachim 113a.
2. Babylonian Talmud, Eruvin 41b.
3. Babylonian Talmud, Berachot 57b.
4. Babylonian Talmud, Pesachim 113b.
5. Ecclesiasticus 25:2.
6. Babylonian Talmud, Niddah 16b–17a.
7. Babylonian Talmud, Avot 5:12.
8. Babylonian Talmud, Avot 5:15.
9. Babylonian Talmud, Pesachim 113b.
10. Babylonian Talmud, Avot D'Rabbi Natan 36:5.
11. Babylonian Talmud, Sotah 22b.
12. Fried, Heshy. "Guide to shuckling," *FrumSatire*, May 24, 2010. http://www.frumsatire.net/2010/05/24/guide-to-shuckling/
13. Ausubel (1948, 638).
14. Babylonian Talmud, Kiddushin 49b.
15. Babylonian Talmud, Pesachim 94a.
16. Ausubel (1948, 644).
17. Babylonian Talmud, Kiddushin 82b.
18. Babylonian Talmud, Kiddushin 82a.
19. Babylonian Talmud, Kiddushin 82b.
20. Babylonian Talmud, Nedarim 49b.
21. Babylonian Talmud, Bava Kama 85a.
22. Midrash Leviticus Rabbah 3:1.
23. Babylonian Talmud, Bava Batra 110a.
24. Babylonian Talmud, Chullin 84b.
25. Also Proverbs 15:15.
26. Babylonian Talmud, Ketubot 110b.
27. Babylonian Talmud, Menachot 109b.
28. Midrash Tanchuma Leviticus 3.
29. Babylonian Talmud, Soferim 16:8.
30. Babylonian Talmud, Gittin 56b.
31. Babylonian Talmud, Shabbat 34a.
32. Babylonian Talmud, Shabbat 31a–31b.
33. Midrash Leviticus Rabbah 1:15.
34. Babylonian Talmud, Pesachim 112a.
35. Babylonian Talmud, Berachot 58a.
36. Babylonian Talmud, Pesachim 86b.
37. Babylonian Talmud, Kallah Rabbahti 9.
38. Babylonian Talmud, Gittin 45a.
39. Babylonian Talmud, Taanit 16a.
40. Deuteronomy 28:3.
41. Babylonian Talmud, Bava Metzia 107a.

42. Ausubel (1948, 639).
43. Babylonian Talmud, Eruchin 16b.
44. Babylonian Talmud, Sotah 22b.
45. Numbers 25:1–16.
46. Leviticus 4:3.
47. Midrash Leviticus Rabbah 5:6.
48. Babylonian Talmud, Sotah 21b.
49. Jerusalem Talmud, Sotah 3:4.
50. Babylonian Talmud, Gittin 56a.
51. Babylonian Talmud, Bava Metzia 85b.
52. Berkovits (1990, 3–37).
53. Proverbs 1:25.
54. Isaiah 3:16.
55. Isaiah 3:16.
56. Genesis 18:10.
57. Numbers 12:1.
58. Genesis 30:1.
59. Genesis 31:9.
60. Genesis 34:1.
61. Midrash Genesis Rabbah 18:2.
62. Midrash Genesis Rabbah 47:9.
63. Babylonian Talmud, Megilla 13a.
64. Babylonian Talmud, Ketubot 65a.
65. Babylonian Talmud, Sanhedrin 7a.
66. Babylonian Talmud, Eruvin 100b.
67. Babylonian Talmud, Yuma 66b.
68. See Babylonian Talmud, Bava Metzia 59b.
69. Judges 4:6.
70. II Kings 22:15.
71. Babylonian Talmud, Megillah 14b.
72. Babylonian Talmud, Temura 16a.
73. Babylonian Talmud, Eruvin 100b.
74. Babylonian Talmud, Ketubot 5b.
75. Proverbs 17:28.
76. Babylonian Talmud, Pesachim 99a.
77. Rabbi Yehuda in Babylonian Talmud, Megilla 18a.
78. Babylonian Talmud, Megilla 18a.
79. Babylonian Talmud, Bava Metzia 59b.
80. Babylonian Talmud, Megillah 14b.
81. See I Samuel 25:23–42.
82. Genesis 9:6.
83. Midrash Leviticus Rabbah 34:3.
84. Babylonian Talmud, Derech Eretz Rabbah 3.
85. Babylonian Talmud, Avot 4:4.
86. Babylonian Talmud, Bava Kama 92b.
87. Midrash Genesis Rabbah 45:7.
88. Babylonian Talmud, Sukkah 52b.

89. Babylonian Talmud, Shabbat 152a.
90. Babylonian Talmud, Berachot 61a.
91. Babylonian Talmud, Sotah 10a.
92. Babylonian Talmud, Pesachim 112a.
93. Genesis 24:67.
94. Babylonian Talmud, Bava Kama 92b.
95. Genesis 24:67–25:1.
96. Babylonian Talmud, Yevamot 63a.
97. Ecclesiastes 7:26.
98. Babylonian Talmud, Sanhedrin 7a.
99. Babylonian Talmud, Taanit 31a.
100. and purposely arrive while the men are getting dressed—Rashi.
101. Babylonian Talmud, Gittin 90a–90b.
102. Babylonian Talmud, Niddah 31b.
103. Babylonian Talmud, Eruvin 54a.
104. Babylonian Talmud, Eruvin 54a.
105. Ausubel (1948, 648).

Chapter 13

1. Stern (1991).
2. Babylonian Talmud, Sotah 40a.
3. Babylonian Talmud, Bava Kama 60b.
4. Babylonian Talmud, Avodah Zarah 54b.
5. See Deuteronomy 4:24.
6. Babylonian Talmud, Avodah Zarah 55a.
7. Exodus 5:1–2.
8. Midrash Exodus Rabbah 5:14.
9. Midrash Leviticus Rabbah 4:6.
10. See Numbers 20:12.
11. Midrash Numbers Rabbah 19:12.
12. Genesis 2:21.
13. Babylonian Talmud, Sanhedrin 39a.
14. Ecclesiastes 7:17.
15. Babylonian Talmud, Shabbat 31b.
16. Exodus 33:20–23.
17. Babylonian Talmud, Chulin 59b–60a.
18. Babylonian Talmud, Sanhedrin 91b.
19. See Soncino Translation of Sanhedrin, Page 91a, note 7c.
20. Midrash Leviticus Rabbah 25:5.
21. Babylonian Talmud, Kiddushin 39b.
22. Babylonian Talmud, Taanit 25a.
23. Jerusalem Talmud, Bava Metzia 2:5.
24. Midrash Rabbah Deuteronomy 1: 10.
25. Midrash Leviticus Rabbah 28:2.
26. Deuteronomy 30:20.
27. Babylonian Talmud, Berachot 61b.
28. Midrash Ecclesiastes Rabbah 5:14.

29. Ecclesiastes 5:14.
30. See Babylonian Talmud, Gittin 7a.
31. Genesis 8:7.
32. Babylonian Talmud, Sanhedrin 108b.
33. Midrash Genesis Rabbah 64:10.

Chapter 14

1. Exodus 22:30
2. Jerusalem Talmud, Demai 1:3.
3. See Babylonian Talmud, Avot D'Rabbi Natan 8:8.
4. Babylonian Talmud, Chullin 7a–7b.
5. Babylonian Talmud, Shabbat 112b.
6. Babylonian Talmud, Berachot 32a.
7. Babylonian Talmud, Berachot 17b.
8. Babylonian Talmud, Sanhedrin 65b.
9. Babylonian Talmud, Chullin 105b.
10. Psalms 126:1.
11. Babylonian Talmud, Taanit 23a.
12. Babylonian Talmud, Berachot 56b.
13. Babylonian Talmud, Berachot 18b.
14. Babylonian Talmud, Berachot 18b.
15. Babylonian Talmud, Berachot 18b.
16. See Babylonian Talmud, Ketubot 103b.
17. Babylonian Talmud, Pesachim 50a.
18. Babylonian Talmud, Bava Metzia 85b.
19. Babylonian Talmud, Bava Batra 58a.
20. Babylonian Talmud, Sanhedrin 102a–102b.
21. Babylonian Talmud, Avot 2:5.
22. See II Kings 21.
23. From Psalms 95:7.
24. Babylonian Talmud, Sanhedrin 98a.
25. Babylonian Talmud, Sanhedrin 113b.
26. Babylonian Talmud, Shabbat 53b.
27. See Iyun Yaakov.
28. Babylonian Talmud, Megillah 7b.
29. Isaiah 41:2.
30. Babylonian Talmud, Taanit 21a.
31. The blessing recited on wine to sanctify the Sabbath.
32. Babylonian Talmud, Megillah 27b.
33. Babylonian Talmud, Berachot 7a.
34. Deuteronomy 9:25.
35. Numbers 12:13.
36. Babylonian Talmud, Berachot 34a.
37. See Exodus 23:5.
38. Babylonian Talmud, Bava Metzia 30b.
39. Babylonian Talmud, Sanhedrin 11a.
40. Babylonian Talmud, Derech Eretz Rabbah 7.

41. Yalkut Shimoni Numbers 12.
42. Midrash Leviticus Rabbah 33:1.
43. Proverbs 18:21.
44. Babylonian Talmud, Eruvin 53a.
45. Babylonian Talmud, Eruvin 53b.
46. Babylonian Talmud, Bava Metzia 84a.
47. Babylonian Talmud, Bava Metzia 85a.
48. Babylonian Talmud, Berachot 46a.
49. Babylonian Talmud, Sanhedrin 37a.
50. Berachot 10a.
51. Babylonian Talmud, Avodah Zarah 17a.
52. Fringes on the corners of a four cornered garment.
53. According to Rashi, so that they should allow her to convert.
54. Babylonian Talmud, Menachot 44a.
55. Berkovits (1976).
56. Babylonian Talmud, Kiddushin 40a.
57. Babylonian Talmud, Kiddushin 81a–81b.
58. Babylonian Talmud, Shabbat 53b.
59. Jeremiah 9:4.
60. Babylonian Talmud, Yevamot 63a.
61. Yevamot 62b–63a.
62. Exodus 15:17.
63. Exodus 25:8.
64. Babylonian Talmud, Ketubot 62b.
65. Babylonian Talmud, Nedarim 66b.
66. Babylonian Talmud, Nedarim 66a.
67. Babylonian Talmud, Ketubot 65a.
68. Babylonian Talmud, Nedarim 66b.
69. Babylonian Talmud, Nedarim 66b.
70. See Numbers 5.
71. Jerusalem Talmud, Sotah 1:4.
72. See Numbers 5:11–31.
73. Babylonian Talmud, Nedarim 66b.
74. Babylonian Talmud, Bava Batra 12b.
75. I Kings 1:15.
76. Babylonian Talmud, Sanhedrin 22a.
77. Exodus 20:11.
78. Midrash Genesis Rabbah 68:4.
79. Sotah 2a.
80. Babylonian Talmud, Shabbat 118b.
81. Mallow (2005, 49).
82. Midrash Song of Songs Rabbah 1: on verse 1:4.
83. Babylonian Talmud, Bava Batra 58a.
84. Mallow (2005, 84).
85. Babylonian Talmud, Shavuot 30b.
86. Babylonian Talmud, Bava Kama 37a.

87. Babylonian Talmud, Pesachim 113b.
88. Novak and Waldoks (1981, 25).

Chapter 15

1. Babylonian Talmud, Chagigah 15b.
2. Babylonian Talmud, Chullin 31a.
3. Babylonian Talmud, Shabbat 30b.
4. Babylonian Talmud, Shabbat 77b.
5. Babylonian Talmud, Pesachim 10b.
6. Babylonian Talmud, Chagigah 14b–15a.
7. Deuteronomy 24:1–4.
8. Babylonian Talmud, Gittin 20b.
9. Deuteronomy 22:10.
10. Babylonian Talmud, Bava Kama 54b–55a.
11. Babylonian Talmud, Bava Kama 55a.
12. Babylonian Talmud, Bava Batra 22a.
13. Babylonian Talmud, Shabbat 149b.
14. Babylonian Talmud, Sanhedrin 55a.
15. Psalms 104:21.
16. A *yarod* is a desert bird possibly related to an ostrich.
17. Babylonian Talmud, Sanhedrin 59b.
18. Deuteronomy 23:19.
19. Micah 1:7.
20. Babylonian Talmud, Avodah Zarah 16b–17a.
21. Soncino Avodah Zarah 17a, note 3a.
22. Babylonian Talmud, Menachot 69b.
23. Leviticus 23:17.
24. See Babylonian Talmud, Nedarim 50b–51a.
25. Babylonian Talmud, Menachot 37a.
26. Babylonian Talmud, Chullin 70a.
27. Deuteronomy 22: 6–7.
28. Babylonian Talmud, Chullin 139b.
29. Babylonian Talmud, Niddah 23a.
30. Babylonian Talmud, Bava Batra 23b.
31. Jerusalem Talmud, Kelaim 9:3.
32. Exodus 25:2.
33. Deuteronomy 34:6.
34. Isaiah 40:12.
35. Isaiah 66:15.
36. Numbers 31:23.
37. Babylonian Talmud, Sanhedrin 39a.
38. Psalms 72:16.
39. Babylonian Talmud, Sanhedrin 90b.
40. Babylonian Talmud, Sanhedrin 90b–91a.
41. Jerusalem Talmud, Bava Kama 4:3.
42. Babylonian Talmud, Horayot 13a-13b.
43. The Nazirite is described in Numbers 6:1–21.

44. Babylonian Talmud, Nazir 34a.
45. Babylonian Talmud, Gittin 84a.
46. Babylonian Talmud, Gittin 84a.
47. Babylonian Talmud, Gittin 78b.
48. Babylonian Talmud, Bava Kama 26b.
49. Babylonian Talmud, Sanhedrin 77b.
50. Babylonian Talmud, Sanhedrin 77b.
51. Babylonian Talmud, Sanhedrin 75a.
52. Deuteronomy 22:9.
53. Leviticus 23:7.
54. Leviticus 25:4.
55. Deuteronomy 22:10.
56. Deuteronomy 15:19.
57. Leviticus 21:1.
58. Babylonian Talmud, Maakot 21b.
59. Numbers 6:6.
60. Babylonian Talmud, Shabbat 35a.
61. Babylonian Talmud, Zevachim 22a.
62. Babylonian Talmud, Zevachim 43b.
63. Proverbs 30:15 and 16.
64. Babylonian Talmud, Berachot 15b.
65. Deuteronomy 31:16.
66. Babylonian Talmud, Sanhedrin 90b.
67. Leviticus 21:14.
68. Babylonian Talmud, Derech Eretz Rabbah 1.

Chapter 16

1. A piece of this routine may be found in Novak and Waldoks (2006, 60).
2. See, e.g., Novak and Waldoks (2006, 151).
3. See, e.g., Kerr (2005).
4. Negaim 2:1.
5. E.g., Leviticus 19:33–34.
6. Genesis 38.
7. Even the name, Moab, means "from my father."
8. Babylonian Talmud, Pesachim 87b.
9. Jerusalem Talmud, Berachot 2:8.
10. See http://www.ajhs.org/publications/chapters/chapter.cfm?documentID=231.
11. Novak and Waldoks (2006, 87).
12. Babylonian Talmud, Nedarim 50b.
13. Sacks (2005, 186).
14. Berger (1997).
15. Berger (1969, 118).
16. Babylonian Talmud, Taanit 22a.
17. See, e.g, the *Wilmington Morning Star* or the *Hartford Courant* (April 1, 1983).
18. Babylonian Talmud, Shabbat 31a.

Bibliography

Aleichem, Sholom. *Selected Stories of Sholom Aleichem*. New York: The Modern Library, 1956.

Ausubel, Nathan. *A Treasury of Jewish Folklore: Stories, Traditions, Legends, Humor, Wisdom and Folk Songs of the Jewish People*. New York: Crown Publishers, 1948.

Beattie, James. "Essay on Laughter and Ludicrous Composition." In *Essays*. Edinburgh: William Creech, 1776.

Ben-Amos, Dan. "The 'Myth' of Jewish Humor." *Western Folklore* 32, no. 2 (1973): 112–31.

Berger, Arthur Asa. *The Genius of the Jewish Joke*. Northvale, NJ: Jason Aronson, Inc., 1997.

Berger, Peter. *A Rumour of Angels*. New York: Anchor, 1969.

———. *Redeeming Laughter*. Berlin: Walter de Gruyter, 1997.

Berk, Ronald A. *Professors Are from Mars and Students Are from Snickers*. Madison, WI: Mendota Press, 1998.

Berkovits, Eliezer. "A Jewish Sexual Ethics." In *Crisis and Faith*, edited by E. Berkovits, 41–82. New York: Sanhedrin Press, 1976.

———. *Jewish Women in Time and Torah*. Hoboken, NJ: Ktav Publishing, 1990.

Berrin, Danielle. "Judd Apatow's Kind of Judaism." Retrieved from http://www.jewishjournal.com/hollywoodjew/item/judd_apatow_i_couldnt_be_more_jewish_20090730, July 30, 2009.

Bonham, Tal D. *Humor: God's Gift*. Nashville, TN: Broadman Press, 1988.

Brand, Ezra. "Talmudic Humor and Its Discontents." Retrieved from http://seforim.blogspot.com/2013/02/talmudic-humor-and-its-discontents.html, February 22, 2013.

Brodsky, David. "Why Did the Widow Have a Goat in Her Bed? Jewish Humor and Its Roots in the Talmud and Midrash." In *Jews and Humor*, edited by L. J. Greenspoon, 13–32. West Lafayette, IN: Purdue University Press Studies in Jewish Civilization, 2011.

Brown, Ronald N. *The Enjoyment of Midrash: The Use of the Pun in Genesis Rabbah*, Hebrew Union College Dissertation, Cincinnati, OH, 1980.

Buber, Martin. *Tales of the Hasidim*. New York: Schocken Books, 1947.

Burkhart, Ford. "Healthful Humor." *The New York Times*, April 14, 1998: F7.

Chajes, Z. H. *The Student's Guide through the Talmud*, 2nd edition, Translated by Jacob Shachter. New York: Philipp Feldheim, Inc., 1960. Reissued in 2005 through Yashar Books, Brooklyn, NY.

Cohen, T., ed. *Jokes: Philosophical Thoughts on Joking Matters*. Chicago IL: University of Chicago Press, 1999.

Currid, John D. *Ancient Egypt and the Old Testament*. Grand Rapids, MI: Baker Books, 1997.

Davies, Christie. "Jewish Jokes, Anti-Semitic Jokes, and Hebredonian Jokes," In *Jewish Humor*, edited by A. Ziv, 75–96. New Brunswick, NJ: Transaction Publishers, 1986.

———. "Exploring the Thesis of the Self-Deprecating Jewish Sense of Humor." *Humor - International Journal of Humor Research* 4, no. 2: 189–210, ISSN (Online) 1613–3722, ISSN (Print) 0933-1719, DOI: 10.1515/humr.1991.4.2.189, July 2009.

Feinsilver, Alexander. *The Talmud for Today*. New York: St. Martin's Press, 1980.

Fishkoff, Sue. "Badkhn Belt? Jewish Humor Was Born in 1661, Prof Says," *The Jerusalem Post*, March 3, 2011.

Frank, David A. "Arguing with God, Talmudic Discourse, and the Jewish Counter Model: Implications for the Study of Argumentation." *Argumentation and Advocacy* 41 (2004): 71–86.

Freud, Sigmund. *Jokes and Their Relation to the Unconscious*. Translated by James Strachey. New York: W. W. Norton, 1960 (original work published in 1905).

Friedman, H. H. "Humor in the Hebrew Bible," *Humor: International Journal of Humor Research*, 13, no. 3 (September 2000): 257–85. (Also, Friedman, H. H. "Is There Humor in the Hebrew Bible? A Rejoinder," *Humor: International Journal of Humor Research*, 15, no. 2 (June 2002): 1–8.)

Friedman, H. H. "He Who Sits in Heaven Shall Laugh: Divine Humor in Talmudic Literature," *Thalia: Studies in Literary Humor*, 17 (March 1998): 36–50.

Friedman, Hershey H. and Lipman, S. "Satan the Accuser: Trickster in Talmudic and Midrashic Literature," *Thalia: Studies in Literary Humor*, 18, (March 1999): 31–41.

Friedman, Hershey H, and Friedman, Linda Weiser. "Humor and the Omniscient God." Retrieved from SSRN: http://ssrn.com/abstract=2112655 or http://dx.doi.org/10.2139/ssrn.2112655, July 18, 2012.

Friedman, Linda Weiser, and Hershey H. Friedman. "I-Get-It as a Type of Bonding Humor: The Secret Handshake" Retrieved from SSRN: http://ssrn.com/abstract=913622, 2003b.

Gerard, Alexander. *An Essay on Taste*. London, 1759.

Goldin, Eugene, and Terry Bordan. "The Use of Humor in Counseling: The Laughing Cure." *Journal of Counseling and Development* 77, no. 4 (1999): 405–10.

Good, Edwin M. *Irony in the Old Testament*. Philadelphia, PA: The Westminster Press, 1965.

Gordon, Mel. "Nazi 'Proof' that Jews Possessed the Worst Humor in the World." *Israeli Journal of Humor Research* 1, no. 2 (2012): 97–100.

Grotjahn, Martin. *Beyond Laughter*. New York: Blakiston Division, (McGraw Hill), 1957.

Gruner, Charles R. *The Game of Humor: A Comprehensive Theory of Why We Laugh*. New Brunswick, NJ: Transaction Publishers, 1997.

Guri, Yosef. *Let's Hear Only Good News: A Dictionary of Yiddish Blessings and Curses*. Hebrew University Press, 2004.

Hecht, Esther. "Maledictions of the Mamaloshen." *The Jewish Week*, June 4, 2004, 28.

Henkin, Hillel. "Why Jews Laugh at Themselves," *Commentary* 121 no. 4, (2006): 47–54.

Herford, R. Travers. *Christianity in Talmud & Midrash*. New York: Ktav Publishing House, Inc., 1975.

Hobbes, Thomas. *Leviathan*. London: Crooke, 1651.

Holden, Robert. *Laughter, the Best Medicine: The Healing Power of Happiness, Humor and Joy!*. New York: Thorsons (HarperCollins), 1993.

Honeycutt, James M, and Renee Brown. "Did You Hear the One About?: Typological and Spousal Differences in the Planning of Jokes and Sense of Humor in Marriage." *Communication Quarterly* 46, no. 3, (1998): 342–52.

Hyde, Lewis. *Trickster Makes This World: Mischief, Myth and Art*. New York: Farrar Straus & Giroux, 1998.

Hyers, M. Conrad, ed. *Holy Laughter*. New York: The Seabury Press, 1969.

———. *And God Created Laughter: The Bible as Divine Comedy*. Atlanta, GA: John Knox Press, 1987.

Hynes, William J, and William G. Doty, eds. *Mythical Trickster Figures: Contours, Contexts, and Criticisms*. Tuscaloosa: University of Alabama Press, 1993.

Isbell, Charles David. "Humor in the Bible." In *Jews and Humor*, edited by L. J. Greenspoon, 1–11. West Lafayette, IN: Purdue University Press Studies in Jewish Civilization, 2011.

Jemielity, Thomas. *Satire and the Hebrew Prophets*. Louisville, KY: Westminster/ John Knox Press, 1992.

Jonsson, Jakob. *Humor and Irony in the New Testament*. Leiden: E. J. Brill, 1985.

Kant, Immanuel. *Kritik der Urteilskraft*. Berlin: Lagarde, 1790.

Kantor, Mattis. *The Jewish Time Line Encyclopedia*. Northvale, NJ, Jason Aronson Inc., 1989.

Keith-Speigel, Patricia. "Early Conceptions of Humor: Variety and Issues." In *The Psychology of Humor*, Jeffrey H. Goldstein, and Paul E. McGhee, 3–39. New York: Academic Press, 1972.

Kerr, Audrey E. "The Paper Bag Principle: Of the Myth and the Motion of Colorism." *Journal of American Folklore* 118, no. 469 (2005): 271–89.

Klein, Lillian R. *The Triumph of Irony in the Book of Judges*. Sheffield: Almond Press, 1989.

Knox, Israel. "The Traditional Roots of Jewish Humor," In *Holy Laughter*, edited by M. Conrad Hyers, 150–65. New York: The Seabury Press, 1969.

Koller, Marvin. *Humor and Society*. Houston, TX: Cap and Gown Press, 1988.

Kranc, Moshe. "Workplace Heaven or Hell." *Being Jewish, Passover 2005/5765*, http://www.beingjewish.org/magazine/spring2005/article2.html, July 18, 2005.

LaFollette, Hugh, and Niall Shanks. "Belief and the Basis of Humor." *American Philosophical Quarterly* 30 (1993): 329–39.

Leibowitz, Nehama. *Studies in Bamidbar (Numbers)*. Jerusalem: The World Zionist Organization, 1980.

Lipman, Steve. *Laughter in Hell: The Use of Humor during the Holocaust*. Northvale, NJ: Jason Aronson, Inc., 1991.

Maccoby, Hyam. *The Day God Laughed: Sayings, Fables and Entertainments of the Jewish Sages*. New York: St. Martin's Press, 1978.

Mallow, Jeffry V. *"Our Pal, God" and Other Presumptions: A Book of Jewish Humor*. New York: iUniverse, 2005.

Margalioth, Mordechai, ed. *Encyclopedia of Talmudic and Geonic Literature*. Tel Aviv: Yavneh Publishing House, 1981.

Martineau, William. "A Model of the Social Functions of Humor." In *The Psychology of Humor*, edited by J. H. Goldstein, and P. E. McGhee, 101–25. New York: Academic Press, 1972.

Miles, John R. "Laughing at the Bible: Jonah as Parody." In *On Humour and the Comic in the Hebrew Bible*, edited by Yehuda T. Radday, and Athalya Brenner, 203–15. Sheffield, England: Almond Press, 1990.

Novak, William, and Moshe Waldoks, eds. *The Big Book of Jewish Humor*. New York: Harper Collins, 2006. This is the reissued 25th Anniversary edition of the classic 1981 book.

Oring, Elliott. *Jokes and Their Relations*. Kentucky: University Press of Kentucky, 1992.

———. *Jokes and Their Relations*. New Brunswick, NJ: Transaction Publishers, 2010.

Philologos. "Man Thinks, God Laughs, a Reader Writes and a Columnist Contemplates." *The Jewish Daily Forward*, May 10, 2013.

Price, Lucien, ed. *Dialogues of Alfred North Whitehead*. Boston, MA: Little, Brown and Company, 1954.

Radday, Yehuda T. "Humor in Names." In *On Humour and the Comic in the Hebrew Bible*, edited by Yehuda T. Radday, and Athalya Brenner, 59–97. Sheffield: Almond Press, 1990.

Radin, Paul. *The Trickster: A Study in American Indian Mythology*. London: Routledge and Paul, 1956.

Rothstein, Robert A. "'If a Jew Has a Dog ...': Dogs in Yiddish Proverbs." In *A Jew's Best Friend? The Image of the Dog throughout Jewish History*, edited by Phillip Ackerman-Lieberman and Rakefet Zalashik, Eastbourne, East Sussex, UK: Sussex Academic Press, 2013.

Sacks, Jonathan. *To Heal a Fractured World: The Ethics of Responsibility*. New York: Schocken Books, 2005.

———. "Covenant & Conversation: Vaera—Of Lice and Men." Retrieved from http://www.chiefrabbi.org/2013/01/07/covenant-conversation-vaera-of-lice-and-men/, January 7, 2013.

Schachter, Stanley J. *Laugh for God's Sake: Where Jewish Humor and Jewish Ethics Meet*. Jersey City, NJ: Ktav, 2008.

Schopenhauer, Arthur. *Die Welt als Wille und Vorstellung*. Leipzig: Brockhaus, 1819.

Soncino Press, *The Babylonian Talmud*. London: Soncino Press, 1960, edited by I. Epstein.

Soncino Press, *The Midrash Rabbah*. London: Soncino Press, 1977 translated and edited by H. Freedman and Maurice Simon.

Spalding, Henry D. *A Treasure-Trove of American Jewish Humor*. Middle Village, NY: Jonathan David Publishers, 1976.

———. *Joys of Jewish Humor*. Middle Village, NY: Jonathan David Publishers, 1985.

Spencer, Herbert. "The Physiology of Laughter." *Macmillan's Magazine* 1 (1860): 395–402.

Stern, David. *Parables in Midrash: Narrative and Exegesis in Rabbinic Literature*. Cambridge, MA: Harvard University Press, 1991.

Telushkin, Joseph. *Jewish Humor: What the Best Jewish Jokes Say about the Jews*. New York: William Morrow, 1992.

Veatch, Thomas C. "A Theory of Humor." *Humor: The International Journal of Humor Research* 11, no. 2 (1998): 161–75.

Weinberger, Marc G, and Charles S. Gulas. "The Impact of Humor in Advertising: A Review." *Journal of Advertising* 18, no. 2 (1992): 39–44,

Whedbee, J. William. *The Bible and the Comic Vision*. Cambridge, England: Cambridge University Press, 1998.

Whitfield, Stephen J. "The Distinctiveness of American Jewish Humor." *Modern Judaism* 6, no. 3 (1986): 215–60.

Winston-Macauley, Marnie. "Yiddish Curses for the New Millennium." Retrieved from http://www.aish.com/j/fs/Yiddish_Curses_for_the_New_Millennium.html, October 24, 2011.

Wisse, Ruth R. *No Joke: Making Jewish Humor*. Princeton, NJ: Princeton University Press, 2013.

Witkin, Stanley L. "Editorial: Taking Humor Seriously." *Social Work* 44, no. 2 (1999): 101–4.

Ziv, A. ed. *Jewish Humor*, New Brunswick, NJ: Transaction Publishers, 1998.

Ziv, Avner, and O. Gadish. "Humor and Marital Satisfaction." *Journal of Social Psychology* 129, no. 6 (1989): 759–68.

Index

351